Believing in Place

Believing in Place

A Spiritual Geography of the Great Basin

Richard V. Francaviglia

University of Nevada Press

RENO & LAS VEGAS

University of Nevada Press, Reno, Nevada 89557 USA
Manufactured in the United States of America

Design by Omega Clay

Library of Congress Cataloging-in-Publication Data
Francaviglia, Richard V.
Believing in place : a spiritual geography of the Great Basin /
Richard V. Francaviglia.
p. cm.
Includes bibliographical references and index.
ISBN 0-87417-542-9 (alk. paper)
1. Great Basin—Religious life and customs. 2. Great Basin—
Social life and customs. 3. Great Basin—Description and travel.
4. Religion and geography. I. Title.
BL2527.G74 F73 2003
917.9–dc21   2003001847
The paper used in this book meets the requirements of
American National Standard for Information Sciences—
Permanence of Paper for Printed Library Materials,
ANSI Z39.48-1984. Binding materials were
selected for strength and durability.

First Printing

12 11 10 09 08 07 06 05 04 03   5 4 3 2 1

The Unicorn, p. 39, © Hollis Music, Inc.
Used with permission.

TO ELLEN
who has traveled
so many roads
with me

The most beautiful and most profound emotion we can experience is the sensation of the mystical. It is the sower of all true science. He to whom the emotion is a stranger, who can no longer wonder and stand rapt in awe, is as good as dead.

—ALBERT EINSTEIN

Contents

Illustrations

Introduction

At the dawn of the twenty-first century, two very different events reminded Americans and the world about the power of religion in defining place. The first, which occurred on September 11, 2001, will live in infamy as a horrendous act perpetrated by the darkest side of religion. That religion, a brand of radical Islamic fundamentalism, revealed to the world how exclusive, intolerant, and fanatical some faiths can become. Those unforgettable events on September 11 also had a geographical dimension, for they revealed how tempting symbols on our East Coast—the World Trade Center towers in New York and massive public buildings in Washington, D.C.—had become to international terrorism. Significantly, the terrorist attacks on the World Trade Center quickly transformed a commercial location into what Mayor Rudolph Giuliani called "a Holy Place." Six months after September 11, twin beams of white light soared skyward from the World Trade Center site to commemorate the victims, a moving tribute underscoring the important role that places play in our search for meaning.[1]

Several months after September 11, a second event also focused the world's attention on the role of religion in defining place. In February 2002, some two thousand miles west of Ground Zero, the Winter Olympics were held in Utah. Although the possibility of terrorist acts kept security on high alert, the three-week-long event was serene if not entirely free of controversy. Television broadcasts from the Winter Olympics repeatedly conveyed one reassuring image that consisted of three components—the snow-covered, bedrock-solid Wasatch Mountains, at the foot of which lay Salt Lake City's jeweled skyline, which was in turn crowned by the spires of the Mormon Temple. Religion had played a significant role in the Winter Olympics, but this time it revealed religion's positive and nonsectarian side. The Mormons—as members of the Church of Jesus Christ of Latter-day Saints are called—were instrumental in conceiving, orchestrating, promoting, and hosting the Winter Olympics. In a remarkably sensitive move, the Mormons had decided not to push their faith on others by proselytizing, thus unconditionally accommodating visitors of diverse faiths. In addition to enabling the Mormons to showcase their increasingly inclusive religion, the "Salt Lake Olympics" subtly reinforced the belief that the Intermountain West is somehow buffered or sequestered from the terrors of the outside world. Symbolically, the prospect of peace from a violent outside world is exactly what had brought Mormons to this stunning, mountain-protected location in the first place.

The isolated region that the Mormons first encountered in 1847 is the subject of this book. This region beyond the Rocky Mountains is sometimes called the Intermountain West, but was widely known as the Great Basin when the Mormons arrived. Although the Latter-day Saints transformed portions of the Great Basin into their spiritual homeland shortly after their arrival, this region was, and remains, home to people whose ancestors have lived here for thousands of years. These Native peoples' spiritualities were, and remain, closely linked to all aspects of the place—its climate, topography, plants, animals. In this book, I hope to tell the story of how the Great Basin's environment resonates in the spiritual lives of all people, Native and non-Native, Mormon and non-Mormon, resident and traveler.

Believing in Place takes readers on a journey (or rather journeys) into one of America's most unique and underappreciated regions. In the process, it addresses two important and interrelated, but sometimes overlooked, issues—spirituality and place—that are of growing interest to academics and our popular culture. Well before September 11, 2001, *a renewed interest in spirituality* was apparent in America, evident in the success of the popular television show *Touched by an Angel*. How significant was this quest for spirituality at the dawn of the twenty-first century? According to James Redfield, a 1998 Gallup poll "contains a revealing finding: Eighty-two percent of those surveyed reported that spiritual growth was a very important part of their lives."[2] Part of a broader search to "rediscover the world's mysteries," this growing belief in the importance of spirituality is predicted to be among the five most significant trends that will characterize human behavior in the twenty-first century.[3]

That search for something profoundly spiritual has coincided with a second major movement in recent years—*a growing interest in the meaning of place.* On one level, this focus seems to coincide with a popular secular concern for protecting both the quality of habitat (as in environmental protection) and preserving the character of the built environment (as in historic preservation), but it goes far deeper. Increasingly, place is becoming recognized as an essential element in the human drama.4

There is a point at which these two trends—*spirituality* and *place*—converge.5 This convergence is welcome to me, for I have been interested in the relationship between spirituality and place for thirty-five years as both a historian and geographer. Like my former colleague, geographer Yi-Fu Tuan, I strove for decades to infuse a humanistic, even phenomenological, perspective into geography. Over the years, I also found myself becoming closely affiliated with historians. Through close association with my colleagues in the History Department at the University of Texas at Arlington, where I now teach, I've come to appreciate the art of bringing history to life—always, of course, in the context of place. Although I call this book a "spiritual geography," it is actually a fusion of spiritual history and spiritual geography because they are inseparable. *Believing in Place* seeks to reveal that elusive but palpable quality we call the "spirit of place" in light of human spirituality. That quality is often revealed through the inspirational stories that people tell about their experiences here.

If there is one underlying philosophical message in this book, it is that stories are always about places, more specifically what happens to people as they are exposed to those places. Story and place have a venerable connection: From ancient literature to popular film, they have been interdependent. Can you imagine the *Odyssey* without the rugged coast of Greece? *A River Runs through It* without the Rockies? *The Wizard of Oz* without Kansas—or Oz? The Bible without the Holy Land?

But consider this dilemma: the more caught up we become with both *character* and *plot* in storytelling—that is, the more engrossing a story becomes—the more we tend to relegate place itself to the background. This is especially true when we condense stories into, say, an hour on television or two hours on film. Consider the consequences. Although Americans invented the short story, we became so good at abbreviating tales that we often shortchange the stories' settings. If this streamlining or condensation of storytelling is a characteristically American phenomenon, it has one lasting consequence: Our interest in cutting to the chase (sometimes quite literally) means we are no longer as likely to savor the meaning and significance of place.

I realized this when I came to know Native Americans and listened to their stories, in which details about the topography, weather, and vegetation are woven into the plot and are inseparable from it. Consider N. Scott Momaday's *The Way to Rainy Mountain,* in which the buzzing insects and dancing heat waves play important roles in the drama. Or Diane Glancy's *Firesticks,* in which the red soil of Oklahoma's fields, and the red brick of Oklahoma's towns, are part of the narration's kindling. In reading such stories, my students often express frustration, and no wonder: For a culture in a hurry, it is easy to think about elements of place as just so much "atmosphere." Trees and hills become props to be moved around strategically in order to "set the scene," and no more. But to Native Americans, place figures in—and is inseparable from—the actual content of the story.

I confess to not only to being obsessed with place generally, but to being fascinated by the Great Basin in particular. For readers unfamiliar with this region, which often appears as a blank on people's mental maps of the U.S., the Great Basin is a huge, physically diverse region that lies between the Sierra Nevada and the Wasatch Mountains. I define the region hydrographically—the huge contiguous area of the western United States that drains internally, its rain and snowmelt never reaching the ocean (fig. o.1). I know that other definitions, such as floristic patterns and physiography, would result in a slightly different shape and a slightly smaller region.[6] However, I deliberately selected the definition that also fairly closely coincides with the delineation of the region provided in the classic *Handbook of North American Indians: Great Basin,* by William Sturtevant et al.[7] I did so because that definition emphasizes cultural connections that sometimes transcend physical parameters like vegetation and geology. There is, therefore, considerable geographic variety in the Great Basin as I define it in this book. To begin with, the region includes much of *two* biologically defined North American deserts—the Mojave Desert and the Great Basin Desert that lies immediately north of it. But, as I shall show, these two deserts are seamlessly woven into the larger region's cultural history, both ancient and modern.

Although the word basin suggests one huge bowl-shaped depression, this is a very complex region of interior drainage consisting of almost a hundred separate basins that are occupied by either playas (seasonally or mostly dry lakes) or perennially water-filled lakes. The latter are either salty (as in the Great Salt Lake) or fresh (for example, Pyramid Lake). The Great Basin is an area of active mountain building, and throughout much of the region those playas and lakes are bordered by mountain ranges, most of which run in a north-south direction. Because the Great Basin lies in the rain shadow of mountains that block most moisture from getting here, the climate is generally arid to semiarid. Therefore, large areas consist of scrub vegetation like creosote bush (in the Mojave Desert) and sagebrush (throughout the central and northern part of the region). However,

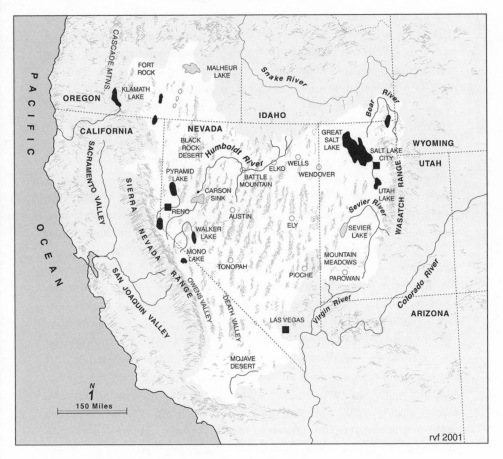

Fig. 0.1. The hydrographically defined Great Basin a huge region of interior drainage. (Map by author based on definitions in Donald K. Grayson's *The Desert's Past*)

because the mountains tend to be cooler, moister "islands" that rise from the desert valleys, the vegetation there is lusher: piñon and other pine trees are common at the higher elevations.

Like much of the West, the Great Basin's human story is largely scripted around the drama of North American/European American conflict. In addition to a rich Native American past, this region also has an intriguing European American political history. Since about 1520 it has been claimed by a succession of countries: Spain (until 1821), Mexico (until 1848), and the United States. Beneath the veneer of European conquest, however, this region has been—and still remains—home to several groups of American Indians. Two of the region's dominant Native groups, the Shoshone and Paiute, are Numic peoples who speak Uto-Aztecan languages. The Washo

Indians are also part of the region's prehistory and history, although they occupy a much smaller area and their language is different. Most Indians in the region lived in small bands, and their lifestyle was fairly mobile. Regional population density was low.

The Great Basin was an enigma to early Europeans. Several factors—its location far from the coast, its aridity, and its scattered human population—ensured that it would be infrequently visited. In fact, the Great Basin was the last region in continental North America to be explored.[8] Spanish explorers had visited its extreme eastern edge in the 1770s but were unable to cross it. Although known by mountain men in the 1820s and 1830s and traversed by explorers like John Charles Frémont (who named it in 1844), the Great Basin remained virtually untouched until settlers began to trek westward on the Oregon Trail in the 1840s. Two factors in the late 1840s—the arrival of the Mormons in the area near Great Salt Lake (1847) and the discovery of gold in California (1848)—set the tone for what was to follow. By the 1850s, miners had worked their way eastward from California, searching for mineral wealth overlooked by those who had traveled overland in search of El Dorado. Those miners encountered Indians, and the results of this contact were sometimes catastrophic (as in the Pyramid Lake War) but more often disruptive to Native lifestyles (as when miners cut down the piñon pines for use in their charcoal ovens and smelters). By the late nineteenth century, the region's political geography was fixed. Although it is today part of one nation, the Great Basin region cuts across state boundaries: It occupies most of Nevada, about half of Utah, and adjacent portions of Oregon, California, Idaho, and Wyoming.

So much for a historical and geographical primer. This will also be a personal story, because the Great Basin's interdigitated geography and history fill me with a sense of awe. The environment features stunning vistas of rugged mountains rising from pancake-flat dry lakes; arid to semiarid climates with intense sunshine; bracing diurnal temperature variations with frost sometimes tingeing cold mornings that yield to hot afternoons; aromatic vegetation like sagebrush and piñon pine whose scents trigger a sense of adventure and nostalgia. My fascination is also triggered by the rich and sometimes tragic human history here. The Great Basin has witnessed prophets and religious conflict that would do the Holy Land proud. But my appreciation of this region goes deeper than any one particular aspect of the place or its history. Rather, it is the *totality* of those sensations that combine to affect both my intellect and my emotions. More than forty years ago, this synergy led me to the realization that I feel more closely connected to the universe here than in other places. That epiphany has made my many trips into the Great Basin since 1960 pilgrimages, for I never fail to come out of this region restored and reenergized. I attribute that to feeling closer to both creation and the creator here.

I am not alone in experiencing the region's magic and recognizing its strong association with spirituality. When I began serious study of the region as a graduate student in 1967, I asked residents in the southern Great Basin—from southern Nevada into California's Mojave Desert—to identify the type of environment that most conveyed a sense of religion or spirituality. Looking at a set of ten photographs, my informants could choose from several environments that ranged from fertile and well wooded to arid and austere. They could also choose from a series of words, from forest to grassland to desert and a number of alternatives in between. Significantly, when 95 percent of them chose "the desert" in both word and picture, I was not surprised—for I, too, felt this connection. In 1968, my wife Ellen and I traveled across the Great Basin and encountered the part of the region settled by the Mormons. So intriguing was this landscape to me that I wrote my doctoral dissertation—and later published a book—called *The Mormon Landscape* about it.

From the late 1960s to the late 1980s, I visited the Great Basin many times, usually alone, overwhelmed by the region's vastness but realizing that *something* helped unify it in my mind. Based partly on my experiences here, I wrote the book *Hard Places* (1991), which describes and interprets mining landscapes. That book began by noting the stark contrast between two Nevada communities, the Mormon town of Panaca and the mining town of Pioche. They were only about a dozen miles from each other, but worlds apart in design and ideology. The contrast between Panaca and Pioche reflects one of the profound schisms in American landscape history. In popular thought, that contrast between communities covenanted with God and those based on commercial risk endures,[9] but I hope to show how faith affected both communities.

By the late 1990s, I came to realize that one factor in particular—*the search for something beyond normal experience*—characterizes life in the Great Basin. Many people don't just find themselves living here: They are here for a reason, even if that reason is sometimes mystical and beyond immediate comprehension. Wanting to better understand this region's hold on both myself and others, I set out to determine what gives the Great Basin its *genius loci.* That is when I realized that spirit and spirit of place and spirituality are inextricably tied. As a historical geographer, it occurred to me that the place itself—its topography, vegetation, weather, climate—could be a major factor in deciphering both the spirit of place and the human spirit.

It could also shed light on how people come to grips with forces greater than, even outside of, themselves—the elusive quality called the spiritual. Then, too, the human drama of how various faiths influenced each other also influences both how people experience, and ultimately shape, places.

In searching for the deeper meanings associated with place, I found additional inspiration in the writings of folklorists and anthropologists. These include James Griffith's *Beliefs and Holy Places*[10] and Keith Basso's *Wisdom Sits in Places.*[11] Like folklorist Griffith and anthropologist Basso, both of whom had studied Native beliefs in Arizona, I had encountered many Indian peoples in the Great Basin's communities, reservations, and out-of-the-way places. The thoughts they shared with me included not only nuances about daily life, but also deep beliefs about spirituality in the Great Basin. Like Griffith and Basso, I feel that the story of *any* American region is incomplete without this Native perspective.

Although desert places possess a power in both Native American and Judeo-Christian thought,[12] they do so in different ways. Writing this book provided me the opportunity to relate two great traditions of communication, one oral and indigenous, the other literary and Western. The former are evident in the Native American creation stories, the latter found in the Bible and other sacred books such as the Koran.

One other tradition—the pagan or pre-Judeo-Christian from the Old World—also must be reckoned with. From it, we inherit beliefs about the deeper meaning of natural phenomena and environment. These beliefs are often downplayed, and sometimes eliminated, in Judeo-Christian texts. As translated by New Agers in search of meaning, however, these pagan spiritualities also play out as one of the multiple interpretations of the Great Basin's spiritual geography.

Multiple interpretations suggests a kind of analytical anthropological approach, which I use to some extent. However, I also want to reiterate that *Believing in Place* is a very personal interpretation; I freely add my voice to the others who tell their stories of the Great Basin's deeper meanings. As will become clear, by spirit I refer to an animating, vital principle or essence; by spiritual, I mean a power that resides *within* something, a power that helps to bring the inanimate to life. Spirituality can be religious in that it involves God as a purposeful being, but it also engages other forces that control our collective and individual fates. This spiritual geography thus embraces both monotheism and other beliefs—notably animism. Using this broad definition of spirituality, I demonstrate that many people in the Great Basin are in search of—and some have found—a spirituality that is both dependent on, and yet transcendent to, the environment.

This book recognizes a fundamental east-west schism in the region's religious geography, wherein the Mormons dominate the eastern half (Utah) while non-Mormons dominate the western portion (mainly Nevada). However, it also urges a reinterpretation of the Great Basin's geographically split personality and simplistic characterizations of "Saints" (that is, Mormons) and "sinners" who frequent places like Las Vegas and Reno. Viewed as part of a complex dialogue between people and environment—which always involves a desire to control fate—spirituality is evident in some surprising locales. I hope to show that churches and casinos, military bombing ranges and New Age sculptures, have more in common with human spirituality than we normally comprehend. These are aspects of place that involve some of humankind's deepest aspirations and fears—emotions that bring us face to face with forces that are well beyond our ability to control.

A word about this book's organization is in order. Where possible, I have integrated my extensive travels with a deeper interpretation of the region's spiritual geography. The events that I describe are based on my many trips through, hikes into, and flights over the region in the past forty years. Each chapter includes references to these personal experiences, and is meant to stand as a separate essay. Yet I use a generally historical approach—what one reviewer called "a remarkably linear design"—in introducing various themes. Therefore, I hope readers will find that the chapters fit together as historically themed, kinetically charged stories that tell a broader story about people's enduring relationship to place here.

While preparing readers for what they are about to experience, I should add a word about maps. Although I have provided a base map in this introduction, it can acquaint readers with only a few of the many geographic features discussed in this book. Therefore, I urge readers to look up the features described herein by consulting either state road maps or a good road atlas of the United States. Better yet, serious readers should consult the state atlases and gazetteers published by DeLorme; now available for all fifty states, these feature "America's Back Roads" (as the atlases' subtitles suggest) in considerable detail.

Like all journeys, my writing this book involved encounter with many knowledgeable people who deserve thanks. David Rumsey of San Francisco kindly shared photographic images of, and insights about, his ranch in northwestern Nevada. Also in the western Great Basin, anthropologists Don Hardesty and Catherine Fowler of the University of Nevada at Reno helped me contact Native Americans willing to share their thoughts on this subject. Their writings also helped me better understand indigenous peoples' relationship to place. Elizabeth Raymond of the UNR History Department kindly provided information about Nevada's historic land-scapes. Of the many Native American people I encountered in the Great Basin, two from Nevada deserve special mention: Bernice Lalo of the Battle Mountain Shoshone band and Marlin Thompson of the Yerington Paiute Reservation provided valuable insights for which I am grateful. At the University of Nevada Press, Margaret Dalrymple wisely encouraged me to write this book before beginning my other proposed book projects about the region. I am glad that she did. I only hope her intuition that "this is a story worth telling" proves correct. I was also heartened by Press director Ron Latimer's strong support of this project from beginning to end. Then, too, on the eastern side of the Great Basin, friend and fellow geographer Gary Peterson of Alpine, Utah, shared photographic images of the region with me. Historians Kent Powell and Phil Notarianni of the Utah Historical Society helped connect me to the literature about communities here. Professor Richard Orndorff of the University of Nevada at Las Vegas provided photographs of Nevada landforms.

Others outside of the region also helped. These include fellow geographer Marshall Bowen of Mary Washington College, who shared information about dry farming in the Great Basin. David Futey of Stanford University provided photographs of scenes in the Basin. Betty Friedrich and Cammie Vitale Shuman of Southern Methodist University's DeGolyer Library in Dallas helped me locate historic images of Utah. Andrew Gulliford of Fort Lewis College in Durango, Colorado, provided me a copy of an illustration depicting John C. Frémont's encounters with Native Americans in the Great Basin. At my university—the University of Texas at Arlington—several fellow faculty and staff members assisted with this project and deserve my thanks. They include Gerald Saxon and Kit Goodwin of UTA's Special Collections. History Department chair Don Kyle was especially supportive. The History Department's Center for Greater Southwestern Studies and the History of Cartography, which I direct, also helped support my effort in several ways. This included valuable input from Linda Pelon, who served as our graduate research assistant and who remains a devoted student of Native American culture. Above all, though, I owe thanks to administrative secretary Ann Jennings, who typed many drafts of this manuscript. Throughout its writing, she offered words of support and enthusiasm at crucial times as this book evolved from rough drafts to the finished work that you are now about to begin.

Landscape and Storytelling

In early October of 1881, three passengers gazed from a train rolling west-ward through Nevada. Although they had spent many hours on the Califor-nia-bound train together, the three did not know each other and had noth-ing in common. One was a Paiute Indian ranch worker who, by virtue of birthright in an agreement with the Central Pacific Railroad,[1] was riding free of charge to a ranch near Walker Lake. The second passenger was a mining engineer headed for the silver mines at Virginia City in Nevada's recently fabled, but now declining, Comstock Mining District. Armed with geological surveys and mining reports, the mining engineer hoped to "breathe new life" into one of the mines there. That would involve explor-ing the secrets hidden deep within Mount Davidson—secrets that yielded both mineral wealth and knowledge of nature's inner workings. The third passenger, an English-born farmer from Utah Territory, was a member of the Church of Jesus Christ of Latter-day Saints. Bound for a religious as-signment in the Pacific Northwest, this Mormon missionary would take the train across the entire width of the Great Basin, ride it over the Sierra Nevada mountain range into California's golden Central Valley, and then continue northward by train and stagecoach to ultimately reach Oregon.

The three travelers were traversing the Great Basin, a vast area of de-sert-mountain topography where vistas are immense and the works of man almost inconsequential. For much of their route across Nevada, they had followed the westward-flowing Humboldt River, which the mining en-gineer recognized as unique, if not peculiar. Unlike rivers elsewhere, the Humboldt never reached the sea. Instead, it terminated in a broad sink rimmed by distant mountains that remained snow-capped until mid-summer. Although lined by trees in a few places, the Humboldt River ran through what travelers called the "Great American Desert"[2] in the 1880s. Unobstructed by trees, the sagebrush-covered landscape here stretches outward to the rugged mountains that define every horizon (fig. 1.1).

1

Fig. 1.1. Enigmatic River: Weaving between sagebrush-covered plains and mountain ranges, the Humboldt River flows westward across a portion of the Great Basin. Scene near Mill City, Nevada, looking toward the Humboldt Range. (May 2000 photograph by author)

As the train emerged from the sinuous Humboldt River Valley, it moved south into an immense desert area. Lulled by the late summer heat and the steady rhythm of the wheels marking their passage over each joint in the rails, the three passengers found it difficult to stay awake as the train rattled through the late afternoon. Then one thing momentarily united them without a word being spoken. By coincidence, all three focused their attention on a large rock-studded mountain range that loomed in the distance to the south. The slanting rays of the sun illuminated the mountains' steep western flanks a copper hue that contrasted with the cobalt blue of the cloudless sky. The mountain range they beheld was one of many that run in roughly north-south, each bordering a long valley. This is "basin and range" country whose alternating mountains and valleys give the landscape a decidedly corrugated quality. Travelers through the Great Basin might agree with a railroad historian who recently characterized the topography as looking as if "God had dragged a rake and left furrows over the land."[3]

To the mining engineer and the Mormon farmer, this landscape's vegetation seemed bleak. The Mormon's roots were originally in a better-watered place, but now those roots would have to rely on diverted water; building on the experience and memory of Mormon ancestors who had settled parts of this desert region for more than thirty years, the Mormon farmer approached the desert landscape with the idea of converting it into a garden. The mining engineer descended from a rich European scientific tradition in geological observation that spanned about a century and a half; expertise learned in these pursuits was helping to distinguish the Great Basin as one of the West's richest mining areas. But it was still bleak country that they beheld: Away from the Humboldt River Valley there was not a tree in sight as far as the eye could see. Though there were scattered piñon pines on the higher slopes, the broad brush-covered plain seemed as vast as the ocean, the distant mountains appearing like islands. As relative newcomers to the area, they were awed by its openness and ever aware of the dominance of one plant in particular—sagebrush (fig. 1.2). About twenty years earlier, explorer J. H. Simpson had noted that the "most abundant plant in the Great Basin is the *artemesia,* or wild sage, and as it is seen almost everywhere in the valleys and on the mountains, it gives its peculiar bronze color to the general face of nature."[4] Just as copper gives weathered bronze the characteristic greenish color to which Simpson referred, the sagebrush lends a distinctive cast to landscapes in the Great Basin.

Fig. 1.2. Basin and Range: The landscape of the Great Basin consists of generally north-south-trending mountain ranges rising from brush-covered plains, as epitomized in this view of the White Mountains and Boundary Peak along the California-Nevada border. (June 2000 photograph by author)

Those explorers were only beginning to understand what the Paiute Indian's ancestors had long known—that the flora and fauna of the Great Basin vary with altitude and are greatly affected by the seasons. The Native peoples usually migrated in search of food, either belt-tightening when it was scarce or feasting when certain resources, like fish or pine nuts, were available. These indigenous peoples conducted elaborate ceremonies both to ensure the bounty of resources and to give thanks for them. The Northern Paiutes, for example, had a keen awareness that some areas were more productive than others. In small bands they seasonally exploited resources, subsisting during the midwinter months, reaping harvest of seeds and waterfowl in summer, piñon nuts in fall. These pine nut harvests were accompanied by ceremonies, with slow circle dances lasting throughout the night; during the ceremonies, the dancers were "sprinkled with water from the branches of sagebrush, evergreen and a symbol of life."[5]

The Paiutes occupied parts of the western Great Basin region, while just east of them the Shoshone Indians ruled. Like the Paiutes, the Shoshone considered sagebrush an essential element in the cosmos. Shoshone spiritual leader Corbin Harney recently recalled that "our forefathers, when they first came to this country, used sage to heal their sick." Its use continues to the present: "Today we're still doing it, the same as we have done for thousands of years." The aromatic sagebrush has strong restorative and regenerative powers. According to Harney, "Sagebrush at one time said, 'I don't care how wet I am; when you ask me to warm your body, I'll burn.'" So reliable is sagebrush as fuel and medicine that "[y]ou can float it in the ocean water, but it will still burn for you, to give you a healing. . . . This is what the sage said." Harney also notes that there "are a lot of things out here to eat. The sagebrush has tiny balls on it," and "[t]hat's what they used to make soup out of, with something else mixed in, like deer meat, jerky, or whatever."[6]

According to the Numu tribal historian Michael Hittman, the "main activities in Numu religion involved praying, sprinkling water or brushing someone down with green sagebrush, devotion to the Sun and belief in the healing power of various plants and herbs found in the natural environment."[7] Numu elder Corbett Mack revealed the significance of sage to individuals' health when he noted, "My grandma, she's never been sick. Never had an Indian doctor in her life." The reason was that she "believes in the sagebrush."[8] He further noted that sagebrush "feels new all the time. Can't be old. That's the belief the Old-Timers had." Hittman underscored the importance of sagebrush to the destiny of the Numu, noting that "When the world is destroyed . . . the planet Earth will tip and any decent living Numu can hang onto the sagebrush plant until Creation begins anew." This, according to tradition, "is the reason for the large amount of sagebrush or 'sawabe' in the deserts of the Great Basin."[9]

If sagebrush is one of the defining plants of the Great Basin Desert, the Europeans and Anglo-Americans had plenty to say about it. In the 1880s a British traveler noted that sagebrush was called "the damnable absinthe" and confirmed that it was "that standard of desolation" which "waves rampant." Twenty years earlier, renowned British explorer Richard Burton had found sagebrush to be, in a word, boring: In his characteristically witty manner, Burton described the Book of Mormon as "utterly dull and heavy, monotonous as a sage prairie." About fifteen years before Burton's wry characterization of sage (and Mormons' reading materials), one of the Great Basin's early American explorers, John Charles Frémont, set the tone. Frémont described his southwesterly entrance into the region, wherein his expedition "entered a defile overgrown with the ominous *Artemesia tridentata.*" Frémont identified sagebrush with the region's "primitive" peoples. "In the Great Basin," he observed, "where nearly naked he traveled on foot and lived in the sage-brush, I found him the most elementary form."[10] Thus it was that in telling stories about this region, the Anglo-Americans conflated the region's Native peoples and native landscape features.

But let us return for a moment to our three westward-bound passengers as they looked out upon this sagebrush-covered land punctuated by rugged mountains in western Nevada. This landscape not only dwarfed the train, it made even the railroad line itself seem like an ephemeral thread. The scale of the scenery was so vast, and the vistas so grand, that it did indeed prompt thoughts about both creation and creator. A writer once noted that "throughout Nevada, I have seen some of nature's finest work." Some of these works, he added, were "oases for the soul."[11] If by soul he meant "the spiritual principle embodied in human beings, all rational and spiritual beings or the universe," as the dictionary defines it, then these three travelers were doing some soul searching. The view from the train had that effect, for each traveler was awed, in a different way, by the view—so awed that each pondered its deeper meaning.

Although the travelers appeared to experience what geographer Yi-Fu Tuan called "topophilia," or sudden encounter with the landscape,[12] they were actually well prepared for what they beheld. To the Paiute, whose ancestors had lived in the region for several thousand years, the mountain range that now came into view was as familiar as the profile of a loved one. Each feature was part of a story that led back to the beginning of time. The mountain range's tallest peak was once the only thing that loomed above the waters flooding the earth. As the elders told in their stories about it, the mountain figured as a major element in the drama of creation before their people wandered forth. The rugged mountain slopes were also part of a story that the Paiute Indian knew well. All Paiute people had heard it since childhood: Here the prankster coyote had tricked gullible rock, breaking him into a thousand pieces that littered the slopes of the mountain. This event had occurred long ago, but because no one ever counted the years it was impossible to say exactly when it had happened.

To the mining engineer, the mountain was a textbook example of a block-faulted range. Its stratified rock read like so many pages in the new geology texts then assigned at the nation's leading universities. The units of rock were like distant but distinguished relatives, recognizable in portraits by both their features and ages. The illustrations in the geology texts enabled the mining engineer to classify these rocks both by their materials—sandstone, limestone, shale—and by their place in the geological time scale—Jurassic, Cretaceous, Miocene. Each was part of a drama that was timed with vague precision, 87 million years for this one; 64 million years for that; and 53 million years for one positioned on top of both the others. The shattered rock on the mountainside was a reassuring example of the weathering that revealed thousands of seasons of freeze and thaw. It remained there, as any good geologist now knew, because the climate was arid. In a wetter place, the land would have been eroded differently, with more material carried away by running water and the resulting landscape heavily clothed in vegetation.

The Mormon farmer held quite a different view of the same mountain range. It appeared as something both reassuring and terrible. Its solid wall had provided the early Mormons a sense of security from the outside world after they fled to the Intermountain West in 1847. Yet at the same time, this mountain was central to an earlier drama. The farmer's parents believed mountains like it bore silent witness to a flood that had covered the earth in Noah's time, destroying all life as it had been known; all except, that is, those fortunate enough to be on Noah's ark. To the people who still believed this story, the amount of time reflected in the landscape was short, only a few hundred generations. All of creation had taken six days, then the human drama played out over about 6,000 years since the creation of Adam and Eve. The Book of Mormon elaborated on, but did not change the timing of, those events recorded with such precision in the Bible.

*

Rolling through this same region about 120 years later on Amtrak's California Zephyr, I note that the landscape hasn't changed very much in places here.[13] The Southern Pacific Railroad's tracks[14] still parallel the Humboldt River Valley and traverse vast areas of sagebrush-covered plains. Today, however, as the westbound train roars through the desert, its air-conditioning insulates me and my fellow travelers from the afternoon heat and the distinctive scent of sagebrush. Here on the silver-colored train named in honor of Zephyrus, the Greeks' divine personification of the west wind, I'm rolling at 79 miles per hour with ample time to think. I reflect back on those three travelers over a century ago. Looking out the wide, tinted window, I ask myself two questions about the travelers' varied accounts of the landscape they beheld: First, how could the same sagebrush-covered plain and adjacent mountain range have been described and appreciated so differently by each observer? After all, wasn't it only one scene—with one real story? That question is natural enough, and lies at the heart of both landscape perception and creation stories about how it all came to be. I recall a study by geographer D. W. Meinig showing that the same landscape can be viewed and interpreted in not just three, but in ten or more different ways.[15]

I consider for a moment Meinig's classic "ten versions of the same scene." As excerpted by geographer Michael Conzen, they cover a broad range of perspectives, including:

- nature (stressing the insignificance of man),
- habitat (as man's adjustment to nature),
- artifact (reflecting man's impact on nature),
- system (a scientific view of interacting processes contribution to a dynamic equilibrium),
- problem (for solving through social action),
- wealth (in terms of property),
- ideology (revealing cultural values and social philosophy),
- history (as a record of the concrete and chronological),
- place (through the identity that locations have), and
- esthetic (according to some artistic quality possessed).[16]

To these, perhaps under the ideological category, I feel obliged to add the *spiritual* perspective. Although normally downplayed by geographers and historians who tend to emphasize the secular,[17] spiritual perceptions are fundamental in shaping attitudes toward place. Although I am a geographer and historian by training, on this issue I feel somewhat more akin to anthropologists and folklorists, who regard spiritual issues as essential to understanding people's relationship to both place and to each other.[18] I feel obliged to interpret both the geography and history of the Great Basin from this spiritual perspective, because so many of the region's residents and travelers conceive it in these terms. This spiritual perspective helps me better understand the significance of communities like Salt Lake City. To some observers, this largely Mormon city possesses "an inland remoteness, a continental isolation," as Wallace Stegner put it. That isolation is a factor in defining places here, for what Stegner described as "barrier deserts" and "rampart mountains" render it a sanctuary to the Mormons.[19] That same feeling, or something close to it, helped make this landscape "home" to the Mormon farmer.

But I also understand that isolation is a relative term. To the region's Native peoples, the area was, and is, full of human memories and spirits, while to the Anglo-Americans it was vacant—a wilderness. A Shoshone track worker on the Western Pacific Railroad at Sulphur, Nevada, told me this in 1964, and it's something I've never forgotten. His words remind me that Anglo-Americans tended to overlook the earlier human—that is, Native American—presence in areas that they encountered as "pioneers." It was this supposed emptiness, this "desolation" as some called it, that both repelled and attracted the first whites who experienced the region. In 1850, traveler Dan Carpenter was so repelled by what he called "[t]his poorest and most worthless country that man ever saw . . . a barren, worthless, valueless, d——d mean God forsaken country," that he quickly corrected his journal entry: "not God forsaken," Carpenter added, "for He never had anything to do with it."[20]

Other travelers through the Great Basin found something mystical about its desert scenes, for they seemed to have been taken right out of those wilderness passages described in the Bible. As they moved westward, the travelers encountered the region's Native peoples. These Indians regarded their ancestral lands with reverence, but their reverence came without the sense of having to prove themselves up to the environment's challenges. Prepared by centuries of biblical interpretation, however, the newcomers viewed the land as testing both their resolve and their faith. Thus it is that landscapes hereabouts involve two fundamentally different types of human spirituality—indigenous and imported.

That issue of landscapes being different depending on who experiences them leads me to the second question that also involves spirituality, if indirectly: Why are individuals so *sure* they know their own explanations about the meaning of landscape to be true? None of them—Mormon, Indian, miner—had personally experienced the actual creation of the landscape. Yet, they passionately understood their beliefs to be true—despite the fact that their truth was not based on personal observation or objective proof. They believed in these explanations because they had *faith* in the stories they had learned sitting in front of campfire hearth, chapel pulpit, and university lectern.

But surely, some might say, the mining engineer's scientific description was the most accurate. Not necessarily, for as we now know, later revelations by scientists themselves would show his account to be flawed. Although the mining engineer recognized that tectonic forces shaped the landscape, the scenery he glimpsed had formed differently than he believed. He was unaware of the continental drift that set large plates into motion. As a body of storytelling, then, science constantly changes; yet, some stories die harder than others because they are believed to be more plausible than alternative explanations. Again, faith comes into play here.

I pause for a moment to ponder and define *faith,* for it has become one of the underpinnings of my story about the Great Basin. The dictionary defines faith in several ways. The first is allegiance or loyalty, and that suggests a kind of tenacity or adherence that makes faith so powerful—and sometimes so dangerous. It also can mean fidelity, as to keep one's word or promises. Fidelity also implies truth, for being faithful means true to one's beliefs or principles. Then, too, faith can mean belief and trust in, and loyalty to, God—as in the belief in a religion's doctrines. Related to these ideas of faith is its ultimate definition as "firm belief in something for which there is no proof."

Looking at the sagebrush-covered landscape of the Great Basin roll past the train window, I realize that the separation between religion and science is somewhat arbitrary, for even scientists trust in something, if only their method of inquiry (the deductive process that states a hypothesis, and proves it in steps based on reason). Then, too, the public comes to believe in—that is, have faith in—scientific theories even though they seem secular rather than religious. A writer describing geologists' predictions of earthquakes and volcanic eruptions at the western edge of the Great Basin near Long Valley, California, put it succinctly: "[I]t takes faith to believe in scientists' interpretation of the geologic record."[21]

Somewhere near Wadsworth, Nevada, I recall that scientists actually have faith in two things—the *method* of inquiry and the likelihood that stories will *change.* Yet the rich historical tradition in science suggests that even explanations once discarded in favor of new theories—as when catastrophism was replaced by uniformitarianism, or when Darwinian evolution was supplemented or superceded by punctuated equilibrium—were "true" at the time they were accepted. This further suggests that narratives, even those based purely on faith, can change through time as more information and experiences enter a people's consciousness. True, some stories remain closer to the original telling than others. But all stories are transformed either by contact with other stories (and the peoples telling them) or by changes in the way the storyteller herself or himself tells the same story through time.

The train provides me a great place to ponder such concepts. As we've rolled from Utah through Nevada, I've been jotting down observations all day in hopes of solidifying some ideas for this book. Now well into western Nevada after a day's train ride, I realize that writing things down somehow seems to make ideas more tangible and stories more permanent; yet, it introduces another element. As the train rolls into the evening about an hour after leaving Lovelock, I consider the words of writer Mary Clearman Blew, who observed that "once I have written about the past, I will have changed it—in a sense, set it in concrete—and I will never remember it in quite the same way. The experience itself is lost; like the old Sunday storytellers who told and retold their stories until what they remembered was the tale itself."[22]

Blew's term concrete reminds me that writing down stories sets them in stone, in a manner of speaking. I remember the stone tablets of Hebrew leader Moses or the golden plates of Mormon prophet Joseph Smith and realize that writing seems to cement ideas into place like the words and dates chiseled into grave markers. This is ironic, for most stories throughout human history changed, albeit subtly, with the telling.

As my Amtrak train rolls through Sparks, Nevada, with Reno just a few minutes away, I think I've discovered something else about the written word, something paradoxical: writing is a relatively recent form of communication, yet it is used to tell (and retell) stories that may predate it by thousands of years. More than a century ago, the Paiute rancher was most closely connected to that oral tradition, for Native Americans did not write stories but passed them down both informally and in storytelling sessions. Some of these stories remain as sacred as any scriptures. That type of storytelling introduces another level of complexity and calls again upon faith—the belief that we are hearing the original. It puts Indian stories at a disadvantage, for our mainstream culture trusts the written word far more than it does "hearsay." That should not make those whose beliefs are based on the written word too cocky, however, for those who believe in the permanence of the written word face a sobering fact: Even though these written words may be preserved more effectively than the writings on gravestones, which ultimately weather away with the passage of seasons, their meanings change through time. This means that we will never exactly know just what those written words meant a thousand years ago or more, even though they may appear to be exactly the same as when they were recorded.

People conceptualize their world in terms of images as well as words. That helps explain the potency of symbols like crosses, stars, and other graphic elements associated with many religions. However, I think of how much we are taught to mistrust imagery when I see the neon-lighted downtown of Reno roll into view. It is animated with flashing images of smiling cowboys, golden nuggets, and silver dollars. These signs remind me that the use of visual imagery figures heavily in most storytelling. Because human beings also communicate using visual symbols, I look to them in their many forms—petroglyphs, pictographs, drawings, maps—to help me understand the stories people tell about places. Victoria Dickenson's words come to mind here: "There appears to exist a distrust of images as true representatives of things in themselves," while "the word itself conveys the 'essence' of the thing."[23] If both academic and mainstream culture inherently mistrust images and rely on narrative, there is probably a biblical root to this mistrust: "Graven images" were scorned, and "the word" was to be heeded and believed. However, although it is true that words may have fewer meanings than images (recall how many stories can be told from the same Rorschach test), that does not mean those images are invalidated. Rather, they have specific meanings at specific times. Although we may not have a clue as to what particular Indian petroglyphs mean, they were rich in meaning when incised into rock surfaces. They still are today, although those meanings may now differ.

As I step down from the train into the rapidly cooling October night, Reno is ablaze with light and filled with sound. I think of how different my arrival by train would have been a century and a quarter ago before electricity transformed night into day. In 1881, the city huddled close to the railroad station, but it now sprawls in all directions along blazing thoroughfares. But after traveling across the Great Basin all day, I realize that portions of the region haven't changed much in the last century. The desert and mountains are still there as dramatic elements of the scenery. My thoughts return to the landscapes that the three travelers beheld with such certainty in 1881. Each believed (that is, had faith in) his own explanation for what the sagebrush plain and adjacent mountain meant. That, too, hasn't changed much, for people still feel a deep need to account for creation—that is, explain how things around us came to be.

Walking a couple of blocks to my hotel, I ponder what the three travelers' stories had in common as well as what made them different. Each of their stories involved some recognition of time (either relative or absolute), or "timing." Because something occurred before something else, chronology is implicit in creation. It is here that I come face to face with yet another profound difference between Native American and European American culture. The Paiute's perception of time was independent of any clock or calendar. I'm tempted to say that the Paiute's beliefs were far less rigid than those of the mining engineer who sought to measure the mountains' formation in recognized time units (geological ages). It occurs to me, however, that the Mormon farmer could trace his roots to a tradition that was even more obsessive about time. Calculating the scene's age in terms of familiar measurements (years) that were extrapolated from stories in the Bible, he fused two traditions—an early narrative of storytelling based on epochal events that only had relative positions in time, with a biblically endorsed measurement, or quantification, of time.

According to some interpretations of Genesis, the earth was literally created in six days, a belief that is still vigorously defended by some who oppose the theory of evolution.[24] The belief in a 6,000-year-old earth, although rapidly becoming archaic, was based on statements by early European church authorities that had become part of folklore. Some Christians at this time still owed their understanding of the earth's age to the painstakingly calculation of Irish Anglican bishop James Ussher. In the mid-seventeenth century, Ussher calculated the time of creation at 4,004 B.C. To do so, he painstakingly tabulated the ages of individuals mentioned in the Bible. Ussher's calculation was widely challenged by scientists in the mid-nineteenth century, and even the Mormon farmer sensed the coming of this new order. Yet knowing the universe's exact birth date was still somehow reassuring. What made it especially so probably involved a linking of mathematics and psychology; through this combination, the earth's age of about 6,000 years seemed comprehensible. For example, during each generation a person experiences about 6,000 days. The alternative dates proposed by earth scientists were staggering, for the earth's age now receded from a manageable thousands to a disconcerting millions, and finally to a nearly incomprehensible billions. By increasing geological time into what John McPhee calls "deep time," scientists distanced humankind farther and farther from creation.[25]

*

After several days' stay in Reno, I rent a car and drive east toward the mountain range that had so entranced those travelers more than a century ago. With a road map in hand, I follow back roads toward the mountain for almost an hour, but it seems to recede until I near its base. I try to see the scene as each of three passengers had—that is, as three different sage-brush-covered plains sweeping up to the adjoining mountains. This, how-ever, is futile because each of the scenes they observed was held in place by philosophical underpinnings as tenacious as the sagebrush and as rigid as the rocks. However, I've joined the three passengers in transforming the scene into a place.

In so doing, I find one fact especially reassuring: that the mountain, for example, had a presence that transcended any individual—or even any cul-ture. This landform was instantly recognized as a mountain through a process of categorization shared by all peoples. Mountains may mean dif-ferent things to different peoples but, thankfully, all peoples exhibit the ca-pacity to consider them different from plains or valleys—even though they may use different words or graphic symbols to identify and depict them.[26] To the Paiute, the mountain had a name that was used in order to differen-tiate it from other mountains. It was a place of critical importance in the tribe's history. To the mining engineer, that name resonated as a place where certain geological events took place. To the Mormon farmer, it was one of a series of mountains that delineated the landscape. Even though it had no name, its shape and position with regard to the surrounding valleys was sufficient to include it as the far western reaches of home. And so the mountain becomes a landmark in the perceptual geography of the region from which it rises. Because it is invested with such belief about creation (and creator), it is also an element in the spiritual geography. The term spiritual is appropriate because it is tied to powerful forces transcending any particular individual; forces linking everyday objects and experiences to creation; forces binding individual and collective souls to place.

Parking the rental car as close as I can get to the base of the mountain, I begin hiking, then climbing its slopes, exhilarated by the view that sweeps to the north. As a place, the mountain has become more than a mere loca-tion to me; it is now deeply invested with *meaning* about human history. The word *meaning* refers to something that one intends to convey; some-thing that is significant or has implications and hidden or special signifi-cance. All three, make that four now, people used the mountain in telling stories that were not only about what happened recently, but also about what had transpired in the distant past. Note that the mountain was not simply a prop in each story, but central to the plot of each. All stories ultimately involve place as well as people, for they occur somewhere that has special characteristics. This is especially true of creation stories, which are inseparable from particular locations.

From a perch high up on the mountainside, I find it easier to comprehend creation itself. The noun *creation,* which is defined as the act of creating, especially the act of bringing the world into ordered existence, is more complex than it first seems. I ponder several things about this word. First, it involves not only *action* but also considerable *drama.* In fact, one of the prime definitions of the word creation is "the first representation of a dramatic role." Second, creation involves the concept of *order* and *organization:* It not only involves making or producing something, but it also assumes that what is created reflects some type of rational or meaningful *design.* When we create something, we make something recognizable either out of nothing or out of something vague. Then, too, there is a suggestion that creation involves grandeur or importance. In fact, one of the synonyms of creation is the entire world, or even the universe; then we use the term "whole of creation" to mean everything we are capable of knowing.

Creation accounts for the birth of everything, and that birth must occur somewhere—that is, in place. In recounting our own individual stories from the beginning, we naturally think of our own birthplace. This individual account plays out for entire cultures, which have places of origin, factual or mythical. Such storytelling seamlessly ties event to location. Nativity means to be born, yet the word is closely related to *nation,* which has geographic boundaries. It also refers to locality: being a native means living in the place of one's birth—again, another reaffirmation of the inseparable link between existence and place. That sounds straightforward enough, and perhaps even comforting, but there is an irony here. Each of the three travelers found meaning in the landscape, and did so with personal certainty. Yet, each built these meanings on a complicated scaffold that had been erected by other architects—ancestors, elders, ministers, teachers.

Consider for a moment the building materials that they used. "Meaning is the most elusive of words," notes a folklorist who has studied in the Great Basin. He adds that "the quest for meaning—is an enigma, since man can understand experience, nature, all that is, only in terms of himself." Like all of us, each of the three travelers did so by first identifying "the form of things—their morphology and configuration," which "is one of the major interpretive tools man uses to place objects living and dead in accepted positions."[27] Without hesitation, each traveler selected, then employed, these objects—the sagebrush-covered plain, bedded rock strata, a mountain peak, a slope of talus—as so many building blocks in constructing an edifice that gave meaning to what he saw. This is a somewhat elaborate way of stating something simple yet profound: by constructing such meanings, each traveler transformed the *space* of the Great Basin into *place,* much like cartographers transform *terra incognita* into known territory through words and images.

Sitting high up on the mountainside, I become aware of the tangible elements needed to construct a spiritual geography here. After decades of traversing this region of far-flung vistas, I now permit myself the luxury of reflection. Inspired by the landscape and awed by people's stories about it, I am in turn empowered to tell a story about this region's impact on the human spirit. In doing so I realize that I will have to weave a fabric of meaning from many threads. I'm not alone in this endeavor. Ascribing deeper meanings to place is one of humankind's natural talents, yet it is fraught with conflict from the outset. As any person learns to employ those building blocks (that is, becomes acculturated), he or she becomes less and less able to build anything different. In other words, landscape is built out of words (and images) and thus becomes a Tower of Babel. We can understand our own landscape constructions but never fully understand another's. Hence, we are fated to never fully understand a landscape's meaning in any other terms but our own.

But I am undaunted. From my mountain vantage point, the Great Basin landscape stretches away to reveal rows of rugged mountain ranges rising from the pale bluish-green sagebrush and dusty-colored shadscale. The air is thin and dry, the sky a deep blue straight above and pale blue at the horizon. Just as two fundamental landscape elements—earth and sky—are everywhere evident in the Great Basin, I realize that there are two fundamental philosophical or religious systems—animism and deism—at work in this place. These two great religious traditions converge in the Great Basin as they do elsewhere in the Americas, but they are more palpable to me here. The Native American tradition, with its animistic interpretation of places, was here first, and it has left its mark in place names and sacred places that dot the entire region. This Native American tradition weaves the landscape into the fabric of creation stories. Looking southward toward the Deep Creek Mountains I am reminded of a Shoshone story about their creation. A tribal elder recounts, "It was Hawk who made the Deep Creek Mountains." This occurred when "Hawk was angry," probably "because someone was fooling around with his wife." The agitated Hawk "flew up high, then dashed himself against the mountain (Mount Wheeler) and broke it all up." According to this elder, Hawk's actions "made all these mountains around here."[28] In these Shoshone and Paiute stories, animals play a part and serve as metaphors for the human condition. I see a contrast here between this Native tradition and that of my imported Judeo-Christian tradition. Mine involves the creation of heavens and earth first, then animals, and—finally—people. My tradition was also born in a desert region, but is monotheistic and patriarchal.

By listening to indigenous peoples, I learn to compare Native American beliefs with those religious beliefs with which I was raised. My Native American friends and associates do not voluntarily talk about religion, but it deeply affects their lives. When we get around to the subject, I learn much by simply listening. Here's what I gather from what they tell me. God in Native religions is a force that shapes and sustains Mother Earth. That force operates more or less serendipitously, that is, without deliberate moral intervention. In Native American religion, people and animals work out their relationships together, and enduring lessons are learned. It seems trite to restate the premise that Native Americans have a deep spiritual connection with the land, but that is at work here. Their Great Basin landscapes were sculpted by the Great Spirit—a creator who is vaguely defined but omnipresent. There is no God in the sense of a judgmental male figure—the LORD—who rewards the good and punishes the wrongdoer. As a consequence, Native American religions are less moralistic than those in the Judeo-Christian tradition. Significantly, because the Great Spirit creator is not jealous or demanding, there is no need for Native Americans to convince others to believe as they do. Native Americans have no need to proselytize, that is, be "fishers of men." In these conversations, we sometimes touch on heaven and an afterlife. Here again I sense profound differences: In Native American religion originally, it appears that there was little or no awareness of the individual's life continuing after death, as there is in Christianity. True, in Native religions there are ghosts, but these are forces that have not yet yielded to their ultimate fate—oblivion after death, a merging into something greater than the individual.

There are other differences, too. The Judeo-Christian tradition brings with it a concept of not only damnation, but eternal damnation, the natural result when one falls from grace with God. I suspect that the Great Basin did not witness such moral life-versus-death (or better yet, afterlife-versus-afterdeath) dramas until the arrival of Christians a little more than two centuries ago. On the other hand, spiritual salvation can ultimately deliver, in Christian thought, eternal grace. The Native Peoples intuitively sense the power of this Christian message, and many believe it today. Nowadays it is impossible to find a Native American who has not been affected by the Judeo-Christian tradition; but then again, I believe that it is equally difficult to find an American believer in the Judeo-Christian tradition who has not been affected, in some way, by Native American spirituality.

On my mountain perch, I think about Moses, Jesus, Joseph Smith, and others who received inspiration from high places to shape religions. That lofty perspective reminds me just how potent the Judeo-Christian heritage is, and how much it has contributed to social, political, and economic life as we know it. Before I prepare to leave, I ponder one last point: The Judeo-Christian tradition nurtured an *individualism* unparalleled in world history. The emphasis on the individual (as opposed to the group) explains what the mining engineer was doing on that train in 1881—trying to both understand creation and benefit other individuals savvy enough to seize economic opportunities. As the engineer gazed out upon the landscape, a scene quite different from what the Paiute rancher saw presented itself. It was also a landscape very different from what the Mormon farmer saw—a landscape that was to be transformed into Eden by communal effort of the Latter-day Saints. But both the Mormon farmer and the mining engineer had common roots in the Judeo-Christian tradition, *and they thus saw the landscape not as it was, but as it might become.*

Being from a different cultural tradition that originated halfway around the world, the mining engineer and Mormon farmer saw a landscape strikingly different from what the Paiute ranch hand saw. The Paiute viewed the landscape as a series of stories involving plants and animals; the mining engineer saw it in terms of raw primordial forces that could be harnessed by humankind; and the Mormon farmer saw one more desolate space ready to be transformed by irrigation into the Kingdom of God. It bears restating, however, that both the Mormon and mining engineer saw a *landscape that could—even should—be shaped into something else, something more productive.* But as they gazed from the train, both the Mormon and mining engineer saw the world at its most primordial. In this desert land, the forces that had originally been unleashed by God in creating the universe were still everywhere visible. These forces had nothing to do with man or animals, except indirectly as some fossils of the latter were entombed by past events. The notion of a mechanistically operating world was an underpinning concept of science. That scientific tradition originated in the areas surrounding the Mediterranean Sea. Its emphasis on a physical world separate from the spiritual was perfectly in keeping with the Judeo-Christian religion that helped nurture the polarity.

By contrast, the Native American's concept of the way things developed involved other actors; even animals had a role in this process. The Paiute thus saw a landscape not empty, but full of plants and animals that were part of creation. Where the Paiute saw existing bounty, the Mormon and mining engineer saw future possibility. But, and this is extremely important, all recognized the hand of some potent force—call it energy, God, or a great spirit—in shaping the landscape.

One element in the Judeo-Christian heritage gave another dimension to this landscape that spreads out below my mountain viewpoint. That is the notion that the *isolation* of the desert poses a spiritual challenge, and in turn offers spiritual sustenance. That belief played out from the beginning of white settlement in the Great Basin, and became a statement of faith in the early 1900s. Consider a 1923 letter to the student body of Deep Springs College, which is located in a remote valley near California's border with Nevada, by college president L. L. Nunn. "The desert has a deep personality," Nunn noted in his missive; "it has a voice; and God speaks through its personality and voice. Great leaders in all ages . . . have sought the desert and heard its voice."[29]

Nunn was not alone in thinking that the Great Basin had religious connotations. At about the same time, 1924 to be exact, amateur archeologist Alan Le Baron wrote a series of startling articles for the *San Francisco Examiner.* In them, Le Baron claimed that he had discovered the Garden of Eden—not in southwest Asia Minor, but rather on a hilltop overlooking the East Walker River about twenty miles south of Yerington, Nevada! Calling the site the "Hill of a Thousand Tombs," Le Baron reportedly found paleontological evidence such as the bones of camels, elephants, and lions and the remains of lush forests. As proof of the site's antiquity to mankind, Le Baron also claimed that the petroglyphs depicting animals and abstract designs were related to, and probably even predated, Egyptian hieroglyphics.[30] Le Baron's claims of a North American Garden of Eden may seem fanciful to some until we recall the idea's deep roots in America; in the 1830s, Mormon prophet Joseph Smith had revealed as much, and Mormons believe it to this day—though the Garden's location is in Missouri. For his part, Le Baron probably took some clues from both the Bible and the Great Basin's powerful—biblical-like—landscape: deep basins, salt lakes, well-watered oases, forested mountains, and remote archaeological sites that suggested a grand past. In the Great Basin, faith and landscape conspire to resurrect old myths and create new ones. I sense this as I gaze southward before I begin my climb down off the mountain. I am still high enough to view the rugged Pine Grove Hills and the kaleidoscopic topography of the East Walker River Valley far in the distance. These places were, and are, sacred to the Paiute Indians, and they possess an allure to European

Americans whose religious roots were first nurtured in a similar-appearing landscape 5,000 years ago and 10,000 miles to the east, the Holy Land.

Arriving back at my rental car physically exhausted but spiritually restored by my time on the mountain, I start the engine and prepare to begin my journey eastward into the heart of the Great Basin. After several days' travel through some of the most wide-open country in North America, I feel confident enough to begin telling its story.

2

Darkness and Light

For the last several days, I've been driving from sunup to sundown, taking in the stunning desert landscapes of the Great Basin. At the end of the third day out of Reno, I've worked my way into the heart of the region. Now, with evening coming on, I'm driving like a bat out of hell between Ely and Pioche, Nevada. Somewhere back up the road, a sign declared Pioche 121 miles, and I took it as a mathematical challenge: could I make it there in under an hour and a half? I calculate that I'll have to average about 85 mph to do it, but the highway is wide open with no traffic in sight. Settling down to a cruising speed of 90, I flick on the radio, hit "seek," and wait for it to lock onto a station. However, here in "cosmic nowhere," as a cowboy poet in Elko once called it, the FM tuner sweeps through all the channels without stopping, endlessly searching for a station. The radio's frenetic hunt for a signal seems to confirm the Great Basin's reputation as 165,000 square miles of emptiness. But I thrive on the openness of the landscape and the momentary separation from civilization. Rolling at about 90, I'm mesmerized by the whine of the engine, the sound of the tires—and enchanted by the beauty of Cave Valley, which stretches off to the south like a worn groove between the two tall mountain ranges flanking it. Hurtling along the desert highway at more than 130 feet per second—so fast that an occasional cattle guard makes just one sound—"bong," as opposed to the "bong-bong" at a more respectable speed—I'm as attentive as I ever get.

After half an hour, I've covered almost fifty miles as long shadows work their way up the western slopes and the horizon turns an inky blue. Driving this fast satisfies more than just my natural penchant for speed; it's a natural reaction for my species, aware of the coming night and wondering where, maybe even if, I'll find shelter. I'm rolling this fast now because I know that I wouldn't be able to do so safely after dark. Like other creatures of my species, I'm better able to see in the day than in the darkness. The daytime has always belonged to me, the nighttime to someone—or something—else. I keep up this pace for a long time, slowing only once in ninety miles for the one car that approaches from the opposite direction. With a wave we flash past each other, then resume our maniacal pace toward opposite destinations.

My attention is riveted to the road as the shadows fill the valley. I calculate that there are now only about thirty miles, or only about twenty minutes of daylight left. At just this time, I reach the crest of a long grade, and the radio finally locks onto a station. As if out of nowhere, a minister's voice booms a line about light and darkness, firmament and heaven. This, I recognize instantly, is the stuff out of which creation stories are made. The minister, it turns out, is broadcasting from Newport Beach, California, a good four hundred miles to the southwest, but his voice is clear. How this channel reaches me while the small channels much closer can't is less a miracle than a carefully calculated mix of initiative, money, and technology. The minister's station is broadcasting the "word of God" at twenty times more power than the secular stations here in the Great Basin.

The minister is expounding on a subject that has captured the attention of people since time immemorial. It's on my mind, too, as I wonder about how these awesome, darkening, brooding mountains came into existence. Somehow, thoughts of creation seem more comprehensible here, far from distractions. With the distant peaks of the Fortification Range in the east now deep in shadow, and only Mount Wilson and Parsnip Peak recognizable as serrations cutting the evening sky, this is a most appropriate place to comprehend creation. One reason is that the topography here reveals some of the cataclysmic forces that shape the earth. Row after row of stark mountains rise from salt-filled basins, each range hinting at those forces. Experiencing this landscape fills me with a sense of wonder—not only about how it developed over eons, but about the original event that started everything developing in the first place. The minister is not alone, for many people have pondered that same question here and elsewhere. The quest for that privileged information—the answer to how everything began—lies at the root of all spirituality and at the center of all religions.

Like many journeys, the search for answers to creation is fraught with not only uncertainty, but ambiguity. As a concept, creation brings to my mind both joy and confusion, for it lies at the root of humankind's most fundamental dilemma. Consider the conundrum that I'm pondering about twenty minutes out of Pioche. First, creation is a subject that concerns only the human animal out of all the species with which we share the earth. I think of them as I race south. Even with the headlights on high beam, human eyesight in these twilight conditions is incapable of seeing much farther than about a hundred yards. Besides, it's the time when many critters with much better nighttime vision, but little sense of traffic hazards, emerge. And so, to give everybody a better chance of surviving, I instinctively reduce my speed to 70, then 60, as night closes in.

I then return to my contemplation about creation, which has a second vexing quality. If it is true that humankind possesses the most inquiring of minds, it is also true that people arrived on the scene long *after* the world was created—in other words, were not present at creation. Ever curious, the human mind knows that *something* both magnificent and overwhelming occurred but is forever denied the ability to know exactly what it was. In other words, humankind is eternally destined to seek answers to what happened, and thus imperfectly comprehend why it happened. The search for answers to creation forces me to expand my definition of spirituality. In two of humankind's most powerful institutions—religion and science—creation is a central issue. We are destined to search for answers, and few places are better suited to that inquiry than the Great Basin. Here the hand of nature is visible as the most elementary of the universe's forces—heaven and earth—are in constant contact.

The heavens are a good place to begin a spiritual geography, for they figure in every creation story. Just as all desert dwellers have naturally looked skyward for answers to the mysteries of creation, those who know the Great Basin encounter that most potent of forces—the sun—here. Sometimes on drives or hikes through the Great Basin, I will seek out a prominent point and contemplate the sun's awesome power. With eyes closed, I feel it penetrate my skin and my consciousness. I felt this power earlier today as I stopped at Pancake Summit, where a dusting of snow still clung in the shadows despite the bright sunshine. Sprawled on the hood of the car, I felt the sun warm my face, and the heat of the engine warm the hood, and my back, a result of the sun-generated fossil fuel I'd coaxed through the car's fuel injection system. This, I recognize, is the force that powers everything, for all energy as we know and use it is derived from the sun.

At night in the Great Basin, the vastness of the universe becomes almost overwhelming. After midnight a couple of weeks ago in western Utah, I'd looked up into the night sky and beheld a Milky Way that looked like crushed glittering glass—or pulverized diamonds—spread from horizon to horizon. That day had been warm, but the thin clear air had cooled to a distinct chill just after nightfall. These stars filling the sky varied in their color because some are hot and some cold, relatively speaking. But they were all icy light to me as I was chilled by both the night air and the thought of the immensity of it all: there is no end to it; I was looking into infinity—and eternity. What I beheld raised the hairs on the back of my neck as if by instinct. In beholding this sight, I realized that I was peering straight into the glowing residue of creation, and I sensed the Milky Way's profound ability to shape storytelling here. One of nature's most awesome sights, this clustering of millions of stars has deep cultural significance in the Great Basin. The Paiute call it *Kus'ipo'* (Dusty Trail) or, more to the point, *Nümü-po* (People's Trail) and believe it to be the path traveled by the souls of the dead as they seek another, more abundant world to the south where there will be good hunting and time for gambling and dancing. The Big Dipper shimmering overhead is *Ta'noa'di,* a heavenly net into which men chase rabbits. To some Native peoples hereabouts, Orion's belt consists of three stars that are either mountain sheep or mountain sheep husbands, while the brightest star in this constellation (Sirius) is a woman called *Tinagidi* (The Chaser). Significantly, the heavens themselves are not the product of remote physical forces, but of Wolf (creator of both Heaven and Earth) and his trickster brother Coyote, who caused his family to flee to the sky.[1]

Night temporarily etches the characters in these stories into the mind, but daytime temporarily erases it. Day and night convey very different moods—and generate very different philosophical questions. As the sun rises, boundaries begin to take form. The world and landscape of the familiar takes shape before our eyes. Once again, it is easy to see why we regard our sun as so important, and so uniquely ours, its rays penetrating and warming both our bodies and souls, its light diffused throughout the atmosphere by dust particles to create the blue sky.

If we have trouble understanding the concept that our sun is just one of countless stars in the Milky Way, we have even more trouble imagining what life would be like without it. The sun evaporates the waters, stirs the winds, and helps sustain life as we know it. And so we have difficulty comprehending, or believing, what it will be like when, in a projected 10 billion years, the sun begins to die. At that time it will likely grow about a thousand times more luminous, slowly turn into a low-luminosity (white dwarf) star, and then ultimately burn itself out. Given the sun's relative constancy in the brief time that human history has evolved, we have less trouble engaging it as a central feature in stories of creation. This is because we implicitly recognize its potent role as the purveyor of light, energy, and life.

The sun illuminates all human storytelling in the Great Basin, as it does in other arid areas. Appearing as a small but very bright disk, it is the largest body in our solar system—a flaming ball of gases about 865,000 miles in diameter. The sun's 10+-million-degree temperature can be sensed even though it is about 92 million miles from earth. When I look toward it, its light both dazzles and repels me, for I am witnessing a sustained thermonuclear reaction as hydrogen is transmuted into helium. The centrifugal force of this explosive reaction is kept in check by the sun's powerful gravitational pull, so that all of humankind tends to think of the sun as an *object* in the sky. At sunrise, or especially at sunset when its rays shine through dust in the earth's atmosphere, we can gaze at the sun and behold an orange (or red) disk. In midday, the sun is potent enough to enable us to see the pulsing veins in our closed eyelids.

The nuclear reaction that gives life to our sun is remarkably stable—at least in human terms. The sun has burned brightly for the several billion years that the earth has been in existence and so is our constant companion in the heavens. In bright sunshine, out in the Great Basin earlier today, I had trouble believing that, impressive as the sun is, it is pretty much typical of the yellow dwarf stars in the universe. Even in November, it floods through the car's windshield, heating up the interior. Now, as night falls, I switch on the car's heater to compensate for the disappearance of the sun, always remembering that I am using the sun's captured energy to heat the car's darkened interior and propel me through the gathering darkness.

It is easy to think that the sun is strong today, but according to Shoshone and Paiute Indian creation stories, it was once far more potent. They recount a time, long ago, when the "sun wasn't like it is today" because it "didn't just go across the sky" and "didn't set in the evening." Instead, as related in the Paiute story "Cottontail's Encounter with Sun," it stayed motionless in the sky; at that time, "the land was very hot . . . too hot" and the sun "burned the earth." To rectify this situation, Cottontail Rabbit shot his arrows into the sky hoping to hit—and kill—the sun. At first, the arrows were burned up, so the enterprising Cottontail "shot a fire stick," which killed Sun. Cottontail then found the dead sun lying on the ground, cut its heart out, and "threw it high into the sky." Perhaps realizing the gravity of his actions, Cottontail told the sun that he hadn't actually killed him, but rather caused him to behave: "I have shown you the way to go. Now you go that way." As a result, the sun always rises in the east. It always sets in the west. It is now "high in the sky" and so "it doesn't burn the earth."[2]

This story is noteworthy for several reasons. First, it breathes life, even personality, into the most potent force in our solar system. The story is characteristically Native American in that it is animistic—that is, it attributes consciousness to natural objects and provides animals with deliberate intelligence. Furthermore, the story is classically Native American in that animals have an active role in history, or prehistory. Cottontail is one of many animal actors in such dramas; he is wily and bold enough to get the sun to behave, it is true, but he is only one of many animals—such as Elk, Bear, Wolf, and Coyote—who also have power.

Compare this story with one from the minister's Judeo-Christian tradition, which permeates Western culture. In it, humans are the actors and God both the producer and director. In Western thought, a cottontail rabbit is only an animal and would not really think, speak, or be capable of such action. Moreover, the sun would be considered an inanimate object incapable of deliberate action or thought. Instead, another force—the omnipotent being called God—directs the motion or actions of such objects or animals. Neither the objects nor the animals have either personalities or powers. In a sense, Western culture would consider the Paiute story a fable, or mythical story about supernatural happenings, especially one in which animals speak or act like human beings to teach humankind lessons. Western culture has a rich set of such fables, but they are normally considered separate from religion. They are, I suspect, remnants from a time before Judeo-Christian culture came to dominate the religious beliefs of much of the Middle East, then Europe, and ultimately more than half of the earth's surface.

I am reminded of this contrast as I near Pioche, which I did reach in an hour and a half—noticing that the rental car's engine sounded somehow different now that I'd put it through a racelike pace for the last 120 miles. It's now broken in. Just before reaching Pioche, I note a yellow glow building in the eastern sky. Nearing the town, the glow intensifies. What, I wonder, could the light be? Surely not Pioche, which is home to only about eight hundred souls and no traffic lights. Within a few minutes, my question is answered. As I swing around the last curve into town, a full moon lights the eastern sky, appearing huge on the ragged eastern horizon. The moon brightens the dark night here, but it is actually our sun that illuminates the moon's stony and dusty surface. Tonight the moon is so bright I can almost read by it; yet, in another couple of weeks, it will be bathed in its own shadow and the night will be filled with millions of stars made invisible tonight by the moon's radiance. So go the phases of our constant companion, the moon, whose twenty-eight-day cycle is so much like women's menstrual cycle. This connection once again speaks to the inseparability of the geophysical world from the biological. These thoughts are on my mind as I pull into the motel parking lot after having driven about five hundred miles through the Great Basin since sunrise.

How I located the motel is a story in itself worth retelling, for it underscores the faith placed in the Bible hereabouts. When I first arrived in town I passed a long, one-story building that looked like a motel but had no sign. There was only one old car parked in front, and it also looked abandoned in the evening light. A quick look around the former mining town revealed there were no hotels or motels. I figured I'd have to sleep in the car, but inquired at the local speedy-mart just in case I had missed something. The woman behind the counter said, "Call this number and ask." Perplexed, I called the number and explained I was a professor studying the history and geography of the Great Basin. The elderly woman on the other end said I'd be welcome to stay at her motel, and she described its location. "But," I said, "I thought it was closed." "No," she responded, "Just drive to the motel and let yourself into room 14. You'll find the key under the doormat." She explained that I would find everything in order, and upon leaving in the morning, I should "put twenty dollars in the Bible." Incredulous but tired, I drove to the motel, found the key, slipped it into the lock, turned the doorknob, and walked into a clean room. There, as predicted, was a Bible sitting prominently on the nightstand next to the bed.

This book—really a compilation of several books spanning many centuries—firmly traces its origin to the Middle East. Its roots are Mesopotamian, but its story plays out through a tortuous recounting of Hebraic genealogy. At the book's end, in the New Testament, one finally arrives at the teachings of the book's last prophet, Jesus. Some of the teachings in this book inspired yet another of the world's greatest religions—Islam—about six hundred years after Jesus' death. It is, however, the beginning of the Old Testament I seek tonight, as I want to compare what I read in it with what the minister on the radio was discussing earlier. I also want to compare the Bible's Old World perspective with that of the religions in the New World—that is, Native American—creation stories I've encountered in my travels throughout, and readings about, the Great Basin.

I encounter the first mention, or rather suggestion, of the sun at the very opening of the Old Testament. In Genesis, God first creates heaven and earth. But all is in darkness until God says, "Let there be light, and there was light." This is a defining, highly qualitative act, for "God saw that the light was good; and God separated the light from the darkness." We suspect that the sun has been created, though it is not actually named in that passage. Nevertheless, because "God called the light Day, and the Darkness he called Night" (Gen. 1:3-5), we intuitively know that our sun is the illuminating force. Throughout the Bible, the sun is a powerful object that suggests God's power. God's omniscience is confirmed by his seeing everything "under the sun" (Eccles. 10:5), an expression that commonly refers to everything that has been created. Moreover, in the Bible, the light from the sun is good, cleansing, and associated with rectitude, as when God says "I will cover the sun with a cloud . . . and put darkness upon your land." (Ezek. 29:7-8).

In these accounts, we can immediately sense the power of God as creator and destroyer. He commands the sun, and only he is to be equated with the light which suggests both power and truth. We also realize that darkness suggests something disapproved by God, an effective metaphorical device that has far-reaching cultural implications. One unfortunate consequence of such binary thinking is the equation of light or white with good and darkness with bad, which in turn leads to racism that ultimately equates lightness/whiteness with purity/goodness and darkness with alienation from God, if not evil. This, as we shall see, will play out in the cultural and religious history of the Great Basin as whites encountered Indians. The Bible is loaded with complex meaning and suggests a strong dualism in its storyline. Is it, I wonder, the Bible that reflects a binary either/or reality? Or does the binary reality we believe in reflect our dependence on this venerable book's interpretation of nature—both physical and human nature?

As I go out to my car to retrieve some maps, I look up into the night sky. Spotting Polaris, the North Star, I realize that there is another, positive side to darkness—its thought-provoking quality. Immersed in darkness, we think our deepest—that is most profoundly philosophical—thoughts. Unencumbered by the appearances of objects, we use our imaginations to order the unfathomable, to give meaning to that which is beyond meaning. We can think spiritual thoughts during what musician Louis Armstrong called "the dark sacred night." Then, too, night can help us get our bearings in the universe. Those people who have mastered the universe by developing agriculture and commercial networks are those who have come to reconnoiter and navigate from the night sky. They take pinpoints of light and weave the darkness into the fabric of knowledge—knowledge of both space and time as the positions of stars help us understand the seasons. Those points of light would have no meaning without the blackness of the void in which they are set.

Speaking of darkness, consider the next potent symbol in many creation stories—the cave. In the Great Basin, there are many caves where peoples instinctively grouped in prehistoric times. Because a cave's temperature is far more isothermal than its surroundings (often equaling the average annual temperature of a particular geographic location), caves offer protection from temperature extremes in both winter and summer. Today these mysterious sites are festooned with petroglyphs and pictographs whose meaning may forever be lost. Of all the places we may experience, a cave is the most primordially uterine and symbolically feminine, for it draws us into Mother Earth; thus the analogy of cave and womb is deeply rooted in human prehistory and history. This is landscape at its most elementary— and most forbidden in Western culture—landscape as a metaphor for human genitalia. A cave in this context denotes the most mysterious and magical of dark places, the female reproductive tract.

The vulva appears in a number of Paiute stories that I've encountered in my travels throughout the Great Basin, including "Orion's Belt." In it, Mountain Sheep's wife neglected her digging of roots and instead decided to play with string and then turn herself into a deer: "So," a Paiute storyteller relates, "she sat on the ground and made tracks with her vulva." As might be expected, the wife's act creates discord, as does the men's taking the woman's willow stick. In confronting her husband and the other men, the storyteller continues, "She became so angry, she cut off her vulva and threw it at him." The vulva then "hit her husband on the back on his neck and stuck" there. In one version of this story, the band of mountain sheep continue until they came to a big rimrock; in another they become the constellation Orion. The woman turns into a deer.3

This Paiute story reveals more than just a close connection between animals and people. It suggests that animals have an important role in the creation of natural phenomena. It also reveals a rich anthropomorphic and anatomical connection between place and creation narratives. This is the stuff of spiritual geography, wherein both the landscape and all natural features are linked to creation narratives. Note, too, that something ethereal or special is linked with something common but naturally hidden—the power of parts of the human body: the vulva is an important element in a dialogue about power because it both transforms and is transformed. The story also suggests a deep connection between the human body and landscape, as exemplified by one of the body's—and the landscape's—most elementary forms of enclosure. The artist and writer William L. Fox notes the symbolic connection between caves and vulviform petroglyphs in many parts of the Great Basin, a correlation "that reinforces the interpretation that the vagina sign represented an entrance to the spiritual underworld."[4]

These stories remind me of my first encounter with a significant pictograph site in Joshua Tree National Monument in 1968. Fellow geographer Jim Leonard had joined me in exploring the area, and we found ourselves inquiring about Indian rock art sites. One site, which was off-limits to all but the most serious of archaeological researchers, was shown to us by a park ranger who made an exception for us as interested geographers. I am glad that he did, for the site is so potent in its natural and cultural symbolism that I've thought about it many times in the last thirty-five years. The abundant pictographs here represented people and animals, but the cave's *configuration* itself was most compelling as a depiction of the passageway to the womb (fig. 2.1). I have shown this image in many presentations, and it never ceases to elicit an audible reaction from audiences—so close is it in appearance to the human female genitalia. Even more revealing is the site's relation to hydrology, for when it rains, water courses from this suggestively realistic feature—an irrefutable connection between the vulva and the flow of life. In this equation, the vulva equals the *source* of life, and the water the element that *sustains* all life. This cave is at the southern edge of the Great Basin, and its Mojave Desert location may be significant, for that is where Numu culture may have originated several thousand years ago.[5]

Far to the north, the cave at Fort Rock in eastern Oregon is another Great Basin site associated with origins. Here in the high desert where the region's character is determined by vulcanism and strong seasonal temperature extremes, Fort Rock rises like an island from the sagebrush sea, a wave cut bench at its base testifying to an ancient shoreline. Fort Rock's porous basalt yielded perfect natural caves—places of refuge from storms. Sandals found here are among the oldest artifacts (ca. 11,000 B.P.) found in North America. In Nevada, Fishbone Cave has yielded artifacts and fossils confirming that people coexisted with prehistoric horses and camels some time between 5,000 and 10,000 years before present. In Lovelock Cave, a wealth of artifacts, including baskets, sandals, and mummified human remains, have been dated to about 4,000 years before present.[6] Those two basic topographic features associated with life-giving water and life-protecting security—springs and caves—sustained early mankind here in the Great Basin.

Consider for a moment those conditions that encourage humankind to equate the vulva and cave: both are dark, isothermal environments that offer an element of safety from external conditions. Both also inevitably in-

Fig. 2.1. The Power Within: Hidden in a cave in Joshua Tree National Park, this cleft in the rocks evokes the vaginal entrance to the womb. (July 1968 photograph by author)

troduce a factor of mystery, even fear of the unknown, and hence both possess considerable power. In a number of stories, caves are associated with procreation. For example, in the Paiute story "The Cave," Gray Wolf and his younger brother Coyote are hunting deer. When asked how he finds the deer, Gray Wolf states that "I go and remove rocks and a deer will come [out]." Coyote imitates this technique; removing a rock, and a deer does come out, but Coyote misses it. In order to improve the odds, Coyote foolishly removes "a lot of rocks from the entrance" of the cave. This causes many of the animals—including mountain sheep, antelope, elk, and bear—to flee before they can be shot. Gray Wolf says that "Coyote has no sense and has opened the door," freeing too many animals at once. As a consequence, "Now they roam the earth and we will have to hunt for them." Realizing how much has been lost by Coyote's actions, Gray Wolf chastises his younger brother: "How foolish you have been!"[7] Having some idea of Coyote's nature, I suspect this dressing down only made him more irascible.

But it is the topography, the earth itself, that captures my attention in this story for Native peoples believe that all life was born from it. Note well that the cave is again associated with fecundity as it is a crucial element in a tale about procreation. Note, too, that animals are important elements in the Native American [pro]creation stories. The earth, in effect, gives birth through its womb—the cave. European American readers may be a bit put off by my recounting sexual stories in a spiritual geography. What, they might ask, do these cave stories have to do with spirituality?

Let me respond by noting the numerous references to caves in the Bible—including the very first in Genesis, where "Lot went up out of Zoar, and dwelt in the hills with his two daughters, for he was afraid to dwell in Zoar; so he dwelt in a cave with his two daughters." (Gen. 19:31) If one senses a sexual tension here, there is good reason, for Lot's daughters are both nubile and wily. Here in the cave the daughters conspire to seduce their father; each gets him drunk, lying with him on two consecutive nights so that "we may preserve offspring through our father" (Gen. 19:31-38). This event suggests a connection between caves and procreation, even though that procreation occurs through trickery.

In the Book of Joshua, caves also serve an obliquely survival-related purpose; one that ensures the Jew's survival as a people. When five fleeing kings hide in a cave, Joshua orders great stones to be rolled "against the mouth of the cave, and set men by it to guard them." After destroying the kings' troops, Joshua next orders his men to "open the mouth of the cave, and bring those five Kings out to me from the cave," whereupon the kings are slain and hanged from trees. Joshua's men then throw the kings' bodies back "into the cave where they had [originally] hidden themselves." To seal the cave, Joshua's men again "set great stones against the mouth of the cave, which remain to this very day" (Josh. 10:22-27). In this story, caves are the site of mayhem and retribution but serve a purpose related to the perpetuation of a race of people. In Isaiah, caves are places of refuge where the wicked will flee a vengeful god: "And men shall enter the caves of the rocks and the holes of the ground, from before the terror of the LORD and from the glory of his majesty, when he rises to terrify the earth" (Isa. 2:19). In the Bible generally, darkness signifies that which is hidden from God's eye—but only temporarily. There is, in other words, no place to hide. Small wonder that caves are associated with considerable fear in Judeo-Christian thought. They become, in some biblical stories, tombs rather than wombs.

Settled in the motel in Pioche, I read passages from the Bible late into the night—passages that reveal just how palpable darkness is to our culture. About 1:00 A.M., I turn off the light and the motel room is plunged into darkness. After a few minutes, as the features of the room slowly come back into view though still deeply bathed in shadow, my mind begins to entertain a thought that I never would have had in the daylight. How, I wonder, can I be sure that I am safe here? After all, if I could pick up the key to this room from under the doormat, couldn't someone else? But then I think, no, the place is as safe as it is clean.

Somewhere in that delightfully buoyant state between being awake and asleep, suspended between light and dark, I remember once reading about another nighttime encounter that took place in the Great Basin about 150 years ago. It happened on John Charles Frémont's third expedition into the region. With the intrepid Kit Carson among its members, the expedition had made camp and were completing their supper at a place called Sangundai's Spring in what is today west-central Nevada. As Frémont later described it in his memoirs, "Carson who was lying on his back with his pipe in his mouth, his hands under his head and his feet to the fire, suddenly exclaims, half rising and pointing to the other side of the fire, 'Good God!, look there!'" (fig. 2.2). The sight that had so shocked Carson was an Indian woman, whose face was illuminated by the fire. Frémont described her as "apparently eighty years of age, nearly naked, her grizzly hair hanging down over her face and shoulders." Frémont's group was not alone in experiencing shock at this encounter: The woman evidently thought she had entered a camp of her own people when she realized her mistake, or as Frémont describes it, "when her open mouth was paralyzed with fright, as she saw the faces of the whites." Frémont's men caught the frightened woman and gave her food, but she later escaped into the night. Frémont concluded that the food, and the fire that they left for her the next morning would likely "prolong her life."[8] I feel reassured knowing that most encounters with the unknown are usually benevolent. With this thought beginning to swirl, my edginess slowly fades as I drift off to sleep.

The next morning I awaken refreshed as the rising sun's rays filter through the curtains. After washing up, I prepare to leave this mysterious motel. As I place a twenty-dollar bill into the Bible, it occurs to me that this book figures heavily in the invisible relationship that the motel owner and I have entered into: she trusting me enough to give the key to her property to me sight unseen, I trusting her enough to spend the night here. The twenty-dollar bill's "In God We Trust" underscores the faith that permeates even a simple monetary exchange in our culture. That Bible was a silent intermediary in my transaction with the mysterious but trusting motel owner.

Fig. 2.2. Out of the Darkness: As illustrated in John Charles Frémont's *Memoirs,* the unexpected arrival of an old Indian woman in camp prompted a startled Kit Carson to exclaim, "Good God! Look there!" (Courtesy Special Collections Division, University of Texas at Arlington Libraries)

Emerging into daylight reminds me about what we've left behind, metaphorically speaking, in our journey from darkness to light. Some travel literature for Lehman Caves, about eighty miles north of Pioche, stands in a rack at a service station where I fuel up for the day's drive. The brochure suggests that caves are almost alien places with oddly shaped rock formations and even odder creatures. Humankind no longer lives in caves. We distanced ourselves from them when we began to construct houses. Caves are often considered the dwelling places of animals, and so it seems likely that a society holding man above animals, as we do in Judeo-Christian tradition, would hold caves in disdain. In the Book of Job, caves become the dwelling places of outcasts. In experiencing great tribulation, Job finds himself losing his possessions and social position. He laments that "men whose vigor is gone" are—like dogs—destined "through want and hard hunger" to "gnaw the dry and desolate ground" where "in the gullies of the torrents they must dwell, in holes of the earth and of the rocks." (Job 30:2-6) This description is worth remembering, for it will play out later when westward-moving Anglo-American settlers encountered the Native peoples of the Great Basin and considered them inferiors because they dug the earth for food. In Judeo-Christian thought, the underground is associated with falling from grace or, worse, Satan's home in the underworld—hell.

Although the Judeo-Christian tradition and the Native Americans' Great Basin traditions regarding caves are different, they do have some things in common. Consider, for example, a revealing Paiute story about a giant living in a cave above a valley. This giant is strong and fearsome, so fearsome that all animals wished him dead. Again animals assume powerful roles in the drama, not only as players, but as heroes. As related in the story "Cottontail Fools the Giant," only Rabbit was brave enough to attempt the task of killing the giant. Climbing up the mountain, Rabbit spied the giant "sunning himself in front of his cave." Rabbit managed to trick the sleepy giant and hammer a stake through him. This brave act was followed by a big explosion that scattered flintlike bits of the giant's body far away into the distant valleys—except for one piece of flint that cut off most of the fleeing Rabbit's tail (hence his short tail today).

Aside from describing how the landscape of that area acquired its veneer of flintlike rocks, this story suggests that caves can have also an ominous quality, for a malevolent giant lived therein. That is understandable, because the very thing that adds to a cave's mystery—the unknown that may lie within—is the same element that can generate a sense of fear and apprehension. Note, however, an important difference here. In the Native American story, it is the giant who is bad—not the cave—yet, the association links the cave with apprehension.

At the far western edge of the Great Basin, close to the California border in the Sierra Nevada, Cave Rock near Lake Tahoe is the site of a "legendary cave." Here the Washo Indians "said the Great Spirit formed the cave when Lake Tahoe rose high and threatened to drown the Washo, who lived near a tremendous rock." According to this story, the Great Spirit "thrust his spear into the rock and made a cave where the water could drain." Richard Moreno noted that there is a second version of this story, one that reflects the "fierce turf battles" that sometimes occurred between the Washo and Paiute peoples regarding fishing and hunting rights at Lake Tahoe. In this story, the "cruel and evil Paiute" people attempted to enslave the Washo. But the "God of the World" came to the Washos' rescue "by creating the cave and imprisoning the Paiute inside of it" and "transformed the evil ones into demons who were afraid of the lake and so could never leave the cave." This legend claims that their "cries and moans can sometimes be heard coming from Cave Rock."9 This story (or rather stories) confirms the power of caves as places of salvation as well as imprisonment. But above all, these stories reaffirm the role of place in storytelling.

That brochure advertising Lehman Caves reminds me of the numerous caverns north of Pioche in the vicinity of the White Mountains, some of which are difficult to reach even today. One spectacular cavern was called "Pockage Cave" by George W. Bean, a Mormon exploring this region for Brigham Young in 1858. Bean said he adopted the name from the Indian word for pocket, which also meant hole or cave. This was no ordinary cave, but rather a well-developed cavern. Although it at first appeared to be one large chamber, it soon revealed itself to be very complex, featuring "smaller caves or branches . . . from ten feet to one hundred yards in length and from ten to twenty five feet wide"[10] (fig. 2.3).

Fig. 2.3. Wonders Underground: In Lehman Caves, Nevada, varied textures of travertine hint at the mysteries of creation. Features include "cave popcorn" (covering the center and lower portion of wall at left) and smooth fluted columns (right). (Photograph by David Futey)

James Martineau, a prominent member of the expedition, described the cave as having been penetrated "more than a mile without finding any sign of its end." He described it as having "hundreds of passages branching off in every direction." Whereas the Mormon explorers approached the cave with curiosity, the Indians reportedly refused to enter it. They told the explorers several stories about this cavern. One involved "two squaws [who] went into the cave, a long time ago, and remained six months." Although they had entered "in perfect nudity," the women "returned dressed in fine buckskin, and reported they had found a large and beautiful valley inside clothed with vegetation, timber and water, and filled with game of the choisest [sic] specie."[11] The belief that caves represent connections to other worlds is common. Note, too, that the idea of riches or abundance at the other end of the journey through the cave, perhaps a subliminal reference to their mysterious, womblike quality.

These legends persisted for a long time after whites arrived in the region. In the 1860s, miners traveling through the Cave Valley and White Mountain area of Nevada reported that an Indian guide "told us all manner of stories about the cave." The Indian guide predicted that the explorers entering the cave would "after traveling three days . . . come to a new world, where there was another sun and moon, and another race of human beings, who had horses, cattle, sheep, etc., and plenty of women." As late as 1890, James Martineau noted that "[t]o this day, no Indian will venture to enter its gloomy recesses, fearing he may be spirited away as were the squaws."[12] The Mormons, however, held a different opinion about the cave. Upon originally entering it, they sang a hymn, "For the Strength of the Hills We Bless Thee," that included the words "For the dark resounding caverns / Where thy still small voice is heard / . . . we bless Thee, Our God—our fathers' God."[13]

Caves play a significant role in a deeper drama that reaches across cultures. The prophet Muhammad's search for spiritual fulfillment led him not only into the desert for solitude, but to a cave on Mount Hira when he could communicate with God. Muhammad used the darkness as a key, just as he reveled in the light that flooded the desert by day. And yet humankind seems forever destined to regard light and darkness with ambivalence. The sun provides the light and energy needed to sustain life, but that force can also destroy. So, too, darkness provides us the comfort we need to quell the sun's heat, and to enable us to sleep deeply; yet the darkness contains many mysteries that man—with eyes suited to see only in the daytime—fears. So with these musings I arrive at another realization about religion, which also has two sides—one that encourages us to seek answers, the other to sustain our natural fear of the unknown. We encounter both these emotions as we seek answers to some of existence's deepest mysteries.

I am tempted to think that these mysteries are confined to the distant past, and that places like caves might no longer possess power in helping us find answers to these mysteries. But then I remember my conversations with people and the stories they tell. Consider the words of Mormon writer Terry Tempest Williams, who seeks the darkness to see the light. "There is," she writes, "a holy place in the salt desert, where egrets hover like angels." This holy place, Williams reveals, "is a cave near the [Great Salt] lake where water bubbles up from the earth." Shattered by the loss of her mother to cancer, Williams finds renewal in this most elementary of landscapes—the amniotic womb where creation is reenacted. Here, Williams confesses, "I am hidden and saved from the outside world." This cave, she adds, "is the secret den of my healing." It conforms to Williams's body and nurtures her soul: "Leaning against the back wall of the cave, the curve of the rock supports the curve of my spine." Here Williams is renewed as "my skin draws moisture from the rocks as my eyes adjust to the darkness."[14]

Hidden in the recesses of the cave, Williams carves chevrons ("the simple image of birds") and sings "without the embarrassment of being heard."[15] By drawing, she has done something fundamentally human—made a sign or a mark to affirm her presence. And by singing alone, she has raised her voice to no one but her creator, who alone hears all, without judgment. Only after these rituals does she return to the world outside, renewed.

Williams's anecdote about the cave is important for several reasons. At one level, it confirms the power of *place* in the process of spiritual renewal. But note more closely how the place itself is interpreted, or rather empowered, by its close connection to human anatomy. The cave represents the womb, which, in Williams's words, is "the first landscape we inhabit." Like the cave, "our maternal environment is perfectly safe—dark, warm, and wet. It is"—again in Williams's words—"a residency inside the feminine."[16] Note, too, that Williams's account suggests that the power of certain places is associated with certain types of beliefs. Although her anecdote is personal or idiosyncratic, it has broader cultural implications. A particular place, by its association with spiritual renewal, answers a broader spiritual need. Thus it is that places become associated with *ritual*: by its repeated role in storytelling that reached an ever greater number of people through time, the cave attains a sanctity, that is, becomes a holy or sacred place. Viewed thusly, the cave—like the womb—becomes central to a drama of creation. Like Williams, countless people have ventured forth into the daylight, invigorated by what they have encountered, and learned, in the dark.

The chasm between light and dark is on my mind as I prepare to leave Pioche. I am reminded of a group of Mormons who were camped in the Moapa Desert in southern Utah about 150 years earlier. Surviving an Indian attack during the night, "they sat in awe and wonder" when "morning came, [and] the sun rose in all its splendor over the hills and desert wastes, turning them into a haze of glory." At this point, their leader began singing "one of our most beautiful hymns."

> The morning breaks, the shadows flee;
> Lo! Zion's standard is unfurled.
> The dawning of a bright day
> Majestic, rises on the world.[17]

Here in Pioche, the air is still cold but warming as the sunlight works its way into the purple shadows of buildings and vegetation, bringing the old mining town to life. Invigorated, I get into my rental car, start the motor, slip the gearshift into drive, and point it west toward Big Pine, California, at the western edge of the Great Basin. With a road map spread out on the passenger seat, I'm anticipating another day of intriguing desert landscapes bathed in glorious sunlight; and, as always, wondering somewhere in the back of my mind if I'll make it to my destination before nightfall.

3

Water and Memory

Sun looked at the earth. It was very dry.
Sun looked at the people. They were thirsty....
Then Sun said, "I know what to do. I will make it rain!"
—The Sun and Moon Story in MARY L. POPE,
Let Me Tell You a Story

But the Lord seen some sinnin', and it caused him pain.
He says, Stand back, I'm gonna make it rain.
—*The Unicorn* (Song)

Rolling out of Pioche, Nevada, I take one last look at the town in my rear-view mirror. Like most mining towns in the Great Basin, this one is chiseled into a canyon and flanked by mine dumps veneering the steep hillsides. Here, at about 6,000 feet above sea level, piñon pines cling to the rocky slopes of the Highland Range (fig. 3.1). To the Native peoples, the piñon pines provide harvests of seeds in the fall, and annual ceremonies still give recognition and thanks for this upland bounty. The presence of these small pines reveals one of the truisms about environment in this region. Trees flourish here because these mountain ranges receive more precipitation, and are cooler, than the adjacent valleys. Most of this precipitation occurs as winter rain and snowstorms, but some also falls as summer thundershowers that form over the mountains first, then trail off over the valleys. This water ultimately either evaporates or finds its way into the region's groundwater. In some places, springs flow year round, and they have drawn human and animal populations for millennia. Not surprisingly, the oldest known site of human habitation in Nevada is Tule Springs, a well-watered oasis near Las Vegas that nurtured the region's inhabitants between 10,000 and 11,000 years before present.[1]

Fig. 3.1. Upland Bounty: As seen here in southwestern Utah's Wah Wah Mountains, the piñon pine (*Pinus monophylla*) is one of several types of conifers found in the moister uplands of the Great Basin. (June 2000 photograph by author)

Just out of Pioche, the road leads down into Dry Lake Valley, which is bordered by the Pahroc Range. The root word of Pahroc—*pah*—refers to water in Paiute, and this root word is frequently encountered throughout the entire region—for example, Tonopah, Ivanpah, and Pahrangat. This reminds me that the name "Paiute" is not what these Indians called themselves, but rather what the whites called them—Pah-Utes; that is, Ute Indians who knew where water was to be found and lived close to it. That root word *pah* for place names is not only common geographically but significant geosophically. Its prevalence is both a tribute to the Native peoples of the region and a constant reminder of the significance of water here in the Great Basin. The contrast between desert and water is also suggested in many Anglo place names hereabouts, such as the evocatively named Burnt Springs Range that frames equally evocative Dry Lake Valley on the east.

From the valley floor, mountains are in constant view, and in the morning light they remind me of elongated islands. Although the German term *inselberg* (island mountain) is used for mountains like these that loom upward from the desert, these islands appear to be more of an archipelago rising from a sea. Sometimes, when the light is right, as it is now, the nearly flat desert floor is easy to mistake for the ocean. The bluish green of sagebrush adds to the effect and to an aptly named book about this region, Stephen Trimble's *Sagebrush Ocean*.[2] Trimble's desert-as-ocean analogy is part of a long tradition. Ever in search of the dramatic, Samuel Clemens (Mark Twain) invited readers of *Roughing It* to "imagine a vast, waveless ocean stricken dead and turned to ashes." Twain's words are on my mind as I roll along a graded road leaving a pale plume of dust in my wake: "imagine a coach creeping like a bug through the midst of this shoreless level, and sending tumbling volumes of dust."[3] Twain experienced the landscapes of Nevada at a speed not much greater than a walk, but I am moving at twenty times that speed, sweeping through the oceanic expanse of Dry Lake Valley, my bearings dependent on the mountainlike islands rising in the distance.

Two elements—water and land—are present in almost all of mankind's innumerable stories of creation. Significantly, these forces are not in harmony, but rather vie for supremacy before the permanent settlement of humankind can occur. Water, the giver of life, either rains down from the heavens or rises to cover the earth outright. Land, as the foothold for all future activities, welcomes mankind only after the waters finally subside. This is the point at which people enter the scene. The archetypical epic creation story, or rather combination of stories, is about that formative event that yields a recognizable landscape as waters recede and land comes into view. In these stories, landscape means more than a single vista or the image of a farmstead suggested by the German word *Landschafts-bild*. Instead, it has more in common with the Chinese word for landscape, *shenshui*, which is based on two elements—water and mountains (*shen* for mountains, and *shui* for water). Like the perennial yin-yang (light/dark, male/female, up/down), these two elements harmoniously complement each other yet are in perpetual conflict.

So it is with the landscape of the Great Basin, that generally arid and perpetually landlocked region between the Sierra Nevada and the Wasatch Mountains. To those with an eye trained to read the landscape, vistas here bear the shape of two major forces—mountain building and running water. The former is evident in the many parallel mountains, the latter in the eroded gullies and ever-present lakebeds (fig. 3.2). Most of these lakes are now dry, but some of them—like Mono Lake, Pyramid Lake, Walker Lake, and the Great Salt Lake—remain as vestiges of a time when water occupied more than one-third of the region's surface. Today some of these lakes are salty, some fresh, but all are important elements in the story of creation. A quick look at a map reveals that the Great Basin's lakes are located on either the western or the eastern edge of the region, fed by rain and snowmelt from either the Sierra Nevada or the Wasatch. These lakes are the remnants of two much larger lakes—Lake Lahontan and Lake Bonneville—that once inundated portions of the region.

Perceptive observers have long noticed signs of these immense lakes in parts of Utah and Nevada. Far up on the flanks of mountains, terraces indicate ancient shorelines—tangible evidence that water once covered a much larger area than it does today (fig. 3.3). Locally called "benches," these terraces are visible along the mountain slopes near Salt Lake City, Orem, and Provo, where residential neighborhoods now replace fruit orchards that flourished a century ago. In Nevada, the west side of the Lahontan Mountains near Grimes Point provides a less urbanized example of such ancient shorelines. Here, Lake Lahontan reached a level of 4,360 feet above sea level by the end of the Pleistocene era about 13,500 years before present. That was apparently the lake's maximum level, and the timing is significant, for it coincides with some of the region's early archaeological sites. That high-water level was perhaps the result of extensive snowmelt from the Sierra Nevada and other smaller mountains. For about 45,000 years the lake's level had fluctuated; then it began to drop before that sharp increase that left its mark highest up on the mountainside.[4]

Fig. 3.2. Mountain Islands, Desert Seas: Two processes—mountain building and running water—are especially significant in shaping the landscapes of the Great Basin. Columbus Salt Marsh, Nevada. (May 2000 photograph by author)

Fig. 3.3. Landscape as Repository: The legacy of water is everywhere apparent in the Great Basin, as seen in these benches or terraces on the flanks of Nevada's Lahontan Mountains. (Photograph by Richard Orndorff)

We get another glimpse of this dramatic past after occasional periods of heavy rainfall or runoff, when normally dry lakes become sheets of water that fill the bottoms of these enclosed basins. Rolling through the desert, I recall the eastern Great Basin in a very different mood a decade earlier. In the mid-1980s, lake levels began to rise due to a series of unusually wet winters. The rising waters threatened Salt Lake City, forced the relocation of the Southern Pacific Railroad across the Great Salt Lake, and helped create an ominous mood for Terry Tempest Williams's book *Refuge.* From my vantage point on a westbound Greyhound bus during those turbulent mid-1980s, those cold, storm-tossed waters reminded me how the landscape may have looked to the region's early inhabitants. Yet the wet weather ultimately subsided in the 1990s, conquered by the sun's triumphant return. Under blistering summer suns in subsequent years, the waters receded, and the bone-dry land once again emerged.

Those interested in divining water's enduring role in human affairs ought to listen carefully to the Native Americans. Their stories reveal a profound awareness of water's presence—or former presence. Anglo prospectors and settlers respected the Indians' knowledge of the often-hidden water sources here in the Great Basin. That is the reason why water-revealing Indian place names were adopted, then stuck. The Native Americans' creation stories demand our close consideration, for they resonate with ancestral memories of water that was more plentiful than it is today. They recount a legacy of environmental change as waters rose, then receded to reveal the landscape we know today. In one story relating the distant past, "This World Was All under Water," animals fled to the highest point (now called Mount Grant) to escape the waters. According to Paiute storyteller Corbett Mack, the animals "have to" find land here as their world is almost completely inundated. They find land "Cause that's sticking out a little. Have to stay up there on account of that's the only dry spot." This peak, Corbett notes, has a name: "Kuruggwa," or "Highest Mountain."

Some good came of this widespread inundation. The flood drowned giant cannibals who had threatened women and animals. The animals waited on Kuruggwa for an indeterminate amount of time: "That's when the Water goes down, keeps on going down, going down. Then there's Nevada." According to Mack, "Woman wanted that that way"—in other words, she played a role in both the demise of the giants and the rise and fall of the water. "You know how woman made the Flood? She's smart. Just make the water raise up. Make this country to be all covered with water." Mack concludes: "She's a pretty smart woman, by God. Got to [be], to know how to make that" happen.[5]

There are several important aspects to this story. First, it is not simply one man's story but rather conveys a rich, shared storyline passed from elders through all people in the Northern Paiute tribe. Note, too, both the content and cast of characters. The story puts woman at the center of the drama. She has power—Paiute or Numu call it "*bbooha*"—that can control the weather.[6] Such power could be used for good or evil purposes, but in this case clearly it was good. Note that the water in this story, even the flooding that virtually covers the earth, is portrayed in terms of a recognizable point of land. According to this Paiute story and local lore, Mount Grant was an island at one time in humankind's—or at least this tribe's—history/prehistory.

The story also suggests a subliminal association with climate change, for it helps account for the richness of life high up on the mountain. Mack tells us, "They say every kind of Animal's on top [of] that mountain. Deer, Mountain Sheep, Antelope, Sagehen. He keeps his tail in the water." Such mountains are veritable garden spots, with a higher density of animals sustained by the rich growth of vegetation that is in turn a result of the higher precipitation received there. One of the Native peoples' most dependable foodstuffs, piñon pine nuts, are harvested from the mountains annually—again a result of wetter conditions here than in the valley bottoms.

In the Old World, water also shaped humankind's memory. There, too, the Pleistocene was a time of wetter (and cooler) climate. In North Africa and the Middle East, streams ran perennially where today they are only ephemeral; caves across the region are filled with depictions of animals that long ago either retreated to areas having wetter climates or disappeared with increasing aridity. It was in this belt of increasing desiccation and shrinking streams that the Judeo-Christian heritage took root. The peoples of this region would come to regard water as sacred (so sacred that it would figure in a central ritual of Christianity—baptism) and the desert wilderness as man's vexation and temptation. When the Judeo-Christian tradition spread into the Great Basin about two centuries ago, its practitioners brought with them the legacy of water as nurturer of both spirit and flesh.

But that statement must be tempered by an observation that desert dwellers are surprisingly ambivalent about water. Life-giving on the one hand, water had a menacing side in biblical stories, as it did in the Paiute flood story. Consider a similar inundation story that was first told in another part of the world—the great flood as recounted in Genesis. This, too, has a moral purpose: it rids the world of iniquity. God warns Noah, "I will send rain upon the earth forty days and forty nights; and every living thing that I have made I will blot out from the face of the ground" (Gen. 7:4). As in the Paiute story, animals are saved. Noah, accompanied by his wife and sons, shepherds them onto an ark built especially for the purpose of physical escape and spiritual salvation. In a drama similar to that in the Paiute story, the waters rise to inundate the land. As recounted in Genesis 7:11, "the fountains of the great deep burst forth, and the windows of the heavens were opened."

In comparison to the Paiute flood, however, the biblical inundation was more complete—and more deadly. No place remained above the waters, which "prevailed so mightily upon the earth that all the high mountains under the whole heaven were covered" (Gen. 7:19). The deluge destroyed everything that was not aboard the ark: "And all flesh died that moved upon the earth, birds, cattle, beasts, all swarming creatures that swarm upon the earth, and every man" (Gen. 7:21). After a specified amount of time—150 days, to be exact—the waters abated; and at a precise time—on the seventeenth day of the seventh month—the ark came to rest on the mountains of Ararat.

As in the Paiute flood story, a mountain figures heavily in the salvation of life. A fixed geographic position—some elevated point above the water—not only saves humankind from oblivion, but also enables humans to retain essential contact with terra firma. However, several important differences between the two stories should be pointed out. In the Paiute story it is a woman (not a man) who orchestrates the salvation—a reminder, perhaps, that a female (Mother Earth) is the creator of life. But more important, Noah acts on God's command, whereas in the Paiute story the woman herself is the major shaper of events. In other words, Noah is obedient, while Woman is omniscient. Note, too, that the Paiute story never loses sight of at least one recognizable point of land (Kuruggwa), while in Genesis humankind loses sight of all land for several months. The ark and all on it become *separated from the earth,* and all are in the hands of God (through Noah's obedience), but the Paiute story *retains the earth* as a foothold or touchstone. This suggests a fundamental difference between both the stories and the cultures they represent. The Paiute story uses the destruction to emphasize the power and intelligence of woman and the wisdom of a Great Spirit; the biblical story emphasizes the power and will of God. Yet both are united in one essential: They both employ catastrophe as a major metaphor.

Sequential destruction of life (animals and people) suggests some vestigial memory of environmental catastrophe. A closer look at creation stories reveals that both fire and flood may cause destruction. Both are accounted for in Numu creation stories. Consider this one from the Smith and Mason Valley Numu in Nevada, as related by tribal elders: "Following the Fire which destroyed the Animals and the Great Flood which destroyed the animals a second time, Coyote decided to visit the Woman who was destined to become 'Mother-of-Us-All.' This Northern Paiute woman lived on an island in the Big Ocean." This woman, the story relates, was extraordinarily beautiful, and Coyote was very much in love with her. Yet, because Wolf is his older brother, Coyote suggests that Water Woman marry Wolf instead, as was the custom. Water Woman finds Wolf near present-day Fallon, Nevada—a site rich in lakes and marshes. They bear four children—a number sacred to the Numu—two daughters and two sons. However, much to Water Woman's despair, these children grow up fighting; the brothers shoot arrows at each other, and the sisters strike each other over the head with grinding stones. Upset with their behavior, Wolf takes hold of one set of siblings, sending the brother and sister "flying toward the North." These two, Wolf tells them, "shall be called 'Sáe.'" The other set of siblings he kicks in the seat of the pants into Smith and Mason Valleys, where they "shall be called '*Numu*.'" After this act, Wolf retires from his earthly life. He urges his wife, "Don't cry.... I am leaving this world." Wolf tells her that he is "going up into the sky" and that they will someday be reunited: "When you die, you can join me in my other home beyond the clouds."[7]

As for the Water Woman—or "Mother-of-Us-All"—she "finally retired to the mountain springs and lakes such as Mono and Walker Lakes close to Smith and Mason Valleys," where "now she is called 'Water Baby.'" Over the years, both Paiute and Shoshone have told me about "water babies." When I first heard the term, it sounded innocuous, perhaps even endearing. But that was soon dispelled when I learned about the water baby's terrible powers. Water babies are potent spirits who lure the unwary to death and destruction. As recounted by a Shoshone woman: "When you hear the crying [of the water baby], it means someone is going to die." In this regard, she noted, the water baby is similar to an owl, for "[w]hen Owl comes around the house at night talking, that is a sign there is going to be a death."[8]

Another Shoshone story describes a spring called *Paohmaa* (literally, water baby), where "long time ago a water baby lived." The women did all the work at this time, and they had to set their babies down to do other chores. When the baby cried, the woman would pick it up and nurse it. But that was when the water baby would reveal its truly terrible character. The water baby "would swallow the breast and then the whole mother"[9]—a story that reveals something of the horror associated with water babies and the springs where they lived. Numu tribal historian Michael Hittman quotes tribal elder Corbett Mack as saying that "there are really *two* types of Water Babies":

> One is a mature woman with long black hair which drags on the ground behind her, no taller than a twelve month old infant. The other is like a twelve month old infant just beginning to walk. Numu tell their children to ignore them if they should be seen as their presence may bring harm or misfortune to them and their family. "Throw a rock at Water Baby and tell her to leave you alone" Numu are instructed. "But above all else, never tease or make fun of the Water Baby, for she can create whirlpools of water drowning you and yours."[10]

This Numu story is compelling for several reasons. First, it again gives Woman a central position in creation and ties her origin to water. Second, it helps explain why no wolves inhabit Smith and Mason Valleys.[11] Third, it suggests a fear of one of nature's mysteries, the swirling vortex. Lastly, it indicates a strong ambivalence toward water. Water Woman is aquatic in origin yet has human form. Her being is linked to a large body of water (the sea); yet she today inhabits the lakes of the Great Basin. The double persona she assumes as Water Baby suggests something deeply troubling and perennially unresolved. In any case, these powers must be heeded, for failing to do so can cause disaster. The Water Baby is called Paoha by the Numu, and her/their presence is immortalized in the place named for Paoha Island, one of two islands (the other is called Negett, or Canadian goose in Numu) on Mono Lake (fig. 3.4). Lastly, the Numu story's use of the concept of immortality, and reunion in heaven after death, may suggest that this part of the story might have been adopted from Christian settlers.

But it is above all the use of water as a *theme* that unites these stories from both cultures. In both the Great Basin and the Holy Land, water is never taken for granted. Moreover, it is always regarded with ambivalence. In Genesis, Jacob admonishes his son Reuben for being as "unstable as water" (Gen. 49:4). In various books of the Old Testament (for example, 1 Kings 13-14 and Num. 5) water is used to test one's truthfulness to God. Here it connotes a purifying influence, as in the sprinkling of "water of expiation upon them" (Num. 8:7) for purification and atonement. In the New Testament, water is even more clearly linked to goodness and salvation and rejuvenation. When Jesus insists that a person be "born anew," Nicode-

Fig. 3.4. Perilous Waters: In Mono Lake, California, the dark Paoha Island immortalizes the Water Baby, an ominous force in Paiute lore. (June 2002 photograph by author)

mus asks, "How can a man be born when he is old? Can he enter a second time into his mother's womb and be born?" to which "Jesus answers, 'Truly, truly, I say to you, unless one is born of water and the Sprit, he cannot enter the Kingdom of God.'" (John 3:4-5) To leave no doubt about the meaning of water Jesus later proclaims, "He who believes in me, as the scripture has said, 'Out of his heart shall flow rivers of living water'" (John 7:38).

This water, of course, is figurative; it symbolizes a spring from which flows new purifying spiritual power. This linking of water to redemption not only reaffirms the spiritual significance of water in Judeo-Christian thought; it also provides an interesting comparison to water in Native American Great Basin stories. In both stories, water is something that behaves in response to external powers (God's in the Old Testament, Water Woman's in Paiute). However, the Paiute story lacks the misogynistic paternalism found in the Old Testament, where water may be mixed with impure substances (i.e., be deliberately tainted) to put a woman through the test of proving whether she is answering truthfully her husband's accusations of infidelity (Num. 5). In the New Testament, water seems miraculously free of this misogyny, instead sparkling with truth and light itself.

In his travels to the Intermountain West in the early 1850s, Solomon Nunes Carvalho visited Salt Lake City. As a sophisticated Sephardic Jew, Carvalho was well aware of Judaic traditions long associated with water, and with Christianity's deep dependence on it for metaphor. In early spring, as the Wasatch Mountains were still snow-clad, streams from them flowed into the valley below. Using wording right out of John (7:38), Carvalho observed that a "stream of living water, twelve feet wide, fresh from the mountains, runs along between the sidewalk and the road—the Temple Block." As Carvalho approached a group of Mormons here, "some of whom had already undergone the ceremony of baptism, and others patiently waiting," he noticed a priest prepare a woman for immersion into the cold water. Standing up to his waist in the stream with his coat off, the priest placed one hand on the woman's back and the other on her head. He then "reported the following words: 'I am commissioned by Jesus Christ to baptize you, in the name of the Father, and Son, and of the Holy Ghost. Amen.'" Ever aware of the stark conditions in the Intermountain West, Carvalho also observed the water's effect on the woman, or rather "the shock on her system which a sudden plunge into cold freezing water must naturally have produced."[12]

In short, when the priest tried to immerse the woman, she resisted. As Carvalho described it, she "struggled to get out of the water, but her husband remarked that the whole of her head had not been submerged, and insisted that 'his wife should be perfectly baptized.'" The priest heeded the husband's words: "She was consequently dipped effectually a second time, and the poor woman finally made her escape, almost frozen."[13] When Carvalho next witnessed a seventy-five-year-old woman voluntarily baptized, he asked, "Would persons submit to those extraordinary feats if they did not possess faith?" Of a third person baptized—"a young man of about twenty years, with a calm, placid countenance" who "underwent the operation without flinching," Carvalho was so impressed that he "should have liked to have painted him as a study for 'St. John.'"

After the streamside ceremony, Carvalho noted, those present "went each on their respective ways, many of them, I dare say, with the seeds of consumption sown at the moment, fully determined to live a life of piety and virtue."[14] Carvalho's reference to consumption (tuberculosis) suggests the deleterious physical effect this baptism may have had on the participants; yet each felt a sense of renewal, even rebirth, as a consequence of the immersion in life-giving—which is to say eternal life-giving—water. Carvalho rightly notes that "faith" is an important element here, for through it a purely physical act (immersion) is transformed into a spiritual event.

Water's more ominous side seems to be equated with older stories that plumb deep memories. In Old Testament and Paiute creation stories, floods come close to eradicating all life. These stories have a number of elements in common, and they may represent deeply embedded memories of a time (the late Pleistocene) when conditions were very different—far less desertlike—than they are now. In both the Great Basin and the Holy Land, water is regarded with an ambivalence that appears to confirm its continuing presence as a destroyer. True, it is an essential ingredient for all life, replenishing and sustaining. At the same time, it is extremely dangerous. Consider this strange fact: In desert regions like the Great Basin, more people drown than die of thirst.

The Mormon pioneer John Pulsipher relates a story about Elizabeth Pratt, wife of Mormon leader Parley P. Pratt, who "came near loosing [*sic*] her life" on the Weber River at the eastern edge of the Great Basin in 1848. Elizabeth was swept from the river's bank into the rushing water, where "the force of the currant [*sic*] had worn under the roots of the bushes and held her under so strong I could not pull her out." Imagine the desperation and urgency that Pratt and others felt as they fought the powerful waters pulling poor Elizabeth under—"just her head and arms were above the water and she nearly lost hold." In the end, it took three men to pull Elizabeth from the stream. Pulsipher recalled that Elizabeth "was so scared and chilled and trembled for hours" after her rescue. He related this tale "as a caution for you all to be careful."[15]

About thirty miles out of Goldfield, Nevada, I recognize the distinctive shape of Coyote Cuesta and I recall another important difference between Old World and New World creation stories. Animals figure as important characters in Native American stories, whereas they are secondary—that is, subservient to man—in those from Judeo-Christian heritage. I'm headed toward eastern California, where the Great Basin slams into the abrupt wall of the Sierra Nevada. Here, in Owens Valley, ethnographer Dorothea Theodratus notes that Coso Hot Springs "holds meaning for life before there were people—when animals and Sun held the worldly balance of life." The site remains important because "[s]ome creatures (bear and frog) remained there after people came, and the locality holds strong in the minds of Owens Valley people for its physical and mental health potential and the camaraderie experienced . . . there."[16] Note that it is water that subliminally links prehistory and history to place, but that animals have a major role in the process.

A story from the Numu sums up the significance of animals' actions, and their power to create landscapes. It also signifies the power of landscape to shape human history. According to the Paiute story "Why People Die," death itself is a direct result of Coyote's foolish actions. "Long ago," the story begins, "one mountain stood vertically on end." Wolf and Coyote were arguing at the top of this mountain, where there was a special spring. Old people would "climb up on top of this mountain and drink from the spring and bathe in it, so that they could regain their youth." Coyote, being very contrary, did not like this, for he felt that "old people should die." While arguing with Wolf, "Coyote became so angry that he kicked this Bald Mountain," which "toppled over and into the valley below." So great was this fall that it not only "flattened the mountain" but the water also "splashed all over, forming Honey Lake, Pyramid Lake, Eagle Lake and several other lakes in the region." As a consequence, the old people could no longer bathe in the spring, and thus could not regain their youth. In other words, they lost their immortality, and were forever fated to die—all by the selfish actions of Coyote.

This story is significant for several reasons. In addition to addressing an important element in spiritualism, humankind's ongoing quest for immortality, it also links the environment to a spiritual crisis. It describes massive topographical change that is associated with severe earthquakes; Coyote the trickster is the cause, but the consequences of his actions are similar to the catastrophic forces that have been known to cause regional changes to drainages elsewhere in the basin and range province.[17] Next, note that the water once had curative powers but has lost them; in other words, the magical waters were once concentrated but now are dispersed—hence losing their regenerative powers.

These stories vary through time and space. Consider, for example, another story about the creation of that deep blue jewel of western Nevada, Pyramid Lake. It, too, is associated with loss, but the account is different. According to former Paiute tribal chairman Mervin Wright, Pyramid Lake was created when Stone Mother (a prominent rock formation on the eastern side of Pyramid Lake) wept at losing her two sons (who were banished for their fighting and ultimately formed warring tribes) as well as her husband ("who went away, leaving the Stone Mother all alone"). Stone Mother's grief was so great that her tears "drained all the water from her body, which created the lake; her body then turned to stone." For their part, the lost sons' tribes are represented by other area lakes, namely Summit Lake and Eagle Lake to the north, and Honey Lake to the west.[18] Throughout time, there is an enduring theme of *loss* recounted in creation stories, for they seem to relate a time when things were better (lusher, milder, etc.) than they are now. In the case of the Great Basin (and the Middle East) I suspect that there is some truth to this sentiment, for the area was once better watered and could sustain life more easily than it can today.

But that is only part of the story. Here in these desert regions, I sense a wistfulness, perhaps nostalgia, for better times that may be as bound up in the human soul as it is in the environment. If, once upon a time, rivers flowed, but now they have dried, perhaps things were better then for mankind generally. Once, perhaps, there was no suffering, not even death, but now they stalk us everywhere. I suspect this may be another truly vestigial memory of all individuals, the time when we all effortlessly floated in the amniotic fluid of our mothers' wombs buffered from the storms. But even though we speculate about a world once free from hazards, this is likely wishful thinking: the environment is fraught with danger and always has been. The landscape of the Great Basin reveals the scarp lines of catastrophic earthquakes that reshaped the local topography and reoriented the waters. If one message emerges from creation stories, it is that the earth and its waters are in constant flux. Humankind is paradoxically always at risk in Native lands, yet is prone to ponder a place, and a time, when all was placid and safe. As the keynote story of Judeo-Christian tales goes, if only we hadn't been driven from the Garden of Eden, we would live forever. Creation stories, as they employ water and other forces, always address humankind's vulnerability and reveal humankind's penchant for wistfulness.

Yet it is that very same impending loss—our own mortality—that prompts us to ponder imponderables. As Yi-Fu Tuan has wisely noted: "Death, surprisingly, also has gifts. It consoles, it gives an extra edge to life, and it is the ground of virtue."[19] The ultimate irony, of course, is that the death we try so hard to avoid is what gives such immediacy to the lives we lead. Out here in the vastness of the Great Basin, I find myself agreeing with John Cowper Powys, who stated, with considerable bravado and insight: "I tell you the foundation stone of all human happiness is the thought of death."[20]

The Great Basin is the perfect place to ponder such thoughts. The landscape everywhere reminds us of our own mortality: it is huge, we are small; its changes are measured as epochs, ours as mere lifetimes or generations; it offers hope of regeneration, but that regeneration forever eludes humankind. There is an odd mix of hope and despair in all landscapes generally, and those of the Great Basin in particular. In their bold form, we see evidences of creation and destruction, of revelation and erasure. Like all landscapes, the scenery of the Great Basin is a repository of imagination. Because we sense a connection to its very form, and find both solace and terror in the waters that course through it, we are destined to use it as a yardstick against which all myths—and all history—are measured.

It is easy to think that mythology is confined to the past, until we look closely at our own stories today. Then we see that water, and the immensity of time and space, remain a vital part of Great Basin culture to the present day. Filmed in part near Goldfield, Nevada, and in the Mojave Desert, the 1999 Morgan Freeman film *Desert Blue* builds on the theme of the close connection between water and destiny. *Desert Blue* begins with an enigma —a sign in the middle of the desert proclaiming the location of "Baxter Beach." To add to the enigma, the film's action opens with a young man named Blue, who is making a boat in the desert as his friends look on. The viewer soon learns that the beach is the dream of Blue's family, who hoped to divert aqueduct water to the site and to create an Ocean Park after Baxter's gold-mining boom ended. But things haven't worked out: "The water's not coming," one of Blue's friends states. "It didn't come when your father built this place; I'm sorry, but its not going to just appear." Undeterred, Blue answers, "And Noah was stupid for building an ark, right?" Incredulous, one of Blue's friends asks: "Did you just compare yourself to Noah?"

That line hints at Blue's vision and his ability to connect with something beyond his immediate surroundings. "The water," we learn from Blue, "was supposed to be my dad's," and would draw people from miles around. His father must also have been a visionary, for Blue tells his friends, "My dad always said we have all this sand and no beach, and that aqueduct is just passing on by with more water than the friggin' ocean." But that was before a soft drink company appropriated Blue's family's share of the water, leaving the place desolate and the father despondent. Despite his father's untimely death and his friends' criticism, Blue perseveres. In the process, he meets a young television actress, Sky, from Los Angeles, who happens to be stuck in the town of Baxter after a hazardous waste spill on the only highway through town results in a federal quarantine.

As one might anticipate from two characters named so obviously, and so symbolically, Blue and Sky are attracted to each other from the outset. Predictably, their friendship and romance develop during Sky's brief exile in Baxter. Walking through the desert outside of town, Sky asks Blue, "If you could do anything you wanted to right now, what would you do?" Without hesitation, Blue answers, "Go swimming in the ocean." Sky then asks, "You've never been to the ocean?" to which Blue answers, "Nope." Picking up some fossil shells, Blue says, "Maybe it's because *these* are everywhere." Bewildered, Sky asks "Sea shells in the desert?" to which Blue answers "Yeah. I think this used to be an ocean—and right now we're walking on the ocean floor." To viewers versed in pop culture, this reference brings to mind the enigmatic lyrics of "A Horse with No Name" (1972) by the group America: After traveling for nine days in the desert, the rider finally had to let the horse go free because the desert had turned to sea. Desert and sea have much in common in this song, which portrays ocean as an enigma—a desert with its life underground.[21] The desert is associated subliminally with the ocean in many cultures; we need only recall that camels are considered the ships of the desert. Continuing his desert-as-ocean analogy, Blue points to the creosote bushes and other desert scrub: "And you see those bushes? They used to be kelp." Caught up in the scene and its pathos, Sky responds, "It's beautiful."

Blue secretly hopes that nature will intercede in human affairs, "Even if the state doesn't give us the water," he tells Sky, "the big one [earthquake] will wipe out L.A. and we'll be sitting on beachfront property." As they recline on two beach chairs in the desert, Sky adds, "You know, if you close your eyes . . . you can pretend there's water." As it turns out, they do not have to pretend for very long: One of Blue's friends, an explosives-wielding young woman in Baxter, blows up the aqueduct. The film ends as water courses into the water park. Metaphorically, perhaps even metaphysically, closure is reached as two elements, desert and water, are reunited.

The drama that plays out in *Desert Blue* reminds me of the persistent role of water in all creation stories. It is an integral part of the creation stories of the Paiute and Shoshone peoples who lived here for thousands of years before whites arrived in the late eighteenth and early nineteenth century. Water also figures as a critical element in stories of regeneration. At the western edge of the Great Basin, with the well-watered Sierra Nevada as a backdrop, Anglo-American writer Mary Austin lamented the Los Angeles Aqueduct's removing water from Owens Lake in the early twentieth century. By the 1920s, Austin had experienced personal spiritual crises triggered in part by social isolation and environmental change. Adopting a Native American style for her 1927 poem "Song of the Maverick," Austin noted, "I am too arid for tears, and for laughter, too sore with unslaked desires. . . . For I am crammed and replete, with the power of desolate places."[22] In one of the classics from this region—*Land of Little Rain* (1901)—Austin's tears and thirst mingle as she recounts how water was stolen from both the Native peoples and the settlers in Owens Valley. There is, of course, a connection between this modern tale of water loss and the older stories. The enduring story of desiccation here in the Great Basin is climatic in its initiation, as the area became drier and drier following the Pleistocene era, but cultural in its ultimate consequences. Nature herself has been instrumental in increasing aridity here, but humankind compounds her frugality.

Related stories—most of them much more modern—center on another type of loss, the decline in the *quality* of water found here. These stories might be considered "objective," though they too are often related at emotionally charged levels. Are people not only using up the waters here, but also fouling them by pollution? The importance of protecting water comes to mind as I ponder a news story describing a debate raging in Fallon, Nevada. An agricultural town that bills itself as the "Oasis of Nevada," Fallon's trim houses, green lawns, and beautiful old shade trees seem an unlikely backdrop to a question all too typical of the modern age: Why would eleven children here, all from different backgrounds, have leukemia? That figure is much higher than what one would normally expect in a town of 8,300 people. Only 2,000 cases were recorded in the entire nation annually, so this makes Fallon one of 108 "cancer clusters" in twenty-nine states and five countries. It has long been known that Fallon's groundwater has arsenic rates ten times higher than federal water quality standards, but arsenic has never been linked to leukemia. Could it be a result of residual radioactivity from nuclear testing near Fallon in the 1950s, even though no radiation has been detected? The news story offers further possibilities—"agri-cultural chemicals. Or something from industrial plants. Or, of course, the water"—but there are no answers as yet for a community waiting for some clue. One resident opines, "I think it's just a freak thing."[23] That gets me to pondering about how fate expresses itself spatially; randomly, for the most part of course, but perhaps in clusters as we have more and more ways of reporting and interpreting the information.

Both the landscape and our collective memory reflect the reduction and degradation of the aquatic environment in the Great Basin. Water, the sub-stance of life and tears, is ever vanishing. The land is becoming saltier, the waters more concentrated. That, perhaps, explains why the greatest decep-tion in the desert is its truest paradox—the aquatic mirage, wherein the re-lentless blue of the sky mocks the desert's aridity by floating on the sur-face of the land like a sheet of pure water. These images both perplex and enchant me as I travel through the region. Is that sheet of blue stretching across the bottom of Eureka Valley water, or another atmospheric sleight of hand? Nearing the valley floor at 75 miles an hour, it seems as if I'm about to drive right into a lake that I know shouldn't be there; then, sud-denly, that sheet of water recedes, and the desert continues to engulf the speeding rental car.

I am part of a long tradition of perplexed travelers here. While exploring Utah's Great Salt Lake Desert in 1852, Howard Stansbury observed that the "minute crystals of salt which cover the surface of the moist, oozy mud, glisten brilliantly in the sunlight, and present the appearance of a large sheet of water so perfectly, that it is difficult, at times, for one to persuade himself that he is not standing on the shore of the lake itself." Stansbury noted that other features of the landscape complement the illusion: "High rocky ridges protrude above the level plain, and resemble great islands ris-ing about the bosom of this desert sea." He concluded: "The mirage, which frequently occurs, is greater here than I ever witnessed elsewhere, distort-ing objects in the most grotesque manner, defying all calculations as to their size, shape, or distances, and giving rise to optical illusions almost beyond belief."[24]

Like water in most desert folklore and history, the mirage vanishes as we reach it. But it is too easy to dismiss mirages as mere deceptions caused by the intense heating of air at ground levels. Rather they suggest an inherent truth and paradox of arid-land geography—that desert landscapes are largely shaped by water. Like our search for answers to creation, the mi-rage distorts our perception, yet it subliminally reminds us of a truth that floats just beyond our consciousness—that water may have an even greater role in shaping, even reclaiming, this land in the future. Blue's prediction that his father's dream of oceanfront property might someday come true is not as farfetched as it might seem. Geologists predict that the Great Basin will, in another fifty or so million years, become a sea as California further separates from the North American landmass. In the ultimate of ironies, this desert region will once again return to the sea. Then the Paiute story of Mother-of-Us-All, who lives on an island in the ocean, may not be a story rooted in the past, but also a prediction of the distant future.

Stories in Stone

Indeed, this whole Basin region of the Continent is full of the strangest anomalies of nature, puzzling the science and defying the industry of man, and almost insulting the beneficence of God.
—SAMUEL BOWLES, *Our New West* (1869)

The geology of the Great Basin presented a bewildering variety of land-forms to nineteenth-century observers. I'm thinking about this as I travel across the region with maps in hand, trying to figure how everything fits together. Maps help greatly here, and one is especially helpful. Among my most prized possessions, an early-twentieth-century geological map of the western United States shows the Great Basin as a buff-colored matrix laced with brightly colored, elongated lens-shaped features. The buff color represents the alluvium-filled valleys, while the multicolored lenses signify the geologically complex mountains. This map was prepared by the U.S. Geological Survey, but it also comes in handy when deciphering the region's intricate spiritual geography.

Listen closely to the inspirational stories about this region and you will find that they are rooted in bedrock. The rocks and mountains themselves have an important role in this drama. They help us tell stories of immense forces that shape the landscape, and they color our belief about what it means. Consider again the diverse types of rocks and the varied fossils of animals and plants that have intrigued and bewildered humankind since ancient times. To the geologist, they are so many clues used in helping decipher a story of the earth's history, a history set in motion and operating more or less regularly as rocks take form and then erode; even an occasional catastrophic event—a localized meteor hit, volcanic explosion, a regional earthquake or flooding, continental-scale drought—is a part of the equation. When a meteor smashed into central Nevada in the early twentieth century,[1] it not only lit up the night sky but collided with a landscape contorted by eons of volcanic and tectonic violence.

Viewed geologically, the Great Basin is a fragmented landscape created by episodic events that are ultimately linked to the movement of the earth's crust. The region's corrugated quality—mountains alternating with valleys—is a direct outcome of catastrophic forces. It inspired geologist Kenneth Deffeyes to state that "the lesson is that the whole thing—the whole Basin and Range [province], or most of it—is alive." This suggestion of a living geology is unusual, for we have come to think of rocks as dead (that is, inanimate) and the biosphere as alive. Deffeyes clarifies: "The earth is moving. The faults are moving. There are hot springs all over the province. The world is splitting open and coming apart."[2] This constant motion may seem contradictory, for people often mention the region's "solitude" and "quietness." But both the abrupt scarp lines of fairly recent earthquakes and the large areas covered by fresh lava flows suggest otherwise. Once I was shaken awake by an earthquake while camping out in southern Nevada. The trembling sensation lasted for seconds, but seemed like minutes. What had seemed so solid now seemed to be twitching and shrugging.

To most people who speed through this region, it seems more dead than alive. On a trip into the Great Basin in late spring of 2000, I met a European traveler—actually a Danish scientist—in Fallon, Nevada. He had driven from Salt Lake City to Fallon, where he'd stopped for the night on a two-day trip to California. Eager to learn about his perceptions of the Great Basin, I asked him what he thought of the drive along Highway 50 across Nevada. He looked over at me, paused for a moment, and then said, "God, that country's dull . . . and so much of it!" How, I wondered, could what he saw as a "dull" landscape resonate so strongly, even spiritually, to me and to others? In order to register as more something than monotonous, landscape must touch a certain chord in an individual, then be articulated as meaningful and incorporated into broader patterns of storytelling. The Danish scientist had no stories upon which to ground this immense region, and so it remained terra incognita to him.

Spiritual geographies require an appreciation of humankind's experiences *in situ.* Although the word spiritual may suggest something disassociated from both body and its earthly corollary, landscape, the spiritual is in many ways dependent on the physical. I should begin by reaffirming that the landscape literally embodies humankind in both his/her physical anatomy and ethereal musings and longings. Its varied landforms—from phallic pinnacles to vulviform caves—are evident in parts of the Great Basin. This, in fact, points to one of the ironies of the region's geography. To those who do not live in the Great Basin, the vastness of this desert is numbing. As William Fox observes, "The desert has few easily discernible landmarks and is thus a topography where few if any memories accumulate." To him, "The desert more often appears to us as space, not place."[3] Not so for people who live here day after day, century and century, however. They come to know it intimately with the passage of time.

To that Danish scientist trained in microscopic plant cytology, the landscape of the Great Basin appeared similar all the way from the Wasatch Mountains to the Sierra Nevada. I realize that he has been jaded into thinking that the place is uniform throughout. He might have had a different impression had he traveled a bit more slowly with the new guidebook to the "Loneliest Road in America"[4] in hand. U.S. Highway 50 reveals a remarkable transect as it rises and falls repeatedly over a corrugated landscape of north-south-trending mountain ranges separated by salt-filled basins. This quintessential Great Basin landscape deserves a closer look, for while the basic geomorphology suggests a serrated uniformity, even monotony, the rocks themselves along this 500-mile traverse tell a different story.

On a trip across the Basin over Highway 50 in 1989, I decided to collect a rock specimen from each of the mountain ranges I crossed. This, I figured, would give me a firsthand understanding of the petrology and a better grasp of the region's overall geology. By so doing, I'd make my colorful USGS map come alive. The road map showed about a dozen and a half mountain passes along the route, and to ensure some randomness, I decided to collect a rock sample from the rock cut nearest the "summit" sign at each pass. Anticipating about two-dozen specimens, I asked a motel owner near Carson City if she had a couple of empty egg cartons. Regarding my plan as delightfully eccentric, she complied. "You must be a college professor," she correctly assumed as she handed me the empty egg cartons. How strange, I thought, that the places recently filled by high protein DNA would soon be filled by rocks.

At sunrise, I pointed the rental car east after collecting a specimen of salt-and-pepper-colored granite in the Sierra Nevada behind the motel. Driving into the morning sun, I stopped at each summit, hammering an egg-sized sample from the rock face with my Estwing geologist's rock pick. This tool, by the way, is my second-oldest possession, given to me Christmas of 1955 by my parents; the oldest is a 1909 geology textbook given to me in 1954. After breaking off each specimen with the rock pick, I carefully marked its location on a piece of paper, sticking both the specimen and the label into the egg carton.

As the day progressed, I worked my way from mountain range to mountain range. Stopping the car, I'd scamper up to a rock face and break off a specimen. This probably looked strange to any observers who rushed by on the highway. This frenetic rock breaking and collecting reminded me of the early geologists in England, whose seeming insanity was immortalized in a poem by Sir Walter Scott:

> and some rin up hill and down dale,
> knapping the chucky stanes to pieces wi' hammers,
> like sae mony road-makers run daft—
> they say it is to see how the world was made!

The road makers here had helped me considerably as they usually left steep cuts into bedrock in an effort to ease the road's grade across the summits. After collecting each specimen, I'd then jump back into the car, step on the gas, and head down into another valley with my eye on the next intriguing summit. By day's end, I had reached Utah, aware of the spectacular diversity of specimens now filling both egg cartons: purple rhyolite, black basalt, white limestone, green slate, pink quartzite, red sandstone. The rainbow of colors and the variations in texture—from glasslike to coarsely granitic—suggested a kaleidoscope. This collecting enabled me to see firsthand that the distribution of rocks in the Great Basin varied spatially. In the western Great Basin, igneous rocks were common, but in central Nevada they changed abruptly to metamorphic rocks, and farther east, sedimentary rocks. This egg-carton collection confirmed a truism about the region's geology: it is highly complex, but patterns exist. With enough experience, one can identify certain rocks as being common in certain parts of the region and absent in others. Miners and mining engineers finally understood these relationships after considerable trial and error and systematic study. Like them, I see that landscapes are built upon the bedrock geology, which in turn becomes fair game for speculation about how and when—not to mention why—the landscape took shape (fig. 4.1).

These rocks have a story to tell for anyone interested in *explanations* about landscape—regardless of whether one's motives are scientific or religious. Geologists propose three basic models to explain the creation of the region's distinctive basin and range topography. The first involves a system of structural blocks that have rotated along curving, downward flattening (listric) faults: the uplifted part of the block is the mountain, while the valley is the downslope part. The second theory proposes that the mountains are uplifted blocks (horsts) and the valleys are depressed blocks (grabens). The third hypothesizes that the landscape is a series of elon-

Fig. 4.1. Topography and Belief: Likely a place of spiritual significance for early Native Americans, the spectacular Lunar Crater in Nevada suggests the awesome geological forces that create landscapes and influence human beliefs in the Great Basin. (Photograph by author)

gated, rhombohedral blocks formed by the fragmentation of the upper crust through high-angle faults; the uplifted part is the mountain, while the part that titled downward is the valley. Geologist John H. Stewart suggests that the "basin-range structure may involve elements of each model."[5]

Geologist Bill Fiero, in his *Geology of the Great Basin,* offers a systematic interpretation of the development of the region's landscapes. He tells a story that reaches back more than 200 million years, and involves long-understood processes of sedimentation, faulting, and volcanism—plus more recent revelations about plate tectonics and exotic terrains. Fiero confirms that, although "virtually all geologists are in agreement that the thinning of the crust beneath the Basin and Range is directly related to the fault-controlled uplift of mountains and down-dropping of basins," there is disagreement as to how the mountain masses came to be oriented. Simplifying things just a bit, he presents two theories that might explain the Great

Basin's topography: one suggesting that mountain blocks rotated along curving planes (listric faults), with mountains representing the uplifted part of tilted blocks while the valleys are their downslope portions; the other suggesting that the basin and range topography consists of tilted blocks that moved upward or downward along high-angle faults of about sixty degrees, the resulting uplifted chunks being mountains, the down-dropped being valleys.[6] Note that each theory explains a process, and thus addresses a central aspect of creation—how something came to be.

Current scientific theories about the creation of the basin and range province center on plate tectonics, in which huge blocks of the earth's crust are in constant motion. When the plates collide, these blocks are forced upward in some places, but in others they are dragged under into areas where hot liquid magma works its magic on them. In these zones of subduction, the blocks are transformed by heat and pressure. This reconstitution helps explain the texture of rocks in parts of the Great Basin that appear to have characteristics that are, at best, transitional rather than definitive. These rocks may have been sedimentary at one time but are once again rendered igneous through the process of subduction. In one place, I encounter a magnificent example of this, where three types of rocks grade into each other almost seamlessly—indisputable proof that the three main classes of rocks involve somewhat arbitrary classifications. I realize the incredible leaps of faith that I must take, however, in assuming that I know that (and how) these rock units actually moved as the geologists say. I agree with Donald Baars, a geologist who puts the entire process in philosophical perspective. Baars begins by noting that the "concept of plate tectonics may be likened to a new religion. Since hard facts are lacking, if one is not a 'believer' one is considered an 'atheist' with regard to the many theories and interpretations of the 'clergy': The oceanographers and geophysicists." I like Baars's use of the term "clergy" here, for by this he means the arbiters of faith. In this scientifically inspired religion, says Baars, "Many of the concepts are plausible and exciting, and sometimes they fit the hard geologic facts." But Baars continues: "Many times, however, they are contradictory and totally incongruent with known geologic facts, at which time the facts are ignored." Here Baars means that the social forces within an institution, as mediated by the clergy, are powerful; theories thus become accepted as fact by the faithful practitioners. Science is not supposed to function this way, of course, but all institutions are subject to both abuse and excessive control. As Baars puts it, "With enough 'faith,' every known earth event is compatible with the religion, especially with respect to oceanography. On land, however, where outcrops and fossils abound, it is often extremely difficult to be a 'follower.'" Baars here refers to the fact that not every aspect of the geology, especially in a complex region like the basin and range province, is perfectly harmonious with the prevailing theory, which must be accepted on faith that becomes doctrine. He concludes: "The entire doctrine may in time be proven true, it may be completely disproven by geologists, or a compromise may be reached. I prefer to think the last possibility is likely."[7]

Setting aside for a moment the validity of plate tectonics theory in explaining how this basin and range topography took form, I ponder the concept of being offered either two or three alternatives that might explain how mountains and basins came to be juxtaposed with such regularity. The set of two alternatives suggests an either-or choice, and it is as reassuring as any binary set of explanations (for or against, up or down, right or wrong, left or right). The suggestion is that one is true, one false, though each might have some validity. The set of three alternative explanations, however, is somehow even more reassuring—not only because it provides more alternatives and nuances, but because it subliminally suggests a stronger foundation. I ponder this as I set up my tripod for an evening photograph of the White Mountains bathed in a salmon-colored afterglow. Rock steady, the tripod mimics the architecture of Trinitarian Christian mythology, with its Father, Son, and Holy Spirit supporting all existence and knowledge. It also recreates one of the Old World's most potent geometric forms, the pyramid.

Consider the naming of Pyramid Lake, which John C. Frémont's party encountered and named in January of 1844. Frémont was impressed by the lake's "green water" that "broke upon our eyes like the ocean," but it was one "remarkable rock in the lake which had attracted our attention for many miles." As related by Frémont, the rock "rose, according to our estimate, 600 feet above the water; and, from the point we viewed it, presented a pretty exact outline of the Great Pyramid of Cheops" (fig. 4.2). That pyramid in Egypt was, and remains, one of the architectural and spiritual mysteries of the world. It is associated with a quest for eternal life, and its pure three-part composition, anchored onto the earth but pointing toward heaven, continues to engage the imagination. The potency of the pyramid's symbolism is made explicit in its depiction as the all-seeing eye of God that became an integral part of the Great Seal of the United States shortly after the Republic's creation. The pyramid's deeper meaning was widely discussed in the 1800s, and so Frémont must have found it an irresistible symbol to equate with American expansion into the Great Basin. As if to justify his naming of the feature, Frémont added an enigmatic if not boastful comment: "and though it may be deemed by some a fanciful resemblance, I can undertake to say that the future traveler will find a much more striking resemblance between this rock and the pyramids of Egypt than there is between them and the object from which they take their name." About fifteen years later, a group of Mormons traveling through the eastern portion of the Great Basin described a "high pyramidal peak perfectly white"[8]—hence the name White Mountains—with this type of tripartite geometry in mind.

When glimpsed from certain directions, some of the region's mountains seem like isolated triangular pyramids, but they are in fact usually part of larger, more complexly shaped ranges. Those mountains are the region's dominant landmarks—a reminder that we tend to emphasize the singular quality in the environment that most captures our imaginations here in this area of corrugated basin and range, mountain-and-valley topography. Throughout most of its varied 165,000 square miles, the Great Basin consists of classic horst-and-graben (i.e., structurally controlled/faulted mountain-and-valley) topography on a huge scale, so huge that it is difficult to comprehend without generalizing. The repetition of alternating mountain-valley-mountain-valley topography was described by three geologists as "looking from the air like so many caterpillars headed north and south."[9] This topographic repetition may lull one into thinking that the story of its creation is repetitively dull, but that is not the case at all. The Great Basin is one of the most geologically complex areas on earth. I recall Howard Stansbury's expedition to the Great Salt Lake in the early 1850s (fig. 4.3). His descriptions are almost mind-boggling in the variety of rocks encountered and the positions that they assumed with regard to one another. For example, at the northern edge of the Great Basin, he describes "an escarpment of dark limestone . . . lying on and conformable with layers of feldspathic rock," while a "short distance further on, the same rock is again seen, overlaying the dark limestone." In describing the geology, Stansbury states, or rather understands, that "It is plainly [sic] to see that this has been a region of great disturbance." And in one brief passage about the topography near the Great Salt Lake, Stansbury notes that "the rocks were thrown up at a very high angle, and in some places were per-

Fig. 4.2. Envisioning Egypt: When John C. Frémont's expedition beheld this scene in 1844, they named the lake Pyramid after this island rock's likeness to the mysterious Pyramid of Cheops in Egypt. (From Frémont's *Report of the Exploring Expedition to the Rocky Mountains, 1845;* author's collection)

Fig. 4.3. Recording the Region's Wonders: Howard Stansbury's 1852 *Exploration of the Valley of the Great Salt Lake* revealed some of the complex geological wonders of the Great Basin, as this sketch of "west side of Promontory, Flat Rock Point," Utah, suggests. (Courtesy Special Collections Division, University of Texas at Arlington Libraries)

pendicular, and rested, as far as could be ascertained, on a primitive [i.e., older] formation below." But "[t]oward the southern end of the promontory, the limestone disappeared, and the surface rock was formed of conglomerate composed chiefly of the older sedimentary rocks, and some boulders of serpentine and porphyry," which is to say one formation contained rocks from all three known groups—sedimentary, metamorphic, and igneous.[10] Here we encounter another trinity. And again, like father, son, and holy spirit, there is something strangely reassuring about it.

But earlier in the day, as I stood on one of the passes I crossed, I had pondered something else about the geological information underfoot. Given the incredible variety of rocks present on the earth's surface, it is remarkable that most religions are silent about their meaning. I suspect that the variation in color, texture, and composition of rocks—from chalky white limestone through a kaleidoscope of colors and textures to glossy black obsidian—was, and is, either daunting or too disconcerting to comprehend. Of course, most places provide far less complex geology than the Great Basin, but there is still quite a bit elsewhere. Understandably, the idea that rocks themselves, or rocks of different types compared, could be used to date major events in the earth's history was unsettling. It created concern when first introduced about two hundred years ago, especially when those dates accelerated the ages of rock formations to thousands, then millions of years. In one of the great ideological coups in history, geologists appropriated the very materials that reflect the earth's, and ultimately humankind's, origin. Then again, geologists had a different motive. More than two thousand years ago, Euripides suggested the geologist's attitude when he wrote:

> Happy the man whose lot it is to know
> The secrets of the earth. He hastens not
> To work his fellows' hurt by unjust deeds
> But with rapt admiration contemplates
> Immortal Nature's ageless harmony
> And how and when her order came to be,
> Such spirits have no place for thoughts of shame.

Not everyone holds a sanguine view of such "secret" knowledge. According to Yi-Fu Tuan, geologically diverse mountainous landscapes, with their uplifted and contorted sediments, "too powerfully remind me of time." Tuan notes that "[a]nyone with a modicum of geologic knowledge might feel dread—the sensation of being sucked into a yawning temporal abyss—in the face of exposed strata, once laid flat, now grotesquely contorted, clear evidence of a paroxysmic and unimaginably remote past."[11]

In retrospect, the *variety* present in the geology of the earth's crust seems to suggest a story so complex that it would need to be either ignored or simplified. The alternative is to embrace that variety and its inherent complexity, but the result might be uncertainty, even *confusion*. Consider the words of Western Shoshone spiritual leader Corbin Harney, whose Native religion addresses this diversity. Harney explains it using a story: "You see, the coyote and the wolf were talking long ago. The wolf was arguing that we [people] should all look alike; the rocks should be the same, the sagebrush the same, all the humans the same." Although Wolf believed that "we should think alike and act alike and so forth," Coyote had a different plan. According to Harney, "the coyote always said, 'No, we should all be different. We shouldn't look alike at all.'" Thus, Harney notes, "the rules and regulations were set by the people who were here before us as animals." This had far-reaching consequences: "And so, today, we look around us and nothing looks alike. Rocks are not alike. Humans are not alike."

This, Harney concludes, has deep and lasting social and moral consequences. It lies at the root of why "we don't believe in each other."[12]

Harney's story equates variation with discord. According to this story, it is the result of a trickster who wishes us to oppose each other, to divide us on fundamental meanings, to lead us astray. Harney observes that we can learn to find truth and harmony if we take care of the things around us, restore them through prayer. Things from Mother Earth have life, Harney notes. "The rocks are the same way. The rocks talk—they eat like we do; they breathe air like we do. They have the same age as whatever was here thousands of years ago." Harney adds with much pleasure: "Some of your people are just beginning to realize that the rocks have a life."[13]

As I traversed the Great Basin, stopping at each pass with rock hammer in hand, I found a fossil shell in one of the limestones in eastern Nevada. Consider for a moment the spiritual significance of such an encounter. Finding a seashell embedded in strata at about 7,500 feet above sea level, more than six hundred miles from the ocean, is inherently delightful only if one embraces a story of endless change through geological time; this story was generations in the making, pieced together from fragments of ancient natural history and Leonardo da Vinci's stunning realization, in contradiction to his earlier belief in the deluge of Noah, that "the distribution of land and sea had not always been as it was then." With faith in the old explanation shaken, da Vinci now concluded that "at one time the sea had covered those parts of the dry land where fossils now occur."[14]

Leonardo has been called the father of paleontology for his revelation, but that makes fossils no less bewildering and no less potent to many people of faith. Consider again the words of Corbin Harney: "Other humans were here before us. Animals were here before us. But they didn't follow the rules and regulations that were given to them. So now we find them in the sand. We find them in the rocks. Then we say, 'They *were* here; they *used* to be here.'" As before, Harney's concern is moral and ethical. He adds, "That's what they're going to be saying about us, if we don't take care of this Earth." To Harney and many other Western Shoshone, the landscape is rich in evidence of such transformations from animal to stone. He notes that "there is still a place where I've been, right out of Ely [Nevada], between Ely and Kern Creek—there's a big mound where the animals actually sat in a circle, where they talked about a lot of different things." To Harney, the topography itself tells the story: "All those rocks piled up there, those were all the different animal life that became stone." Like many stories about landscape, this Shoshone story is rich in both imagery and morality: "And all the rocks and the birds and the animals, they used to talk; they had voices, and, as I realize it, they've still got a voice today." That voice is extremely important to the spirituality of the Shoshone. It tells them that "you have to take care of all those things in order to be able to continue." In Harney's words, it warns: "If you don't[,] when they die off, you are going to die with them." Harney believes that "what we would call stories today" had deeper meaning and veracity. He now solemnly concludes "they weren't stories, but history . . . what the Indian people talked about was really true."[15]

These stories are indeed history in the sense that they passed down via the oral history tradition. Like many such stories, or parables, they have deep cultural roots and philosophical dimensions. Harney vividly offers the demise of earlier life-forms as evidence of their role in a cyclical chronology. He mentions those from "the last cycle," which "ended with those huge monsters who lived here a few thousand years ago." Those creatures "came to an end because they didn't understand what the earth was doing, or how to work with nature." Harney uses two metaphors that resonate among desert dwellers—wind and sand—to describe that end: "The wind took their life with blowing sand, and today you can find them in sandstone all over the country. Looking at them, I think that's true."[16]

So potent is the topography of the Great Basin that it figures in all storytelling. To the Mormons, the Great Basin's mountains offered protection and hence helped them nurture their religion. This in part explains the reverence that the Latter-day Saints feel for such topography. In this sense, mountains are sacred—but only to a point. Consider, instead, Spirit Mountain, a prominent peak in the rugged Newberry Mountains near the southern tip of Nevada. As historian Ferenc Morton Szasz notes, Spirit Mountain typifies American Indian "sacred space," a vital attitude that all Native Americans "share in common . . . a deep reverence for the forces of Nature, an awareness of the interconnectedness of life, and a special relationship to the land itself."[17] As with most such sacred places, Spirit Mountain figures in a story that is associated not only with tribal history generally, but with specific supernatural events or conditions recounted and deeply believed by that tribe. According to Helen Carlson, Spirit Mountain is "said to have been so named because of the Indians' belief that it was the dwelling place of departed chieftains."[18]

I suspect that Spirit Mountain's distinctive shape and its peak's elevated position (5,639 feet) above the surrounding valleys contribute to its cultural visibility. For even though the valley floors here at the southern edge of the Great Basin are several thousand feet lower than Spirit Mountain's summit, this peak's elevation is actually lower than many of the valley floors in the central Great Basin, which lie at about 6,000 feet above sea level. (That difference in elevation accounts for the furnace-hot summers in the region's southern reaches, but it also explains the delightfully warm winter days here.)

As related by whites who traversed the area, Spirit Mountain held special meaning for Indians as a locale in which "spirits congregated." This attitude appears to have much in common with beliefs about the mountains of ancient Greece. Those mountains rimming the eastern Mediterranean were abodes of the gods. Moreover, those spirits who dwell on Spirit Mountain are the souls of mortals who, by virtue of their esteemed social positions, now dwell in spirit. Lest we think that such a place would be attractive to visit, we need only remember that what many people today innocuously call the "Newberry Mountains" were once the "Dead Mountains"—an ominous name that suggests why they were "given wide berth by the Indians who called them Spirit Mountains."[19]

Then, too, the actual shape of the topography can suggest the presence of spirits or ghosts. I will never forget the feeling of awe and unease that I experienced one evening upon encountering a valley full of weirdly eroded spires. In the descending gloom of impending nightfall, these sculpted landforms set even my scientific mind to recognizing how much like ghosts they appeared. Nevada has commemorated one such locale in Nye County, the Goblin Knobs, which were "so named because 'local tuff weathers into hoodoos and weird knobs.'"[20] In south-central Nevada, the hoodoos of Cathedral Gorge are awesome reminders of the powers of earth building, water erosion, and wind erosion (fig. 4.4). Seeing how much sediment is flushed from this area after a brief downpour, I am reminded of the Roman scientist-poet Lucretius' question: "do you not see that stones even are conquered by time, that tall turrets do fall and rocks do crumble?" These weirdly shaped landforms are also awesome reminders of the power of the human mind. Although the term hoodoo is used by geologists to refer to fantastically sculpted rock formations, it originated in Africa as a term for something that arouses resentment. In the Voodoo religion, the word refers to something that brings bad luck. Since the 1880s it has also signified the casting of a bad spell. No matter how rational one is, it is difficult to spend a night in such a valley without one's imagination discerning a resemblance between people alive and dead.

Few encounters better illustrate the differences between Native American and Judeo-Christian traditions than that which involved the Utah chief Wakara and Solomon Nunes Carvalho, a Sephardic Jew. Wakara accompa-

Fig. 4.4. Landscape and Spirit: In Nevada's Cathedral Gorge, a hoodoo, or erosional remnant, conveys a sense of mystery, even foreboding, to some. (Photograph by David Futey)

nied Carvalho on John C. Frémont's fifth expedition into the region. At the southeastern edge of the Great Basin in 1852, Wakara informed Carvalho that "a few miles from our present camp there was a most extraordinary vinegar lake, where all bad spirits dwell; a place where a living animal was never seen, and near which there was no vegetation." Carvalho here pauses to add an important element of drama in his account. He notes that "our interpreter told me he had heard before of such a lake, but he placed no faith in it." As if to accept the challenge—proving the native voice over that of an outsider—"Wakara said he would go along and show us the place."

We might pause here and note that the willingness of Native Americans to share information about place was an important aspect of early contact, and that explorers like Carvalho learned much about the soul or spirit of the countryside from it. As Carvalho resumes his account, he builds on the drama of discovery: "Before the lake was in sight, the atmosphere gradually became unpleasant to inhale"–"mephitic" was his word for it–"leaving a sulphurous taste on your palate." So "charged with sulphuric hydrogen gas" was the air that Carvalho and his party had "an inclination to vomit." As if to vindicate Wakara, the group arrived to find a sunken depression that "had evidently been a lake" but "now looked like the dry bed of what was once a lake." Walking onto its surface, the party discovered "that it undulated with the weight of our bodies." Adding to the drama and danger, Carvalho notes that he felt as if he was "walking on thin ice, which bent, without breaking beneath my weight." The thin ice was both metaphorical and literary, for he was challenging readers' assumptions about the authority of white interpreters and the fallibility of primitives regarding matters of science. The men now heard a roaring noise beneath the surface that "our Indian said was caused from 'big fire below.'" In characteristically scientific fashion–he felt obliged to discover the source–Carvalho jabbed his pickaxe into the crust. As a yellow muddy liquid gushed out, the ever-curious Carvalho just had to taste it to determine what it was. To his chagrin, "it was strong acid, which immediately set my teeth on edge."

Wakara had been right about the place. Carvalho confirmed its desolation, noting that "there are no signs of vegetation." The "wonderful lake," as he called it to signify that it was both awe-inspiring and interesting, emitted a "sulphurette hydrogen gas which impregnates the atmosphere, [and] prevents birds or animals from inhabiting or resorting near its neighborhood." Carvalho was perhaps correct that this "extraordinary place had probably never before been examined by a white man." As proof, he noted that "[n]one of the many Mormons who were present, and to whom I related the particulars, [had] ever explored it."[21] Carvalho's words remind me just how ingrained is the explorer's need to be first, if not the first person, then the first white person, to experience a place. In my many hikes throughout the most sparsely populated areas of the Great Basin, it was always easy for me to think just that–that I am seeing something that no one else has ever seen–and then just as quickly realize that many Native people had walked here long before I arrived.

If Carvalho's description of the lake abounds in geological terminology, that is understandable. Most well-educated travelers were cognizant of earth science at this time. Here we again see the scientific mind at work as enlightener. Where the Native peoples sense a place of much mystery and danger, Carvalho encounters clues. He tells us, for example, that upon nearing the lake "[o]ur path was covered with large quantities of obsidian [volcanic glass], and presented every indication that the lake we were approaching was of volcanic origin." Moreover, in explaining the lake's mysterious roaring sound, he concludes that it was "evidently produced by the force of the liquid through some subterranean cavern." It is important to note that Carvalho used deduction in explaining what he saw. As if expounding from a treatise on geology, he demystifies and depersonalizes the site: "in the neighborhood of some volcanoes," he observes dispassionately, "sulphuric acid is found impregnated with lime and baryta, both of which are abundant on the margins of this wonderful lake."[22] The term "wonderful" is appropriate here, for by that he meant remarkable—but not unique, because other places in the world also possess similar qualities. Carvalho's words reveal that our perspective about particular places changes when we experience many places in our travels. True, we can find wonder in them, but they are now judged in light of the other places throughout the world that we have experienced, or read about. By this process, we systematically reduce the magic of individual places, while increasing an awareness of how they compare to similar places.

One might argue that Carvalho's increased awareness was simply a result of technology: The steamship and railroad brought places closer together, and the printing press brought words (and then images) of places to an ever-increasing number of people. But we can never separate such technology from the religious systems that first encouraged and then sustained them. By first separating people from place in the most profound (that is, spiritual) way, Judeo-Christian thinking enabled the objectification—that is, the despiritualizing—of such places. In Judeo-Christian thought, place and spirituality play out on separate planes—or stages—while in Native thought, place and spirituality are closely linked.

But to return to the mysterious lake in southwestern Utah that Carvalho so readily explained in 1852, consider a more profound aspect of topography, again in relation to the body. By the time Carvalho encountered the lake, his Judeo-Christian culture had (with assistance from Islamic and other sophisticated traditions) begun to demystify not only the landscape, but also human anatomy and physiology. To Native peoples (and perhaps Carvalho's ancient Jewish forebears), the chthonic forces of volcanic topography were essentially gastrointestinal. It is no coincidence that he related mephitic, sulphur-laden liquids and vomiting in the same passage. The sulphurous exhalations and fluids of the earth—hot, fetid, mysterious—are flatulence and excreta on a grand scale. These exhalations and secretions we tend to give wide berth, and they are frequently contrasted with the purity of springs (cool, clear, odorless). We are strongly repelled by, and yet drawn to, places of volcanic origin. Certain springs and features in the Great Basin help point to subterranean connections to the volcanic past—a catastrophic past that left sheets and mounds of volcanic materials strewn across the earth's surface. These places foam and fume with mephitic gases that our eyes interpret as exotic but our noses remind us are as near as our own bowels.

These are the places that are likely to be associated with evil spirits by Native Americans, and that newcomer to the Great Basin—the devil—by those from the Judeo-Christian tradition. The devil, lord of the underground, thrives in this fiery realm. But his handiwork is seen in surface features. The devil is commemorated in several topographic features in the Great Basin. A mountain peak in the southern end of Nevada's Spring Mountains close to the California state line was named Devil by early travelers, apparently "because of its forbidding aspect." Then, too, there are two Devil's Gates in Nevada—one located between Gold Hill and Silver City on the Storey-Lyon County line, the other at the north end of the Fish Creek Range in Eureka County (fig. 4.5). Of the former, J. Ross Browne is said to have commented that its name aptly conveyed "a forcible impression of the unhallowed character of the place." The other, a spectacular entrance into a canyon on today's Highway 50, was presumably given its fanciful name because it—like other topographical and hydrological features named after the fallen angel—possessed an "unpleasant or forbidding" aspect.[23] To these we can add about a dozen other features in Nevada, including an entire mining district, a creek, a cave, an unusual vertical sided hole in an alluvial fan (Devil's Throat), a peak in the Dead Mountains (Devil's Thumb) and a group of hot springs in the Monitor Valley called the Devil's Punchbowl.[24]

Utah also has its share of features named after the devil. Here, too, they are especially common in areas of volcanic topography. This is a natural enough connection as volcanic landscapes reveal the effects of potent subterranean forces. Consider, for example, the Devil's Kitchen of west-central Utah, where an escarpment of pockmarked, chocolate-colored basalt cuts across sagebrush-covered landscape. A local guidebook observes: "Perhaps Devil's Kitchen was named after the strange faces that eerily peer at you from the rock wall as the shadows lengthen in the evening."[25] The deepening shadows do indeed reveal a menacing countenance, a roughly elongated triangle, the lower point forming a chin, the two upper points becoming the horns—just the way the devil is commonly depicted in art. It is easy to think that such allusions are totally fanciful, until we recall that hu-

Fig. 4.5. Tribute to the Devil: To early travelers, certain topographic features in this region suggested the work of the devil—as in Devil's Gate near Virginia City, Nevada. From J. Ross Browne, "A Peep at Washoe," 1860. (Courtesy Special Collections Division, University of Texas at Arlington Libraries)

mans have a well developed natural ability to render abstract forms into recognizable faces—including that of Lucifer, the king of the underworld.[26] Reading the landscape is like taking a Rorschach test, but there are points of convergence where many people see the same things—at least when those things resemble cherished, or feared, icons.

Devil's Throat and Devil's Thumb suggest something else about those landscape features—that is, how often we equate the form of the landscape with the shape of the human body—as in the *mouth* of a river, *head* of a stream, *foot*hill, *shoulder* of a mountain. Our culture, with its puritanical influences, stops short of analyzing this relationship carefully, for it leads to some uncomfortable territory. The relationship between body and landscape is not only very deep, it is also very sexual. Here is an example of how we touch upon it, but then draw away for fear of censure. Rich Moreno and Larry Prosor recently noted that "Nevada writer David Toll once described some of the mountains in Nevada 'like sleeping women, sprawling languorously across every horizon.'" These authors conceded that "indeed, if you look long and hard enough, you begin to see there is something sensual in the curves and rises of these ranges"—but then quickly countered that "of course when you start to see women in the mountains, that is probably a good indication that you should take a break from driving."[27]

There is ample evidence that many early travelers did not take such a break. Traveling through the Great Basin in the late 1850s, Samuel Bowles wrote a revealing passage about the mountainous topography near the booming mining town of Austin, Nevada: "Do not think such a country is altogether without beauty or interest for a traveler. Mountains are always beautiful; and here they are ever in sight, wearing every variety of shape, and even in their hard and bare surfaces presenting many a fascination of form—running into sharp peaks; raising up and rounding out into innumerable fat mammillas, exquisitely shapen, and inviting possibly to auriferous feasts."[28] This passage is more than a little reminiscent of the erotically charged Song of Solomon with its reference to the topography of the human body and the riches of the earth. In that most enigmatic book in the Old Testament, a woman reveals that she has "breasts like towers" and makes reference to "the mountains of spices" that awaken a lover's passion (Sol. 8:11, 14).

Reading Bowles's statement and the Song of Solomon reminds me that men have often characterized landscapes in terms like these. Although I am prone to agree with geographer Douglas Porteous on one point—that the metaphorical connection between body and landscape "is, in fact, an interacting system, whereby landscape is seen as body but, also, body is regarded as landscape, that the body in question, in male-dominant cultures, is very often the female body"—I cannot go so far as to believe his conclusion that "the culmination of 'body as landscape' is pornotopia."[29] Pornography assumes a prurient interest in sex and, in this case, an interest in the domination of women, but I suggest we look a bit more openly, and less puritanically, at the subject of landscape as body.

That need to expunge the landscape of its sexual content is understandable enough in polite company or politically correct subcultures, but it denies an inherent human recognition of body in landscape. That we continue to purge both our minds and our maps of this connection recalls two geographic features, one in California, the other in Oregon, that are explicit enough: "Nellie's Nipple" in the Mojave Desert is unmistakably breastlike in appearance and female in name to suggest a prospector longing for a woman whose form was once commemorated as a toponym—but then removed from maps by more sensitive authorities. But even less acceptable is the aptly named feature "Cock Rock" in southern Oregon, a fifty-foot-tall column of basalt that bears an uncanny resemblance to its namesake; but alas, one will not find this landmark named on USGS topographic maps because of its risque suggestion of frontal nudity.

It is tempting to think this equating of anatomy with landscape is so much male fantasy, until we remember that women are now empowering themselves to do it too. Mormon writer Terry Tempest Williams notes that "there are dunes beyond Fish Springs. Secrets hidden from interstate travelers." Here, in Utah, "wind swirls around the sand and ribs appear." Williams discerns "musculature in dunes." This is not just any body, but that of a woman—Mother Earth. These dunes, Williams observes, "are female. Sensuous curves—the small of a woman's back. Breasts. Buttocks. Hips and pelvis. They are the natural shapes of Earth"[30] (fig. 4.6).

To cave-as-womb we now add other anatomical features to our earth—flanks of hills, clefts of canyons, tips of summits—that once again remind us of our deep connection to both our bodies and the earth. Just as the Song of Solomon is something of an aberration in the Bible, a celebration of sensuality, the Judeo-Christian tradition distances us from these feelings. Small wonder that early Anglo-Americans worried about the temptation of both wilderness and the "savages" who dwelt there. The Great Basin's Indians remind us of the landscape's sexual connotations as we plumb their stories for content both sacred and profane.

Let us again turn to the Paiute of the Great Basin, whose frank recognition of human genitalia in the landscape is enduring enough that it has survived in many stories. This one, too, is about stone. As related by an-

Fig. 4.6. Landscape and Imagination: Geologists interpret Sand Mountain, in central Nevada, as a wind-deposited feature whose sinuous crest parallels the direction of prevailing winds, while artists and writers may see the shape of a reclining woman in its sensual contours. (Photograph by Richard Orndorff)

thropologist Kay Fowler: "Coyote and Wolf (brothers) were living together. One day Coyote was propositioned by a woman, but she changed her mind and ran away. Coyote pursued her. She stopped to relieve herself and when Coyote found the spot, he left his penis there as a marker. (Northern Paiute still refer to particular geologic features as 'Coyote's penis.')"[31] The story does not end here, for "Coyote found where the woman's mother lived" and realized the place was good. He also learned that consummating a union with the woman would be dangerous because "she had sharp teeth in her vagina and she invariably dispatched all suitors." Through his resourcefulness, however, Coyote "defanged" the woman and they "lived together." In this story, children materialize in a big willow jar that had been placed between Coyote and the woman by her mother. Coyote is commanded by the mother-in-law to carry the jug back to his home and not open it, lest the children escape. These children represent various Indian groups in the region, including the Bannock and Paviotso. Other peoples in the Great Basin, including the Washo, have similar narratives.[32] But note the significance of the jar, a sealed container that functions as a place of incubation and ultimately, procreation.

Sexuality and procreation are important aspects of this story of creation and diaspora. Note, for example, several underlying themes. First, Coyote is male—curious and crafty, potent and impetuous; second, the woman is both powerful and dangerous, so much so that she requires a defanging in order to bear children; third, there is a constant tension between male and female—an enduring, perhaps universal element. The suggestion that sexual trauma has occurred to both male and female is noteworthy, both in the implication of castration (which is represented as penislike rock features) and a defanging of the perilous vulva (perhaps a subliminal reminder that most cultures find ways of subduing "natural" predatory female sexuality). Of special interest, though, is the comparison of a vulva to a jar, the container of human life, while the penis is exiled to the position of an isolated topographic feature. Those distinctions—vulva and penis as internal and external—thus play out psychologically as they do topographically.

There are other stories in the region's landforms. I consider the name Beowawe as I drive slowly along a back road paralleling the Southern Pacific's polished steel tracks in northern Nevada. This former railroad community with an Indian name intrigues me. Local Anglo-American storytelling by those who grew up along the railroad suggests that Paiute or Shoshone Indians witnessed a portly railroad official relieving himself here and, awed by the size of the man's buttocks, named the location after their word for "great posterior."[33] I like this story, but I think the name may predate the railroad official's call to nature. "Beowawe" in Paiute (Numu) means "gate"—a possible reference to two hills that suggest an open gateway in the topography here, and this in turn may link the place to the Shoshone word for "derriere" or, more to the point, "big-ass Indian woman."[34] Although the answer to this riddle may never be known, it may indeed lie in the Indians' designation for one indelicate part of Mother Earth. And this again reminds me how earthy spirituality is, at least in some places, and among some peoples who've not forgotten their connections to the earth.

5

Encounters with the Wind

I find the signature of wind everywhere I look.
—JAN DEBLIEU, *Wind*

Flying over the Great Basin in a commercial airliner, I gaze down into the Salt Lake Desert near the Utah-Nevada state line. It is late spring and the sky cloudless; from 23,000 feet the dark mountains appear like rows of purplish cinders, the broad valley floor is bright white. Looking closer, I see that the wind has stirred the surface of the dry lakes into dust storms that race from south to north. From here the scene seems serene, but on the ground the air is full of stinging sand and flying tumbleweeds. Traffic on Interstate 80 slows to a crawl in places as visibility drops to near zero. In a few places, trailer trucks have been flipped onto their sides by the strong shearing winds. Smart motorists driving campers have heeded the warning signs and pulled off the highway. In the lee of mountains the wind is tolerable, but out in the open, it's blowing at 50 miles per hour and causing havoc.

The view reminds me of a fact of life in the Great Basin. Although the geology helps define the landscape, everything is always at the mercy of the weather. The aridity keeps the region a basin (actually more than one hundred basins),[1] while running water erodes the mountains and fills those basins with silt. But in addition to mountains and water, a third element—a restless atmosphere—gives this region much of its character. The incessant movement of the atmosphere here gives me pause to recall those times when the wind isn't blowing. They are rare, strangely silent, like the unnatural silence of a missed heartbeat or a stopped clock. Those times when there isn't a breath of air moving, when stillness briefly reigns, catch me by surprise. They seem unusual because the wind, like me, seems to be always moving about in search of something. Here still air seems to be living on borrowed time, for the region is positioned in the path of the westerlies and is so diverse that a differential between a heated surface here or a cool slope there sends the air moving in a futile search for equilibrium. So it is that this moving air is ever present in the Great Basin and always has work to do in shaping both life and landscape. It helps evaporate water and move fine particles of rock into sensuous sand dunes. As motorists hereabouts know, it can also abrade windshields, paint, and chrome. As geomorphologists know, it leaves ventifacts—rocks that have been worn smooth by sand-filled wind.

The addition of wind to the formula for shaping places reminds me of the Chinese concept *feng shui* (literally wind and water), in which the wind must be taken account of in all aspects of environmental design. In *feng shui* the wind is not an inanimate force; rather, like the other elements, it is alive. Appropriately, the term *feng shui* is also used more broadly to refer to the living earth. This belief that the wind is "alive" suggests that it is an animate, rather than a purely physical, force.

When conditions are right, the Great Basin's landscape becomes animated as buff-colored columns of dust churn across the valleys (fig. 5.1). The term "dust devil" is commonly heard today but was not used until the twentieth century. In describing one of these whirling winds in 1877, Nevada writer William Wright (more popularly known by his pen name Dan De Quille) noted that they do not appear until about one o'clock in the afternoon, when "tall slender columns of dust, rising often perpendicularly to the height of a thousand feet" march across the desert. De Quille added that they may commence as a single column, "but soon another and another rises and like stately giants, they chase each other across the plain, till soon all mingle into one confused, flying mass, and so continues till sundown or after."[2] These "dust devils" are chimneys of heated air that rotate skyward as they travel with the prevailing wind. Their power is physically palpable as stinging sand and bits of vegetation are carried along in their otherwise invisible columns; some are strong enough to damage sheds and other loosely built structures. In the center of a dust devil there is a brief calm, only to be replaced at the other side by debris-filled air moving the opposite direction.

The veering of the wind is an inevitable element of the dust devils' passage. Driving through the Great Basin, I've learned to anticipate their antics as they cross highways. The dust devil's reversing flow of air is predictable as I drive into one. Because they almost always rotate counter-clockwise, I'm prepared: No matter which way I'm headed, I anticipate that their wind will pull first from left to right, and so instinctively I tug the steering wheel to the left to counter the rushing air. For a split second all is

Fig. 5.1. The Whirlwind: Common in the Great Basin in summer, the dust devil is a rotating column of heated air that is regarded uneasily by some Native peoples. (June 2000 photograph near Coaldale, Nevada, by author)

still, but I then quickly compensate for the counter-tugging of the wind by a twist of the wheel to the right as I enter the rushing air at the backside of one of these remarkable whirlwinds.

In describing conditions around Lander and Eureka Counties in Nevada during the 1930s, mining historian William O. Vanderburg observed that "during the summer . . . winds are frequent, and they may have sufficient velocity to send sand and dust clouds high into the air." Vanderburg further noted that a "peculiar phenomenon during the summer months is the whirlwinds or miniature tornadoes of sand and dust that twist and gyrate in huge columns, majestically traveling through the valleys for miles."[3] As might be expected, these impressive dust devils figure in both the folklore and literature of the Great Basin and the West. As recorded by anthropologist James Mooney, a verse from the Paiute "Songs of Life Returning" captures the power of the towering, rotating winds:

> There is dust from the whirlwind,
> There is dust from the whirlwind,
> The whirlwind on the mountain.[4]

Anglo-American literature also mentions dust devils, which help set the mood for fiction. In *Parowan Bonanza* (1923), B. W. Bower described the landscape of a playa: "a dry lake lay baked yellow, hard as cement, with dust devils swirling dizzily down its bald length."[5] As an astute observer and rancher, she knew the dust devil to be a phenomenon of the arid and semiarid West. In *The Giant Joshua* (1942), Mormon writer Maureen Whipple observed: "The blue of the sky was washed white with brilliance, and dust-devils whirled in southward-sweeping clouds."[6] These dust devils were characteristic of Whipple's desert landscape in Utah. Although fairly objective, even these writers' descriptions suggest the power of the wind by use of such phrases as "whirling dizzily" and "towering majestically." Nevada even has a valley named in honor of these desert winds: Whirlwind Valley near Beowawe, in Lander and Eureka Counties commemorates the dust devils that are common there.[7] Similarly, there is a Whirlwind Valley in the Sevier Desert of Millard County, Utah. Like its counterpart in Nevada, this valley trends generally north-south (in this case, between the House Range/Swasey Mountain and the Little Drum Mountains) and it, too, is alive with whirling dust devils during summer.

Out in the open on foot, I crouch when I find myself in a dust devil's path. The sound of the wind increases to a hiss, and debris fills the air. I always viewed this type of encounter as a minor inconvenience: I simply shut my eyes and hold my breath; these whirlwinds are gone soon enough, and I'm none the worse for wear. But the name dust devil suggests real mischief, and it brings to mind a less beneficent interpretation. To the region's Native American inhabitants, dust devils were more than intriguing nuisances; they were visits from the spirit world—ghosts that stalked the land by day.

At the Yerington Indian Reservation just south of Wabuska, Nevada, Paiute tribal administrator Marlin Thompson repeated words of advice about dust devils that he'd heard from the elders: You don't ever want to get caught in one of them because they change you by taking something from you. Thompson used an interesting phrase when he described dust devils as "going through" the unwary: whereas most non-Indian observers would describe the dust devil as passing or going by, Thompson's mentioning that the dust devil goes *through* them hints at the power of the whirlwind to intrude or invade. This invasion is not only physical but spiritual. According to many Paiute and Shoshone stories, dust devils are a manifestation of spirits who endlessly stalk the earth in search of the unfortunate: they rob a person of spiritual strength, and such weakening exposes individuals to illness and misfortune.

I had always wondered why these whirlwinds were called dust devils, and now I have an idea that the term likely derived from Indians. If, as the *Dictionary of American Regional English* suggests, the term devil denotes unpleasant or dangerous qualities, then a dust devil can be much more than

simply "a small whirlwind which picks up sand and dust."[8] In *Blue Highways,* Native American writer William Least Heat Moon notes that "people
of the Old Testament heard the voice of God in desert whirlwinds, but
Southwestern Indians saw evil spirits in the spumes and sang aloud if one
crossed their path."[9] As early as the mid-nineteenth century, John Wesley
Powell reported that the whirlwind (*turó ni at*) was said by the Numa to be
caused by an "angry witch."[10] In this belief the Paiute and Shoshone are
not alone. According to Jan Deblieu, "Many aboriginal cultures believe
wind to be the restless souls of the dead."[11]

Marlin Thompson's words were fresh on my mind the day after I met him
in early June 2000. It was one of those transitional days when several conditions announce summer's arrival: the sky is virtually cloudless, the high
sun feels focused as if shining through a magnifying glass, and the winds
shift from the northwest to southwest; these are perfect conditions for the
formation of dust devils. Just west of Tonopah at noon, I noted a couple of
dust devils churning across a dry lake. One of them looked more or less
typical, but the other seemed especially intense. Intrigued, I pulled off
Highway 6 to take a closer look. Impressed by the size of the dust devil
closest to me, I observed it closely for several minutes as it approached
from the southwest. It was not only perfectly developed, a column of rotating air that rose like a pillar; it was huge. Towering about 1,500 feet into
the air, it must have measured a couple of hundred feet across. Buff in
color, it moved northeast at about 25 miles per hour. Something about this
dust devil was different. Out of the hundreds, perhaps thousands, of dust
devils I'd seen, this one seemed more powerful. As it passed within about
two hundred yards of me, I was awed by what happened next. In the center
of this huge dust devil, another formed before my eyes, this one churning
even more rapidly inside. This dust devil within a dust devil was different
in color—almost pure white—probably because it had passed over the snow-
white center of the dry lake. Something else was different about this dust
devil within a dust devil. It was so well developed that it looked like a twirl-
ing rope rising upward from the lakebed. As if this were not awesome
enough, what happened next amazed me even more: rising from each side
of the central dust devil, two smaller dust devils began to form. These, too,
were white, but instead of developing into tight columns, they remained
closer to the ground, assuming goblinlike forms. Flanking the center dust
devil, these ghostly forms pulsated, changing shape simultaneously but always maintaining humanlike proportions of height and width. From one
second to the next, they seemed to march, or dance, within the huge dust
devil.

This was one of those events so awesome, and so riveting, that I did not even attempt to reach for my camera. Besides, doing so would have been futile; first, the dust devils' *motion* would have to have been recorded to be believed—and I did not have a video camera. Second, the creation of these flanking dust devils took no more than ten, perhaps fifteen seconds; so that by the time I would have gotten the camera out of the camera bag, removed the lens cover, set the correct aperture, and adjusted the focus, it—or rather they—would have been gone.

And disappear it did. Almost as quickly as it had formed, this whirlwind lost its character, assuming the form of a normal dust devil; that was still awesome enough but not as, well, *supernatural.* With a sense of disappointment, I watched as the interior column of rotating white dust dissipated into the dust devil and the two goblins became fainter, then indistinct, then vanished. In its entirety, this spectacular event had taken less than half a minute, yet it transformed me. I could imagine being a Paiute Indian in, say, 1800, watching this display. It was so breathtaking—and those two smaller dust devils within the whirlwind so humanlike, or rather ghostlike—that I could now understand why the Native peoples considered them "spirits" rather than natural phenomena. Although the scientist in me insisted on drawing a picture of this magnificent dust devil (fig. 5.2), neither words nor an image can adequately capture the experience of watching nature act so anthropomorphically.

Three thoughts occurred to me after this experience. First, I was left with a question: I had observed many dust devils, but had I ever *really* seen them? I had thought so, but now I wasn't sure. Second, I realized that even though I could explain what I'd seen in meteorological terms, I had been privileged to witness the kind of rare natural event of which stories are made. Third, I now believe that my meeting with Marlin Thompson was crucial in my being in the right place at the right time. I am sure of this because I know I never would have paid such close attention to this particular dust devil had I not talked with Mr. Thompson the day before. I can remember thinking at the time I first saw the dust devils—that I must pay better attention to these phenomena to better understand what the Paiutes see when they experience a dust devil. This experience I count among the many gifts that have come to me in my field of work. These gifts are provided by people along the way, those whose experiences make the landscape resonate with greater, and deeper, meaning than the casual traveler, or even the scientist, will ever experience.

Understanding the nuances and significance of this dust devil came as a real surprise. I had seen innumerable dust devils during my many years of living in the West but never one this spectacular . I was reminded of Mary Clearman Blew's revelation about such encounters. The first time Blew recognized petroglyphs on a basalt formation in the Columbia Plateau, it came almost as a revelation: "They had always been there, etched into the face of the basalt, and yet they had suddenly materialized before my eyes." As if afraid to lose the image, Blew adds that she "looked at them for a long time . . . unwilling to take my eyes off them lest they vanish again."[12]

Unlike petroglyphs, dust devils are transient, constantly changing. Try photographing one: to begin with, they look different through the viewfinder; then, by the time you focus on these apparitions, they change density. You hope they will intensify so you can catch one for posterity, but most of the images will be pale specters of what seemed so spectacular to your eye. This makes me realize something fundamentally important as I dust myself off and get back into my rental car: *Some phenomena apparently survive better in the telling than the recording.* In other words, science

Fig. 5.2. Stories Within: Sketch of a huge dust devil containing several dust devils within it, suggests both the power of the wind and the presence of human-like forms. (Sketch by author, based on experience west of Tonopah, Nevada, June 2000)

can only take us so far: Being human, we are destined to translate some things phenomenologically rather than objectively. That is where the spirit resides. This point was brought home recently as Comanche elder and storyteller Carnie Saupitty related a series of stories about the "Spirit of Place." After recounting numerous stories, Saupitty paused and then uttered one of the most profound statements I've ever heard about sacred places—that they *become sacred only after some transforming experience has occurred there.*[13] So, too, for natural phenomena such as the wind.

I have never forgotten an experience I'd had in the southern Great Basin while I was still in high school. Two friends and I had climbed to the top of a small mountain in southern Nevada. It was June, and the sun blazed down on the clinkerlike volcanic rocks. Sitting on the rocks, we were awed by the view of similar volcanic mountains rising from the salt-white valleys below. A few desert plants had managed to grow here, and one rabbit brush nearby drew our attention as a strong breeze started it to rattling. The wind increased and soon turned into a strong upward draft that pulled the entire bush, roots and all, out of the ground. That was certainly peculiar, but nothing compared to what happened next. The bush did not fly away, but stayed suspended for perhaps half a minute, floating, as it were, in thin air. Then, slowly, the plant began to fly away, straight up into the clear blue sky. We looked at each other in amazement as it disappeared out of sight, estimating that it had been carried aloft a thousand or more feet. "Thermal," one of my friends declared, and I added a new word to my vocabulary.

Consider for a moment another encounter with the wind—and with place—from a very different perspective. This encounter happened not on the ground but several thousand feet above the Great Basin during the 1940s. It was related by Warren A. Roquet, a military navigator aboard bombers in World War II. As part of his training, Roquet was based out of Tonopah Army Air Base in western Nevada from November 1944 to March 1945. Roquet flew on numerous test flights that winter—flights that were made all the more difficult because "at almost any distance it was almost impossible to see where the snow covered mountains stopped and the white clouds started." With wry humor he noted that "white clouds with rock centers were a worrisome hazard." On one particularly memorable flight in January of 1945, Roquet found himself navigating after dark in especially troublesome conditions—an approaching cold front, intense St. Elmo's fire that covered the airplane's wings with "dancing blue and pink flames," and static electricity strong enough to incapacitate the plane's radios.

This electrical activity also disrupted the airplane's navigation system, and Roquet could only guess where he and the crew of the B-24 were. The only certainty was that they were lost somewhere over Nevada. Using a sixth sense, Roquet guessed that a sharp bump they'd just felt might "be the updraft of the north winds as they crossed the Toiyabe range." Using this possible clue, Roquet marked an "X" on the map, "hoping for a second bump" that would indicate the Toquima Mountains. As if on cue, they felt the second bump, and Roquet marked another "X" on the map. To verify their position, however, Roquet needed a third bump that would indicate their passage over the Monitor Mountains. And sure enough: "In a few minutes, I got the third bump." These bumps proved to Roquet that the aircraft was northeast of Tonopah. Sure of their position, he gave the pilot a new course that brought them safely into the Tonopah Army Air Base just minutes before a blizzard hit.

I like this account because it again subliminally suggests the power of the trinity, as three points are so much more believable than two. Roquet himself believed the incident had deep spiritual significance. He concluded his harrowing account by observing that although it was "the best navigation of my career," it was also something far more mystical: "I also know the lord had been with us in the St. Elmo's fire as our safe return was more than mere luck."[14] That concept—"more than mere luck"—suggests a higher power "looking out" for someone. This belief further suggests that one's fate is not always in one's own hands—at least not entirely so—but is in fact affected by divine intervention. Roquet credits "the lord" with intervention, not only in assuring a good *outcome,* but in having a hand in the actual *process*—in this case, brilliant navigation based on clues provided in the environment. The Numu (Paiute) Indians who were somewhere below Roquet's B-24 would recognize this as a spiritual communion—the connection of an individual with a power that in turn empowers the individual.

Roquet was heir to a long Judeo-Christian tradition that recognizes the power of the wind. The Bible is rich in references—more than 150, in fact—to the wind as both sustainer and destroyer. The wind is first mentioned in Genesis 8:1-2, when Noah and the Ark were afloat and "God made a wind blow over the earth, and the waters subsided; the fountains of the deep and the windows of the heavens were closed, the rain from the heavens was restrained, and the waters receded from the earth continually." The wind here has a beneficial role in human affairs, but later in Genesis (41:26-30) a searing east wind signals seven years of famine. Later in the Bible, the severely tested Job learns that the terrible power of the wind is one of many calamities that he must endure. It destroys his family as a test of his belief in God: "and behold, a great wind came across the wilderness, and struck the four corners of the house, and it fell upon the young people, and they are dead" (Job 1:19). This description leaves little doubt that the wind was a cyclone, or tornado, with its rotating winds shifting to all quarters of the compass and its power to destroy buildings. The early peoples of the Holy Land attributed such winds to God's anger: "Therefore thus says the Lord God: I will make a stormy wind break out in my wrath . . ." (Ezek. 13:13). Although an east wind might bring drought, it was the whirlwind that was most definitive in its power to positively enlighten ("And Elijah went up by a whirlwind into heaven"–2 Kings 2:11) or utterly humble ("For they saw the wind, and they shall reap the whirlwind"–Hosea 8:7). In either case, the wind symbolizes humankind's dependence on the will of a powerful and demanding God.

Like the Holy Land, the Great Basin lies in the general belt of the mid-latitudes, where westerly winds alternate with those from other directions. The Great Basin region experiences variations from the gentlest of breezes to sustained winds. Although the term *zephyr* is often used to mean a breeze in many places, it usually signifies a strong wind in the Great Basin. The zephyrs in the vicinity of Virginia City, Nevada, are legendary, as they are funneled down off the Sierra Nevada. They may come from any direction, depending on the season and other conditions. In 1860, J. Ross Browne described a wind that "blew in terrific gusts from the four quarters of the compass, tearing away signs, capsizing tents, scattering grit from the gravel banks with blinding force in everybody's eyes, and sweeping furiously around every crook and corner in search of some sinner to smite" (fig. 5.3). To Browne, this wind seemed demonic in its perseverance: "Never was such a wind as this–so scathing, so searching, so given to penetrate the very core of suffering humanity." Browne concluded that this wind seemed to have a will of its own in tormenting mankind, "following him wherever he sought refuge . . . in short, it was the most villainous and persecuting wind that every blew, and I boldly protest that it did nobody good."[15]

Like others of his time, Browne was familiar with the Bible, and his references to the wind's searching for "some sinner to smite" reminds us of the Old Testament. Jan Deblieu makes this same connection: "It is little wonder that the authors of the Old Testament perceived of wind as an agent of a nurturing yet jealous and vengeful God." That is because "in the biblical Holy Land (and throughout the world), the force and direction of the wind largely control the level of moisture in the air." Deblieu concludes that, as a result, "the wind's mood through the seasons often dictates

Fig. 5.3. The Wrath of God: Using a biblical metaphor, J. Ross Browne illustrated a strong wind "in search of some sinner to smite." From "A Peep at Washoe," 1860. (Courtesy Special Collections Division, University of Texas at Arlington Libraries)

whether the authors of the Bible feasted in comfort or suffered the hardships of severe deprivation." Tellingly, the Hebrew word *Neshawmaw* connotes not only wind or breath, but also "divine inspiration, intellect, . . . soul, spirit." As related by Deblieu, the Jews likely inherited their ambivalence about the wind (and water) from the Babylonians, whose gods Apsu and Tiamat struggle with their unruly sons; the parents give life to a sky god representing inert forces, while the sons give life to storm gods and raging waters; through such powers, one son ultimately creates sky and earth.[16]

Never one to miss irony—or to embellish a story—Samuel Clemens (Mark Twain) also commented on the "Washoe Zephyrs" that blow through western Nevada. Almost as if on cue, one was blowing upon Twain's arrival to Carson City in 1860. He called it a "peculiarly Scriptural wind" and observed that it brought with it "a soaring dust-drift about the size of the United States set up edgewise . . . and the capital of Nevada Territory disappeared from view."[17] Experiencing a Washoe Zephyr in the pass between Virginia City and Gold Hill, Twain swore that he witnessed "a Chinaman flying an iron door for a kite here, on this divide"[18] (fig. 5.4). Although the iron door was an unlikely kite, the Chinaman flying it was perfectly in character. Kites are said to have originated in China about A.D. 1000 and served both spiritual and aesthetic purposes to those who flew them. Kites unite humankind with the wind and enable their flyers to communicate directly with the spirits aloft. The Chinese god of wind is an old man (Feng Po) who "carries the breezes in a sack slung across his back. When he wants the wind to blow from a certain compass bearing, he points the mouth of the sack in that direction." According to Jan Deblieu, this deity can also take the form of a dragon called Fei Lien.[19]

Fig. 5.4. Witnessing the Celestial: One Washoe Zephyr was so strong that Mark Twain swore to witnessing "a Chinaman flying an iron door for a kite." (As reproduced in Sarah Ann Davis et al., *Guide to Virginia City, Nevada, and the Comstock Lode Area*, 1959)

Another aspect of the wind in desert regions like the Great Basin deserves mention, and that is its power to convey pestilence—or manna—in the form of locusts. The Book of Exodus states that "Moses stretched forth his rod over the land of Egypt, and the Lord brought an east wind upon the land all that day and all that night; and when it was morning the east wind had brought the locusts . . . a dense swarm of locusts . . . [that] . . . covered the face of the whole land, and they ate all the plants in the land and all the fruit of the trees" (10:12-16) Shortly after their arrival in the Great Basin, the Mormons were beset by a similar plague as countless crickets descended upon their fields. There was a considerable difference between the biblical locusts mentioned and the Mormon crickets, which marched like armies; nevertheless, it was easy for the Mormon settlers to view this scourge as being identical to those mentioned in the Bible. In the Mormons' bout with this voracious insect, it was *salvation* that descended from the sky: Flocks of seagulls fell upon and devoured the crickets. This act seemed miraculous at the time, for seagulls in the desert were difficult to comprehend. Those who professed the seagulls' intervention miraculous were countered by those who speculated that the gulls were migrating at the time and happened to intercede; others contend that the gulls are more or less permanent residents of the marshy regions in the vicinity of Great Salt Lake—and that this miracle was not really that miraculous after all. Nevertheless, the story of the gulls' fortuitous arrival has become part of the region's folk history—another way of proving the Mormons' divine right to be here.

Although an insect invasion is catastrophic to agriculturalists, it may be otherwise to nomadic peoples. Of John the Baptist it is said that "his food was locusts and wild honey" (Matt. 3:4), and that seems credible given his modest and peripatetic lifestyle. Similarly, the region's Native inhabitants ate a wide variety of insects and insect larvae—to the disgust of many nineteenth-century Anglo-Americans who had come to depend on domesticated crops and animals. Yet the Mormons cited the Indians' diet as yet more evidence that these people were descendants of the lost tribes of Israel. We have distanced ourselves from consuming nature's bounty, such as toasted locusts, as we've become ever more particular about what we define as food.

In the Great Basin, the wind rarely ceases to move, and it may arise at a moment's notice. One minute may transform a still campsite into chaos as a wall of wind—sometimes carrying dust and sand—roars through like an express train. On rare occasions, tornadoes visit the Great Basin. These most awesome of windstorms usually occur in late springtime, but because of the region's light population density, they rarely do any signifi-cant damage—an exception being the tornado that struck Salt Lake City in the spring of 2000. The Paiute "Songs of Life Returning," one of the promi-nent Ghost Dance songs, appears to feature a tornado. It begins by describ-ing a wind that "stirs the willows" and "stirs the grasses" but soon reaches a crescendo:

> Fog! Fog!
> Lightning! Lightning!
> Whirlwind! Whirlwind![20]

I imagine the rare but awesome tornado twisting amidst lightning and thunder and can appreciate the awe such storms can generate. Rotating winds of any type suggest a column between earth and sky, and between this life and another. It is here that I recall the potency of the spiral in my-thology, for its very motion suggests transformation.

Many Native Americans in this region give such displays of nature wide berth, for those phenomena are potent manifestations of force beyond humankind's control. How different this attitude is from that of Anglo-Americans like writer John Randolph Spears, who related a strange me-teorological phenomenon at Walker Lake, that "picturesque body of water" at the western edge of the Great Basin. While traveling on the Carson and Colorado Railroad's train that ran along the eastern side of the lake in the early 1900s, Spears wrote: "If the tourist is lucky he will pass this lake when a sudden squall comes out of the mountains." He added: "The way the wind pounces down on the water and whirls it along in towering eddies, hundreds of feet high, is a sight that alone counterbalances even the dis-comforts of a day's ride on the Carson & Colorado." These awesome water-spouts excited Spears's curiosity, but to Native peoples they would have been terrible indeed. Of these and whirling gusts of wind that create "lofty whirligigs" or "sand-spouts" on dry land, Spears observed: "It is no wonder that the Arabs of this desert country, the Piutes, believe in witches and supernatural powers in the air."[21]

Winter brings an entirely different, usually more stable, weather pattern to the region. The storms that do occur are usually larger in size but gen-tler in nature. In my travels through the Great Basin, I've witnessed snow-falls that transform the landscape, softening its edges but accentuating vegetation like pinions, whose dark green contrasts with the dazzling white of the snow. Crowning the higher mountains of the Great Basin well into the summer, but covering even the valley floors during part of the winter, snow was (and is) regarded with awe. A good snow cover ensures a bountiful crop of pine nuts and other herbs; then, too, snow assures steady runoff to sustain fish populations in the streams. Snow seems straightforward enough to Western culture—the frozen equivalent of water. Yet, like rain, this seemingly pure compound needs hygroscopic nuclei, such as dust, before it can occur.

This contrast, the purity of snow requiring a particle of foreign matter as a catalyst, is intriguing. Western Shoshone spiritual leader Corbin Harney notes that "some people might have noticed that when you pick up snow, or when you disturb the snow, there are little tiny black bugs there." According to Harney, "They're the ones that make the water." However, Harney is concerned that "today, for the last several years, I haven't been seeing those bugs anymore." Harney worries that "[w]e have killed them off," in part "because we're monkeying with this nuclear poison that's affecting the whole world."[22]

Harney's words about snow remind me of an incident that occurred in the early 1850s. On May 14, 1853, Solomon Nunes Carvalho was accompanying Brigham Young's caravan of wagons along the eastern edge of the Great Basin. Carvalho spied what he thought was gunpowder leaking from one of the wagons. Young normally kept a supply of gunpowder that he gave to the Indians, so it wasn't an unusual cargo; but Carvalho was concerned that the powder was being wasted as it fell into the snow. Then he noticed that "the powder was only in the ruts made by the wheels of the wagons." He stopped to obtain a sample to show Young. Upon examining the powder closely, however, Carvalho was amazed to discover "minute living insects of the beetle tribe, but no larger than a grain of rifle gunpowder." These bugs were not visible ahead of the wagons, but "the weight of the wheels seemed to have pressed them through the snow, with which the whole valley was covered." Carvalho viewed this spectacle with wonder. The contrast of these minute, black insects on the dazzling snow was remarkable: "for ten miles, it appeared as if two continuous trails of gunpowder, from three to five inches wide, were laid the whole length of the Parvain Valley." According to Carvalho, "Neither the Governor nor the gentlemen who accompanied the expeditions, had ever remarked a similar phenomenon before, although they had frequently travelled over the same road."[23]

The Indians could have told Carvalho and his fellow travelers about this phenomenon, for it signaled the coming of spring, when the snow would melt to replenish the earth. But few of us have gained the Native perspective of this landscape because we approach it with such preconceptions. Small wonder, then, that those of us who think we know the Great Basin never cease to be amazed when something unexpected happens. This place is still full of surprises and wonders for those who stay still long enough to listen to the wind.

I was reminded of this in February of 1988 as I brought my rental car to a stop on the lone, snow-covered road in the Owyhee River country at the northeastern edge of the Great Basin. It was still the deep of winter, and I shut off the motor to catch the full effect of the wind's passage across the clumps of sagebrush and piñon. Stepping out into the snow brought me calf-deep in white crusts that crunched underfoot as I walked—old snow, but all the signs suggested that more was on the way. Judging from the way the hair in my nostrils pinched, I estimated that it was only about 5° Fahrenheit, seemingly a bit too cold to snow very much right then—but that northeast wind and the increasingly cloudy sky, not to mention that the air had that distinctive "smell of snow" on the way—suggested I'd better get moving toward civilization. After about five minutes of such reverie, I started the car and began navigating through the small drifts that challenged my way here and there. This was 4-wheel-drive country, but I'd been having a good time with the rental car, barely maintaining traction as I slalomed down the road, leaving wobbly tracks in the deep snow like an intoxicated skier.

By about 2 P.M. it had warmed up, although still well below freezing. The sky was leaden and spitting snow that began as pellets but soon turned to big wet flakes that clung everywhere. The windshield wipers did their best, but the snow was getting the upper hand. Here, miles away from the nearest weather station, it was snowing at the rate of about two inches an hour. The car's radio antenna bristled with snow and ice, and it was piling up on the hood. By 4 P.M. I was glad to see the snow letting up as I neared Elko, slipping and sliding along the back road; then again, it always seems to snow less in the valleys than in those lonely mountains. Upon my arrival in Elko I learned that the road back up to Mountain City was impassable, and so I counted myself luckier than the married couple who tried to travel this road about ten years ago, the woman freezing to death as their vehicle bogged down in three feet of snow. It is times like these that remind me how aptly named Nevada is, in Spanish, for the snow that graces the mountains and usually, but not always, spares the lower elevations.

Long Great Basin winter nights with snow depths poorly calculated figure prominently in the Shoshone story of Coyote and Mouse. "A long time ago," the story begins, "when animals talked and were relatives and friends, Coyote and Mouse lived together." The two animals were hungry, and it was winter. Being somewhat crafty, they hoped for some snow that would enable them to track the rabbits. Coyote started to chant, periodi-

cally asking the mouse how deep the snow was. Without even looking carefully, Mouse answered that the snow was "only the height of the shadows of
my droppings." This was not true—the snow had really begun to pile up—so
Coyote redoubled his chanting for more snow, thinking that his "medicine
must not be strong." By the time that Coyote stopped chanting, however,
they both realized that there was "too much snow for us to track rabbits
in." Coyote's temper flared, and he intended to hit Mouse, but Mouse fled.
The furious Coyote pursued Mouse, hoping to kill him. Using his charm at
times, Coyote tried to lure Mouse back, but Mouse ran to the snow-covered
mountains, where he encountered his uncle Porcupine, sitting high up in a
cedar tree. Mouse climbed up to Porcupine for protection, while Coyote
continued his ruthless search. Porcupine's house consisted of two sets of
ribs of a mountain sheep. When Coyote came sniffing after Mouse, Porcupine urged him to stand under the heavy set of ribs, which he tricked Coyote into thinking that he should grab as they fell. But alas, the ribs were so
heavy that they crushed and killed Coyote. The story ends with Mouse now
living safely on the mountain, where he had a supply of pine nuts for
food.[24]

This story reveals how seamlessly the Great Basin's Native stories
involve weather, animals, and environment. The enduring antics of the
trickster Coyote finally result in his downfall; a kind of cosmic order is restored as the less calculating Mouse is assisted by Porcupine, who in turn
personifies knowledge and truth. The measurement of the snowfall is the
issue that precipitates Coyote's problems, for he is so angered by Mouse's
innocent miscalculation that he would do harm to his own relative. Here in
the Great Basin, the snow blankets the mountains and the drama of life
continues unabated year after year, ever dependent on snowfall to ensure
next year's crop of pine nuts; in beholding these snowy landscapes on the
back roads of Nevada, and I am reminded of the purity of a winter in which
snow is not measured for skiing, but rather for storytelling.

6

In Search of the Great Spirit

Long ago there were no white men. There were no white men in the valleys of the Numu. There was plenty of food. No one ever went hungry. There was peace in the land.

—from "How Water Lilies Came to Be," in MARY L. POPE,
Let Me Tell You a Story

As I drive the highways and graded back roads throughout the Great Basin, or hike back into the region's isolated valleys and mountains, I sense the Native American presence everywhere. It is palpable in the names and the features of the landscape, like the Pequop Mountains and Mono Lake. It is also evident in the handsome faces and intriguing stories of people I've come to know and respect—people like a Shoshone track worker on the old Western Pacific Railroad line near Sulphur in northwestern Nevada who told me about his people's early relationship with the region's traveling ministers, or like the Paiute Indians who've shared their history and stories about sacred places with me. Like most people, these Native Americans are curious about strangers: they want to know who I am and what brings me here. Until they get to know me, they are naturally—and correctly—suspicious. And why not? For more than a century and a half, white people have relentlessly criticized and exploited these original inhabitants.

It was not always this way. In fact, the first contacts between Europeans and Indians in the Great Basin were relatively peaceful, though they do reveal that Christianity's proselytizing zeal put the Indians' spirituality at something of a disadvantage. The very first recorded contact occurred in the late 1700s as Spain intensified its efforts to explore the area. This contact brought two religions, Native spirituality and Roman Catholicism, face to face when the region was nominally part of New Spain but still candidly designated as Terra Incognita on maps. This encounter occurred near Utah Lake in 1776, as the fabled Domínguez-Escalante expedition traversed the eastern edge on the Great Basin in search of a route from Santa Fe (New Mexico) to Monterey (California). Although the expedition failed to cross the Great Basin, turned back by the punishing environment, it nevertheless marked a watershed in the region's spiritual geography. In his report to the king of Spain in 1777, Captain Don Bernardo Miera y Pacheco downplayed the expedition's failure to reach the Pacific coast. Beginning with words calculated to underscore both his loyalty to crown and devotion to church, Miera emphasized his success as proselytizer: "Because within me there burns a desire to spread our Holy Faith," he attested, the expedition had succeeded in its religious goals. He elaborated: "It is certain, My Lord, that many tribes [there] desire the water baptism, especially the Timpanogos and Barbones [Long Beards] of the Valle Salado and Laguna de Miera, for those people, with tears in their eyes, manifested their ardent desire to become Christians."[1] To those familiar with the geography of the Great Basin, Miera's reference to the Indians' tears in this passage seems fortuitous—perhaps a subliminal reference to the salinity of the waters he encountered at the eastern edge of the region, as in the aptly named Valle Salado.

But Miera was as much strategist as spiritualist. In his report, he strongly recommended that the crown establish three settlements in the interior West. The chief settlement would be in the vicinity of today's Salt Lake City-Provo area, "on the shores of the lake of the Timpanogos, on one of the rivers that flow into it, for this is the most pleasing, beautiful, and fertile site in all New Spain." Miera further noted that "[t]his lake and the rivers that flow into it abound in many varieties of savory fish" and other animals, and that "the meadows of these rivers produce abundant hemp and flax without cultivation." Significantly, however, Miera's report neglected to mention something about the geography that was dutifully recorded in the expedition's notes—namely, that the "other lake with which this one communicates, according to what they told us, covers many leagues and its waters are extremely noxious and salty, for the Timpanois [Indians] assure us that a person who moistens any part of his body with the water of the lake immediately feels much itching in the part that is wet."[2] This, of course, is the formidable Great Salt Lake, which the expedition did not visit, but about which the Indians had plenty to say. Miera and the expedition were under the impression that Utah Lake and the Great Salt Lake were part of the same huge lake —Timpanogos—when in fact they are two separate bodies of water linked by a river.

Despite Miera's urging that settlements be built at the base of the Wasatch Mountains near Utah Lake, Spain pretty much ignored the region, as did its successor—Mexico. As part of Mexican Alta California, however, this region was of increasing interest to others, including Anglo-Americans. Some of them began to explore the area in the 1820s, expanding the frontiers of the fur trade. Like the earliest Spaniards, these explorers had fairly peaceful relationships with the Indians, but many were less zealous about spreading the gospel of Christianity; some, in fact, married Native women and their resulting lifestyle suggested either assimilation of Native spiritualities or a fusion of European American beliefs with those of the Indians.

That accommodation or coexistence, however, began to break down with the arrival of American expansionists in the early 1840s. With the increase in movement toward Oregon in the mid-1840s, things began to worsen as skirmishes occurred in the northern part of the region. Although occasional violence had marred some early contact here, one single event, the California gold rush of 1849, seems to have marked the turning point. For those traveling overland, the Great Basin lay directly in their path. Many forty-niners crossed it on a developing network of roads and trails, and their encounters with Indians created some conflict. Through the 1850s, relationships continued downhill. When J. H. Simpson explored the Great Basin as part of a military expedition in 1859, he commented on both the region's cultural and natural history. On cultural matters, Simpson frequently deferred to, and often quoted, Dr. Garland Hurt. As Indian Agent of the General Government in Utah, Hurt was ostensibly helping the Indians. However, he perpetuated a number of stereotypes about his Indian charges. Typical of Hurt's statements about—actually condemnations of—the Indians is his generalization that the "To-Si-witches (white knives), inhabiting the Humboldt River—who take their name from a beautiful white flint, which they procure from the adjacent mountains, and use as knives in dressing their food—are a very treacherous people; and the Bannacks, Go-Sha-Utes, and Cum-um-pahs are not much less so."[3]

Outright warfare with Indians ushered in the 1860s in the Great Basin, and by about 1870 conditions had so deteriorated for the Native peoples that it bordered on despair. The mining industry's voracious appetite for wood (both for mineshaft props and for charcoal to feed the smelters) had resulted in the cutting down of piñon pines and the increasing impoverishment of the Native peoples dependent on them. As John Wesley Powell and George W. Ingalls traversed a portion of the Great Basin, they reported to the federal government on the "miserable" status of Native peoples. With a combination of sadness and imperialism, their 1874 report helped seal the fate of Indians as both endangered and unwanted. Consider their summary opinion about one of the region's most important Native American groups: "There are no Indians in all the territories visited by your commission," they noted, "whose removal is so imperatively demanded by consideration of justice and humanity, as these Shoshones of Nevada."[4] This soon occurred as the Shoshone and others were removed to reserved areas that amounted to fragments of the original lands they had but recently occupied. In the Great Basin, those fragments remain today as Indian reservations, rectangular patches of land where bands like the Shoshone, Paiute, and Washo live.

I am ambivalent about what happened more than a century ago. Although the process of sequestering Indians onto reservations was often cruel, it did ensure their survival instead of the annihilation that might have occurred if relentless Anglo-American expansion into the region had not provided places of refuge. Native American culture was severely tested by the process of forced assimilation, but through it, somehow, the Native peoples persisted. The historian in me wants to know how this cultural survival occurred in the face of such nearly insurmountable odds. In the process, I encounter more than I want to know about both racism and religious intolerance. I consider again the words of Dr. Hurt. From his outspokenly Christian perspective, Hurt found it easy to generalize about the Indians' religion: "Their religious ceremonies are quite simple and primitive, being nearly the same among them all." When Hurt observed that Indians "recognize but one God, or Great Spirit, whom they call by different names among different tribes," readers of his report might have thought the Native Americans inherently monotheistic, and hence salvageable. However, Hurt quickly added that "their conceptions of the attributes of the Deity are generally limited and erroneous." Among the reasons that Hurt cited were the Indians' use of substances in worship: "Smoking seems to be one of their religious ceremonies, and is generally indulged in with great solemnity."

But even worse, Hurt claimed, were these people's animistic beliefs. Indians were, he asserted, "very superstitious, and frequently attribute natural events to supernatural causes, as the changes and eclipses of the moon." Then, too, Hurt observed that the "sun appears to be with the most of them the embodiment or representation of the Great Spirit, and supplications are frequently made to the rising sun as to a rational being." Here Hurt reveals one of the great differences between Judeo-Christian tradition and Native religions—the belief that objects are alive with spiritual power; more particularly, that natural phenomena *are* manifestations of the Great Spirit. Not to be misunderstood, Hurt observed that Indians were an "inferior" race—incapable of becoming civilized because "there seems to be a want of some of those higher intellectual endowments which render our own race"[5] capable of civilization.

In describing the Indians' predetermined plight, Hurt compared Native religions with Christianity. Tellingly, he felt that both his scientific philosophy and his Christian religion were "rational." Lamenting the Natives' tendency to worship objects, he concluded, with a moral certainty, that "in all these ceremonies, their conceptions seem to fall infinitely below a rational comprehension of the object of their adoration, and often developing an inconsistency not easily reconciled with an enlightened idea of true religious devotion."[6] Little did Hurt realize that developments in both psychology and science would someday challenge the rationality of *his* religion too.

It is easy to dismiss Hurt's ideas as antiquarian, but they make several points about nineteenth-century beliefs. Deeply ethnocentric and environmentally deterministic, they equate human progress with the settings in which people live. For those trained to think that the well-watered lands of northern Europe (and, by extension, the eastern United States) helped sustain civilization, it was a short leap to assume that impoverished envir-onments like the Great Basin yielded impoverished peoples. Respected scientists and philosophers of the era were prone to ascribe cultural development to race, and race to environment. Portions of the Great Basin, according to J. H. Simpson, rivaled "the deserts of Asia and Africa in sterility,"[7] and it was here that observers found the most "miserable" and "wretched" of the Native peoples. If these Indians were "reduced to the most extreme state of want" (to use Indian agent Hurt's term), nineteenth-century observers linked that deprivation to the Great Basin's environment. Drawing deadly aim at the region's Native peoples, J. H. Simpson opined: "They are of the very lowest type of mankind, and illustrate very forcibly the truth which the greatest physicist of our country, Prof. Arnold Guyot, of Princeton College, has brought out so significantly in his admirable work, 'Earth and Man,' to wit: *'That the contour, relief, and relative position of the crust of the earth is intimately connected with the development of man.'*"[8]

Simpson's emphasizing of these last words is significant. He even named the Guyot Range in Utah in honor of this famous, if opinionated, physicist. That name, of course, replaced an Indian name for the same mountains. Westward-moving Anglo-American Christians thus transformed the region's geography, which in turn was said to exercise an effect of both mind and spirit. Even though Guyot's environmentally deterministic philosophy was ultimately doomed to revision, many people still believe it in principle to this day.

History is never separate from place, and I sense this as I encounter Indian reservations that look like postage stamps on my road maps of Utah,

Oregon, and Nevada. Some of these reservations were established in the late nineteenth century, and there was considerable public opposition to them, for they seemed to keep Indians together, and hence to reinforce Native traditions. The Dawes Act of 1887 (amended in 1891, 1906, and 1910) attempted to make yeoman farmers out of Indians; yet the Indian Reorganization Act of 1934 ended these allotments and helped Indians reestablish a sense of tribal identity. Given these seesaw changes, Indian reservations are both time- and place-dependent, yet represent arbitrary halfway measures, like purgatory or limbo. They hang suspended in time between the latter half of the nineteenth century, which witnessed tremendous turmoil in relation to prevailing thoughts about Indian culture and spirituality, and the twentieth century, which witnessed a regrouping of Native heritage. I take some solace in the historic national dialogue about Indians, which was based on hope as well as cynicism. To his credit, even J. H. Simpson attempted to distance himself from Garland Hurt's racist interpretation of Indian culture as hopeless. Interestingly, however, he used religion as part of his philosophical argument. Simpson, in effect, believed the only way to redeem Native peoples was through Christianity. In his preface to Dr. Hurt's letter (Appendix O of Simpson's report), Simpson stated:

> I cannot agree, however, with the doctor in the idea which he appears to hold forth as to the original disparity of the races. . . . [because] I know it is the habit of many excellent and scientific men, as the doctor has done, to leave out in their philosophy a great truth—the greatest that has been divulged in the world— that the great I AM has spoken to man in his ignorance, and has given to him certain primary truths, which if he regard, he will assuredly live in light; but which if he disregard, he will assuredly walk in darkness himself, and lead others into darkness.[9]

Simpson went on to note that he believed in "the unity of the [human] race," which he based on his understanding and "knowledge of the Holy One, the Bible." This, in Simpson's words, was "the grand text-book of individuals as well as nations."[10] The Bible was brought to many Native peoples in the Great Basin, but it never completely replaced their own spirituality— many people of the time hesitated to call it religion.

For generations, American popular culture has tended to equate the Great Basin Indians' modest material culture with cultural and spiritual impoverishment. Ethnographers have also suggested the connection. Julian H. Steward and Erminie Wheeler-Voegelin's explanation of why different areas of the Great Basin were designated by food types may be taken as typical: "Since the Paiute were largely preoccupied with food—as evidenced by the time and effort spent on obtaining food, the frequent starvation, and the comparative absence in their culture of activities of a purely social, religious, or recreational nature–they came to designate the people who lived in different portions of the territory by some important or unusual food obtained there."[11]

Steward and Wheeler-Voegelin speculated that, like other "simpler, hunting and gathering peoples of the world," the Paiute lacked "collective ceremonialism" and that "[i]n the absence of such collective enterprise religion rarely serves as an integrative factor."[12] Their words bring up an important point: *religion,* generally defined as the service and worship of God or the supernatural, is more specifically defined as either a personal set or *institutionalized* system of religious attitudes, beliefs, and practices. *Spirituality* is defined as something that in ecclesiastical law belongs to the church or to the clergy, but its definition can also mean the *quality* of or state of being spiritual–that is, of or relating to supernatural beings or phenomena. Thus the two words *religion* and *spirituality* are not synonymous. Elaborate religious systems such as Catholicism or Islam are canonical, complex, and hierarchical–in part because they involve so many people and represent considerable accumulated resources; the elaboration of churches and mosques alone hint at this power and complexity. Smaller groups of people–especially mobile people–have less need to sustain such infrastructure. That does not mean, however, that their religion is any less significant or less valid.

The suggestion that the Indians' "impoverished" condition also equals an impoverished spirituality was, and is, both ethnocentric and deterministic. It is based in part on our culture's belief that material wealth translates into cultural development. Using this premise, the organized religions usually qualify as advanced because they manifest such accumulated wealth. This wealth is based on tithing (the provision of a portion, usually 10 percent, of one's earnings) and other donations to the church. They also embody detailed and complex rituals. The reverse argument–that the Indians' simplicity of lifestyle equals a purer spirituality–tempts those who see mainstream religions as out of synch with nature. But this argument, too, is flawed and deterministic. The elaboration of organized religions has always brought with it a reverse reaction–the quest for simplicity, as manifested in asceticism. And yet, people still hunger for elaborate rituals–a reminder that spirituality is complex, and always conflated with culture, history, and environment.

Contrary to what some of the Christian missionaries and others of the time reported, the Indians did indeed possess a moral sensitivity that was in turn tied to spirituality. To better appreciate this I turn to the early rec-ollections of Sarah Winnemucca, who related a reprehensible incident that occurred in 1857. Symbolic of the increasingly violent actions on the fron-tier during the 1850s, the incident involved the murders of two whites and the covering up of the affair by Captain Jim, a Washo Indian. When whites demanded that Captain Jim bring in the guilty parties, he brought in three innocent Washo Indians instead. When these three Indians bolted from custody, they were shot to death by a group consisting of both Paiutes and whites. Believing the innocent Indians to be victims of Captain Jim's du-plicity, the mourning Washo women cried out to those who had killed them: "Oh, may the Good Spirit send the same curse upon you!" After the Washo Indians' bodies were burned, as was their tribe's custom, Captain Jim lamented: "It is true what the women say—it is I who have killed them. Their blood is on my hands." Although the language "blood on my hands" is indeed reminiscent of Pontius Pilate's concern about Jesus' blood being on his, Captain Jim's next words resonate with a kind of Native American, per-haps even universalist, moral recognition: "I know their spirits will haunt me, and give me bad luck while I live."[13] These words remind me that spiri-tuality is ultimately connected to beliefs about the *consequences* of ac-tions. These beliefs form the underpinnings of all human society and are expressed in both ethics and morality.

Driving through the Great Basin, I have lots of time to think about the re-gion's historical tragedies and moral triumphs. This enduring drama is in-timately linked to spiritual traditions. It resonates in both the region's cul-tural history and its physical geography. Like most other large regions, the Basin is not uniform throughout geographically, or culturally. Several places *within* the Great Basin are associated with intense spirituality. On its western side, the corrugated countryside in the rain shadow of the Sierra Nevada in California is spiritually charged. Here the Coso mountain range rises abruptly from salt-filled basins that surround it. The rocks here, as in much of the Great Basin, are veneered with a durable, mahog-any-colored coating called "desert varnish." Pecked into their surfaces are more than 20,000 petroglyphs. These markings have long puzzled non-Native peoples, and their meaning is not clear even to many Indians. I'm tempted to think of these petroglyphs as simple symbols for, say, the sun, or mountain sheep. But they have meanings that likely transcend individ-ual objects (or creatures, or people) and reveal much about the dialogue be-tween individuals and the environment, and between people and spirits.

I decide to spend a couple of days in the Cosos in an effort to make some sense of out these enigmatic petroglyphs. Hiking back into a canyon flanked by nearly vertical walls of basalt-colored rock, I come across a cluster of petroglyphs that appear to be a flock of mountain sheep frozen in stone (fig. 6.1). It is obvious that someone spent considerable effort at some distant time to represent these animals. Dating these petroglyphs with precision is impossible, but it is safe to say that many are hundreds of years old, and some may be a thousand or more. Here and there, a petroglyph depicts something, say a horse, that suggests it was done within the few hundred years since the Spaniards arrived. Most, though, appear to considerably predate the Europeans' arrival.

I suspect that anthropologists are correct in suggesting that not just anyone made these petroglyphs, and that they are probably the work of shamans. Closely linked to spirituality, a shaman is defined as a priest or priestess who uses magic for the purpose of curing the sick, divining the hidden, and controlling events. The word magic—that is, the use of means (such as charms or spells) believed to have supernatural power over natural forces—denotes a key element associated with shamans, although other meanings of the word magic suggest mere illusions or sleight of hand. I also suspect that shamans have had some very bad press, criticized from one side by Judeo-Christian religion (which considers itself rational despite its dependence on miracles) and on the other by science (which demands verifiable proof for assertions). At any rate, here in this remote canyon I recall the reports of anthropologists who've noted that these mountains are closely associated with shamans.

The Coso Range is, according to the anthropologist David S. Whitley, "widely recognized as a nexus for weather control power." Many of the petroglyphs depict mountain sheep, "the special helper of the rain Shaman." Whitley concurs with Carling Malouf that spirit helper places were called *pohaghani,* which translates as "house of supernatural power."[14] Numic rock art is commonly associated with certain types of sites, namely, permanent sources of water, mountain peaks, rock outcrops, and caves—which are in turn associated with power. Although they might be located at a great distance from the actual tribal home of any particular shaman, these potent sites were likely visited by shamans from different tribes.

Ceremonial uses of plants also figure into the equation of shaman and site. It is widely believed that shamans placed themselves under the influence of mind-altering substances that induced trances and visions. One plant in particular, jimsonweed, is often mentioned as a source of power. Jimsonweed (*Datura stramonium*) goes by many names—angel's trumpet, devil's trumpet, devil's apple, nightshade—most of which suggest its toxicity. It is native to much of the United States (though some sources claim

Fig. 6.1. Frozen in Stone: Petroglyphs of mountain sheep chiseled into the desert varnish coatings on rock in eastern California's Coso Mountains are typical of depictions by shamans. (Sketch by author)

India as its source) but found its way into ceremonial use in some places in the Great Basin. The intense reactions that jimsonweed can induce were summarized as "red as a beet, dry as a bone, blind as a bat, mad as a hatter," and with good reason.[15] Chemicals in the plant's flowers and stem are potent enough to cause anything from confusion to delirium, euphoria to ecstasy. Whitley notes that "rain shamans had mountain sheep as their spirit helpers; that is, they were themselves mountain sheep." To enter the supernatural, the shamans symbolically "killed" themselves to make rain. The rain fell when they "died," or when they entered an altered state of consciousness brought on by consuming a mind-altering plant such as jimsonweed. The altered state of consciousness may account for the bizarre elements of some petroglyphs, such as two-headed mountain sheep.

Here I sense another profound difference between Native and Judeo-Christian religion, the use of mind-altering substances (such as peyote) to induce states that permit individuals to experience visions. By contrast, the Judeo-Christian heritage encourages sobriety. Does this veneration of altered states, I wonder, in any way contribute to the widespread drug and alcohol abuse on Indian reservations? Some Native American leaders, including Paiutes, no longer recognize deliberately altered states of consciousness as desirable; yet the U.S. Supreme Court's recent recognition that Native peoples have a right to use peyote in worship ceremonies suggests that it will endure. At any rate, the entrance into an altered state reminds me of the description once written by a student on LSD: "I had the palpable impression of being in a bright sandy desert beneath a raging sun in a deep blue sky, but this was not what I was looking for—I wanted visions, not impressions."[16]

Visions! By studying the petroglyphs with the notion of altered states of consciousness in mind, some anthropologists now see them as entopic (behind the eye) patterns that are experienced by shamans in many places and cultures—for example Africa, upper Paleolithic Europe, and the Great Basin. Through the use of hallucinogens, shamans experience phenomena—call them hallucinations—that are then depicted in stone. Interestingly, several states of being or experiencing, such as flying, drowning, and orgasm, are associated with shamanism. The latter may explain both the legendary sexual vigor of Southern Paiute shamanism, as well as the translation of the Paiute term for "understanding, intelligence" as, literally, "having semen."[17]

I find it fascinating that anthropologists equate rock art sites with sexual symbolism. If rock art sites are "entrances into the supernatural, placed at numinous locales having great potency," that may account for the symbolic relationships and associations that connect baskets, vaginas/wombs, and rock art sites.[18] Is it this sexual undercurrent, I wonder, that makes these petroglyphs and these rock art sites at once so intriguing and so easily dismissed as "primitive" and "misguided" by many Christians?

The Coso Mountains' repository of shamanistic art documents revelations about both nature and culture. The density and diversity of petroglyphs, as well as their rich patina, suggest a confluence in time and place here. In the silence of the Coso Mountains, I sense that some places are so potent that they transcend any one culture. Farther south, a similar concentration of petroglyphs at Little Lake appears to be associated with both "hunting magic" (which explains the prevalence of mountain sheep petroglyphs) and shamanic vision quests, "in which shamans sought to draw on the powers of the world around them by inducing hallucinations."[19] The idea of shamans from different tribes journeying here to find inspiration makes me ponder another difference between Native American and Judeo-Christian heritage, where the holy city of Jerusalem is a hotly contested battleground among Jews, Christians, and Muslims, each of whom claim it as their own. The individualism embedded in those religions makes a holy site in effect a public place, while these remote petroglyph-strewn sites in the Great Basin were likely off-limits to all except a few keepers of power and wisdom.

However, in the way shamans are regarded—with respect and awe—by their people, they remind me of the patriarchs and priests in the Judeo-Christian tradition. Some of these religious men also had, and have, immense sexual appetites as religion sometimes brings spirituality and sexuality into close harmony through states of ecstasy (as in "the sex was heavenly" or "I went to heaven"). The idea of a prophet, one who possesses extraordinary moral or spiritual insight, seems to be linked to desert lands where, as Yi-Fu Tuan recently noted, the individual becomes important by virtue of his (or her) standing above all else in the landscape—casting a long shadow, as it were.[20] I recall this as I drive north out of the Coso country toward western Nevada. The area around Mason and Yerington, Nevada, also resonates with spiritual history, and spiritual geography.

Like the eastern portion of the Great Basin, which is associated with the Mormon patriarch Brigham Young, western Nevada is closely linked to a spiritual leader who intrigued the American public with tales of miracles and spiritualism toward the end of the nineteenth century. He was a Paiute Indian whose Paiute name was Quoitze Ow, or Wovoka, and whose Christian name was Jack Wilson. This Anglo-sounding name was given by the ranch family with whom Wovoka lived. His nickname, the Ghost Dance Messiah, further enhanced Wovoka's reputation about a century ago.

By whatever name he is called, Wovoka has become a part of the history and folklore of not only the Great Basin, but also the entire American West. Wovoka's message of racial tolerance, coupled with his intense fascination with controlling natural phenomena, have ensured his status as western American icon. He has been embraced by all the western Nevada peoples, Indian and white, as suggested by his inclusion in an exhibit at the historical museum in Yerington (fig. 6.2). He fits seamlessly into the Great Basin's complex spiritual history and geography—a man at once part of his local culture yet also of broader religious events. His popularity coincided with the precipitous decline in the fortunes of Native Americans, who found themselves in increasingly desperate straits in the latter half of the nineteenth century.

The biographical facts about Wovoka are somewhat nebulous, yet we do know some revealing things about his life and his personality. At least three traits or powers distinguished him. First, he is said to have been able to perform *miracles*—or to prophesy (and cause) events such as rainfall or snowfall; this type of weather control awed both Paiutes and whites in an area so dependent on moisture for survival. Second, he is said to have gone into deep *trances*—so deep that some felt he was transported to the "Heavens through the Dipper or the Milky Way." Some observers stated that Wovoka's body was "rigid as a board" and that he was immune to pain while in these trances. Lastly, Wovoka claimed *invulnerability* to harm. He was widely considered to be bulletproof. He is reported to have survived being

Fig. 6.2. Commemorating a Prophet: The Paiute (Numu) spiritual leader and prophet (*puhagamu*) Wovoka, as depicted in a life-size diorama at the Yerington, Nevada, Historical Museum. (May 2000 photograph by author)

shot, the key to his survival being a shirt that miraculously offered protection.[21] Given Wovoka's proximity to the Mormons, who possess sacred undergarments, some have been tempted to claim that he got this power from them; yet Hittman observes that the concept of invincibility to projectiles is also found in Native American culture well *before* the arrival of Mormons. Protection from certain harm by belief in a supernatural power is also found in many other peoples and is likely one of humankind's basic beliefs.

Here in western Nevada, I think about Wovoka as I drive the back roads along the Walker River Valley, where layers of rock are piled on one another like teetering stacks of misshapen pancakes. By all accounts, Wovoka was physically impressive, about six feet tall, with heavy eyebrows, a prominent jaw, and a nose that looked "decidedly Greek" to one observer. The peripatetic ethnographer James Mooney described him as "a dark full blood, compactly built, and taller than the Paiute generally." Mooney added that Wovoka "was well dressed in white man's clothes, with the broad-brimmed white felt hat common in the West." In words that subliminally both suggest breeding and attribute a wildness to Indians, another observer stated that Wovoka "visibly stood out among his fellow Indians like a thoroughbred among a bunch of mustangs." Wovoka's most thorough biographer, historian/ethnographer Michael Hittman, noted that Wovoka had a "fondness for neckerchiefs, eagle feathers, and five and ten gallon Stetson hats" (fig. 6.3). Wovoka's demeanor also drew comment, for he was humorous and even a prankster at times. He also had a "solitary and contemplative disposition, one of those born to see visions and hear still voices." There was "a stillness about his mien that one senses." Yet Wovoka possessed a temper and was known to call upon nature in his threats—as when he became so incensed at being overcharged for watermelons by one of the early settlers that he "threatened to cause the Walker River to rise and destroy her watermelon patch, flooding the entire valley as well."[22]

The Walker River figures prominently in Wovoka's deeds. In one of his earliest miracles, he reportedly caused ice blocks to materialize in the river in the middle of summer—an act considered to be outright fraud by one of his more critical biographers.[23] But Wovoka is largely remembered for one thing or event—the Ghost Dance in 1888–89. From its point of creation in western Nevada, Wovoka's Ghost Dance spread rapidly among western Native Americans.

I reflect on songwriter/singer Robbie Robertson's poetic observation that "news of the Paiute messiah, Wovoka, the prophet of the ghost dance. . . . spread across the badlands like a prairie fire from tribe to tribe."[24] I like to think that Wovoka's words were swept along on the west wind, but at this late date (1890) the railroad could have conveyed them eastward out of Wovoka's ancestral lands in western Nevada. By train, which Indians rode on many occasions, Wovoka's ideas could have spread across the Great Basin along the Central Pacific Railroad to the Shoshone Indians, thence up the Wasatch front into Wyoming on the Union Pacific, and then all the way into the badlands of the western Dakotas, where they played out so tragically for the Sioux and other Plains Indians.

So highly suspicious were white authorities of any hint of power among Indians that the Ghost Dance figures as a central catalyst in the disastrous 1890 Battle of Wounded Knee. The Natives' belief that bullets could/would not harm them while they were wearing the ghost shirt disquieted whites. Then, too, the Ghost Dance's patent resurrection of Native traditions was also disconcerting at exactly the time that Natives were supposed to either assimilate or die off. The dance itself can be traced to Numu ceremonial round dance traditions in which, as James Mooney put it, a "large circular space had been cleared of sagebrush and leveled over, and around the circumference were the remains of low round structures of willow branches which had sheltered those in attendance."[25] But in contrast to regular Numu round dances, which often centered on either spring fish runs or fall pine nut harvests, and likely featured a sacred cedar, willow, or pine tree, the Ghost Dance featured Wovoka himself in the center. Hittman notes that anthropologists traditionally offer two possible hypotheses regarding the motivation for the Ghost Dance: first, that it is a classic "Prophet Dance" that centers on preparing followers for doomsday; second, that it represents acculturation as Indians sensed their increasing deprivation and employed the dance as a response to crises brought on by the arrival of the whites in the region. As Hittman astutely suggests, several factors evidently come into play here, but it is noteworthy that Wovoka's Ghost Dance ceremony was universalist in that it offered racially integrated salvation in the hereafter.[26]

Two other place-related aspects of the Ghost Dance religion deserve closer scrutiny. The first might be called its environmentally apocryphal quality. As part of a revelation, which came as a result of a "great noise" above him in the mountains at around age twenty, Wovoka saw Heaven. What Wovoka viewed, according to Numu reservation chief of police James Josephus, "was the most beautiful country you could imagine"—not the landscape of the Great Basin, but rather a land that was "nice and level and green all the time" where "there were no rocks or mountains." The place was paradisiacal, for there were "all kinds of game and fish," and even the dead were "dancing, gambling, playing ball and having all kinds of sports." To reach this land, Wovoka claimed that people must not fight (all men are "brothers" and should be good to each other) and should not steal.[27] This is yet another indication that Wovoka appears to have been inspired by Judeo-Christian moral principles.

The second place-related aspect of the Ghost Dance focuses on how Wovoka used environmental symbolism—that is, aspects of the natural environment in concert with his *bbooha.* In this he probably tapped deep roots of Native American cultural history. He could, for example, anticipate signs of what was going to occur meteorologically: "One was a straight high cloud. This was for snow. The other cloud was dark and close to the

Fig. 6.3. Ghost Dance Prophet: A drawing of Wovoka made in 1892, when the Paiute spiritual leader was already a legend. (Courtesy Smithsonian Institution)

ground. It was for rain." This may sound like so much good empirical observation, but it was claimed that Wovoka could also actually *control* natural outcomes. A historical marker erected by the Yerington Paiute tribe in 1975 states that "after a mystical revelation, he was given power by our Great Father to control natural elements." These powers included rainmaking and drought, as well as earthquakes. Shortly after Wovoka's death, a series of earthquakes rattled Mason Valley, and many whites as well as Paiutes believed them to be caused by Wovoka. As Claude Keema, son of a rancher whose father had employed Wovoka, put it: "Son-of-a-gun, Jack! Said he was gonna shake this world if he made it [to Heaven], and, by God, he did!"[28]

Thus Wovoka was connected to the heavens, waters, and earth. Michael Hittman suggests that there is a strong connection between the prophet's powers and certain natural phenomena, such as "unusual earth tremors, etc., and climatological incidents such as heavy fog, etc. in Smith and Mason Valleys in the late 1880s, and . . . the severe regional drought of 1889-1890." Hittman further notes that "Wovoka's Great Revelation coincided with the January 1, 1889, eclipse and night was the optimal time for obtaining and demonstrating bbooha." By calling upon his powers, the Ghost Dance Prophet had not only "restored environmental normalcy to the Walker River area," but also "had personally delayed the Apocalypse."[29]

Hittman concludes his interpretation of Wovoka by linking various red and white mineral pigments found in the Great Basin with powerful spiritual/cultural symbolism. For example, "the color white = 'white radiance' (of the Sun) = Thunder = cloud = rain = eagle feather = curing" was associated with Wovoka, the Rainmaker. A white horse also figured in Wovoka's prophecies. This whiteness is also associated with the brightness of the sun, which is central to Numu beliefs. Brightness is further associated with the "white dirt" in the caves of the Wabuska Hills. According to Numu Marlin Thompson, this white earth is still considered sacred by some Numu.[30] Hittman notes that Wovoka would chew (but not swallow) the white paint, and use it for purification by blowing its dust on patients.[31] I recall hearing a story that Paiute Indians thought that the ubiquitous white flour brought by settlers also possessed supernatural powers. But, alas, when the Indians dusted themselves with it, this powder became sticky and was soon revealed to be useless for that purpose.

Also common in curing (and in the Ghost Dance) is the red ocher paint (peʌape). It likely derives from the iron oxides present in the form of soft hematite or limonite found in some locales. As related by Hittman, "if red = Sun = eclipse = rattle-snake = the power to cure," then might not it "also symbolize the Prophet's divinely revealed weather control power?"[32] In other words, rather than thinking of red and white as binary or opposite, Hittman asks "can we then say, white = red?" If we can, then this is a "balanced equation which the 1890 Ghost Dance Prophet himself surely would have positively endorsed."[33]

Wovoka's teaching was prophetic, and his legacy both enduring and syncretic. His teaching and actions fused certain aspects of Judeo-Christian heritage with Native American animism. To him, the sun and other elements represented potent forces that, with the correct *bbooha,* could be harnessed to do good. Wovoka's close involvement with "nature" was also a concern to Christians, for it deviated from their strict philosophy that placed God above nature. Jan Deblieu puts it succinctly: "For nearly three thousand years Judaic culture and its Christian progeny have steadfastly separated God from 'nature'–that is, the forces and creatures that man and woman evolved from."34

Wovoka's freely employing these forces opened Pandora's box and placed him in the category of "false prophet" to many in both the region and outside it. This is ironic, for Wovoka was deeply influenced by both Numu spirituality and Judeo-Christian thought. He had come in contact with "saddle-bag riders," those itinerant preachers who–like Jesse L. Bennett of the Methodist-Episcopal Church and the Reverend R. Carberry of the United Community Methodist Church–rode from place to place in the western Great Basin bringing the word from both the Old and New Testaments. Thus, according to one source, "Jack [believed he] could save Indians from hell fire." Then, too, Wovoka himself explicitly wrote that "I am the only living Jesus there is. Signed, Jack Wilson" on the back of a photograph in 1917. If these words are Wovoka's, they reveal that he never lost faith in his own Native powers, but that he recognized the power that Jesus possessed. Although words equating mortals with Jesus still upset many Christians (recall the outrage that the late John Lennon caused when he opined that the Beatles were "more popular than Jesus"), it should also be recalled that Wovoka did not call himself Christ, but rather linked himself to the spiritual bearer of good tidings, the humble Jesus. Although Wovoka died in 1932, and by then the Ghost Dance was merely a historical footnote in many places, it still resonated among many Numu in western Nevada. Whereas the earlier 1870 Ghost Dance had failed to endure, Wovoka's later version did. He is still held in high esteem by Numu and many whites alike.

Here in the Great Basin, I see a conflation of Indian and Christian traditions almost everywhere I search. Although it is tempting to posit Christianity as the opposite of Native American culture and spirituality, they become dependent on each other. In fact, Christian religion worked closely with Native peoples, who were frequently parceled out to various religious groups, like the Baptists and Methodists, for assimilation.35 Mainstream religion even had a role in the creation of Nevada's reservations: In 1902, when the Baptist missionary Lillie Corwin moved to Reno, Native Americans seemed on the verge of disappearing. In the years following her arrival, Corwin founded the Nevada Indian Association. By 1916 she became a key force in establishing the "Indian Colonies" in Nevada. According to the historian of religion Ferenc Morton Szasz, these small reservations were "scattered in a dozen towns throughout the state, thus assuring Native Americans at least a modest land base"—an action that is commemorated in the Washo tribe's museum.[36] Thus we add another irony to the list of axioms about religion in the West: although helping to contribute to the near demise of Native religions, organized religions have also helped to preserve Native spirituality through an increasingly compassionate interpretation of others' beliefs. Throughout the twentieth century in the Great Basin, Native American religion persisted as a potent undercurrent of mainstream religion. It promises to become even stronger in the twenty-first century.

The complex relationship between Native beliefs and imported views is on my mind as I cross from southern Nevada into Utah. Rolling along on one of the lonely graded roads that alternately sweep across sagebrush-covered plains and into Joshua tree forests, it occurs to me that the vegetation of the Great Basin serves as a metaphor for the region's spiritual perceptions. Although both the big sagebrush (*Artemisia tridentata*) and the Joshua tree (*Yucca brevifolia*) are native in this transition area, one remains associated with Native spirituality, the other with imported religious beliefs. The omnipresent sagebrush, bluish-green in color and velvety in texture, is so commonplace that it is easy to forget its deep significance to Native peoples. When burned, sagebrush "purifies the living in the presence of ghosts or when a person dies," and "in girls' puberty ceremonies celebrants use the plant for costuming or for other purposes."[37] Crushed sage serves as "a medium through which messages are taken to the spirits, for example, as an offering in the spring to ripen the pine nuts or as an offering for health after a specific illness."[38] Like Native American culture, sagebrush is easy to overlook and easy to oversimplify. And like Native American culture, the sagebrush has thrived despite the alteration of its native habitat.

Great Basin sage is really several species of shrubs that survive in a wide range of conditions here. They belong to the genus Artemisia, and that name suggests a female association. I wonder if even scientific names subliminally suggest not only gender but also spirituality. The entire genus is named after Artemisia of Asia Minor, who erected a structure to house the body and honor the memory of her deceased husband Mausolus in 353 B.C. (hence the word *mausoleum*). But the genus has another possible connection to powerful women. It is said to have been named after the Greek goddess of wild nature, Artemis.[39] Somehow the name Artemisia seems appropriate, for the sagebrush resonates with a fragrance that, like the scent of a lover, simultaneously arouses and sedates.

As I roll into southwestern Utah, I've reached the domain of the peculiar treelike yucca plant whose popular name—Joshua tree—resonates with Old Testament religion (fig. 6.4). These impressive yuccas were reportedly named by the early Mormons, to whom the branches suggested a prophet pointing the way. This encounter is said to have occurred on the Mormon Trail from Salt Lake City to San Bernardino—a trip that required a trek across the Mojave Desert. Interestingly, however, the early journals that I've consulted usually simply refer to the tree's distinctive form, without reference to the biblical figure Joshua. In 1852, Solomon Nunes Carvalho traversed the Mormon Trail to San Bernardino with a group of Mormons. He makes no mention by name of the Joshua trees that abound in parts of the area. To Carvalho, the vegetation here was strange, but he tried to characterize it using familiar terms. As the group neared Cajon Pass, he describes "a forest" of peculiar trees, some of which grow "to an immense size; some as large as the greatest oak tree I ever saw." To Carvalho, this was indeed "a curious tree, the trunk is cylindrical, as if it were turned; its limbs are leafless, except at their extremities, on which grow long narrow leaves, with a sharp prickle at the end."[40] Many people confused *Yucca brevifolia* not with human or biblical characters, but with another family of plants, the cacti. In fact, by the 1870s, the term "cactus tree" was often used for what we would later call a Joshua tree.

In the folk imagination, however, it was easy to see something patriarchal about these strong, spiny trees. The name "Joshua tree" did not enter the region's vocabulary until the twentieth century, but when it did, it took root quickly and firmly. If, by 2000, the Joshua tree was one of the most recognizable of western desert plants, its countenance and religion closely linked, that conflation involved several vehicles of popular culture. In the 1994 film *Joshua Tree*, a woman named Rita comments on a group of these bristling trees, "It's funny, they kind of look like people." Her friend Santee quickly responds: "The Mormon settlers thought they looked like the prophet Joshua." Although it is tempting to think that this is both a natural and deeply historical connection (that is, stickery tree naturally equals grizzled patriarch), this association took hold rather recently through a partnership between the written word, film, and music.

Literature evidently had a formative role in the transformation of this tree from botanical ("cactus") to religious ("Joshua") in the popular mind. Maureen Whipple's popular novel *The Giant Joshua* (1942) helped perpetuate the image of the book's symbolic namesake—Mormon leader Brigham

Fig. 6.4. Desert Patriarch: The Joshua tree (*Yucca brevifolia*) is associated with both the Old World prophet Joshua and with Brigham Young, leader of the Latter-day Saints. (Photograph taken near Goldfield, Nevada, by author, June 2000)

Young—as a determined patriarch. Whipple's book also associated this "cactus-like tree with spiny branches," which "looked like a gnarled dwarf with weird, extended arms," with the Old Testament religious prophet. "When Brother Brigham called the Saints who were colonizin' San Bernardino back to Salt Lake at the time of Johnston's Army," one of the story's characters, Abijah, tells a pretty young woman named Clory, the party "had to cross a big desert which stretches many miles to the south and west of where we be now." Abijah relates that "at the beginning of the desert they ran into whole forests of these trees," which deeper in the desert "grow to be giants. 'Giant Joshuas.'" He explains that "[t]he Saints called 'em that because their twisted branches made 'em look like Joshua with his arms outstretched pointing the Israelites toward the 'Promised Land.'"[41]

Note these trees' male quality. Later in the book, Clory asks another of the characters, Free, "And the Joshua Trees? Did you see the Giant Joshuas?" He answers, "Yes—whole forests, some young fellers with flowers at the ends of their arms, and others so old—so old and crippled, like giants with the rheumatiz.'" "'But," she adds wistfully, " . . . still pointing to the Promised Land."⁴² Later in the novel, the meaning of these "thousands of years old" trees to the early Mormons is related as part of the drama of religious diasporas: "'Here,' said the Saints, 'these trees are like Joshua leading the Israelites;' and so they traveled in the direction the strange trees pointed and at last came to the Promised Land."⁴³ Throughout *The Giant Joshua,* Joshua trees are associated with both the patriarchs' and the Mormons' (which is to say latter-day Israelites') trials and tribulations in the desert, and Brigham Young's leadership is conflated with the biblical prophets through this literary use of the plant. By contrast, Whipple's characterization of the "velvet fingers [of] the sagebrush"⁴⁴ suggests a female countenance that may subliminally link the Indians with femininity, hence something needing protection.

The male ruggedness and searching spiritual associations of the Joshua tree made it a perfect symbol for the rock group U2's album *Joshua Tree* in 1987. Although many of U2's songs suggest a spiritual quest, one song on the *Joshua Tree* album has strong spiritual connotations. "I Still Haven't Found What I'm Looking For" narrates the difficulty of the journey through life: "I believe in Kingdom Come," U2's lead singer proclaims, adding, "but I still haven't found what I'm looking for." As might be expected, some conservative religious people found this verse irreverent, yet it poses an interesting question: Can one believe and yet still search for more answers? After forty years of traveling through this region, my answer is yes.

Others, however, find the end to that searching here. Maureen Whipple's *The Giant Joshua* suggests that these contented souls' journeys are ultimately both personal and collective, and that they have geographic boundaries. Kingdom Come suggests heaven, yet we search for such places on earth. The Promised Land, "a land flowing with milk and honey" (Deut. 6:3), is what all prophets ultimately seek in the Western tradition; yet the fact that Wovoka, the "sagebrush prophet," was also on that journey to find both deeper spiritual meaning and the reward of a more fertile place than the Great Basin through *belief* is significant. It suggests that there is a temporal, even corporeal, aspect to soul searching. That connection between the physical and the ethereal lies at the base of all spiritual geographies.

Whipple's characterization of the Joshua tree and sagebrush reminds me of some of the differences between Native American and Judeo-Christian thought. In the former, vegetation exists as part of storytelling, linking peoples and animals with place. In the latter, plants are employed as symbols for the deeds of particular named people (e.g., Joshua), usually patriarchs. In this regard, burning bushes and Joshua trees have much in common as signifiers of communication and deliverance. Yet both traditions employ vegetation, animals, topography, even weather and climate, as essential ingredients in the search for endorsement by a higher power. That usually brings spiritual searches down to earth, in a manner of speaking, even as we seek things that usually remain just beyond our reach. I see sagebrush as a signifier of Native spirituality because it is always present, underappreciated, unspectacular, yet deeply grounded in collective traditions that require faith to survive.

Zigzagging across the central Great Basin on the roads that run like transects shot at weird angles, I work my way back up into Nevada's Railroad Valley after leaving the armies of twisted Joshua trees. The "Ghost Dance" song by Native American singer-songwriters Jim Wilson and Robbie Robertson is chanting on the car's CD player, and I realize the repeated refrain "We shall live again" is both political and spiritual. There is a complete irony here, for high technology like this CD is largely an importation of the Judeo-Christian tradition via the European industrial revolution, yet it is one of those factors that can help ensure the survival of Native American beliefs. That has been true since writing, and then the tape recorder, were used to rescue threatened Native languages. That notion—that human ingenuity and technology can be used to keep folk spiritual traditions alive—is somehow very reassuring as I drive along the Utah-Nevada border into the heart of what was called the "Great American Desert" a century ago. It seems "a thousand miles from nowhere"—well, not exactly, but metaphorically—as a CD by Dwight Yoakum is now playing as I roll north. Out in these wide open spaces, Yoakum sings, "Time don't matter to me," and I know exactly what he means.

When I am in the Great Basin, I sense that time is passing by elsewhere, but there is a timelessness here that I savor. With my CDs playing, I pretend I've isolated myself from everything; and yet I secretly know that technology has brought me here, that I'm even using it to hear inspirational messages, as well as to propel myself from place to place in the Great Basin like a missionary searching for souls. Yoakum's words get me to thinking that time may not only be immaterial, but might not exist at all. What if, as physicist/metaphysicist Julian Barber suggests, time "is nothing but a measure of the changing position of objects"? Barber goes on to assert that "[w]e don't live in a single universe that passes through time.

Instead, we—or many slightly different versions of ourselves—simultaneously inhabit a multitude of static, everlasting tableaux that include everything in the universe at any given moment." The ultimate consequence of this concept is that nothing really has a past, but that there is an infinite array of sequences that coexist. That has awesome implications for spirituality, especially for the individual's life span in relation to eternity. In short, Barber says, "immortality is all around us." But rather than endorsing the idea of an individual's living forever, Barber means something even more profound—that nothing ever actually dies. Rather, it constantly exists in every state in which it ever existed. This would mean that the universe is timeless, and so, as the writer/philosopher Tim Folger puts it, "instead of life after death, there is life alongside death."[45]

Rolling along with one eye on the speedometer, which measures the distance between experiences, I see that Barber means we don't pass *through* time; each instant is an *entirely different universe.*[46] I suspect that my ongoing quest to understand the Great Spirit is ultimately bound up not only in spirituality, but in physics, which has deeply spiritual implications and repercussions. Time is central to most religions, for we comprehend that our lives are finite. Even though time may not exist, it is the way we conceptualize life so that we can ponder what happens as we change from one state (life) to another (afterlife). Yet spirituality introduces a new way of addressing, and then negating, time. I try to forget about time, banishing it temporarily as I drive along a road out in the middle of nowhere, straddling the Nevada-Utah border that runs like a dividing line through God's country. That ecstasy of timelessness only lasts so long, however, for I'm traveling on a road separating two time zones, Mountain and Pacific, pretending that I'm an hour older, or younger, depending on which way the road jogs.

7

Chosen People, Chosen Land

In western wasteland . . . where cultures can find no sustenance, can create no lasting images of sacrality or profanity, oblivion reigns; utility is a nonthought, landscape presents only further enigma.
—RICHARD POULSEN, *The Landscape of the Mind*

On the graded road out of Trout Creek and Callao, Utah, I've just left the Goshute Indian reservation and am heading north through the edge of the Great Salt Lake Desert. The folklorist Richard Poulsen's almost nihilistic words about desert places ring clear here, where the Great Basin is at its most desolate in appearance. A blazing white light seems to reflect from both the cloudless sky and the desert floor, enveloping everything in a glare that makes it difficult to judge distances. The shimmering salt flats just west of the Great Salt Lake are quintessentially arid, and the reason that this part of the region was called the "Great American Desert" well into the twentieth century. This country epitomizes what Poulsen had in mind when he wrote about the oblivion of western wasteland.

This desert is so stark that it is used to great effect for filming TV commercials of cars roaring across dry lakebeds. Other products, too, find their way to this austere but strangely photogenic land of salt flats, sparse vegetation, and distant purple mountains that look like cardboard silhouettes. A memorable TV commercial for Sony employs this type of landscape. It begins with a lone tumbleweed blowing across the parched and cracked surface of a dry lakebed. In the distance, rocky, eroded mountains form a stark background. As the camera pans to the right, following the tumbleweed, a Sony Vega television set comes into view amid this desolation. Up to this point, the commercial is in black-and-white, but the TV set's picture is in full color. On the screen, a young boy is shown plunging into a cool blue swimming pool in an idyllic setting. As the camera moves back, it again reveals the desolation of the surrounding desert. Then, we see why the camera has moved back from the foreground: A group of tumbleweeds moves toward the TV set's screen, evidently entranced by what they see. A narrator's voice commands: "Escape to a better place."[1]

This commercial works on several levels, but consider a couple of them that reveal attitudes towards technology and place. Beyond the most obvious suggestion that the color and clarity of the Sony Vega's picture is superior to anything else on the market are deeper meanings, such as the suggestion that a desolate natural environment can be improved by mankind. More to the point, the commercial suggests that the dry desert environment is inferior to the water-abundant environment around the swimming pool. Water equals good, desert equals bad.

This contrast is natural enough, for humankind requires water to survive, and even the hardiest desert dwellers recognize the rewards of the well-watered oasis; small wonder that gardens resonate so deeply in the Judeo-Christian heritage and its offshoot, Islam. But emptiness in a landscape is somewhat relative: Some people transform emptiness into meaning by searching for—and finding—inspiration here amid "complete desolation," as a truck driver once characterized the entire Great Basin from Salt Lake City to Reno. Driving north, I'm about to intersect that east-west interstate highway at a right angle. Up ahead is the little town of Wendover, Utah, whose cluster of welcome signs at the town's entrance announces not only commercial services, but also churches. This in turn suggests that I can find food for both body and soul here.

At a restaurant in Wendover, I overhear two people telling Mormon jokes. Wendover is the perfect place to hear such jokes, for it hugs the Utah-Nevada border. To the east lies seemingly strait-laced Mormon Country, while wide-open Nevada stretches to the west. The joke, which takes one of the men a couple of minutes to tell, reminds me that humor sometimes reveals a great deal about serious matters. Here's what I remember of it:

A man dies and finds himself face to face with a mysterious man who urges him to come forward. After asking the dead man a few questions about the life he led, the mysterious man invites him to step aboard an elevator. As the elevator begins to move downward, the dead man becomes concerned about where he is going. "Oh, no! Could I be headed toward hell?" As the elevator stops at each floor, the door opens to reveal scenes of increasing anguish: first a land burned to cinders, then one is punctuated by flickering flames, then another bathed in fire so intense the man cringes. Fearing the worst, the dead man can barely open his eyes as the door to the next floor opens. But instead of fire, he beholds a scene of tranquil beauty and hears the sound of chirping birds and running water. The landscape is green, with tall trees and fields stretching to the horizon. Before the dead man can ask where they are, the mysterious stranger exclaims in desperation: "Damn those Mormons! Turn your back for just a moment and look what happens!"

This joke is significant for several reasons. First, it is an environmental assessment, equating the physical features of the Intermountain West with hell. It suggests that, in a natural state, the place is infernal. Second, it is a moral fable, crediting the Mormons with the capability of fooling even the devil. Through this industriousness, they transform hell into paradise. The joke also works on deeper levels. Because it is *about* the Mormons, it is ostensibly told by non-Mormons (though Mormons themselves also like such jokes about themselves); note that it includes a subtle allusion to Mormons being damned first. Yet they transform what they have been given as punishment into something wonderful. In addition to validating their position as hardworking westerners, something else is suggested in this joke. The Mormons not only earn that position through hard work; they are also very quick and good enough at what they do to outsmart the devil at his own game. Something else is implied about the Mormons' work ethic in this joke: They must keep working in order to maintain paradise, for if they stop, we assume, the heat and fire will return. In other words, the Mormons are *both selected and condemned* to be hard workers. The joke is especially revealing because it implicitly recognizes that the Mormons *created* this place within the framework of the hostile, hellish Intermountain West. It also suggests that they work like hell to keep it lush and green.

Consider, too, the broader environmental and cultural significance of this joke. In order to have pulled off this environmental coup, the Mormons themselves had to have gone to hell first, then reformed it. The joke views the landscape from a Judeo-Christian or European perspective in which the desert is bad, irrigation good. Other equations are also at play here: indolence is bad, hard work good. And ultimately, the joke suggests that natural is bad, cultivated good. This valuation also played out as a cultural fable in the nineteenth century, when the indigenous nomad equaled a damned soul and the hardworking sedentary transformer was saved. In other words, this is far more than a joke. It is a short story that reflects a series of potent, often unstated, dichotomies about the value of both environment and culture.

Perceptions of places (i.e., environments) are never value free, and are in fact always based on human characteristics or attributes. This good environment-bad environment dichotomy perpetuates an age-old conflict, that of the aboriginal population versus the colonist. On the highway leaving

Wendover, I recall how easy it is to make snap judgments about places and the people who inhabit them. How many people have sped through this region thinking it god-forsaken and pitying the souls who call it home? Not much has changed since the first white pioneers came through here a century and a half ago on their way to California and Oregon. To westward-moving colonists, place and peoples were inseparable. As in other environments across America, colonization occurred at a tremendous price to Native peoples. This may seem like familiar political ground, but I shall till it just a little deeper to show that religion was a significant factor in the encounter between peoples on the western frontier.

Westward-moving settlers had been primed by their religious training, and the Bible was the single most prevalent form of literature that accompanied them. It affected intercultural relationships to the core. By the late nineteenth century, the potent messages and strictures of the Judeo-Christian tradition penetrated even the most isolated places of the Great Basin. Consider for a moment how this tradition affects even the most deeply subconscious of human perceptions, such as the meaning of time. Honoring the Sabbath, or God's day, is a good example.

Harriet Sibyl Irwin moved to Nevada from Michigan in 1891. Undeterred by the isolation, Hattie visited neighbors on far-flung ranches by buckboard. Writing from Duckwater, Nevada, where her uncle farmed and ranched, Hattie described the Indians and other aspects of frontier life. "The morals here," she noted, "are simply unmentionable." Hattie added that "if I had a boy or girl I'd sooner he'd [sic] die at once than be brought up here." In another letter, Hattie describes a trip to an isolated ranch on Currant Creek with her aunt Tat. Before leaving for Currant Creek, Hattie wrote, she "seriously debated whether I'd break the Sabbath more by riding quietly along and beholding nature or staying here and see—well, I went." Upon returning, Hattie was still troubled by her choice: "Of course Aunt Tat and I had a severe attack of conscience when we got home, but we do every Sunday, and so far there hasn't seemed any help for it." Tormented, Hattie noted that "I asked Uncle if he thought we could have a Sunday School and he thought there wouldn't be anybody go."[2] Hattie's mention of "nature" is important here, for it suggests that an appreciation of it might help compensate for her not honoring the Sabbath; yet she remained troubled by her choice. Note the Judeo-Christian preoccupation with a tightly regimented calendar, and the setting of one day a week out to honor God, as decreed in the Bible.[3]

Paiute elder Corbett Mack evidently had no such compunction about Sundays. He related stories about his youthful trysts with "girls"—that is, young women of fifteen or sixteen–at the Yerington Indian Colony. "[T]hey all like that" sweet talking, Mack reminisced, "so what I know I like to do is get 'em under the buckberry bush" on Saturday nights. "Yes, sir! Go to 'em right there! And I can stay with one girl all day long, too, partner! Sunday. "4 Mack's spending the Sabbath in these sexual liaisons was perfectly consistent with his general dismissal of Christianity, but it was not because he hadn't been exposed to Christian teachings. In fact, Mack recalled that when he was a boy at the Stewart Institute, "every Sunday, too, you gotta go to church." Here, dressed in a uniform, he was not able to sit with girls because boys and girls were forced to sit on separate sides of the church. The *tairo* (white) preacher talked about "'The Lord' and 'Jesus' and 'God.'" Although Mack liked carrying and reading what he called "the Bible book" until his eyes went bad around 1914, he said flatly that "I don't get nothin' outta that Jesus business." The general reason he gave for holding this opinion was that "Jesus, he don't help me!" Elaborating, Mack added that the prayers meant nothing to him: "And so, a fellow don't get somethin' outta somethin' else, how can he keep on [believing]? No matter how much he pray! 'Cause, then, its *Karroo'oo,* nothing." Mack ended his discussion by wondering, "But maybe I don't get nothin' outta that 'cause I'm a bad man already. *Ste'yoo,* you know; no good. . . . So maybe that's why Jesus won't listen to me? 'Cause if you believe in somethin' first, well, then, that's different."5 With these honest words, Mack eloquently stated a dilemma that faced, and faces, many Indians–and for that matter, non-Christians: One has to *believe* in the power of Jesus' word in order to be a true believer. However, not everyone can make that connection, especially when other belief systems offer explanations that satisfy the soul.

Significantly, Corbett Mack went on to explain how drinking, and then drug use, began to fill his Sundays. Indians drank, he said, "[t]o feel good, happy." Tellingly, although they drank "heavy on Saturday night. . . . And all day Sunday, too," Mack added that they "never miss Monday's work, though, by God!"6 Although put off by the Indians' reported drinking and drug use–the use of such intoxicants perhaps made easier by the Indians' respect for altered states of consciousness in worship–the Anglo population generally regarded the Native people as having a good work ethic. They were, in fact, among the most dependable ranch and farm hands in western Nevada.

I believe that one must read the history of the Great Basin region as one chapter in a spiritual or religious drama that began to unfold several thousand years ago. In this drama, a chosen people is selected to prevail but must triumph over both the environment and other peoples to do so. According to this story, these others have not seen the light—that is, they are nonbelievers. Common terms for them are infidels, savages, or *barbarians*. We might call this drama the "old eternal contest," because that was exactly the phrase used by a writer in the 1860s. Understanding it can better place racism in a broader spiritual or religious context and may help answer the question as to why such violence occurred in the West generally and the Great Basin in particular.

In several places, the landscape of the Great Basin is haunted by the conflict that ensued when whites and Indians encountered each other with different scripts in hand. Consider the chalky hills along the Truckee River just south of Pyramid Lake, Nevada, where a historical marker documents the bloodshed that occurred here during the Pyramid Lake War in 1860 (fig. 7.1). The story of this war has been told elsewhere,[7] but I see it as a holy war as well as a military engagement. It began with a series of isolated conflicts but soon escalated into warfare despite the admonitions of Numaga, or "Young Winnemucca," who warned his people, "The white men are like the stars over your heads. You have wrongs, great wrongs, that rise up like those mountains before you: but can you, from the mountain tops, reach and blot out the stars?"[8] The answer, of course, was no, but the Paiutes tried. First inflicting heavy losses on the whites, they soon felt the wrath of other whites, who came from as far away as California to avenge their fallen comrades. The outcome of the Pyramid Lake War is simple enough: the Paiutes were decimated, Virginia City boomed, and the Numu became strangers in their own land.

The Pyramid Lake War is fraught with lessons about how "civilized" Christians dealt with the "savage" peoples they encountered. As one reads between the lines, it emerges as one in a long line of Christian victories against pagan infidels. In a situation that has similarities to white encounters with other peoples of color, including in colonial Africa, whites feared these "wild men" who were associated with desolate places. As Hayden White suggests, "from Biblical times to the present, the notion of the Wild Man was associated with the idea of the wilderness—the desert, forest, jungle, mountains—those parts of the physical world that had not yet been domesticated or marked out for domestication in any significant way."[9] To white settlers who equated domestication with "productive" landscapes, the Great Basin landscape was wild indeed. It offered at least two of the environmental ingredients—deserts and mountains—associated with wildness. As additional proof, its indigenous people seemed the epitome of wildness in dress (or lack of it) and manners.

Early white explorers and travelers took great pains to record just how

Fig. 7.1. Haunted Landscape: The Truckee River near Nevada's Pyramid Lake, the site of the tragic Pyramid Lake War in 1860. (May 2000 photograph by author)

incomparably primitive these Great Basin Indians were. Consider, for example, Edward Kern's 1845 statement on the matter. Kern proclaimed the Paiutes near Walker Lake to be "of a much lower grade than any Indian I have yet seen." Not realizing that five old women there were in mourning, he characterized them as "the personification of witches." According to Kern, their appearance "rendered them to me the most pitiable objects I have ever seen."[10] Kern's use of the word *objects* is telling. He viewed these people as something separate from both himself and humanity. But underneath such scornful accounts I sense a deep-seated fear—a fear that the whites might become like those they held in such disdain. Whites in these early Victorian times subconsciously feared that they might be tempted to go native, and hence lose both civilization and their souls.

On a train trip from Salt Lake City westward into the Great Basin in the early 1880s, the travel writer Phil Robinson attempted to thrill readers by observing that "there are plenty of Shoshonees to make the desolation perilous to travelers by waggon." Robinson literally objectified the Native peoples as he continued his description of the Shoshone's "listless men with faces like masks and women burnished and painted and wooden as the figure-heads of English barges." Robinson contended that these Indians were as mysterious as "hieroglyphics altogether" and that there was "something 'uncanny' about them." Yet, shortly before this encounter, Robinson had witnessed several men—"one Englishman, one Negro, three Mulattoes, and a Chinaman"—laughing at an Indian woman and her baby on the railroad platform in Palisade, Nevada. The railroad town of Palisade was bleak enough to Robinson, who called it "a group of wooden saloons haunted by numbers of yellow Chinese." But Robinson had even more scathing words for the racial encounter he experienced there. A self-proclaimed cynic, he noted that the "white man looks down on the Mulatto, and the Mulatto the Negro and the Chinaman reciprocate a mutual disdain." But Robinson notes that he "laughed heartily at them all—at them all except the Shoshonee." The reason, Robinson admitted, lay in the Indians' antiquity. He confessed that "I cannot, for the life of me, help venerating these representatives of a prodigious antiquity, these relics of a civilization that dates back before our Flood."[11] The word relic suggests an object. Then, too, Robinson's reference to the flood revealed his training and suggested that the Indians were connected to earlier races of people that inhabited the world before whites.

This belief that the Indians represented earlier races was commonplace in the nineteenth century. It also found its way into Mormon thinking. In addition to the Bible, the Mormons rely upon the Book of Mormon, which recounts the early history of the Americas as well as of the Old World. Other books, like *Pearl of Great Price* and the *Doctrine and Covenants,* also offer guidance and explanation to Mormons. According to Mormon ideology, the Indians—or Lamanites as they are called—are representatives of the lost tribes of Israel. How this religious interpretation played out racially on the frontier is revealed in an account by Charles Pulsipher, a Mormon who described an encounter with Ute Indians at the northeastern edge of the Great Basin in 1850. Startled by the Indians, "who were very hostile at that time," Pulsipher decided to go on the offensive, spiritually speaking. He pretended to be looking for their chief, whom he was brought to meet at the Indians' camp. Pulsipher told the chief, "I want you to call all your braves together so they can hear this message I have for you all." The chief summoned the braves, whereupon Pulsipher claims that "I commenced to talk" and "led out on the Book of Mormon saying: 'Many, many moons ago you people were a white people and were loved by the Lord, but because of wickedness and strife they [*sic*] had become so wicked, fighting and killing each other, stealing and so on, the Lord had become displeased with them.'"

Astutely avoiding any further references to racial differences, Pulsipher then brilliantly wove Christianity's universalizing message into his speech. He told the Indians about "how we got the Book of Mormon and that we all were brothers and we should be kind to each other, not steal or kill, but be good brothers." Stressing reciprocity, Pulsipher added that "when we come to see you, you must be kind to us and feed us as you have done tonight, and when you come to see us we must treat you kindly and feed you and then the Lord will be pleased with us all." Pulsipher claims that he "talked for two hours"—it certainly must have seemed that long to him—after which the chief "took out his pipe of peace," which "went the round." In a postscript reminiscent of Alvar Nuñez Cabeza de Vaca's journey across the Southwest in the 1530s, Pulsipher claims that he was then asked to help heal a groaning sick man who, the next morning, was reported by the grateful chief to be "very much better."[12] Pulsipher's suggestion that the Indians were once white people but had become people of color was common in Mormon thought in the 1800s.

Brigham Young himself went even further. In numerous writings and speeches in the mid-to-late nineteenth century, Young claimed that the Negroes' black skin and broad nose were the mark of Cain. That racialist dogma, however, was not the message originally conveyed by the Mormon Church in the East and Midwest, where early church rolls included some African Americans. According to historian Newell G. Bringhurst, "the Saints continued to express a universalistic desire to gather *all* peoples, including blacks, to their new Zion in Nauvoo, Illinois." What had happened to make the Mormons so antiblack? According to a historian of religion in the West, conditions deteriorated after Joseph Smith's murder in 1844, and this trend was exacerbated, perhaps, by the activities of a dark-complected Mormon named William McCary. As "a self-proclaimed black Indian prophet," McCary claimed supernatural powers, including the ability to assume the identity of certain Old and New Testament prophets. These claims, and McCary's sexual liaisons with three white Mormon women, apparently "angered Brigham Young and his followers, particularly the relatives of McCary's female disciples."[13]

The net result was that "Mormon discrimination against blacks increased even more following the Latter-day Saints' migration to and settlement of the Great Basin during the late 1840s and early 1850s."[14] Until amended in the late 1960s, LDS Church policies discouraged proselytizing in Africa and denied the priesthood to blacks, who still make up only a very small minority of church members.

Even though the Mormons' racially conscious thinking was at odds with Jesus' message of universal love, religion always struggles with humankind's strongest passions, including ethnocentrism. Another of those passions—sexuality—also figured heavily in Mormon history, for Mormon men who proved their spiritual prowess could take more than one wife. Mormon women were (and are) counseled to bear children, and birth control is, at least in policy, prohibited. In the nineteenth century, the Mormons' practice of polygamy incurred the ire and the jealousy of Gentiles, as non-Mormons are called by members of the church. I've always felt this to be ironic—that a Jew can be a Gentile in the eyes of the Mormons. But then I remember that Mormons assumed the role of Jews, driven into the desert by persecution and emerging as a chosen people in a promised land. This American diaspora helps explain why Mormons are, somewhat surprisingly for Christians, so passionately supportive of Israel's claims to the Holy Land. Like all peoples with a strongly developed cultural identity (including Israelis), the Mormons operate in the context of a well-defined "other." The categorization of others by race—a convenient, if overly simplified, system of physical appearance—effectively stratified people at a crucial time when technology permitted rapid cultural expansion.[15]

The social/historical context of Mormon expansion was colonialism. Through the process of expansion, places and features in the environment were appropriated in their name. This is evident in the naming of a common plant, Mormon tea (*Ephedra spp.*), that grows in parts of the region. To further connect the Mormons with this plant, it is sometimes called Brigham tea or settler's tea. As the name suggests, *Ephedra* served as a social beverage, but it also had medicinal qualities as a blood purifier, curer of kidney ailments, and remedy for colds. The name Mormon tea was likely given to this plant when early non-Mormon settlers saw the Saints brewing it. This implies that the Mormons discovered its use, but they "undoubtedly copied from the Indians" here. In an ironic twist, dried stems of Mormon tea are now marketed under the name "Squaw Tea."[16]

I find the Mormons' dominance in the eastern Great Basin to be pretty remarkable, given that they arrived here just a little over 150 years ago. But then I recall their religious zeal and their incredible passion for the place, and it makes their appropriation of the region more understandable. This place and Mormon history are inseparable. As a people, the Mormons' development, persecution, and rapid move westward were often seen, by both Mormons and non-Mormons, as mirroring the trials and tribulations of the Jews in the Book of Exodus. In moving into already-occupied areas, the Mormons (like all pioneers) needed to construct a framework for interacting with the people who were here before them. Regarding themselves as chosen people, the Mormons found ways to prove it. They used scripture to do so—accounts that suggest the physical consequences of falling from grace. Even though the "mark of Cain" was never clarified in the Bible, it was *assumed* to be racial in a society that was becoming increasingly racist in the nineteenth century. Consider Heidi Nast's interpretation that such racism is a function of paternalistic families subconsciously reenacting Oedipal mythology. Her argument goes something like this: the white father (powerful, judgmental) must protect the white mother (pure, virtuous) from the cast-out (i.e., bad) son—who is marginalized as a beast (wild man, savage, dark person).[17]

Although it is easy to take such arguments to absurdity, the parallels are haunting. Consider how this reasoning may have played out in the nineteenth century on the western frontier generally, and in the Great Basin in particular: Savages are people who used to be like "us" (that is, white) before they were banished for bad deeds. As a further consequence of this behavior, they were branded with racial features different from ours (the mark of Cain) so we could recognize—and judge—them at a glance. Carefully note the implications of such reasoning here. These savages always threaten—or we think they do—to reduce civilization (i.e., order) to savagery (i.e., chaos) if we give them the opportunity This lightness versus darkness drama is of course metaphorical and spiritual. It played out as part of what Denis Cosgrove calls "a world-historical struggle for the light of Christian truth against the darkness of unbelief."[18]

How else might one explain the vitriolic prose of Samuel Bowles, another travel writer edifying Victorian audiences with his florid prose? In 1865, Bowles published *Across the Continent: A Summer's Journey to the Rocky Mountains, the Mormons, and the Pacific States.* In it, he outlines the problems facing the U.S. government in containing the Indians. With seeming Christian charity, he observes that the "government is ready to assist in their support, to grant them reservation." Then, however, he adds ominously, "And if this cannot be secured, short of the [Indians'] utter extermination, why extermination it must be." To Bowles, the alternative was unthinkable: "Else, we may as well abandon this whole region; give up its settlement, its subjugation to civilization, its development to wealth and Christianity." Lest the reader misunderstand Bowles's interpretation, he concluded: "It is the old eternal contest between barbarism and civilization, between things as they have been and are, and material and moral progress."[19]

It is worth spending a little more time out in the Great Basin with Samuel Bowles, for he captured the fascination and admiration that many outsiders felt about the industrious Mormons. Upon leaving "the first Pacific slopes and tablelands of the Rocky Mountains," Bowles noted that travelers "go over the rim of the basin of the Great Salt Lake and enter that Continent within a Continent, with its own miniature salt sea, and its independent chain of mountains, and distinct river courses." I love Bowles's phrase "Continent within a Continent" for it reveals how unique some people thought the Mormons, and the Great Basin, were. Bowles added that this country was "marked wonderfully by nature, and marked now as wonderfully in the history of civilization by its people, their social and religious organization, and their material development." He left no doubt about who had transformed this place: "This is Utah—these the Mormons." Nor did he leave any doubt about the significance of both the place and the people: "I do not marvel that they think they are a chosen people; that they have been blessed of God not only in the selection of their home, . . . but in the great success that has attended their labors, and developed here the most independent and self-sustaining industry that the western half of our Continent witnesses."[20]

Observers like Bowles frequently commented on individual Mormon communities, but this chosen people/chosen land religious drama played out on a huge geographic scale during the first decade or so of Mormon colonization, ca. 1847-1859. The Great Basin was vast, the last unexplored region on the North American continent. The Mormons' movement into it qualifies as nothing less than one of the world's great religious diasporas. The Saints initially spread rapidly through the region from Salt Lake City after their arrival here in July of 1847. This expansion was a direct result of spatially expansive church policy that would create a huge theocratic empire called Deseret (fig. 7.2). Within a few years, they reached southern Utah, including what is today Las Vegas, Nevada. From there they swept westward across the Mojave Desert and claimed San Bernardino, California, as the southwestern entrepôt of Deseret. This expansion, the Mormons hoped, would provide them access to the sea in coastal California. To ensure their claim on as much of the Great Basin as possible, they also spread out to the eastern base of the Sierra Nevada, where they founded Genoa, Nevada (called "Mormon Station") by 1851. The Mormons' claiming of much of the Intermountain West (and virtually all of the Great Basin) as Deseret—the Biblical name for the industrious honeybee—was doubly ironic. The name "Deseret" is so easy to confuse subliminally with "desert," as many a contrite student has noted after finding it on a quiz, that it seamlessly equates the Mormons' geographical ambitions with their desert homeland in the Great Basin.

Few groups better exemplified what was called "moral progress" than did the Mormons. By the time that Bowles visited the Great Basin in the

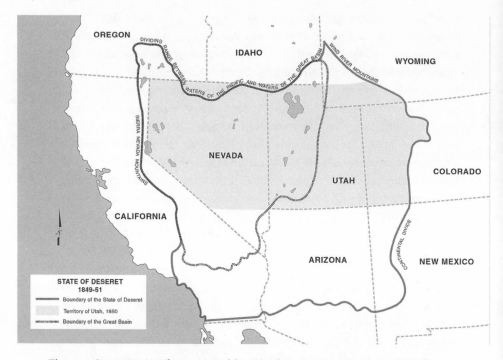

Fig. 7.2. Great Basin Theocracy: Although short-lived and never officially recognized by the United States, the Mormon State of Deseret revealed the Latter-day
Saints' ambitions to dominate much of the Intermountain West. (Map by author based
on maps in Leonard Arrington, *Great Basin Kingdom,* and Dale Morgan, *The State of Deseret*)

early 1860s, they had already transformed the landscape in seeming ac-
cordance with Biblical prophecy. From the mountains overlooking Salt
Lake City, Bowles observed "right beneath, in an angle to the plain, which
stretched south to Utah Lake and west to Salt Lake—'and Jordan rolled between'—was the city, regularly and handsomely laid out, with many fine
buildings, and filled with thick gardens of trees and flowers, that gave it a
fairy-land aspect."[21] Few observers could resist noting the Jordan River's
prominence, for here it connected Utah Lake with the Great Salt Lake, just
as its Holy Land prototype connected the Sea of Galilee and Dead Sea. A
promotional map from the nineteenth century entitled "A Striking Comparison The New State of Utah, Deseret, and the Holy Land" (fig. 7.3) confirms Bowles's assessment of the Mormons' industry while drawing striking parallels to the source region of the Judeo-Christian tradition. Such
maps further conflated the Mormons' Zion with its Old World inspiration.

In defending this new Zion that church leaders hoped to build, the Mormons recalled their trials and tribulations elsewhere in their early years.

Never far below the surface was the memory of their martyred leader Joseph Smith and his brother Hyrum, who were killed by a mob in 1844. After their leader's violent death, the Mormons had been forced to leave their midwestern homes—driven out by Gentiles who despised their beliefs and coveted their property. This memory, and this antipathy, would play out in one of the nation's great religious tragedies—the Mountain Meadows Massacre. The facts are straightforward enough—150 Missourians and Arkansans in a California-bound wagon train were all but annihilated at a remote spot at the southeastern edge of the Great Basin in September, 1857 (fig. 7.4). Today a historical marker commemorates the now serene, but once blood-saturated, site near Enterprise in extreme southwestern Utah.

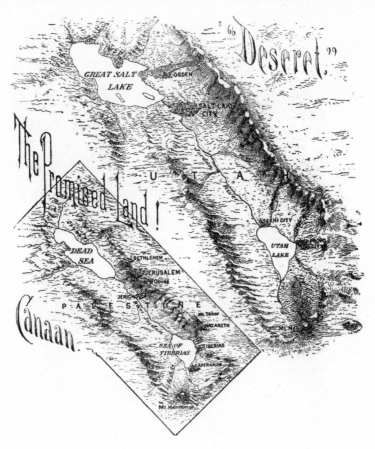

Fig. 7.3. Utah as Zion: In making "A Striking Comparison" between "The New State of Utah, 'Deseret,' and the Holy Land," this 1896 map published by the Rio Grande Western Railway portrays the Mormons as modern Israelites. (Courtesy DeGolyer Library, Southern Methodist University)

The historian Juanita Brooks writes that it is "difficult to visualize a massacre in this setting" with its "peace" and "absolute quiet." Yet, as if to heighten the awful drama that occurred here, she notes that it has changed in appearance: "The lush meadow described with such enthusiasm by early travelers is gone, the stirrup-high grass replaced by a twisting wash." Although ecologists theorize that these changes were likely caused by overgrazing, Brooks also gives another possible explanation: "This land, poisoned and contaminated by the blood that was spilled here, has been cursed by God, old-timers say; He washed it clean and decreed that nothing of value should ever grow upon it."[22] Here we again encounter the significance of storytelling not only in transforming places, but in sustaining them as either holy or unhallowed through both folklore and literature.

Fig. 7.4. Avenging Angels: The Mountain Meadows Massacre (1857) focused national attention on the Latter-day Saints and immortalized a remote spot at the southeastern edge of the Great Basin. (Photograph by David Futey)

The Mountain Meadows Massacre was initially blamed on Indians, and some may have participated in the event. However, the truth soon began to leak out, stunning a nation: Overzealous Mormons had originally promised the wagon train safe passage, but instead orchestrated the massacre in retaliation for anti-Mormon comments made by some Missourians in the party as they traversed the area. Some people who knew the region's "timid and dejected Pi-eed Indians" doubted the Natives' role in the massacre. Captain J. H. Simpson noted in 1859 that the massacre "is ascribed by the Mormons to them, but, as Dr. Hurt justly remarks, 'any one at all acquainted with them must perceive at once how utterly absurd and impossible it is for such a report to be true.'"[23] Simpson reported that "the stigma of this horrible outrage" rested squarely on the Mormons. Sensing the storm that would ensue, the Mormon leadership in Salt Lake City immediately distanced itself from the ugly event by urging the prosecution of the perpetrators. After prolonged investigation, John D. Lee was hanged in 1877. Still, the sordid event further fueled Gentile perceptions that the Mormons were not only peculiar, but also dangerous.

The initial tendency to blame Indians for the Mountain Meadows Massacre seems natural enough, much as the Boston Tea Party was attributed to Indians, but it demands closer inspection. On one level, it was easy to blame this morally reprehensible act on Indians, for they were widely regarded as "savages" capable of great duplicity and cruelty. Yet their being blamed resonates with denial: Christian people could not be capable of slaughtering each other, the reasoning went. Of course, on many occasions, Christians have taken up the sword against each other, as ongoing events in Northern Ireland constantly remind us. And when the followers of different religions consider their differences irreconcilable, as with the modern-day Jews and Palestinians, the results are almost invariably tragic —especially when those religions claim well-defined geographic space and wield considerable political power.

Just such a situation reached a boiling point in the Great Basin by the late 1850s. Religious warfare disguised as territorial dispute seemed imminent as the United States military positioned itself to seize the territorial capital and Mormon city of Salt Lake. Christians again prepared to destroy Christians—in this case, for the practice of polygamy and the dominance of theology in civil affairs. In defense of their newfound homeland, the Mormons prepared for war under Brigham Young's spiritual and military leadership. But, as fate would have it, the federal troops withdrew as Civil War first threatened the nation, then plunged it into its darkest four years.

For their part, the Mormons pursued a two-pronged strategy. First, they made some minor military moves against federal forts at the eastern edge of the Great Basin, but astutely avoided outright warfare. Their second strategy involved flight rather than fight. Under the guidance of Brigham Young, the Saints anticipated the seeming eventuality of federal control by preparing to burn their houses to the ground and then flee deeper into the Great Basin. Some had reportedly even placed tinder, ready to light, in their homes. In preparation for the Saints' flight westward from Salt Lake City, Brigham Young informed Bishop Lewis Brunson of Fillmore City on February 23, 1858, "It is our intention to send out some old men and boys to the white and last mountains to the west of the settlements and find places where we can raise grain and hide up our families and stock, in case of necessity." About a month later, Young spoke to the Saints at the tabernacle. "The prospect of ancient 'Mormonism,' of again leaving our homes," he said, "probably gives a spring to our feelings, especially since we, for the first time, have the privilege of laying waste to our improvements." Young felt that the Saints were physically capable of defending Salt Lake City, but that they needed to "prove to our Father in heaven and to one another that we are willing to hand back to him that which he has given us (which is not a sacrifice) and that we love not the world or the things of the world." God, Young said, "will preserve the people until they can become righteous."[24] The word people is important here, for Young used it to distinguish the Mormons from all others, even though he believed that even non-Mormons might be saved after their eventual conversion.

Hoping to sequester his people from the encroaching power of non-Mormons, Brigham Young selected William H. Dame to lead the expedition. A report confirmed that "W. H. Dame . . . had just returned from G.[reat] S.[alt] L.[ake] c.[ity] with instructions from Pres. B. Young to . . . Penetrate the Desert in search of a resting place for the Saints." Young had "hoped that the co.[mpany] would find a Desert that would take them 8 days to cross, but was affraid [sic] that it would take them only 3 days to cross it." Much like Moses fleeing Egypt, Young hoped to use a buffer of desert to separate the Mormons from their persecutors. This, according to Young, would guarantee "a place of refuge; some valley which should be surrounded by a desert requiring a five-day's [sic] march to cross." The expedition struck out in the spring into what a traveler later described as "scenery . . . grand beyond description," where "the storms of the ages have carved the soft [sandstone] rock into almost every conceivable shape," including "huge castlelike piles with spires and turrets innumerable" and "grotesque groupings of figures differently shaped from five to twelve feet high and appearing more like monuments in a churchyard than anything else," as well as rock formations that looked like "sentinels on duty" and "groups of cone-shaped mounds appearing like the tents of a vast army."[25]

Dame was less romantic, but he did write a wistful letter to his "Affectionate wives" when he was "[o]ne hundred and fifty miles from you." Dame told them that he had "just come down from the top of a big mountain" where he had "looked hard to see you, but alas; the distance too great, though felt you were well and had not forgot to pray for me." Mountains were on the minds of everyone on the expedition. As the group continued deeper into the Great Basin, they glimpsed a "high pyramidal peak perfectly white . . . which Pres. Dame pronounced to be the White Mts." This part of the Great Basin resonated as sacred to these Mormons in search of a refuge. Its "mountains and deserts were dedicated to God," and they asked to be "led to the place appointed by his holy spirit that we might know the place when we see it."[26] The expedition never found that place of sanctuary where all Mormons could be protected. Although a disappointment at the time, this failure ultimately ensured Salt Lake City's role as both spiritual and secular capital.

But at this time, when Mormons were contemplating fleeing ever deeper into the Great Basin, the White Mountains held great spiritual significance as a potential refuge. I find it telling that the expedition found flat stones and erected an altar on one of the mountains. There they sang a recently published Mormon hymn entitled "For the Strength of the Hills We Bless Thee." The hymn's words reveal the Mormons' belief that they were selected to be in the Great Basin. Consider this stanza:

> Our God, our fathers' God
> Thou hast made thy children mighty
> By the touch of the mountain's sod
> Thou has fixed our ark of refuge
> Where the spoiler's foot ne'er trod.[27]

It occurs to me that hymns of this type are a continuation of stories in the Bible, but that their wording and music also transform them into anthems. They endorse the Mormons' presence in a locale that is seemingly pure and unsullied. Note how seamlessly place is woven into the design of the following stanza:

> For the dark resounding caverns
> Where thy still small voice is heard,
> For the strong pines of the forests
> That by thy breath have stirred.[28]

These words remind me of Terry Tempest Williams's personal discovery of spiritual strength and guidance in a cave near Great Salt Lake. The concept of anthem is appropriate for such hymns because they reaffirm the individual's personal and spiritual belief that the place is his or hers, while politically reaffirming that it belongs to his or her *people* collectively. The hymn confirms how closely a people connect aspirations and belief with topography. It concludes with reference to "the strength of the hills," for which the Mormons again give thanks to "our God, our father's God."[29]

In their search for sanctuary, the Mormons had traversed some of the Great Basin's most formidable and remote country. Here tall mountains rise so high above bone-dry valleys that their summits are above the tree line. Seeking the most remote part of the region for solitude, I've hiked back into these mountains on two occasions. On my first trip, I clawed my way up out of the desert and into the glacial country, where steep scree slopes rose above stunted forests of bristlecone pines. The valley below was hot, but at more than 10,000 feet above sea level, this mountain stood with its peak in the jet stream. The wind howled and the temperature dropped well below freezing at night—and it was still mid-August. What impressed me most about the White Mountains was their awe-inspiring silence. Solitude reigns here in one of the last refuges of its kind in the American West.

I'm a stranger here at this elevation, in this high country of shattered granite and perennial ice. Just below the timberline, bristlecone pine trees (*Pinus aristata*) (fig. 7.5) cling to the mountain slopes, their contorted branches bearing testimony to the winds, their roots anchored in seemingly barren rock. The trees' gnarled bark and twisted limbs remind me of grizzled, wizened prophets, and the setting enhances their character. Look closely at a bristlecone pine and you may sense some of the potent divinity of God separating light and darkness in Michelangelo's Sistine Chapel ceiling painting; then, too, some of the wilder bristlecone pines look a bit like depictions of John Brown in his daring raid on Harpers Ferry, disheveled but inspired—perhaps divinely—with a kind of certainty that only possessed, even mad, men exhibit. This stunning mountain setting confirms botanist Michael Cohen's observation that "Great Basin bristlecone pines are, in the most radical sense, strangers [to us] because of the way they live and where they live." People, Cohen perceptively notes, "do not grow up in environments surrounded by these trees, but come to them casually or deliberately as visitors."[30]

Like the Mormons scouting for a New Zion away from Zion, I'm here in the White Mountains deliberately: my goal is to understand the Mormons' longing for such isolation. From my location on the steep rocky slopes just

below the timberline, I see the bristlecone pines as the embodiment of solitude, growing in the dry cold of America's driest cold region. All across the
Great Basin, wherever mountains rise to about two miles above sea level,
similar alpine habitats offer such solitude. In this regard, both Nevada's
White Mountains and California's White Mountains (home to the aptly
named Ancient Bristlecone Pine Forest Reserve, where there is even a
"Grove of Patriarchs") have much in common. The antiquity of bristlecones, which may live to be thousands of years old, adds to the effect. They
are easy to associate with biblical patriarchs who thrive in, or are regener-
ated by, such grand isolation. Even today the Great Basin region's tall

Fig. 7.5. Mountain Patriarch: The contorted, burnished
trunks and branches of bristlecone pines high in Nevada's Snake Range bear testimony to adversity, suggesting to some the ancient patriarchs and prophets.
(Photograph by David Futey)

mountains offer hypersolitude, and I can understand Cohen's reasoning regarding spending "more time in the mounts of the region than in the valleys." Perhaps, as he suggests, "this has been a way to hide from modern realities too frightening to confront on a daily basis."[31]

Here in the White Mountains of present-day Nevada, the Mormons planned to resume their efforts to build Zion unmolested—even if they had to destroy what they had created. That plan suggests ultimate sacrifice, but a closer look at Brigham Young's words confirms that they secretly hoped to return to Salt Lake City. At the beginning of the city's evacuation, Young admonished the Saints to "cache window and door frames and casings, etc., and thus save all that we can," because "we may come back here."[32] History proved kind to the Mormons, who avoided that apocalyptic conflict with federal authorities. That is yet another reason why the Great Basin still figures as their land chosen in tribulation and occupied through triumph.

The Mormons' preparation to flee into the Great Basin's wilderness in the late 1850s had a biblical tone, as did the gathering of the Saints in Salt Lake City preparatory to the impending war with the United States. One story notes that Orson Hyde, upon being ordered back to the city of the Saints, attempted to sell his property at Franktown, Nevada, which the Mormons had settled in 1852. "Wishing to obey the edict," the story goes, Hyde "received very little for his sawmill and farm." Hyde was so perturbed at the turn of events that he reportedly "cursed the area before departing: 'Ye shall be visited with thunder and . . . with floods, with pestilence and with famine, until your names are not known amongst men.'"[33] If there wasn't a verse exactly like this in the Bible, it was close enough to suggest a connection.

In point of fact, the Saints' regrouping from the margins of Deseret back toward Salt Lake City reoriented the cultural (and spiritual) geography of the Great Basin. Although the Mormons did spread elsewhere in the Intermountain West, they lost a presence in much of Nevada at exactly the time that miners poured into the region from California. Thus decisions that were meant to unify the Saints in preparation for a confrontation with the United States had a permanent effect on the character of the region. Nevada early on became the Silver State (1864), but Utah remained a territory under the control of a religious group for another thirty years.

The Mormons attracted ample commentary at this time, for their religion seemed at once ancient and yet progressive. Ever drawn to things peculiar in culture—especially exotic religions—travelers flocked to Utah in the late nineteenth century to see these peculiar people. In describing Salt Lake City in the early 1880s, the irascible Phil Robinson noted that "the City of the Saints puzzles me." For him, "the charm of this place" was due to the city's being a combination of Western and Eastern, "Oriental in its general appearance, English in its details." According to Robinson, many factors "combine to invest Salt Lake City with the mystery that is in itself a charm." He noted that "the future is full of promise, for the prosperity of the city is based upon the most solid of all foundations, agricultural wealth, and it is inhabited by a people whose religion is work."[34] Although Robinson recognized the presence and importance of non-Mormons to the city, he was especially enchanted by its deeply religious character. He conceived of Salt Lake City as "the young rival of Mecca, the Zion of the Mormons, the Latter-Day Jerusalem." In verbiage typical of the era, he further lauded it as "also the City of the Honey-bee, 'Deseret,'" the encampment of "'Shepherd Kings'—the rural seat of a modern patriarchal democracy; the place of the tabernacle of an ancient prophet-ruled Theocracy—the point round which great future perplexities for America are gathering fast; a political storm center—'a land fresh, as it were, from the hands of God.'"

Several of Robinson's comments—that Salt Lake City was "a beautiful Goshen of tranquility in the midst of a troublous Egypt," and "the templed city of an exacting God—a place of pilgrimage in the land of promise," help cast the city in a decidedly biblical context. His statement that Salt Lake City was "the home of the 'Lion of Judah,' and the rallying point of the last days of the Lost Tribes, the Lamanites, the Red Indians," foretells the city's role as a major center for a universalizing religion that might ultimately assimilate the Native peoples into what one writer in 1881 called "Our Western Empire" of the larger "Empire of Christendom."[35] Time has shown that this cultural and religious assimilation was only partial in the place the same writer said had been "a howling wilderness" before the Mormons claimed it.[36] In the Great Basin as elsewhere in the West, Native peoples would never completely lose their own religions despite aggressive attempts by Mormons and others to thoroughly convert them to Christianity. But time has also shown that the Mormons were the most assiduous of the new arrivals, heeding their leaders' call to build up Zion by taming the wilderness and converting its Native peoples. With their words in mind, I roll into the City of the Saints in an early evening rain shower that throws yellow light and purple shadows onto one of America's most distinctive urban places.

8

Vanishing Cities of Zion

To many Americans Utah is even yet a land of mystery—the home of strange rites and unhallowed religion; but to me, in its physical features, it is already as the home of the soul. As more and more I become familiar with it, I see how little Mormonism has to do with its real greatness, how small a space it will occupy in its future history, and what countless other matters there are of wonder and interest.

—J. H. BEADLE, *Western Wilds and the Men Who Redeem Them*

I think about J. H. Beadle's observations and prophecies as I look out at the skyline of Salt Lake City on a bright summer day. True, the grand physical landscape of Utah overshadows most works of humankind here, as is plainly evident in the spectacular Wasatch Mountains that loom off to the east and the vast sweep of the Great Salt Lake to the west. But everywhere I look I realize that Beadle grossly underestimated the tenacity of the Mormons who claimed this area as home and set deep roots into its soil. Beadle's classically anti-Mormon sentiments aside, these people would indeed have something to contribute to Utah's "real greatness." As early as 1858, the perceptive traveler Henry Howe knew as much. He noted that "Brigham Young's object in selecting Salt Lake as the site of his new city and the center of his new Kingdom, was to separate his people from the rest of the world, and the place was admirably chosen for the purpose."[1]

The Mormons showed incredibly shrewd judgment in selecting the site of Salt Lake City. Its location at the apex of an alluvial fan (safe from flooding), in close proximity to a perennially flowing stream (ensuring an ample water supply), and at the base of a strategic pass (making it a natural stop on the route west) was uncanny. Plus, the Great Salt Lake itself proved to be one of the region's most potent landmarks as it glistened in the afternoon sun or caught the moods of the region's tempestuous weather. Consider the words of traveler Phil Robinson, who visited the area in the early 1880s. Robinson found himself between Ogden and Salt Lake City as night descended along the Wasatch front. The trip was "two hours . . . of dullness" until "on a sudden I saw out in front of me a thin white line lying under the hills that shut in the valley." When Robinson asked a fellow traveler what the line was, the traveler responded, "That, sir? That is Salt Lake."[2]

Many people commented on the city's peculiar location, which served as a model for later communities. Despite his anti-Mormon sentiments, J. H. Beadle himself commented on how the Mormons' communities were proliferating in these sheltered sites along the Wasatch front: "the traveler along one side of the valley sees all the Mormon villages on the other side, each set back in a little cove, but those near him are hidden by projecting mountain spurs."[3] Some observers were mystified as to why these communities were built so close to the mountains, but a closer look at Mormon doctrine and folklore reveals the importance of mountains to the Saints. They provided not only water, but also a connection with the Mormons' Judeo-Christian spiritual roots. The Mormons were well aware of the prophecy in Isaiah 2.2., "And it shall come to pass in the latter days that the mountain of the house of the Lord shall be established as the highest of the mountains, and shall be raised exalted above the hills." Although he never lived to see the West, Joseph Smith reportedly urged the Saints to prepare to move to the fastness of the Rocky Mountains. To folklorist Richard Poulsen, the mountain in Mormon thought "is the central issue of a dream of freedom." In the Mormon version, "the mountain is transformed to a cultural center, to the house of the Lord." Here in Mormon Utah, "[m]ountain and people become inseparable, because they both know and express the subtle nuances of cultural validation. . . . The mountain, then expresses a landscape of belief." Poulsen concludes: "The mountain is a holy place not merely because a prophet wandered up into it and came down out of it transformed, but because the people are transformed by its presence."[4]

Salt Lake City's location probably resonated as biblical for many reasons, not the least of which was its subliminal similarity to a passage in Revelation: "And in the Spirit he carried me away to a great high mountain, and showed me the holy city Jerusalem coming down out of heaven from God" (21:12). The Wasatch Mountains' power to transform human belief and to enhance Salt Lake City's importance as a spiritual place is evident in the accounts of early travelers to the region from the East. Approaching the Wasatch in September of 1848, early Mormon convert Hosea Stout reported that from "the top of the mountain which is the highest one we had to ascend on this journey," the scenery was inspirational: "Here we had a view of the south part of the Valley & like old Moses could 'view the landscape o'er' while many hills and bad roads yet intervened" (fig. 8.1). Many early Mormons noted similar experiences upon nearing Salt Lake City. When Stout's group arrived in Salt Lake City three days later, they were commended by Brigham Young, who stated that "this is the place he had seen before he came here & it was the place for the Saints to geather [sic]."5 Brigham Young is widely credited with the expression "This is the place"—or, even more emphatically, "This is the *right* place." It is noteworthy that Young suggests that he had recognized the landscape here in an earlier vision or dream. This precognition further endorses Salt Lake City as *the* place.

Ever aware of the exotic and ever in search of human spirituality, explorer Richard Burton put Salt Lake City on his itinerary in 1861. Burton was clearly impressed with the city's appearance. He noted the Mormons' belief that the city was "New Hierosolyma, or Jerusalem, alias Zion on the tops of the mountains, the future city of Christ, where the Lord is to reign over the Saints, as a temporal King, in power and great glory." Always aware of landscape's role in dramatic encounters, Burton described his first view of the Salt Lake Valley "from the gates and portals and deep serrations" of the Wasatch Mountains, where "the valley presently lay full before our sight." Here, at about the place where Brigham Young is purported to have uttered his famous affirmation, Burton's fellow travelers had an epiphany: "At this place the pilgrim emigrants, like the Hajis of Mecca and Jerusalem, give vent to emotions long pent up within their bosoms by sobs and tears, laughter and congratulations, psalms and hysterics." Despite his attempts at objectivity, Burton himself understood these pilgrims' belief that "the 'Spirit of God pervades the very atmosphere,' and that Zion on the tops of the mountains is nearer heaven than other parts of the earth." Caught up in the pilgrims' ecstasy, Burton confessed that "even I could not . . . gaze upon the scene without emotion."6 Outsiders like the sophisticated Burton were not the only ones who sensed an Old World biblical quality to this landscape. When Hosea Stout left Salt Lake City to assist in developing Mormon communities elsewhere, he gazed wistfully back toward it: "At noon we found ourselves on the point of the Utah mountain where we took our last look at Salt Lake City." The view was evidently both sublime and evocative, for Stout observed that a "light cloudy fog rested on it, in which we could see President Young's House, like Solomon's Temple in the midst of the glory of God."7 This was the most arid country that the Kentucky-born Stout had ever experienced, and it seamlessly translated as biblically inspired, as did the actions of his leader, Brigham Young.

The Wasatch Mountains' semiaridity added to their allure, just as the desert confirmed the Mormons' mission here. As Mormon church leader G. A.

Fig. 8.1. Encountering Zion: "First View of Great Salt Lake Valley from a Mountain Pass" reveals the anticipation of travelers to their first glimpse of Zion. From Stansbury's *Exploration*, 1852. (Courtesy Special Collections Division, University of Texas at Arlington Libraries)

Smith told the Saints in 1861, "If the mountains were covered with beautiful timber, and plenty of grain could be grown without irrigation, there is no doubt but our enemies would overrun us, or at least make a great deal of trouble; but as it is, we inherit the chambers of the mountains, and the oases of the desert our homes."[8] This is a hard land, one that requires sustained work to yield a livelihood. Thus it was that the Mormons were forever destined to toil—a sacralization, if you will, of the American work ethic.

The Mormons' work and initiative is everywhere apparent in Salt Lake City, where one of America's most remarkable buildings—the Mormon Temple—rises at the base of the Wasatch Mountains. Even the name of its architect—Truman Angell—resonates with a sense of the ethereal. Constructed of durable gray granite quarried from the Wasatch, the Temple took forty years to complete (1847-1887). It is topped by a gold statue of the angel Moroni, who faces east toward the mountains and the rising sun. A popular question-and-answer joke in Salt Lake City implicitly recognizes the potency of Mormon Temple's position:

Question: "What's going to happen when the angel Moroni blows his trumpet?'"
Answer: "Salt Lake City is going to be knee-deep in pigeon shit."

This irreverent joke is likely based on the numerous references to seven angels blowing their trumpets in chapter 8 of the Book of Revelation. It works so well because it conflates the mundane (bird excrement) with the Mormons' loftier mission (the angel's awakening humankind to Christ's second coming). It also reaffirms the angel's prominent position in church ideology. The golden angel's looking east is symbolic for two reasons: It not only focuses on the Holy Land and the dawning of each new day, but is also symbolic of the Saints' constant awareness of the mountains. From the earliest days of Mormon settlement in the Great Basin, the mountains have served to protect the Saints from the perils farther east, which is to say corrupt civilization advancing westward. In truth, the Mormons from the very beginnings of their settlement here could not escape the wrath of harassers from the eastern United States; in lighter moods, travelers cast them as the butt of jokes—their wit sometimes barely concealing hidden admiration. Yet, the Mormons always knew how to make the most out of, that is, profit from, the presence of the Gentiles. Historian Leonard Arrington noted that commerce with the throngs of gold-seekers bound for California helped the Mormons build up their Great Basin kingdom.[9]

Mark Twain was among the early travelers who commented on what the Mormons had created here in Salt Lake City. Not an advocate of Mormon religion, but ever in search of the humorous, Twain opined that Mormon men should not be condemned for practicing polygamy. Rather, he suggested, they should be applauded for rescuing so many homely women from otherwise certain spinsterhood. However, Twain's witty and acerbic comments are only part of what he wrote. Note his admiring description of Salt Lake City, with its "block after block of trim buildings, built of 'frame' and sunburned brick—a great thriving orchard behind every one of them, apparently—branches from the street stream winding and sparkling among the garden beds and fruit trees—and a general air of neatness, repair, thrift and comfort, around and over the whole"[10] (fig. 8.2). Humor and criticism aside, early observers could not refrain from commenting on those industrious aspects of the Mormons as well as their peculiarities. As the crown jewel of Mormon settlement, Salt Lake City seemed to exemplify these traits.

The "Americanization of Utah," to paraphrase Mormon historian Charles S. Peterson's interpretation of how the Saints' rural way of life began to change, involved a number of compromises after just about the four decades that it took the church to complete the temple.[11] Statehood' in 1896 followed the Mormons' renunciation of polygamy several years earlier. It should be noted, however, that this renunciation pertained only to

Fig. 8.2. "Right with the Compass and Right with God": Salt Lake City's orthogonal plat and isolated site are apparent in this lithograph of "Great Salt Lake City from the North." (From Richard Burton, *The City of the Saints*, 1861; author's collection)

earthly polygamy: a Mormon man who has been married to more than one woman will be reunited in heaven with all of his wives. And as I've traveled throughout the eastern Great Basin, I've encountered excommunicated Mormons who still practice polygamy: When I asked a woman in western Utah when the house she was living in was constructed, she answered: "I'm not sure; you'll have to ask our husband when he comes home."

Observers like explorer Richard Burton could not resist casting the Mormons' polygamy in the light of the harems of the Middle East. As part of an elaborate popular-culture appreciation of "the Orient," which "in those days, meant Egypt and North Africa, Turkey and the Holy Land," observers often reported on mysterious and titillating sexual practices.[12] If Orientalism's prerequisites included the "equating of deserts with romance" and "a voyeuristic fixation on harem life,"[13] then the Mormon kingdom of Deseret served as America's counterpart. Virtually every observer had something to say about the Mormons in this regard, for their sexual practices broke with European-American conventions as they sought to live more like the peoples depicted in the Old Testament. For the Mormons, polygamy also answered certain cultural needs, including the care of a surplus of women, and the simultaneous reaffirmation of the power of patriarchy and the growing power of sisterhood. Early accounts of Mormon life stressed either the harmony of such sisterhood or the evils of such enslavement of women—the latter resonating in recent times as polygamy was challenged in a recent Utah court case against a self-proclaimed Mormon man with five wives.

The contrast between Mormonism as it once was—polygamous, quasi-socialistic, and marginal—and what it is today—monogamous, free-enterprise oriented, and mainstream—has fascinated me for some time. This church can reaffirm or slightly shift its philosophy, for as its name suggests, revelations are still possible in the Latter-days—that is, in the time since Jesus Christ. For example, the church recently emphasized the words "Jesus Christ" in its official name because many people felt the Mormons to be practitioners of an unusual, non-Christian, religion. In the spring of 2001, the church further reinforced this emphasis by urging that the organization not be called the "Mormon Church" or even the "Latter-day Saints (LDS) Church," but by its full and rightful title, the "Church of Jesus Christ of Latter-day Saints."[14] The reaffirmation of the church's name gets to the heart of a question posed by writer Scott Anderson. "Who are the true Mormons?" Anderson asked. "Are they the ones who cling to the original tenets of the faith, no matter how obsolete or distasteful they seem today? Or are they the ones who have gone along with the modifications and revisions the modern world demands?"[15] Ever obedient to church authorities, most Mormons in Utah subscribe to the latter; yet, scattered throughout the Intermountain West are excommunicated Mormons who seek to recapture the energy and nonconformity of the early Saints. Those fundamentalist Mormons, I suspect, will always be with us, and forever a thorn in the side of the official LDS Church.

And so I'm thinking about Salt Lake City's origins and transformations as summer sunlight pours down upon it, the city's oasislike quality distinguishing it from its desert setting. The city is perennially "Mormon" and yet always attracts the attention of non-Mormon commentators. At around the time that Utah Territory became a state and Salt Lake City its permanent state capital, a perceptive observer named F. A. Bailey described Salt Lake City as "a typical Mormon village, one of a line of closely connected settlements running along the valley between the Wasatch and the great lake." Well aware of "Brigham Young's shrewd policy of centralization," Bailey recognized the city's pivotal place in Mormon affairs despite its bucolic character. Its "picturesque low stone houses," he wrote, "were set back in bushy yards, each house with its orchard beside it—delightful old overgrown orchards, in which children played and the calves grazed in dappling sunlight."[16]

But Salt Lake City has greatly changed in the last 150 years, and with that progress has come a steady loss of its Mormon character—except, that is, in Temple Square, one of the most significant religious centers in the New World: America's equivalent, in fact, of Rome (though many Mormons might recoil at the idea of their faith's being likened to Roman Catholicism). Even the church office building appears like almost any other high-rise building, and its placement seems to both dwarf the Mormon Temple and isolate that building from its granite Wasatch Mountain roots.

So it is that I set off southward to find some Mormon communities that retain more of the early features of Mormon towns; communities like those described half a century ago by the sociologist Lowry Nelson in his classic book *The Mormon Village*.[17] As I begin my trip, I steer my rental car toward Interstate 15 through a maze of construction barrels readying the city's roads and streets for the 2002 Winter Olympics. As I swing through the south side of the central business district, I'm aware of something that geographer D. W. Meinig pointed out about forty years ago:[18] There is a potent Gentile presence in part of the city, giving it something of a split personality. The older buildings in this section, including the stock exchange and the numerous large commercial buildings bankrolled by mining magnates, are associated with the Gentile mining booms in the nearby mountains and stand in contrast to the impressive, historic ornate facade of the Mormon-built ZCMI (Zion's Cooperative Mercantile Institution) department store and Brigham Young's "Lion House" closer to Temple Square. Finally finding my way to a freeway on-ramp, I set out to look for that vanishing face of Mormonism—the utopian, self-sufficient villages that church leaders encouraged as they settled this part of the world a century and a half ago using Salt Lake City as their prototype.

Although Interstate Highway 15 was completed in the early 1970s, most Mormons hereabouts will tell you that Brigham Young had envisioned it more than a century before. This road of Young's dreams connects the city of the Saints with what was once a small Mormon village—Las Vegas. I'm traveling in Young's footsteps as I traverse country he visited annually. Clinging to the eastern edge of the Great Basin, I-15 now makes quick work of this 400-mile journey. Like most interstates, however, it gives one a different, more detached view of the landscape than the older, slower roads do. I'd normally take Highway 89, which cuts deeper into Mormon Country, but I've got business in Las Vegas tomorrow (honestly!) and have given myself only a day to get there. With the Wasatch Mountains still on my left, the freeway traverses a variegated landscape of desert rangeland alternating with green irrigated fields.

I've got the air conditioner on and NPR's "Fresh Air" on the radio. Terry Gross is interviewing the maverick Mormon writer Terry Tempest Williams, whose work repeatedly has shaken up the Mormon Church. I wonder how Williams's writings sit with the most conservative Mormon folks who live in these valleys they've occupied since the early 1850s. I sense some of Williams's persistent passion and incessant questioning in a recent magazine interview. Starting with the Mormon premise about procreation and reproduction, she allows that "it could be argued that sex is like land, it must be used for something. Develop the land. Sex is about having children." But then she adds a thought disturbing to many Mormons: "What happens if it's about love? And what happens if it's between two men, [or] two women?" Williams concludes that this possibility "threatens the patriarchy."[19] The Mormons' potent undercurrent of fertility is apparent in a recent book of short stories, *In Our Lovely Deseret,* that takes its title from Mormon song and scripture but is so explicit in places that it has embarrassed many traditional Saints.[20]

In the process of transforming the Great Basin's landscape into Zion, the Mormons converted topographical features into spiritually charged icons. I am aware of this as I continue south on I-15 near Kanosh, where Tabernacle Hill is visible to the west. A local visitor's guide states that this extinct volcano "is named after the Mormon Tabernacle located on Temple Square in Salt Lake City due to its shape."[21] Farther off the interstate to the west, travelers encounter a series of fascinating topographic features that evidently resonated with the Indians but have been given a Mormon identity. Consider, for example, the "Great Stoneface." Located not far from Old Fort Deseret, which was constructed to protect settlers during the Black Hawk Indian War in 1865, the stone face is a prominent landmark in west-central Utah. Rising about forty feet above the surrounding lichen-splashed volcanic topography, the Great Stoneface, also known as the "Guardian of Deseret," is intimately linked to Mormon folklore. A local travel brochure asserts that the early Mormon pioneers here encountered, to their surprise, "the spitting image of their recently slain prophet naturally carved in stone." This likeness of Joseph Smith was not dispassionate. "He appeared to be watching over them, like a sentinel sent from God." However, this topographic feature is Janus-faced. The brochure goes on to note: "But the Great Stoneface has a split personality. In contrast to being the image of a prophet of God when viewed from the west, it appears to be

'The Devil's Chimney' when viewed from the east."[22] Few features are better positioned to define the character of this region than the Great Stoneface, for its two personalities suggest the dualism that is deeply embedded in Judeo-Christian thought: to the east of the Great Stoneface lies Zion and its protection/salvation, while to the west lies the temptation of the desert wilderness, home of pagan, even satanic, forces in the popular mind. Here on I-15, I'm surrounded by the handiwork of the Mormons, who have shaped the desert into a garden—or rather a series of garden spots that stand in stark contrast to the desert.

I'm intrigued by "Mormon Country," as John Codman called it in 1874,[23] and as writer Wallace Stegner popularized it about seventy-five years later. Those highway exit signs along I-15 beckon me to communities I'd studied back in the late 1960s: Lehi, Scipio, Nephi, and Holden. These are classic Mormon villages strung out like beads along the Wasatch front (fig. 8.3). About four hours out of Salt Lake City, I flip my turn signal and swing onto the exit to Parowan, Utah, wondering what I'll find. I've been back to Mormon Country many times since I wrote (and later published) my dissertation about what I coined "The Mormon Landscape."[24] Like all landscapes, this one is in constant flux, yet the framework is distinctively traditional—the open fields at the edge of town intensively cultivated, though pretty much devoid of farmhouses and other related buildings.

Like many towns in this area, the valley around Parowan reveals the handiwork of visionary Mormons who arrived here about a century and a half ago. Turning off of the freeway ramp and onto the old highway that heads into town, I am reminded that these villages were designed as clusters of small farms surrounded by open fields of hay and crops. As I head east, Parowan looms like an oasis within a mosaic of square green, yellow, and brown carpet samples stretching from the mountains' base out into the valley. Had I turned west off the ramp, I would have encountered the Little Salt Lake, an often-dry lakebed in the desert. The name confirms that the original Salt Lake, and the city of that same name, were never far from the thoughts of the Mormon pioneers.

At this slower pace, I shut off the air conditioner and roll down a couple of windows; the sweet smell of cut hay rushes into the car at the same time as a redwinged blackbird's distinctive trilling call reaches my ears. Nothing says "irrigation" like these two signs in an otherwise desertlike setting. Along with the feel of the strong sunlight pounding down on my left arm, they confirm that landscape involves more than just sight, but *all* of our other senses as well.

Parowan was a spinoff of Salt Lake City, and it became the mother com-

Fig. 8.3. With Hills Surrounded: Mormon villages were strung along the Wasatch front like beads on a chain. They often have spectacular mountain backdrops, as seen here at Nephi, Utah, at the base of Mount Nebo. (1969 photograph by author)

munity for other Mormon towns that would be built in this part of the Great Basin. Like all Mormon towns, it is laid out in a grid pattern, "right with the compass and right with God," as a Mormon farmer once put it. I recognize this as a reference to Revelation 21:16, which proclaims that the heavenly city "lies four square." Those words appear in the last couple of pages of the Bible, and they are repeated in the Latter-day Saints' guidance from Joseph Smith, whose City of Zion plan called for Mormon communities also to be laid out four square. The visionary Smith even prepared a drawing of the City of Zion plat in June 1833, also offering specific advice on laying out the city, "should you not understand the explanations" on the map.[25] Another legacy of Smith's plan is evident here in Parowan: the streets are wider than those in non-Mormon towns. This, too, is likely a legacy of Smith's City of Zion plan, which called for all streets to be 132 feet wide.

I head first for downtown Parowan, what there is of it, and find a sleepy but well cared for collection of commercial buildings on Main Street. Most of these no longer serve their original purpose as the interstate now lures people to other, bigger towns for shopping. Like most Mormon towns laid out in the nineteenth century, Parowan has a public square that serves to remind all how powerful the Church was, and is, in civic affairs. On the square of most Mormon villages, you'll find an LDS chapel and other buildings, such as a church relief society or a bishop's storehouse ("for tithes of grain and other crops in the old days," as a Mormon farmer put it). In the nineteenth century, it was not uncommon to see buildings, such as the Parowan Co-op Store, with religious slogans such as "Holiness to the Lord" placed on their facades.[26]

These Mormon buildings remind me of the old Endowment Hall in Spring City, Utah. This simple neoclassical/Greek Revival building features three symbols—a backwards L, a V, and a beehive—in its pedimented gable front (fig. 8.4). I first encountered this building in 1969 while on a trip with two elderly Mormon friends from Nephi. Although my wife and I are not Mormons, this couple had "kind of adopted" us, as they put it. Upon seeing the building's facade, the woman exclaimed "Look! Those symbols are just like the ones on our sacred undergarments!" So close had we become that she had forgotten, just for a moment, that we were not LDS. So startled was she by seeing those symbols displayed publicly that she had blurted out this normally "secret" information. Our Mormon friend was right: those "L" and "V" symbols appear over the nipple of each breast on the undergarments worn by devout Mormons. They translate into "Liberty" and "Virtue," but also have other meanings that are graphic: the "L" is a square used to ensure that a building's construction is true, and the "V" is a compass to be sure that measurements of angles are made accurately. What few people realize is just how similar these L and V symbols are to the compass and square in Masonic ritual. So similar are they that the *Utah Catalog, Historic American Buildings Survey* accidentally identified this building as a "Masonic Lodge" in 1969!

Those similarities are not accidental: most of the early Mormons were Masons until hostilities in the 1840s Midwest led them in separate directions. Long deconsecrated, the Endowment Hall apparently has undergone other changes since my visit in 1969. A folklorist reports that the beehive is the only symbol that remains for the traveler to see, both the backwards L and the V having been removed. You will only see those symbols in more sacred, and secret, places, within the temple and close to the skin—places you do not get to until declaring allegiance to the Mormons collectively and individually. The beehive, however, that wonderful icon of the Latter-day Saints' industry, not only survives but has become the official symbol

Fig. 8.4. Sacred Symbols: Unusual in its open use of sacred Mormon symbols, the decoration in the pediment of this building in Spring City, Utah, features the backwards "L" and the "V" (Liberty and Virtue) symbols reminiscent of the Masonic order, and the beehive, which became the symbol for Deseret and, later, the state of Utah. (1969 photograph by author)

of Utah. It now adorns state highway road signs and stationery. That, some may argue, is symbol enough to honor the Mormons. Somehow, though, those two potent letters L and V continue to excite my imagination, as do all things held secret and kept from view.

Sacred undergarments are very significant to Mormons, some of whom never lose contact with them, even constantly touching them with one hand as they bathe or shower. I remember a Mormon janitor who took care of the church archives in Salt Lake City in 1969. The man, who became interested in my research, must have assumed that I was a Mormon. At any rate, one day he volunteered a fascinating story about how his sacred underclothing had protected him in a construction-site accident some years before: "Believe what they tell you about our sacred undergarments protecting us," he urged before I could caution him that I wasn't LDS. He proceeded to tell me about what happened to him while he was constructing a building. "A wall collapsed on me," he recalled with a painful expression. "But everywhere my sacred undergarments had covered was protected." As his hands gestured in the shape of the undergarments, he described how his chest, back, and portions of his lower trunk had been "miraculously protected." Then, in order to emphasize the real danger he had faced, he enthusiastically added: "But of course my skull was fractured in several places, my hands badly crushed, and one ankle broken." To some, the janitor's having been thus "spared" might seem humorous, but it got me to thinking. Although I was shocked at the injuries he had suffered, his honesty and sincerity made me realize how powerful his faith was. Rather than cursing his injuries, he regarded what was not damaged with profound thanks. *That* is dedication and belief.

These stories, told by devout Mormons, remind me how interwoven visual symbolism and faith are in many societies. Driving a couple of blocks and turning off Main Street, I encounter a scene that takes me back not only to the late 1960s—when considerably more of the vernacular Mormon landscape remained, before Lady Bird Johnson's "Keep America Beautiful" campaign motivated folks to tear down old "eyesores" like abandoned barns and outhouses—but to the nineteenth century. A sturdy brick farmhouse common to the area recalls a time when Joseph Smith's City of Zion plan admonished all devout Mormons to build houses of brick and stone. Also according to plan, each lot had an orchard and garden recalling the Mormon mandate to put up food—at least a year's supply—in anticipation of crises. An irrigation ditch alongside the street (fig. 8.5) testifies to the Mormons' adaptation of this arid land. They likely learned some of these techniques from the Mexican people who lived in parts of today's Southwest, but then, too, the Mormons were well aware of irrigation in the Bible. An 1848 Mormon immigrant guide matter-of-factly encouraged converts to locate in Utah: "The water is good, and very cold, and abundance [sic] for mill purposes, or for irrigation."[27]

Mormon writer Maureen Whipple summed up the deeper meaning of this irrigation when she described the "Biblical peace of tiny green oases set against the savage violence of the hills."[28] The violence, of course, was both environmental and cultural, the peace suggesting the repose of the oasis surrounded by hostility. In 1922, while traveling through Mormon Country, the writer G. W. James described "a sudden encounter" with an irrigated landscape that seemed "to be mere phantasmagoria—when, lo! a magic turn of the road reveals a sweep of emerald with ditches of dancing water."[29] It was here in these oases that the Mormons would make the desert "blossom as the rose"—a fairly close reference to the Old Testament, wherein the "wilderness and the dry land shall be glad, the desert shall rejoice and blossom; like the crocus it shall blossom abundantly" (Isa. 35:1).

This popular conflation of Mormon Country with the Holy Land makes me challenge something that the late J. B. Jackson, the dean of landscape studies, wrote a couple of decades ago. Jackson observed that "no group sets out to create a landscape." He explained: "What it sets out to do is

Fig. 8.5. Life-Giving Water: In hundreds of Mormon villages like Parowan, Utah, the open irrigation ditch is one of the key elements in the landscape, but many are now being covered over. (July 2000 photograph by Nancy Grace)

create a community, and the landscape as its visible manifestation is simply the by-product of people working and living, sometimes coming together, sometimes staying apart, but always recognizing their interdependence." According to Jackson, "It follows that no landscape can be exclusively devoted to the fostering of only one identity."[30] I believe that Jackson's words are probably true in most places, but not here in Mormon Country. Nor would Brigham Young have believed it. In 1852, Young told his people: "There is a great work for the Saints to do; progress and improve upon and make beautiful everything around you. Cultivate the earth and cultivate your minds. Build cities, adorn your habitations, make gardens, orchards and vineyards, and render the earth so pleasant that when you look upon your labors you may do so with pleasure, and that the angels may delight to come and visit your beautiful locations."[31]

Other Mormons of lesser stature appear to have been inspired by Young. Elder M. McCune addressed the Mormons in Nephi in 1854. "I believe that I was lead [sic] by God to settle in Nephi," McCune noted. In what appears to be a folksier version of Young's speeches, he then added that "I hope to see . . . an improvement in all things . . . your habitations embellished—flours [sic] cultivated—shade trees planted—a fit place for the angels to visit."[32]

Many non-Mormon visitors, even doubters like John Codman, also recorded the Saints' passion for building Zion. Of Brigham Young, Codman noted that "[w]hile his promise to the faithful of blessings in the other world are [sic] of an extraordinary and doubtful character, he is evidently instructing them how they can make this world turn to their advantage." Codman revealed how Young deftly fused spiritual enlightenment with landscape building: "On one Sunday he may tell them how they can get a great 'exaltation' in heaven . . . but on ten Sundays he will tell them how to irrigate and drain land, harvest crops, build fences, set out trees, beautify their grounds, raise cattle, saw lumber, and manufacture cloth; and this is the character of the sermons most frequently preached by the clergy."[33]

Perusing the landscape at Parowan, with its looming mountains and sagebrush plains always juxtaposed with irrigated fertility, I do not doubt for a minute that Mormon Country was contested terrain; although many Indians were converted, many others apparently did not appreciate Brigham Young's followers' appropriation of their lands. Because these early Mormon colonists were motivated by a desire to spread their religion into their new Zion, they quickly put their visual stamp upon it. They did so not only at Salt Lake City and Parowan, but at hundreds of other locations as they sought trained converts, then sent those converts out to build up Zion using both their skills and the church's religious instruction and guidance. Tellingly, Joseph Smith's plan for cities of Zion called for each community to be a mile square (population 10,000), surrounded by farming lands. When one community was completed, another would be developed, so that the entire world would ultimately be covered by such cities of Zion. In Smith's own words, "When this square [comprising the city] is thus laid off and supplied, lay off another in the same way, and so fill up the world in these last days; and let every man live in the city for this is the City of Zion."[34] Using such inspired geometry, the Mormons would thus dominate the globe, an inescapable result of the command to multiply and subdue the earth, as mandated in Genesis.

Although these nucleated Mormon villages reflect Joseph Smith's vision as translated by Brigham Young and other church leaders, not all Mormons lived in such splendid cohesion. In parts of the Great Basin one can find Mormon settlements that were less well-ordered.[35] In moving into the Intermountain West, some Saints also lived in more isolated farmsteads. Overall, however, it is the orderly Mormon village that served as a model, and which has captured the attention of most scholars and the general public. As a Mormon farmer in Scipio once told me after reading an article I'd written for the church publication *The Improvement Era,* "My family's records show that the efforts of my grandparents really was a part of a larger plan to settle the Saints according to divine inspiration."[36]

The Mormons were building not only to survive, but to beautify their communities in the eyes of God, and thus thrive as a select people. At Parowan on January 24, 1856, a church leader told villagers, "I feel anxious that you should begin to beautify Parowan, and make it like the garden of Eden." He urged them to plant "at least 2,000 fruit trees, and more if you can. . . . I would like to have you plant the public square to fruit trees, reserving a sufficient space for a public building in the center." He added, "I have seen your Tithing Office, and will say it is the best in the territory—the most substantial and well-finished." He speculated that this building was so sturdy that "[y]ou may fill it with grain without breaking it down." In words typical of the time, he urged the Saints in Parowan to "[c]ease to build temporary buildings, but [instead] put up those of a permanent kind."[37] On September 14 of that same year, Amasa Lyman urged Parowan's settlers to build brick homes, adding "I want you to build . . . as though you intended and expected to live here eternally. When you build your houses . . . build houses *to live in.*"[38]

Like almost everything else they built upon their arrival in the Great Basin, the Mormons' villages were a peculiar combination of pragmatic and spiritual forms. Their housing was solid and utilitarian, conveying a sense of permanence while revealing its New England and midwestern roots. Yet it attained a religious quality as the Saints carefully maintained it in the face of change. One thing that gives Mormon Country a different look than non-Mormon settlements is the architecture's conservatism: Mormons tended to build in styles they had known in the places they were driven from—upstate New York, Ohio, Illinois—while other westerners were more prone to accept newer trends in Victorian-era architecture. So associated with the Mormons did these houses become that they were branded "Nauvoo Style" in Utah and other Great Basin locales. Some Mormons even use the term "polygamy houses" to refer to homes that feature two front doors or two or more chimneys. In reality, these house styles were also found in the non-Mormon East and Midwest. Then, too, most polygamist Mormon men had the wisdom to house their wives in separate homes.

Mormon chapels are the crown jewels of villages like Parowan. They reflect an architectural sobriety that is perfectly in keeping with Mormon philosophy. Often appearing as subdued versions of New England "colonial" architecture, but almost always of brick construction, these chapels are the social and spiritual heart of the community. Mormon practicality is everywhere evident in these rambling church buildings, which often feature adjoining wings for social events. As might be expected, they are devoid of stained glass or religious statuary—they shun even the use of a cross on their steeples. Reflecting on the Saints' architectural conservatism half a century ago, Church President Stephen L. Richards explained: "We don't build elaborately . . . we don't build for show and ostentation, we build so that we may train ourselves in the truths that are everlasting and in the duties and obligations and opportunities that come to us in this glorious work."[39]

I appreciate the steeple's significance to a people who look skyward for inspiration. It is a conduit between heaven and earth, conveying the light of heaven into an uncertain world. A Mormon writer put it this way:

> The church spire catches the sun's last flame,
> A blaze of golden light;
> And holds the gleam on its tapering shaft
> A torch for the coming night![40]

Once again, I am reminded that one of religion's most important roles is to shine light into darkness.

Here in Parowan, I could see the chapel's steeple from almost anywhere in town if it weren't for the profusion of shade trees. This vegetation gives

Mormon towns their oasislike quality. Skillfully employing a mixture of native and imported trees, the Mormons created verdure where sagebrush and saltbrush once dominated. On a whirlwind trip through Mormon Country in the summer of 1938, the peripatetic American writer Thomas Wolfe opined that the "graceless" Mormon houses were hidden by "the merciful screenings of the dense and sudden trees." Wolfe found the Mormon landscape both depressing and exhilarating. In one memorable passage, he described "the windbreaks of the virgin poplars, the dense cool green of poplars in the hot bright light . . . hemmed by the desert peaks—the hackled ridges on both sides—denuded and half barren, curiously thrilling in their nakedness."[41]

I'm fascinated by yet another allusion to desert landscape as unclothed human body, but thinking more of trees when I recall Wallace Stegner's characterization of the Mormons' handiwork in building landscapes: "Wherever you go in the Mormon Country," he wrote, "you see the characteristic marks of Mormon settlement: the typical intensively-cultivated fields . . . the orchards . . . the irrigation ditches, the solid houses, the wide-streeted, sleepy towns." One thing impressed Stegner most of all: "Especially you see the characteristic trees, long lines of them along ditches, along streets, as boundaries between fields and farms. . . . These are the 'Mormon trees,' Lombardy poplars."[42] Native to northern Italy's Lombardy Plains, this poplar (fig. 8.6) is fast-growing but short-lived. Like all poplars, its leaves shimmer in the slightest breeze. You can see Lombardy poplars throughout the West, but somehow they seem perfectly suited to delineating the Mormons' irrigation ditches and property parcels. So captivated by these trees was Maureen Whipple that she choreographed them into a classic landscape description in her historical novel *This Is the Place.* Gazing upon Zion, Brigham Young sees "the trees neat as marching soldiers serried across the land—long lines of Lombardy poplars grouped like pointed spears, cottonwood branches delicate as cobwebs against a winter sky." These trees were part of "a landscape pattern as characteristic as a coat-of-arms."[43]

Sentiments like these prompted sociologist Thomas F. O'Dea to astutely note that the Mormons "feel the West to be their own peculiar homeland, prepared for them by the providential action of Almighty God, and its landscape is intimately associated with their self-consciousness and identified with their past."[44] But a lot has happened since O'Dea made those remarks about half a century ago. Here in Parowan, I sense that this landscape is inexorably vanishing. Some twenty-five years ago, I speculated on the irony

Fig. 8.6. Mormon Trees: Although other people also planted Lombardy poplars, they are so closely associated with the rural Latter-day Saints that they are called "Mormon trees" by many students of the Intermountain West. (Mendon, Utah; 1969 photograph by author)

of the Mormons' permitting their distinctive landscape to disappear, recalling that landscapes serve as a badge of identity and reminder of the Mormons' great past here. It occurred to me at the time, however, that the rural Mormon villages had little place in the scheme of modern Latter-day Saints' ideology. After all, the church long ago relinquished polygamy and the self-sufficient utopian socialism evident in these landscapes. Then, too, since well before the mid-twentieth century, the Mormons had made a point that "we are not peculiar or very different from other Americans," as a Mormon academician once told me in Provo. And yet Mormons can point to many symbols and traditions that make them unique. For example, the Temple is a favored icon on Mormon gravestones; the Salt Lake City temple is often seen, but so are others, such as Logan or Saint George. The temple's appearance on these stones signifies where an important event in a

Mormon's life, like a wedding, occurred. Here in this part of the Great Basin I sense the Mormons' incredibly close attachment to the landscapes of home. Some in the Mormon Church may find such sentiments parochial, for any good Saint will move in a heartbeat whenever called upon to do so by the Church. And they can make a strong point: Although headquartered in Utah, the Church has long set its sights on the entire world. Saving Utah's Mormon heritage, while noble to some Mormons, is not the main objective of a globally oriented church on the move.[45]

Recognizing that its traditional landscape is vanishing, Parowan now features a restored cabin and barn as an example of an early local farm. Throughout town, progress means change. Of the ten traits that identify Mormon towns—wide streets, roadside irrigation ditches, barns and granaries in town, domestic architecture, high percentage of brick homes, hay derricks, Mormon fences, unpainted farm buildings, LDS chapel, and an open landscape surrounding the town—Parowan still exhibited only five in the year 2000, compared with eight in 1969.[46] Although I cited the existence of five of these key elements as the break-off point distinguishing Mormon from non-Mormon towns in the 1970s, I now realize that every year brings places like Parowan closer to their Gentile counterparts. Every year piping replaces another open roadside irrigation ditch, another barn collapses, another Mormon fence falls. In a few towns, like Spring City, which is called "Utah's Williamsburg," preservation will help to retain some of this characteristically Mormon look somewhat longer. But, undeniably, Mormon towns in general are rapidly becoming less visually Mormon.

This attrition is probably natural, but it weighs on my mind as I leave Parowan on I-15. I remember when travelers used old Highway 91, which passed through the heart of each town along its path before being superseded by the interstate. I recall the stories old-timers like my friend Golden Oldroyd used to tell about outsiders visiting their "peculiar" communities. In one story, Mr. Oldroyd overhead a young man telephoning his dad in New York. The young man had left California the day before and was driving home when he stopped at Oldroyd's motel for the night. "Dad," he said, "you surely wouldn't like Utah, just one little town just like the next, set up by the Kingfish for each wife." Amused, Oldroyd realized that this was a reference to Brigham Young. "But, Dad," the young New Yorker then added, "you'd sure like Las Vegas!"

With those words still on my mind from thirty-plus years ago, I merge into traffic rolling south on I-15. Headed into a glorious summer sunset at about 8 P.M., I'm wondering about the works of man in the desert, specifically: When will the sun set on these Mormon villages? But then I feel the road rushing under my tires, feeling the rhythmic thumping of the expansion joints in this magnificent highway, and I get to thinking about very different works, asking myself a technical question: Just how long before I reach Las Vegas will I see its lights beckoning me like jewels in the desert night?

9

Pilgrimages to Babylon

It's nearly 10 P.M., and I'm still an hour out of Las Vegas when I become aware of the city's luminous presence. Even though I'm seventy miles north of the city, the glowing sky to the southwest reveals both its location and its sheer energy. At about 11 P.M., I reach the outskirts, stopping for the night at one of the casinos where I know I can get a reasonably priced room and a drink. The bar provides a great view of the goings-on in the casino, and I soon find myself entranced by what I see. The gambling floor is packed with brightly lighted slot machines, only a few of which are in use. The ceiling reminds me of the night sky, for it is pitch black, invisible except for a few incandescent lights that stare down from it like stars. Tonight, the place is rather quiet, and my attention is drawn to those few souls hunched over the slot machines. With an almost rhythmic regularity, their arms tug the levers that send the displays on the machines spinning and bells softly clanging.

Although I've never been here before, the casino seems strangely familiar. Where else have I seen people so intently focused, so fervently hoping, so mechanistically engaged in an activity, while bells ring and lights illuminate a darkened interior? And then it suddenly hits me: My God! The ambience here is surprisingly like the interior of a Catholic church, serene yet animated, with souls fervently seeking redemption, bells ringing, and candles flickering. Like a church, this casino is the site of incantation to higher powers; both the casino and the church are structural elements in humankind's enduring quest to affect, even ensure, outcomes. The slot machine players' rhythmic bobbing motions remind me of the concentrated fervor I've seen in genuflecting Catholics, bowing Muslims, and nodding Hasidic Orthodox Jews. These similarities prompt me to explore what at first seems like the antithesis of spirituality or religion—gambling—in my increasingly comprehensive spiritual geography of the Great Basin. It occurs to me that individual people have been taking big risks in this region to change their fate. In fact, the landscape of the Great Basin, or more accurately about one-half of it, is an ode to risk taking by successive groups of people, notably hard-rock miners and casino gamblers.

Let me begin by anticipating some readers' reactions to my hypothesis that gambling—or gaming as it is now fashionably called—has a spiritual dimension. After all, about the closest many people get to drawing comparisons between Las Vegas and religion, notably the Bible, are odd jokes like one in a revealing television show, an A&E special about musical performers there: "This is the land of money changers. They take your money, and they change it into theirs." But this is also the land where a musical performer sees a seven-color rainbow and impulsively decides to move here because this is no ordinary place with ordinary five-color rainbows. The place offered him, as he put it, "a sign."[1] If we can agree that *spirituality* taps an inherent power or quality that animates something outside of ourselves, and that *faith* is a belief in forces greater than those we personally control, then the church patron's praying and the gambler's wishing have something in common: they both relinquish personal control and call upon a force outside of themselves to grant a beneficial outcome. Those who consider these two enterprises separate need only remember their conflation in an enduring enterprise of the Catholic Church—Bingo!

Then, too, I recall that the Reverend Tommy Starks of Las Vegas faces plenty of spiritual challenges here. A recent Travel Channel special about Las Vegas observed that "Las Vegas hits the jackpot for saving souls . . . if the ministry is your game." According to Reverend Starks, he has encountered people at slot machines who call out, "Hey father, bless me . . . and my machine." And he does, fervently believing that "God would have to call me several times [for me] to leave Las Vegas because it is an exciting place to minister."[2]

The region's both embracing and disdaining gambling has deep historical roots. Although the "evil" of gambling as an institution has its origin in the Old World, we need to be not only careful in thinking of gambling as a "vice," but also cautious of thinking of it as an imported vice. When an increasingly larger number of Anglo-Americans arrived in the Great Basin around 1850, they often commented on the Indians' propensity to gamble. Although it might seem easy to conclude that the Natives had been corrupted by whites, gambling's roots are much deeper. As historian Ralph J. Roske has astutely observed, "Gambling in Nevada has not only a colorful history, but a colorful pre-history: the Anasazi and Paiutes engaged in rudimentary wagering before A.D. 1150."[3] In the nineteenth century, moralists were offended by the way the Paiute and Shoshone indulged in games of both chance and skill. Writing about the Utah Indians in 1859, Dr. Garland Hurt noted that "[t]heir females are . . . excessively addicted to gambling." "The mode of gambling with both sexes is quite similar," Hurt added, "a number of sticks being used in place of cards." As a measure of their addiction, Hurt reported that the Indians were "so infatuated with this arrangement that I have known parties of them to refrain from eating and sleeping for twenty-four hours at a time, and gamble with little intermission."[4] In Hurt's report I sense the Judeo-Christian (largely Protestant) concern that gambling affects one's ability to be productive and obedient. By the 1860s, a common theme emerged in the Great Basin—the tendency to gamble was cast in moral, even religious, terms, as evident in the strong moral indignation toward such flirtation with chance. As Christians, the newcomers looked askance at the Indians' seeming obsession with letting an unworked-for outcome (fate) dictate the future. Obsessed with faith, Christians generally counseled against the foolhardiness of games of both skill and chance. Undeterred, the Indians continued to play with objects that served much the same purpose as dice—or rosary beads (fig. 9.1).

The propensity to criticize Indians for gambling seems to be deeply rooted in Judeo-Christian culture, until I recall that *the Bible makes absolutely no reference to gambling* or anything like it, such as wagering or betting. Is the absence of gambling in the Bible an aberration or an oversight? Not if we realize that the Good Book's dialogue—whether it uses the word or

Fig. 9.1. Trusting in Fate: Paiute Indian cane dice from southern Utah (left) and stick dice from Pyramid Lake, Nevada (right): were painted red on their convex sides and used for games of chance—the earliest known version of gambling in the Great Basin. (From Stewart Culin's *Games of the North American Indians*, 1907; author's collection)

not—is largely about wagering, which is defined as to make a bet, or to risk or venture on a *final outcome.* Tellingly, the word wager—which we define today as something risked on an uncertain event—has an archaic root that is closer to the spiritual: an act of giving a pledge to take and abide by the result of some action. In this regard, then, the concepts of wage (as in salary) and wager (as in bet) are surprisingly connected. This is revealed by the Bible's few uses of the word wages—as in "And he that reapeth receiveth wages" (John 4:36) or, more to the point, "For the wages of sin is death" (Rom. 6:23). Wages are consequences of actions, or payment for actions. I suspect that the Bible's silence about gambling relates to the omnipresence of risk in those times: as in Ecclesiastes (9:11), "time and chance happeneth to them all"—chance in this case meaning fate. Churchgoers and gamblers share a common credo: By believing, they both try to change an uncertain outcome to one more positive. With characteristic wit and insight, Las Vegas poker player and entrepreneur extraordinaire Bob Stupac recently pointed out that "when Adam bit the apple, he was gambling on Eve."[5]

Nevada has been ambivalent about gambling for a long time. Gambling flourished on the mining and railroad frontier in the nineteenth century, then was outlawed, only to be legalized in 1931. As casinos became a fact of life in Nevada, most religious opposition softened. Jerome Blankenship, a Methodist minister who represented a sect opposed to gambling, ultimately—and correctly—concluded that there is "absolutely no prohibition" against gambling in the Bible. To the amazement of many, he even argued that "gambling helped foster religion, at least in Nevada." He proved it by the fact that "[o]ur congregation received a $2,000 gift from one of the casinos because they just liked us, I guess." According to Blankenship, the congregation "didn't do anything, didn't ask for it." The donation simply arrived in the mail with the notation "Merry Christmas 2000." He concluded: "I think by and large the casinos have been very generous to the community, not just the churches but the community interests at large."[6]

The kind of influence Blankenship refers to is apparent as I look over this thriving community of more than a million people. I drive downtown at 1 A.M., and the city is still ablaze with flashing incandescent and neon lights and pulsing with traffic, the Utah license plates outnumbered by California plates ten to one. This electrically charged landscape offers an incredible counterpoint to those upstanding Mormon towns huddling against the slopes of the Wasatch Mountains in Utah. It reminds me that, for more than a century, the Great Basin has been a battleground between two major forces in Western thought: On one side stands the Judeo-Christian tradition, more specifically Protestant religion, with its emphasis on the straight and narrow. Mormonism epitomizes these values and has made them characteristically American. The Mormon village landscape is their agrarian manifestation, and the Temple block in Salt Lake City the urban counterpart. On the other hand, the region's traditions of risk taking and quick gains loom as a polar opposite. This looseness is evident in the casinos that tempt the traveler and visitor with quick gain on almost every Nevada Main Street, and even out on the interstate; not to mention the sex ranches—"always open"—that lure travelers in the middle of the Nevada wilderness. Their urban counterpart is found in Las Vegas, the city that defined, or rather redefined, temptation. I am reminded of this moral/immoral split when I recall that during the same week in March of 2000, the news media reported that Utah appointed a pornography czar while hospital employees in Las Vegas were disciplined for gambling on which patients would die first.

In the 1999 film *Crazy in Alabama,* the main character, Lucille, is both unconventional and one step ahead of the law. The film is set in the 1960s, and Lucille has done an unthinkable but justifiable deed before heading west. Carrying her abusive husband's head in a hatbox, Lucille writes home to her nephew Pee Joe from Las Vegas, where she's stopped on her trip from Alabama to Hollywood. In that note she tells Pee Joe that "you won't believe what a wonderful time I'm having in Las Vegas. It's a beautiful place, let me tell you, a hundred thousand light bulbs in the middle of the desert." After this glowing description, Lucille confides in Pee Joe: "You know I'm the kind of girl who can resist anything but temptation. That's how I found myself in a casino." Lucille's letter goes on to reveal how she won a small fortune at her "favorite game," roulette. That fortune enables Lucille to pursue her dream of being a movie star.

Once again, Las Vegas appears as a beacon of opportunity in the desert. This theme weaves its way into many films about "Vegas," including *Anywhere But Here* (1999), in which a divorced mother balks at going to Las Vegas with a man she has recently met. Her daughter's advice is simple and to the point: "Go to Vegas, Mom; Take a chance." Naturally, the darker side of Las Vegas also informs our ambivalence about such risk taking. In *Leaving Las Vegas* (1996) the city becomes a magnet for a self-destructive man whose insatiable appetite for its risks and seductions is literally fatal.

In the morning, stretched out beneath a bright sky, Las Vegas possesses a slightly different ambience—a sprawling sunbelt city at the southeastern edge of the Great Basin, where streams and arroyos connect to the Colorado River system; yet its character is wedded to the rest of the region. Driving through downtown, I am ever aware that the city's morphology and imagery are made out of the same alluring glitter. Its stunning new casino resorts mock, or rather replicate, a wide range of attractions, including New York City and Paris. Yet, there is a classical, make that quasi-Oriental, quality to its most enduring attractions that make it Baghdad on the Strip. Caesar's Palace may have suggested decadence and opulence, but that was always framed in a Judeo-Christian context; the Luxor Pyramid somehow seems perfectly at home here—much more at home than a similar-appearing Pyramid in Memphis, Tennessee (that city's Egyptian namesake notwithstanding). Capturing attention as it was meant to do, the Luxor's stunning glass pyramid rises from the urbanized desert floor like an obsidian wedge, a reminder that the western imagination could not rest after simply naming Pyramid Lake in honor of the Egyptian Pyramid of Cheops: Here, in technology-driven Las Vegas, the architects envisioned and pulled off a coup, a replica that is simultaneously derivative and innovative. The Luxor is a perfect testimonial—a landmark to the roots of Western civilization. It joins the Mormon Temple in Salt Lake City as a counterpoint in the region's wonderfully complex spiritual geography. Built around a structural X for the unknown, even the name Luxor itself subliminally suggests the exotic Orientalism of its Egyptian sun-worshiping prototype and the luxury of excess.

Las Vegas is America's tribute to both the exotic and the erotic (I delight that only one letter differentiates these words); yet for all its gaudiness and hype, it reveals America's deep longing to resurrect some of the treasures of the pre-Christian world of the eastern Mediterranean, the birthplace equally of sun worship and Judeo-Christian thought. Although even the best histories of Las Vegas stress its social and technological history,[7] the city's spiritual history has yet to be told. I'm cognizant of this as I drive out of downtown, through some of the city's suburbs, past churches, mosques, synagogues, Mormon chapels. Unless you see this part of Las Vegas in broad daylight, it would be easy to forget that this city of about a million has one face that draws tourists and conventioneers from all over the country, but quite another face for the many citizens who are devout followers of traditional religion(s). The city has about 300 places of worship, including twenty-three Catholic churches, thirteen synagogues and temples, and ten Mormon chapels and stakes (at the local level, of members of the Church of Jesus Christ of Latter-day Saints are divided into "stakes" of, on the average, 4,000 to 5,000 members under stake presidents, and into "wards," each of a few hundred members, under a bishop).

But in the popular mind the Great Basin is home to two classic types of American communities—*covenanted* (with God) like those of the Latter-day

Saints, and *cumulative* (drawing people for monetary gain) like modern-day Las Vegas.[8] The former symbolize sobriety, the latter symbolize the destruction of the soul by vice. Gambling, alcohol, and sex tempt the sojourner here much as the unspeakable pleasures of the flesh symbolized Sodom and Gomorrah. Viewed moralistically, Las Vegas is the epitome of sin—"Sin City" has been one of its nicknames for decades. Nevada's de facto legalization of prostitution (the state permits counties to legalize or outlaw it) and liberal divorce laws simply add to the image of Nevadan cities and towns as sinful places where pleasure comes easy—but always at a price.

Of course, the perils of gambling (and the flesh) have tempted humankind since long before Bugsy Siegel and other shady entrepreneurs aggressively transformed Las Vegas into Sin City. Few people recall that Las Vegas was once a sleepy nineteenth-century Mormon community that had been put on the map in the early twentieth century by the Los Angeles, San Pedro & Salt Lake Railroad (today the Union Pacific). But it is the city's reputation as late-twentieth-century libidinous wonderland that makes it a target and a metaphor for excess. Recall the disapproval of early moralists to Paiute (and Shoshone) gambling, not to mention sermons against the pleasures of red light districts in Utah railroad towns (Corinne and Ogden, to name just two). So strong was the animosity between Mormons and Gentiles that the town founder of Corinne reportedly banned Mormons from owning land there. Then, too, the Great Basin's bawdy mining towns, from Eureka, Utah, to Eureka, Nevada, were early battlegrounds in the spiritual war still being fought here.

I'm addicted to films that take place in the Great Basin. In *Forbidden Highway* (2000), the main character, Elray Dayhart, finds himself Las Vegas-bound and rapidly getting in trouble. The film begins with the line, "Moments of truth; gambling's full of them, for every play leads to one decisive moment." Apprehended by a group of Las Vegas mob thugs, Elray finds himself staked out half naked under the burning desert sun. One of the thugs tells another that "we've got him staked out somewhere between hell and Las Vegas," a suggestion of the infernal nature of both the place and their sinister demeanor. Elray's narrated understatement, "I'm having a little trouble here: I need some divine intervention," reminds me that even reprobates can ask for spiritual help. That comes in the form of a deepening relationship with an otherwise wild woman who helps Elray gain control of his life. As Elray begins a grueling walk, he opines that there's "nothing like a stroll in the desert to give a man perspective." As might be expected, this film features a number of stereotypical characters, including the obligatory wise old Indian man. When Elray asks the Indian, "Isn't there some way you can tell by a sign in the sky if it's gonna rain?" the Indian answers, "I watch the Weather Channel." Their deepening but humorous discussion about signs leads to Elray's reasoning that he can interpret those signs himself. Later, when he comes literally and symbolically to a fork in the road, Elray realizes that "the choice was in my hands." He returns to the woman after the insight that "now we know lady luck to be whoever you want her to be." Elray concludes, "You chose your own luck. Instead of waiting for the signs, you make them up as you go." Through such reasoning, Elray empowers himself to regain control of his life.

The ultimate consequences of obsessions with wagering are portrayed in the edgy, brilliant 1999 film *American Perfekt.* In this tense drama, the desert of the southern Great Basin serves as a perfect setting for a chance encounter between a young woman traveling alone and a mysterious man who personifies the inveterate gambler. Their fates become inseparably intertwined as he bases each future action on the outcome of the toss of a coin. Continually posing two different courses of action (heads he/they will do something, tails he/they will do something else), the man abides by each flip of the coin. Yet it soon becomes apparent that the game is escalating toward disaster, another affirmation of the insanity of relying only on chance. *American Perfekt* reveals the ultimate consequences of binary, either/or thinking yet serves as a metaphor for the many ways, and times, we arbitrarily act as if we had only two alternatives (either/or, yes/no) instead of conceiving of many other solutions or scenarios that might be available.

The outcome of high-stakes gambling of another kind is evident when, a week later, I reach the mining town of Ophir, Utah. Nestled in the forbidding Oquirrh Mountains at the western edge of Mormon Country, about seventy miles west of Salt Lake City, Ophir epitomizes the opposite of the Latter-day Saints' agrarian villages. Now a collection of forlorn buildings (fig. 9.2), Ophir's landscape of visible ore dumps and dilapidated ore bins suggests grander days when it was an important mining town. The landscape of Ophir is similar to that of many mining towns in this region, so much so that anyone ought to be able to identify it as a mining town at first glance.[9] I'd normally study the town's landscape in some detail, but more philosophical thoughts engage me on this trip. I think a great deal about Ophir, not simply as place, but as a name and as an idea.

Ophir! The town's name has been on my mind ever since I can remember, for a line from the Bible suggests its riches and remoteness: "and they went to Ophir, and brought from there gold" (1 Kings 9:28). The name re-

Fig. 9.2. Where They Found Riches: Once the scene of frenetic activity, the biblically named mining town of Ophir, Utah, now rests peacefully in a canyon in the Oquirrh Mountains. (1988 photograph by author)

minds me of my first encounter with the Great Basin four decades ago. It was mining, in fact, that first brought me to the southern Great Basin in 1960. As a high school student in the Los Angeles area, I had made the acquaintance of a Mr. Woodyard, a newspaperman who'd heard about my interest in mineralogy from his daughter, who was a classmate of mine. Mr. Woodyard, to my delight, was a "weekend miner" who was "working some mining claims" in the Mojave Desert. Learning of my interest in geology, he asked if I would like to visit his mining claims. I eagerly accepted when he invited me and a friend to join him. In exchange for this firsthand look at the hard-rock geology and all the mineral specimens we desired, we'd also help Mr. Woodyard dig some shafts using hand tools. When he told us that we'd be going "to the desert" to visit his copper mine, I expected a landscape similar to the Sonoran Desert that I had experienced as a kid in Tucson. But somewhere in the vicinity of Barstow, I realized that this was a far drier and even more formidable place than the (relatively) lush Sonoran, which had huge saguaro cacti and palo verde trees. Here in the Mojave, only low bushes greeted our eyes. Arriving in town, we switched vehicles, leaving the car and jumping into an old army-surplus carryall that would take us to a number of claims "farther out in the desert."

Mr. Woodyard invited us to hop up into the back of the truck, which was open. Riding in the open bed of that dull green truck was an epiphany. We had an unobstructed view of the surrounding desert. The June sun pounded on our bare shoulders; heat waves danced off the desert, creating mirages that set the rocky metallic-hued hills to floating like islands. But two things—the dry lakebeds shimmering in the distance and the sparse vegetation—impressed me most. The northern Mojave Desert felt like the Sahara, and I pretended that it was. Mr. Woodyard seemed to have an uncanny knowledge of the countryside as he drove along the primitive roads. We wound our way across creosote-bush-covered alluvial fans and into hills of shattered rock that looked as if they were piled there just yesterday; the dry, furnacelike air flowed past; the sun shone so brightly we could barely look upward into the dark blue sky. Reassured by the familiar whining of the gears of the old military truck and the low rumble of its big, powerful in-line-six Dodge engine, we were overpowered by the vastness of the scenery. Finally the truck slowed to a crawl. There, up ahead, perched on the rocky hillside, was Mr. Woodyard's mining claim. It was like many I would come to experience in this region—a spot of hope marked by a cluster of old machinery, a small shed, and a small opening in the hillside. With the truck's motor racing, the transmission screaming in compound low, and the gears in the four-wheel-drive transfer case howling, we slowly climbed the last few hundred yards over an even steeper and rockier road.

I was unprepared for what we experienced next. Pulling the truck as close to the mine as he could, Mr. Woodyard shut off the motor. The sudden silence that engulfed us was startling; so overwhelming was it that my ears rang as I tried, in vain, to hear a sound. In Arizona in summer there would at least be *some* sound, perhaps a bird or the buzzing of an insect. Here the silence was deafening, but soon broken by the sound of Mr. Woodyard lifting some gear out of the truck—miner's tools that would enable us to pry secrets from the rocks. "Are you fellows going to help me, or fry like bacon up there?" he asked.

With pickaxes flailing, we hacked our way into the rocks amid stinging chips and flying sparks. After about thirty minutes, this hammering brought us into a vein of cinnamon-colored garnet crystals. Here, at the place where hot magma had encountered limestone perhaps several million years ago, was a classic contact metamorphic zone. The heat had further transformed the chemicals in the once-living seabed where the limestones had formed, turning the calcium and magnesium of shells and bones into honey-colored grossularite garnets. These garnet crystals were an "indicator" to Mr. Woodyard, who informed us that we now had a better likelihood of finding a "zone of enrichment" where metals had precipitated. Sure enough, the rock here was speckled with brassy-golden chalcopyrite and silver-colored cubic crystals of galena. Mr. Woodyard's usage of miners' terms—he noted that we had "gotten into the gossan cap" and were finding plenty of "skarn"—fascinated me. These words were mysterious, arcane, an argot of sorts that helped bond us into the mystical fraternity of miners. Those specks of chalcopyrite and galena were promising, but they had a deeply symbolic meaning: such metals were a sign of ore and historically were regarded with awe. I later learned that Spaniards characterized veins of precious ore as *criaderos,* or breeding places, deep in the womb of Mother Earth. The idea that minerals were bred in places like this, much like seeds, or fetuses, seemed somehow absurd and yet intriguing. I recalled a note from one of my mineralogy texts, that garnet is named for its similarity in appearance to the red color of pomegranate seeds. Mentioned in the Bible, the pomegranate's rich, transparent red fruit suggests mystery and fecundity. To me, the mineral garnet is a reaffirming manifestation of chemistry's order, nature's wisdom, and the Creator's magnificence. I loved the joy of understanding the earth—a feeling that returns whenever I am out in the field studying geology.

Forty years after my encounter with garnets at Mr. Woodyard's mine, the lessons still hold. In June of 2000, while driving in western Nevada, I noticed that the countryside had abruptly changed as magmatic rocks were replaced by limestone. Intrigued, I hung a U-turn and drove back to the point where these two rock units met. Scampering up the slope with my trusty rock pick in hand, I began cracking open the rocks at the contact zone; and there, as if on cue, lay a thin band of honey-colored garnet crystals that uplifted my spirits.

At Mr. Woodyard's mine, we worked most of the afternoon, each drinking several quarts of water. As we worked, we talked about mining and minerals. A history buff at heart, Mr. Woodyard related stories of the mines and mining towns in the area. Their names were magical. Some, like Paranagat and Ivanpah, I'd later learn, were Indian and reflected an interest in water rather than mineral wealth; others, like Calico and Rhyolite, were colorful and referred to the nature of the geology; still others, like Bodie and Pioche, were named after entrepreneurs or investors. These names were wonderful, but one name in particular—Ophir—stirred my imagination. Hearing Mr. Woodyard mention Ophir, I fancied that the Great Basin resembled, in some mysterious way, the mysterious land of Ophir in Arabia, which is mentioned about a dozen times in the Bible.

While driving back to Los Angeles later that day, we crossed the "old Mormon road" into Cajon Pass. The name Mormon itself sounded mysterious to me, and still does despite my close familiarity with these people and their religion. I learned that the Mormons generally shunned the mining of precious metals for a more stable agrarian lifestyle, one self-sufficient and insulated from the seductions of mining. This preference, I would later learn, helped distinguish the miners—largely regarded as sinners—from the Saints throughout the Intermountain West. The "sinners"/"saints" conflict has a long tradition in the Great Basin, and appears repeatedly in the folklore and literature. Like many travelers to the region in the mid-to-late 1880s, Phil Robinson realized that the Great Basin had both a Mormon presence or personality and another, less devout side. As he traveled westward by rail, Robinson contrasted Salt Lake City's character with that of other places, namely, Nevada's mining communities. Mormons, he wrote, "though 'Americans,' refuse to make haste to get rich; to dig out the gold and silver which they know abounds in their mountains."[10] With that distinction, Robinson identified one of the major philosophical splits in the Great Basin—the divide between those who would live on the land as farmers and those who would mine its wealth. That split helped account for what Robinson called "rich and ugly Nevada." As he viewed Nevada from a Central Pacific train, he described miles of sagebrush-covered wasteland, punctuated only here and there by patches of green. According to Robinson, "It is a far cry from the City of the Saints to the city of the Celestials [San Francisco], for Nevada stretches all its hideous length between them, and thus keeps apart the two American problems of the day—pigtails and polygamy."

The dyspeptic Robinson threw vitriolic prose at Nevada's forlorn scenery, but he was also put off by its increasingly ethnic population. Like many writers of the period, Robinson made no secret of his strong racial prejudices; he especially despised blacks and Chinese. His virulently anti-Chinese attitudes no doubt reflected not only his notions about their racial characteristics but his disdain for their non-Christian beliefs. Robinson encountered these "Celestials" in the mining camps of Nevada, including the booming Virginia City.[11] They could also be found working on the region's railroads.

In several fundamental aspects, the religion of these Chinese immigrants stood in stark contrast to Robinson's Judeo-Christian heritage. First, is *man's* (rather than God's) importance in the cosmic order. So important is mankind that people are part of the cosmic triad—matched from the beginning of creation with heaven and earth. This gives the religions of China a humanistic dimension, which is to say they seemed to some critics to have more of an "ethical" than a "religious" emphasis. As a unitary and unifying principle, *jen* stresses the benevolence of man. The individual can spiritually, and hence ethically, advance to noble character through cultivation and learning, while at the same time denouncing force. The religion places no emphasis on a judgmental God with strict moral codes and punishments. In the Chinese religion that Robinson abhorred, one's spiritual fulfillment occurs independently of "scripture." Then, too, I sense a source of conflict between Judeo-Christian thought and Chinese religions in Tai Chen's statement that life-reproducing life is *jen*. Because life involves desire, it is considered a normal part of human nature and is thus harmonious with the cosmic mind. To Robinson, the "heathen" concept that desire is not evil but compatible with goodness was yet another reason to denounce the "pigtailed celestials"–though he probably did so on largely racial grounds.

But it was Nevada's emphasis on wealth–specifically, quickly obtained mineral wealth–that put off Robinson. This comparison–hardworking agriculture versus strike-it-rich mining–helped set the scene for the Great Basin's classification of communities as either virtuous or easy. This distinction, too, can be traced to the Bible. In wording that reminds me of how isolated mining camps can be, the Book of Job observes that men "put an end to darkness, and search out to the farthest bound the ore in gloom and deep darkness." To do so, "they open shafts in a valley away from where men live; they are forgotten by travelers." In a remarkably revealing statement, Job adds: "Man puts his hand to the flinty rock, and overturns the mountains by the roots." The miner "cuts out channels in the rocks" and "binds up the streams so that they do not trickle."[12]

Ministers and miners in nineteenth-century Great Basin were very aware of these passages. So were journalists. When the isolated mining town of Treasure City, Nevada, experienced epidemics of smallpox and pneumonia in 1869, a correspondent there wondered "what in h—l will become of" the miners there? In response, an enthusiastic representative of equally isolated White Pine touted the high altitude, at which "[s]mallpox and pneumonia are mere bagatelles," and where "[s]ilver indications are the thing!" He further chided the weakhearted correspondent, adding: "If our friend . . . had ever opened a Bible he would have made the discovery that the 28th chapter of the Book of Job holds out hope for all who come to White Pine."[13]

But the Book of Job did more than justify miners' pursuing their craft in out-of-the-way places. As one of the most profound books in the Old Testament, Job reminds us that mining empowers (and is empowered by) the knowledge of the earth that the miner possesses: "the thing that is hid he brings forth to the light." Yet Job is careful to caution mankind that the miners' unearthing these previously unseen treasures should not be confused with bringing truly important things to light—that is, discovering wisdom and understanding. That requires a different path. When Job asks, "but where shall wisdom be found?" he quickly adds that "it cannot be gotten for gold, and silver cannot be weighed as its price." Indeed, "it cannot be valued in the gold of Ophir, in precious onyx or sapphire . . . nor can it be valued in pure gold." Job concludes that only fearing the Lord is wisdom, and departing from evil is understanding.[14] The Book of Psalms (119:127) is even more explicit: "Therefore I love thy commandments above gold, above fine gold."

Let us now return to Nevada—which, the moralistically high-minded Phil Robinson sniffed, "is abominably rich, I know." Disgusted by the Silver State's wealth, Robinson grumbled that "there is probably more filthy lucre in it per acre (in a crude state, of course) than in any other state in the Union, and more dollars piled up in those ghastly mountains than in any other range in America." When a fellow traveler remarked that "that hill over there is full of silver," Robinson sarcastically fired back, "Is it?" Robinson then characterized the hill as "the *brute*" (his emphasis), confessing, "I really couldn't help it," for the hill's "repulsive appearance was against it, and the idea of it being full of silver stirred my indignation." Robinson's reason? He compared these barren, mineralized hills with the wondrous fertility of pastoral regions elsewhere, including irrigated lands in Utah, which put to shame "ugly, wealthy Nevada." Indeed, Robinson was so totally enchanted by the agrarian beauty of California's golden hillsides and fertile farms on the west, and Utah's disciplined agrarian beauty on the east, that he summarized the region's geography as succinctly—and as harshly—as anyone ever has: Nevada, he wrote, "lies under the disadvantage of having on one side of it the finest portion of California, on the other the finest portion of Utah, and sandwiched between two such Beauties, such a Beast naturally looks its worst."[15] This juxtaposition endures. A recent anthology entitled *East of Eden, West of Zion* used a biblical metaphor to characterize Nevada's unique position.[16] Morally, too, Nevada is considered the land of Nod—the land east of Eden in the Book of Genesis, where Cain was banished by God after killing his brother (4:16).[17]

I suspect that Robinson inherited his distrust of mineralized desert places like Nevada from the Bible. Their "filthy lucre," won by luck and knowledge rather than the sustained, disciplined work required by agriculture, invited such invidious comparisons. I also suspect that Robinson despised the miner's signature on the land—overturned mountains and bound-up streams that everywhere characterize mining. Job's admonition is joined by numerous other references in the Bible that urge caution about pursuing and using precious metals like gold (after all, some idolatrous statues were of gold) and silver. Yet the Bible is almost obsessed with riches: Precious metals are mentioned frequently in it; gold more than 400 times and silver about 325 times.

On the other hand, references to mining in the Good Book may have motivated travelers in the region to think about the mineral wealth of deserts, more particularly desert mountains, as being much like the Ophir mentioned in the Bible. Although King Solomon observed that "gold is where you find it," or words to that effect, places like Ophir in Arabia were legendary. It is mentioned no fewer than a dozen times in five books of the Old Testament—including Job, Chronicles, Isaiah, Psalms, and 1 Kings 9:28, where Hiram and servants of Solomon "went to Ophir, and brought from there gold."

These biblical accounts were memorable enough to place Ophir on the map as a toponym for mining towns, mining claims, and geographic features in Utah and Nevada: Ophir Creek, Ophir Hill, Ophir Mill, Ophir Canyon. Whereas the mining town of Ophir, Utah, retains its name to this day, Ophir as a town name vanished in Nevada despite its early prevalence. The early name for the Virginia City area was Ophir; there was an Ophir along the Virginia & Truckee Railroad in Washoe County; and Ophir City (about forty-five miles south of Austin, Nevada) was laid out in 1863, but it, too, is today a ghost town.[18] Like much of Nevada's mining heritage, this biblical place name originated in California's gold rush country and migrated *eastward* across the Sierra Nevada with miners in search of riches.

It is tempting to join Phil Robinson in thinking that mining lured only the sinful, until we remember its broad appeal. Although the early Mormons generally shunned the search for precious metals, some devout and enterprising Saints like Henry William Bigler was a prospector in addition to pursuing other careers.[19] That not all Mormons were farmers is further borne out by the woman that historian Ferenc Morton Szasz describes as the "colorful . . . Eilley Orrum, a Scottish Mormon convert who rejected polygamy and moved on to Nevada," where "she allegedly used a crystal ball to locate silver and became known as the 'Queen of the Comstock Lode.'"[20]

The annals of western mining reveal some Mormon investment in gold and silver mines in the 1890s. And, of course, Mormons did not hesitate to mine coal and iron, which would help them build a self-sufficient empire. For the most part, however, they focused on farming. Those Mormons who ignored or defied Brigham Young's admonition to avoid precious-metals mining were, like William Godbe and his Godbeite followers, likely to be excommunicated by the church for their disobedience.

If the lure of precious metals was resisted by most Mormons, at least one other religious group took up the slack. In 1907, gold and silver mining attracted a sect called the "Lost Tribes of Israel" to the area around Goldfield, Nevada. The group had been founded in 1902 by D. K. Eubanks, and the *Bullfrog Miner* observed that this "religio-socialistic community" claimed to be "the only people on earth who accept a liberal interpretation of the Old and New Testament scriptures"—though one wonders if the newspaper writer really meant "liberal" or "literal." Picture if you can a group of "Israelites, as they style themselves," whose "members . . . wear flowing beards, long hair, after the manner of the Patriarchs of Old, are vegetarians and adhere strictly to the teachings of the Bible," joining fiercely independent, often profane prospectors in the Great Basin.[21]

The Book of Job's allusion to miners' bringing to light things once hidden in darkness suggests another often-overlooked aspect of mining. A quintessentially male occupation, mining has been equated with rape—the forcible penetration into Mother Earth, the despoliation of the landscape, the violent transformation of ore to metals that leaves waste, ruin, and smoke in its wake. But that Spanish word *criaderos* suggests that there is another symbolic aspect to mining. Some years ago, I discovered one of mining's most profound secrets while plumbing the historical literature. Miners unlock more than mineral riches as they unleash considerable force in excavating, concentrating, and smelting ores. They play roles that cross gender lines and border on alchemy. Consider this: the activities of miners involve profound transformations from unknown to known. By studying the language and folklore of mining, I came to see it not as rape, but as imitative, symbolic procreation: in a process that imitates conception, gestation, and birth, miners enter Mother Earth, locate her most hidden riches, transform those substances using heat, and through specific amounts of time in effect give birth to new materials.[22] Mining is typically man's work, and women are often denied access to mines for fear that they will bring bad luck. Then, too, in some societies, women are not permitted to be involved in smelting (especially when they are menstruating). It is tempting to think men's controlling reproduction is confined to the past, and acted out only symbolically in mining, but then I recall the contemporary abortion debates and realize that men still have a very powerful role in controlling the process.

There is something primal about mining communities. In frontier areas like the Great Basin, they are at first largely occupied by men; only later do women (and children) arrive as a mining district matures. Those early Great Basin mining towns were rich in symbolism, some of it thinly veiled. Although Christianity made its appearance early here (the oldest Catholic church in Utah is located in the mining town of Eureka), I noted a persistence of references to those gods and goddesses that predated Christianity. In May of 1867, Alex Wise of the Telegraph Saloon in the mining town of Dun Glen, Nevada, posted an advertisement for himself and his establishment. "It isn't every man who knows how to keep a saloon," Wise boasted, "but I think I have discovered the merits of the secret." As owner of one of Dun Glen's "temples of the gods," as he called it, Wise stated that he had "no superior in the proper delivery of fluviatic stimulants," and that he offered "to my particular friends the choicest selection of Wines, Liquors and Cigars, such as the gods, looking down from their etherial [sic] abodes must envy—and all for two bits a single chance!"[23] Wise's allusion to "the gods" is noteworthy, for it recalls an earlier time when Romans and Greeks believed in many deities—each associated with some particular aspect of nature.

There was also a ring of the hedonistic in Wise's advertisement, for he quoted, more or less perfectly, a passage familiar to many in the mid-nineteenth century:

> Man being reasonable, must get drunk;
> The best of life is but intoxication.
> Glory, the grape, love, gold—in these are sunk
> The hopes of all men and of every nation.

One wonders how many of Wise's would-be patrons knew the source of his call to abandon. Dionysian in its implication, this quotation from Lord Byron's *Don Juan* is at once whimsical—even satirical—and deeply nostalgic for a time when men supposedly communed openly with diverse gods and sought pleasures free from modern moral constraint.[24]

It would be easy to dismiss such poetic ramblings—and diligent newspaper advertisement—as misplaced references to the classical age, but I recollect how heavily nineteenth-century romanticism built upon the classical past. Wise's ad was printed at a time when the main streets of bustling commercial towns in the Great Basin were likely to feature Greek Revival facades, which carried two underlying messages: a growing belief in democratic principles and a lingering fascination with polytheism.

Far from Main Street (or red light districts), miners prospected the countryside. Like many others of their time, they had a fascination with classical antiquity. Names for landscape features of the Great Basin hint at this fascination with classical gods and goddesses. Diana's Punchbowl, a group of hot springs in a bowl-shaped valley in Nevada, was named after an ancient Roman deity associated with springs and brooks. Another ancient deity—Aurora, goddess of the dawn—is the namesake of a mining town named by J. M. Corey in the late 1860s. Male deities also found their place in toponyms of the Great Basin. When the U.S. Geological Survey team under the direction of J. H. Simpson encountered a spectacular gap or defile in the Egan Range in 1859, Simpson noted: "I call the place the Gate of Hercules, on account of its stupendous walls." Similarly, Hercules Creek, Nye County, Nevada, was named after "the most illustrious hero of Greek mythology."[25] This reference to more ancient religious traditions—the pagan—clings like a shadow to Judeo-Christian religious thought. These ancient gods had human forms and personalities, and one could appeal directly to them for favors—a situation that has rankled traditional monotheists since the time of Christ. Their presence is murky, yet they persist in a subterranean realm of the Western subconscious.

This conflict between the pagan—which was equated with the sensual and sinful—and the Judeo-Christian tradition—which equaled religious—played out in sometimes-humorous ways. On September 23, 1865, A. M. Sadorus advertised his beef "to the Miners in Arabia," Nevada: "Ho, Ye That Hunger After The Flesh . . . Of Fat Bullocks!" he proclaimed. "I have fitted up a Meat Market in Etna, where the public will at all times finds a display of fresh Fat Beef."[26] That hungering after flesh, of course, is a thinly veiled reference to the pleasures of the flesh, which is to say sex, which is frowned upon in several books of the New Testament. At about the same time, in the Trinity Mining District—whose "three-peaked mountain range"[27] conjures up the Father, Son, and Holy Ghost—the owner of the Trinity Market employed biblical analogies to entice customers: "No superannuated milk cows are brought to this shop to rest their weary limbs; no disabled work cattle come here to pull their last breath; here no veal is served up to a wicked world before its time. I kill the fatted calf and serve up the unctuous loins of round-bodied bullocks."[28] The tone of this advertisement is noteworthy—a sort of tongue-in-cheek admonition or injunction that places the butcher in the role of wisdom provider, even patriarch. And that town name Arabia in turn reminds me of the original location of

Ophir, a distant land whose religious tradition split off from the Judeo-Christian tradition, producing one of its most vigorous offshoots—Islam—about A.D. 600. After years of travel and study in the Great Basin, I've come to see spiritualism as having far deeper roots than narrowly conceived by people who arbitrarily divide the world into believers and nonbelievers, or saints and sinners.

With this expanded view of the potency of early beliefs, I decide to revisit a number of other haunts in the Great Basin with a goal of interpreting their place in a larger spiritual order. Heading west, I decide to press my search for new ways of interpreting spirituality. I'm apprehensive, for I'm about to peer into the gates of Hell, as it were. I'm bound for ground zero, Nevada's nuclear test site, to see what I can find.

Landscapes of Armageddon

Now, for the first time in human history there is no spot on earth where the innocent may find refuge.

—LEWIS MUMFORD, *Faith for Living*, 1941

As I spread a map of the United States before me, the Great Basin's geographical position seems secure, locked safely between imposing mountain borders that buffer it from geopolitical storms. But Lewis Mumford's woeful words are on my mind as I ponder the Great Basin's changing position in world affairs on a drive from Salt Lake City to western Nevada. Mumford's use of the word refuge reminds me of the Mormons' search for sanctuary in the Great Basin, but the state of modern world affairs—with its ever-present concern about religion-fueled terrorism—makes no place really safe. As a closer look at any modern map of the Great Basin also reveals, there is a strategic military presence here. Military bases and gunnery ranges occupy huge areas from Utah's Dugway Proving Ground to Nevada's legendary Nuclear Test Site (fig. 10.1).

A closer look at maps of the Great Basin in two different periods, say the early and late twentieth century, confirms that geography and history constantly intersect. They did so on the eve of the Second World War, when American sociologist-philosopher Lewis Mumford pondered the shrinking size of the world as fascist despots reigned. In despair, Mumford penned his lament as part of a 250-page book that he furiously wrote in less than three weeks.[1] Energized and yet depressed by the condition of the world, Mumford believed not only that civilization was threatened by fascism, but that a spiritual crisis now confronted humankind. The twentieth century had, in Mumford's words, "inherited a morality which it had never worked for." One major reason for this, he claimed, was that "[r]eligion ceased gradually to be a social force and became a private idiosyncrasy; or rather, where it was most active and positive as a social force it tied itself, not to the interests of the poor and lowly, but to the profits of those who governed them." As a disenchanted liberal, Mumford lamented the fact that "Christianity was not practical in this new society: so practice was only in the rare instance Christ-like." True, Mumford conceded, "[t]here was perhaps a closer unity between faith and act among the Jews and the Mohammedans" But, he hastened to conclude, "wherever modern industrial society was strongest, the hypocrisies and dissimulations of the pious expanded."[2]

Mumford recognized an age-old struggle between the forces of "good" and "evil"—forces that, more often than not, involve religion on at least one side, and often both sides. It is one of mankind's great spiritual ironies that religion can be both a creator and destroyer, and can breed both morality and hypocrisy. Ever the perfectionist, Mumford railed at Christianity's "hypocritical" role in world affairs. Although Mumford's blaming despotism on industrial capitalism may have been a bit simplistic, he was right on two counts. Modernity had created a spiritual crisis, and world war was inevitable. When the United States entered that war in December of 1941, it found itself unprepared to wage it on two fronts—Europe and the Pacific—without a massive arms buildup. That forging of swords involved herculean effort, and the Great Basin found itself center stage overnight. Within a short time, the map of the region was festooned with gunnery ranges and military airbases. The dry clear air of the Great Basin made it well suited for war games. The army airbase at Tonopah was a case in point: located in west-central Nevada, the site hummed as military exercises eclipsed the mining that had dominated the local economy and mindset since 1900.

Beginning with World War II training missions, the landscape of the Great Basin came under increasing attack as the military tested its prowess. In one of the classic conflicts of cultural values, distinctive topographic features that were important to the region's Native Americans now became targets for gunnery and bombing practice. For example, northeast of Fallon, Nevada, Job's Peak is the site of creation to the Cattail-eater Northern Paiute peoples; the peak represents the two parents present at creation. But it presented a tempting target and was disfigured by flyers using it for target practice in World War II.

Consider, too, the unique topographic feature named Lone Rock (*mos-ʌi'i*), which is located in a remote part of Carson Sink. Shaped like a wolf's head, it figures in Northern Paiute stories. According to anthropologist Kay Fowler, Wolf's Head is believed to represent the severed head of a wolf. As the Paiute story relates, the head was thrown there during a battle that raged in northern Dixie Valley. After putting the enemy to sleep, Coyote re-

Fig. 10.1. Courting the Apocalypse: Hawthorne Army Ammunition Depot bunkers, Nevada. The numerous military bases encountered throughout the Great Basin underscore the region's role as a major setting in the Cold War against "godless communism." (June 2000 photograph by author)

trieved the head of his older brother. Coyote revived his brother Wolf, and then celebrated victory. To the Paiute peoples, the wolf's head remained in the landscape as a reminder of the battle and resurrection. But look for the distinctive wolf's head today and you will not find it because this remarkable feature was bombed to near oblivion by aircraft using it for target practice.[3] Consider the immense gap in perceptions here: to one people, the landscape is both sacred and a documentary record of the region's history. To another, this feature has no value other than strategic: isolated and distinctively shaped, it made the perfect target. One group is indigenous, the other transient; yet the indigenous group must live with the enduring consequences of these actions. This is a classic example of "landscapes in collision." As ethnographer Don Hardesty puts it, "When people carrying different cultures come into contact . . . worlds collide."[4]

I see this practice bombing as a two-edged sword. Although it destroyed the land, it undeniably made Americans better warriors. The military will tell you that portions of this land were sacrificed to enable the United States to win that war, which did indeed humble "despotism" by crippling the Axis powers in both Europe and Japan. But even before the war's end, the changing map of the world suggested that two formidable superpowers—the United States of America and the Union of Soviet Socialist Republics—would emerge. The United States strongly opposed socialism's industrial stepchild—communism. But looking more carefully, I can see that what I once regarded as a political dispute between private-enterprise-fueled democracy and state-run totalitarian socialism was far deeper. The face-off between these political systems was in fact based on deep ideological and philosophical assumptions about religion.

If Mumford was depressed in 1941, he was likely overwhelmed by 1945. In its all-out effort to end the war and establish its supremacy as a military power, the United States had "let the genie out of the bottle." The nuclear bombs dropped on Hiroshima and Nagasaki in late summer 1945 not only ended the war, they helped begin the new slow-burning political conflict that would soon transform life and landscape in the Great Basin. That event was the Cold War, which lasted two generations (1945-1991).

As I drive across the Great Basin, I pass by huge areas that are off-limits. Signs stating "No Entry—Danger—Bombing Range" warn of dire consequences. Here in this open country that promises such freedom, I find this curtailment of my mobility stifling. The region's geography played a role in this estrangement. I find it fascinating that one of the factors contributing to the Great Basin's reputation as a "spiritual" place—desolation—is also the factor that gives it its reputation as a "wasteland" of both nature and mankind. As the United States military sought places to test its ever-growing arsenal of nuclear weapons, the Great Basin was again deemed a logical place: light population densities and favorable wind conditions helped reduce hazards to the more populated areas. For the first decade and a half of the Cold War, the United States continued its development of nuclear weapons in an effort to deter the Soviets' (and later China's) plans for world domination. The choice, as it was simplistically stated, was either acquiescence or victory.

If, in the twenty-first century, it is a bit difficult to comprehend how and why communism and capitalism faced each other so defiantly, then consider this. Both systems were as universalizing as the most fervent religions; each promised a panacea to all of humankind. Both spread their message through propaganda, and their ultimate goal was conversion. In other words, I now see both systems as closer to proselytizing religions than I was ever able to acknowledge.

Communism was often portrayed as "dull" and "gray," but it excited passions. In her 1977 book describing the complexity of individual communists, and their dedication to the cause, historian Vivian Gornick begins: "Before I knew that I was Jewish or a girl I knew that I was a member of the working class." Gornick notes that her family's working-class background exposed her to communist rhetoric that "dissolved the numbness and transformed the pain back into a moving, stirring, agitating element." She describes her father counseling visitors who no longer claimed external nationhood: "The only nationhood to which they had attained was the nationhood inside their minds: the nationhood of the international working class. And, indeed, a nation it was—complete with a sense of family, culture, history, religion, social mores, political institution." I find the word religion in Gornick's sentence understandable when I realize how wholeheartedly many *believed* in the value of communism as that which could lift the human spirit above selfishness. Karl Marx, in other words, positioned himself as a prophet who preached one of Christ's messages about selflessness and sharing. Despite her early passions for communism, however, Gornick came to realize, with considerable sadness, that "this dream—this passion, this hook on the soul" was destined to fail.[5] I like Gornick's use of the word soul, for it reveals a fervent faith in communism's ability to ennoble the spirit. It was this very passion—communism's religiouslike zeal—that so disturbed the American right during this period.

That may explain Senator Joseph McCarthy's ability to manipulate Congress and badger citizens in his crusade to identify communists. When people claimed that the McCarthy hearings were like the "inquisition" or a "witch hunt," they were closer to the truth than they realized. These hearings had both an underlying religious tone and an aura of religious intolerance: Like the Inquisition, they forced people to prove they were *not* infidels or were *not* possessed. In other words, the accused were guilty until proving themselves innocent. At its most repressive, religion has used this reasoning. McCarthy thus found himself in the time-honored role of ordained inquisitors like Tomás de Torquemada (of the Spanish Inquisition) and Cotton Mather (grand inquisitor of the Salem witch trials). Proving that a person was a communist equaled exposing an atheist. This effectively turned communists into infidels who sided with the dark, powerful forces of the anti-Christ. If that has a ring of the Book of Revelation, that is not coincidental. The Cold War played out as a drama set in the last days before the Apocalypse.

Throughout the 1950s, communism was roundly attacked as "godless" by both secular and religious leaders in the United States. J. Edgar Hoover wrote *Masters of Deceit* in 1958 as "an attempt to explain communism— what it is, how it works, what it aims are, and, most important of all, what we need to know to combat it."[6] This best-selling book went through several printings. So concerned were civic and business leaders about communism that *Masters of Deceit* was given to every member of my graduating class at California's West Covina High School in June of 1961! I recently picked up a copy in a used-book store in Salt Lake City and read it, or rather reread it, with morbid fascination. Few documents better capture the spirit of those troubled times, and I now see Hoover's words as one of the strongest religious manifestos I've ever encountered.

With Hoover's book on the passenger's seat next to me, I drive through the Great Basin aware of its profound impact. In order to set the scene, Hoover observed that Karl Marx "had become an atheist and called for war against religion, a war that was to become a cornerstone of communist philosophy."[7] In citing evidence of "*Communist opposition to religion,*" Hoover claimed that "member after member has related . . . the Party's claims that God doesn't exist and that religion is a myth." These claims, the troubled Hoover believed, "have raised doubts" in the hearts and minds of the young. Hoover noted that Marxist doctrine, according to "one former member, 'purports to reduce man's problems and destiny to an economic formula.'" Hoover claimed that this former member broke from communism because "'I want my children to approach their world and the history behind it, with . . . curiosity and objectivity. . . . I don't want them to feel that the questions are answered, that this or that little system is the slide rule for answering all their questions.'"[8] Hoover, in other words, had used the testimony of a convert who now saw the evil of his former ways.

During the height of the Cold War, I saw a billboard in Utah. Under the words "Get U.S. out of the UN" was a statement about how godless and un-American allegedly United Nations–condoned "socialism and communism" were. Hoover devoted an entire chapter to "Communism: A False Religion." In it, he claimed that Americans faced "a communist mentality representing a systematic, purposive, and conscious attempt to destroy western civilization, to roll history back to the age of barbaric cruelty and despotism, all in the name of 'progress.'" These words nearly freeze me in my tracks for they are so much like Samuel Bowles's statements about Indians a century ago. In a telling comment, Hoover then observed: "In our tolerance for religious freedom, the separation of church and state, we sometimes lose sight of the historical fact; western civilization has deep religious roots. Our schools, courts, legislative bodies, social agencies, philanthropic organizations, as well as our churches are witness to the fundamental fact that life has a significance that we ourselves do not create."[9]

Hoover's emphasis on religion underpinned beliefs about the failings of communism. Not to be misunderstood or ignored, he continued: "The presence of communism in the world and in our own country is a kind of stern reality which should make each of us explore our own faith as deeply as we can and then speak up for its relationship to our 'American way.'"[10] That sentence reminds me of the song popular around the time of the Cuban missile crisis of 1962. A young man sings about the reasons he is willing to serve in the military: "I go for God, country, and my baby." God was a significant element in the rhetoric of the times, yet I've looked in vain for a serious historical study of the Cold War in relation to religion. Some of my historian colleagues think Hoover had ghostwriters help him write about religion, but I suspect that he sincerely felt the message. Hoover was explicit about his values, and supposedly the values of all patriotic Americans, when he declared that the "very essence of our faith in democracy and our fellow man is rooted in a belief in a Supreme Being." To prove this point, Hoover listed "six aspects to our democratic faith"—including "belief in the dignity and worth of the individual," "belief that life has a meaning which transcends any man-made system," and "belief in stewardship, a feeling that a great heritage is our sacred trust for the generations yet to come."[11]

As director of the Federal Bureau of Investigation, Hoover used his pulpit to provide evidence using communists' own words. In restating his disdain for communism, Hoover cited Karl Marx's belief that "religion is 'the opium [sic] of the people.'" He could not resist using William Foster's statement that "God will be banished from the laboratories as well as from the schools" and Lenin's assertion that religion "is a kind of spiritual intoxicant, in which the slaves of capital drown their humanity, and blunt their desire for a decent human existence.'"[12]

In concluding his exposé, Hoover revealed an interesting paradox. "Hatred of all gods was Karl Marx's credo," he stated, and "communists have always made it clear that communism is the mortal enemy of Christianity, Judaism, Mohammedanism, and any other religion that believes in a Supreme Being." But, and this was crucial, Hoover noted that "communism is, in effect, a secular religion with its own roster of gods, its own Messianic zeal, and its own fanatical devotees who are willing to accept any personal sacrifice that furthers their cause."[13] Whether Hoover was right or wrong in his indictment of communism is less relevant than my point in citing his rhetoric: the Cold War was as much a *religious* war as it was a prolonged political or tactical engagement. It is no surprise that the words "under God" were added to the Pledge of Allegiance during the Cold War.

Hoover's zeal was unbounded in its reference to religion. He did not hesitate to "expose" the communists' tactical use of religious icons to further their cause—for example, a "deceptive" Communist Party cartoon that equated Jesus Christ ("Wanted for Sedition, Criminal Anarchy, Vagrancy, and Conspiring to Overthrow the Established Government") with communists facing "political jailings in the United States today." But, Hoover asserted, "the real nature of communism" is that it "is today desperately working to mold atheistic materialism as a weapon of revolution, a revolution which, if it is to succeed, must first sap religion's spiritual strength and then destroy it." In Hoover's words, "the utter elimination of all religion (called 'bourgeois remnants') from the heart, mind, and soul of man, and the total victory of atheistic communism" called for decisive action. "To meet this challenge," he claimed, "no hesitant, indifferent, half-apologetic acts on our own part can suffice. . . . if we are to remain free." Hoover concluded that we must "defend" as well as "nourish" religion—"the source of strength for our land."[14]

I've always been fascinated by such vitriolic prose, and it didn't end with Hoover's bestseller. The concern about communism continued during the 1960s, prompting John A. Stormer to write the provocative *None Dare Call It Treason* just in time for Barry Goldwater's 1964 presidential candidacy. Stormer, a Baptist minister, had an instant hit; his book ultimately sold seven million copies. So enduring was its theme of communist expansion that Stormer wrote a sequel in 1989. In *None Dare Call It Treason . . . 25 Years Later,* Stormer asserted that since the publication of his original book, many of his "warnings, ignored by many, have proven true. The proof? Twenty additional countries have gone into the Marxist camp since 1964." Tellingly, Stormer began his new book with a quote from Jeremiah 13:23: "Can the Ethiopian change his skin, or the leopard his spots? Then may ye also do good, that are accustomed to do evil."[15] The association of evil and communism rang clear in Ronald Reagan's characterizing the Soviet Union as an "evil empire" that had to be stopped. Tellingly, President Reagan used the term *Armageddon* on occasion to suggest the type of all-out battle that might be involved in stopping communism. As it turned out, the end came far more peacefully. The timing of Stormer's second book coincided with the collapse of the Soviet Union, which brought an end to the Cold War in 1991. Although the Cold War ended without the two protagonists ever going head to head, its legacy was palpable in the form of military engagements like Korea and Vietnam, and near catastrophes like the Cuban missile crisis.

The religiously toned works of Hoover and Stormer will haunt the Great Basin for thousands of years into the future. If the landscape of the Great Basin was said by some to be "desolate" before the Cold War, they had meant it in the traditional dictionary sense—devoid of inhabitants and visitors. During the Cold War, however, the region came to signify *desolate* as verb transitive; to "desolate" a place meant to lay waste to it. Whereas desolation had always connoted loneliness, even sadness, to that one could now add palpable devastation and ruin. By the early 1950s, military testing of aboveground thermonuclear explosions shook the landscape of the Great Basin to its core.

As a child of the Cold War, I've long associated the Great Basin with spectacular nuclear explosions that secretly thrilled me as much as they were supposed to terrify the communists (fig. 10.2). There was something strangely appealing about such hot, bright, fast, complete—make that perfect—destruction. Among the ironies that abound in religious history, consider the concept of *holocaust*. Originating from the Greek *holo* (whole, or total, as in holistic medicine) and *kaust* (burnt, as in to cauterize), the first definition of this word means a sacrifice consumed by fire. Both acts of burning sacrifice described in the Old Testament and the consumption by fire of living persons in modern Hindu culture (as a wife perishing on her husband's funeral pyre) are examples of how people conceptualize God's powerful demands. The second definition refers to thorough destruction, especially of loss of life—such as a nuclear holocaust. Whether an act of nature or of God, the effect is the virtual annihilation of, say, a city or a group of people. The third definition refers to the systematic mass slaughter of European civilians, and especially Jews by the Nazis, during the Second World War. Thus it is that holocaust has two principal elements: the one(s) sacrificed and the one(s) who demand(s) the sacrifice. The excessiveness of such sacrifices ensures a historic outcome for both: by cruel irony, the perpetrators are immortalized along with the victims.

In the early 1950s, the term holocaust was widely associated with nuclear warfare. The phrase "letting the genie out of the bottle" both suggests the terrible magic of nuclear energy and implies a profound difference between nuclear and other types of warfare. But there are similarities: World War II taught military strategists that incendiary warfare yielded highly "effective" results, like the devastation wrought on Dresden. However, consider the incendiary effects of a nuclear bomb. To anything at or near ground zero, the distinction between nuclear and incendiary is completely academic: the nuclear explosion vaporizes everything. But far beyond this

Fig. 10.2. Terrible Swift Sword: Detonated at the Nevada Test Site, nuclear bombs like "HARRY" (May 19, 1953) were publicized as a major deterrent to communism and symbolized America's divine right to the ultimate weapon. (Courtesy U.S. Atomic Energy Commission)

zone, the intense heat accomplishes the same feat as an incendiary blast—complete incineration. On one test range in Nevada, a replica of a suburban housing tract was constructed so that the effect of an atomic bomb on our communities could be determined. Its almost instant destruction confirmed the power of our nuclear arsenal, but also underscored our vulnerability. A telling 1950 cartoon, "Back Where We Started" by Jimmy Costello, reminded Americans that there were few places to hide (fig. 10.3). Costello's use of a cave as the ultimate fallout shelter is both brilliant and evocative. In addition to suggesting a high level of unpreparedness, it also contains two subliminal messages; that nuclear war would not only reduce us to a more primitive (cave-dwelling) state culturally and economically, but that it would be so traumatic psychologically that we would indeed go "back where we started"–that is, retreat into the security of the womb (note the figure's fetal position) for protection.

But for all its terrors, nuclear warfare had a strange appeal. Many Nevadans and Utahans describe their fascination with the nuclear tests in the early 1950s. Ranchers would awaken their families in the predawn to witness tests from what seemed to be a safe distance: twenty, thirty, forty,

Fig. 10.3. Back to the Womb: The popular 1950 Costello cartoon "Back Where We Started" uses a cave to emphasize the ultimate consequences of nuclear warfare. (Reproduced from the now-defunct *Knickerbocker News;* author's collection)

even fifty miles away. Regardless of their distance from the blast, one thing is forever burned into the psyches of those observers—the intensity of the *flash*. As one put it, the blast instantly turned night into day. Those viewers were somehow privileged yet cursed. Being present was not only like being a witness to mass destruction, but also like being present at creation: In the midst of creation, God said, "Let there be light." I find it telling that some people describe nuclear explosions in the Great Basin in terms of the sun rising twice on the same day.

Like the miners in the Book of Job, those who wield such knowledge-based power are faced with a dilemma. They freed the ore from darkness and brought it to the light. Yet, as Job notes, this light is really not the light of wisdom. Similarly, with the discovery of nuclear energy, one can look directly into the face of God, by which I mean the only power that can readily transform matter into energy and energy into matter everywhere simultaneously. Although people may question the wisdom of getting in on this act, it is clear that humankind's opening Pandora's box came with awesome responsibilities and consequences. Those nuclear tests in the Great Basin proved that creation and destruction go hand in hand. As I traverse the nuclear landscapes of Nevada, I am reminded of the geological consequences of such blasts, which are both topographical and petrological. A nuclear detonation can create a crater as material is violently displaced; it also creates new geological materials as the high temperature actually fuses rock into glass. In the Great Basin, mankind must be added as the creator of igneous rocks—a direct legacy of the Cold War.

Although the development of the atomic bomb began on the eve of World War II and played out early in New Mexico, its consequences for the Great Basin throughout during the Cold War were profound. Nuclear testing affected the Great Basin in ways that affected no other American region. Here the development of nuclear energy was presented as a two-edged sword. Nuclear tests in the desert were conducted for two reasons—to develop more effective weapons of mass destruction and to harness the power of the atom for peaceful purposes.

Destruction was uppermost in the minds of nuclear advocates. Armageddon beckoned with its temptation of an easy apocalyptic demise that would first flash with the purest of light and then leave the purest of destruction. The Judeo-Christian heritage is filled with accounts of a wrathful god who will someday punish evildoers and nonbelievers. According to the Book of Revelation, which is written in the form of prophesies, seven angels will visit the earth pouring out the wrath of god. At Armageddon the angels will be assembled. As the narrator relates his chilling vision, the seventh angel "poured his bowl into the air, and a great voice came out of the temple, from the throne saying, 'It is done!'" This defining event is followed by "flashes of lightning, loud noises, peals of thunder and a great earthquake such as had never been since men were on the earth." So great was the destruction that Babylon was completely destroyed and "every island fled away, and no mountains were to be found" (Rev. 16:16-21).

Lest we forget, the reason for these pyrotechnical and seismic effects was religious retribution, the ultimate punishment for the failure to heed God's word. Only the faithful can escape this destruction, and the wicked will perish. These verses can be read as metaphorical or allegorical, but many believe them to be literally true. Thus we come to an interesting point in the spiritual geography of the Great Basin. If these words are true, doesn't that mean that these events will someday actually occur? And if we recognize the unfaithful infidel in those leaders who embody evil (as in the Soviet Union's being called the "evil empire" by Ronald Reagan), then do we not have a *responsibility* to use everything in our power—acting with God on our side—to stop this evil power (i.e., the spread of communism) through the use of any weapons at our disposal? Senator Barry Goldwater of Arizona thought so. As the Republican presidential candidate in 1964, he urged deployment of nuclear weapons in Vietnam. The image of Goldwater as prophet was unmistakable. With jaw thrust forward and those clear blue eyes afire, he advocated the unthinkable: nuclear war to achieve offensive ends. From the perspective of the early twenty-first century, this sounds like so much fiction, but it is a matter of record. As a Strategic Air Command officer, Goldwater would throw down the nuclear gauntlet to stop communism in its tracks. Wielding this terrible swift sword had the ring of both religious fervor and political suicide, which it in fact was. The religious right, reborn during this period, supported Goldwater without hesitation. Almost viscerally connected to Goldwater's statements was the familiar image of a nuclear bomb exploding. In fact, Lyndon Johnson's campaign used it to suggest that Goldwater was both an extremist and a madman. Although Johnson beat Goldwater by a landslide, Johnson nevertheless succumbed to escalating use of force—albeit incendiary, not nuclear—to try to stop communism in Vietnam.

Here in western Nevada, I ponder the consequences of early Cold War nuclear testing. I envision a group of observers waiting to witness such a test. Among the most spectacular events imaginable, the above-ground detonation of a nuclear bomb fused itself into the optic nerves of America. These explosions and their aftermath helped perpetuate the image of nuclear desolation and came to be conflated with the desolate landscape of the Great Basin. In addition to the bright flash invariably reported by observers, consider the following: within hundredths of a millionth of a second, a tremendous amount of energy is released—so much so that the temperature can reach 100 million degrees—several times hotter than the sun. The power of the explosion is equally awesome, with the temperature so high that radiant energy exceeds the frequency of visible light by thousands of times. The release of radiant energy at these frequencies is so intense that it does not travel through the air but rather is absorbed *within* it, creating a superheated sphere called—with startling simplicity and honesty—a fireball. This fireball, which begins expanding at several million miles per hour, radiates outward as it releases withering heat and blinding light. Although we commonly think that radiation is a nuclear bomb's most lethal element, the incendiary effect kills most people initially. Nuclear bombs create firestorms that rival Armageddon. But the destruction does not end here. Moving outward ahead of the fireball is a shockwave that can level structures for miles around.

Given the dynamics of the fireball and attendant shockwave, many nuclear bombs are designed to detonate about two miles (11,000 feet) above the surface of the earth for maximum destructive effect. The resulting reaction is catastrophic. Upon reaching the ground, the fireball vaporizes both the soil and the target. Once consumed, these materials now rush aloft in a huge, dirty, mushroom-shaped cloud—propelled there by the heat of the rising fireball. The winds inside this rising "chimney" can reach 500 to 600 miles per hour, and they are capable of lifting boulders weighing a ton or more. When people speak of the brilliant flash of such a nuclear blast, we can objectify their awe. At a distance of 2 ½ miles from the center of the blast, the fireball may radiate more than 1,000 times the heat and light of the noonday sun in the Nevada desert.[16]

Add to this massive destruction two additional factors—direct nuclear radiation and nuclear fallout—and a nuclear blast's impact becomes regional and ultimately global in impact. Radioactive emissions from a nuclear explosion occur in the form of gamma rays and neutrons. Those people nearest the blast, say within five miles, may succumb within days. Those farther away may suffer long-term. Fallout occurs as the waste and debris from the bomb, mixed with other radioactive materials from the fireball, settle as a cloud of radioactive dust. Although the wind currents in the Great Basin carried the fallout over lightly populated areas, many residents of Denver and even midwestern cities claim that they have suffered ill effects. The eastern Great Basin's smaller communities—not to mention the Salt Lake City-Provo area—have reportedly reaped the whirlwind from such tests, as higher cancer rates were reported in some locations. One anecdote is often told: At the height of nuclear testing in the mid-1950s, the cast of *Ghengis Khan* was filming in the desert of western Utah, where they reportedly paused on occasion to observe the spectacular nuclear blasts. As this story goes, they paid dearly for this privilege: The film's cast and crew suffered high rates of cancer and many died prematurely—at least that is the apocryphal story. There is a hint of irony here as the film used Utah's austere landscape to portray portions of Mongolia (note again the orientalizing of the Great Basin), where China would later conduct nuclear tests.

Whatever the real or imagined health consequences of such nuclear testing, the Great Basin had more than its share. From 1950 to the early 1960s, it served as the scene of many nuclear detonations, all in the interest of assuring military preparedness in the Cold War. That, however, was only one part of the nuclear age here. The other focused on using nuclear explosives for peaceful purposes, especially massive excavation projects such as tunnels, canals, and underground mining. These tests represented the sunnier side of Dwight D. Eisenhower's Janus-faced nuclear coin. Developed under the rubric "Atoms for Peace" or, even more evocative of the Bible, the *Plowshare Program,* these tests involved underground nuclear explosions. The reason was spectacularly simple: Underground detonation would not only reduce atmospheric pollution, it would serve as a proving ground to determine nuclear power's effectiveness in earthmoving.

Among the more spectacular of these subterranean detonations was the one that created Sedan Crater in Nevada (fig. 10.4). This 1962 blast was conducted in a valley to determine how well material could be "excavated" by the bomb. It resulted in a 320-foot-deep crater about a quarter mile in diameter. Although the blast itself was not visible because the device was exploded about 600 feet underground, the resultant ominously rising "earth bubble" was. It burst to the surface, sending a cloud of debris skyward. In the process, the explosion had removed about 6.5 million cubic yards of material. Despite the real promise of nuclear devices as the ultimate earthmovers, however, such testing effectively ended in 1963 as the International Nuclear Limited Test Ban Treaty went into effect.[17]

As the development of international treaties suggests, many people seriously questioned how effective—and how sane—the idea of nuclear defense really was. Then, too, widespread criticism of all-out efforts to eradicate communism began to mount in the 1960s. Keeping pace with the political reform—and perhaps even feeding it—were popular films and songs. Of the former, *Dr. Strangelove* was the most potent and enduring. It portrayed the fear of communism as paranoia deeply rooted in the sexual

Fig. 10.4. Landscape of Armageddon: At the Nevada Test Site, underground nuclear testing left spectacular topographic features, such as the Sedan Crater, which vaguely resemble the Great Basin's volcanic craters (see Fig. 4-1). (Courtesy U.S. Atomic Energy Commission)

subconscious and nurtured by a combination of religious righteousness and moral indignation about protecting "our" way of life. Those attitudes were also severely criticized in popular songs like "Eve of Destruction" (1965), which not only proclaimed that we were on the brink of bilateral nuclear annihilation, but that American religious hypocrisy was bound up in the ideological battle. This song also contained a reference to the perils of nuclear warfare, warning that if someone pushed the button, there would be no running away. The song concluded that there would be no one to save, for the entire world would become a grave.[18] This is the stuff of 1960s protest and it resulted in civil disobedience at the gates of, and within, Nevada's nuclear testing grounds.

Ultimately, the Cold War played out in three ways in the Great Basin: First, it created a defense industry that thrived every time the stakes were

raised. The result was a landscape bristling with military bases and sequestered into huge bombing ranges, many pockmarked with craters from
both regular ordnance and nuclear weapons. Second, it helped call popular
or public attention to the area as a place *set aside* from the rest of America.
In other words, the image of the region as one of desolation was exacerbated by its marginalization as a sacrifice zone. I can now see those nuclear landscapes in clearer light: sacrifice, in the biblical sense, is an appropriate term. As fueled by an underlying religious zeal, the devastation
wrought by nuclear weapons was proof of our devotion to our beliefs.
Third, the nuclear age helped galvanize Native spirituality here, sometimes in unexpected ways.

Western Shoshone spiritual leader Corbin Harney notes that "[t]here are
a lot of things going on, like at the Nevada Test Site—when they set off a
bomb a thousand feet within the Mother Earth." Harney contends that "our
water table is getting mixed up with all this uranium and radioactive stuff
that they are blasting down there," a point vehemently denied by officials.
Harney's response is that "our government doesn't tell us the truth about
it, and they try to keep us distracted by telling us it's not dangerous, it's
just a test." He further contends that these tests have led to the deaths of
"our people [who] are dying throughout the country by the thousands"—as
in Utah, where "a lot of people have died and are still dying today on account of the uranium." Harney concludes that "we have to get together to
overcome this and say NO to that uranium," for "[a]s the Indian people said
a long time ago, 'if you don't take care of what you have now, you're not going to have anything.'"[19]

Harney's thoughts are on my mind as I near the formidable Nevada Test
Site, which a guidebook describes as a 1,350-square-mile (860,000-acre)
"multi-use, open-air laboratory" where nuclear weapons were tested for the
first third of the Cold War (1951–1962). Beginning with a one-kiloton bomb
dropped on Frenchman Flat in 1951, ninety-nine more atmospheric tests
were conducted until the Limited Test Ban in 1962. But far more explosions occurred underground than above: 828 nuclear charges were "detonated beneath the landscape," many in the vicinity of Yucca Flat, Rainier
Mesa, and Pahute Mesa. But the literature also presents a bright side, if
one can call it that: Of the entire test site, "[o]nly 110 [square] miles . . . has
been *consumed* by the nuclear testing program, and only 4.6 square miles
of the surface is contaminated with gamma radiation"—leaving an area
about the size of Rhode Island for research, environmental remediation,
and tourism. Although the writer of a guide to the Nevada Test Site admits
that the "irony of a guide to a place that can't be visited is sublime," he also

suggests that things are changing. Tourist interest in the site is growing rapidly. As proof positive that the Cold War's end brought change, and perhaps even nostalgia, consider this additional irony: Until recently classified as "secret," several of the more significant features here are now on, or are being considered for listing on, the National Register of Historic Places. These include "the photogenic debris at Frenchman Flat" and "Sedan Crater, the site of the second Plowshare test."[20] In this nuclear test site I see the evidence of two impulses—exploration and vindication. Here we experimented with the innermost secrets of creation (and destruction), and here we now commemorate our victory in the modern-day crusades. By humbling the infidels who dared to threaten our beliefs in the Cold War, we emerge triumphant.

Things are quiet around the test site today, but I recall the times when the area reverberated with nuclear blasts. The first bombs in Nevada— RANGER (winter 1951) and BUSTER-JANGLE (fall 1951)—were detonated about 1,000 feet above the ground. However, by the fall of 1957, when SMOKY was detonated, the explosions occurred closer to ground level. As related in Carole Gallagher's *American Ground Zero,* a witness recounted that "when the bomb [SMOKY] went off the light was like a thousand suns and the sound like a million cannons." The witness described what happened next: "Then we saw this tidal wave of dirt and dust and sagebrush and rattlesnakes and wires coming after us. It could have been any damn thing out there, but it was coming and [the sergeant] hollered 'Hit It!'" Upon hearing this command, "[w]e went down like damn bowling pins." The crouching and prostrate group then experienced a terrible wind that, "blowing at 150 miles per hour, peppered the hell out of us and everything went flying. There was nothing to hold on to." Looking up into the rising mushroom cloud, the stem of which "was really, really dirty for some reason, long like a stovepipe and deep purple in the center," this observer remembered that it was both "scary" and "awesome standing there looking up and seeing how high that thing was going."[21] Health physicist William J. Brady recently recalled the seemingly unpredictable nature of these blasts. Their "dust clouds—not the mushroom clouds of the initial explosion but the dust clouds that were thrown up and resuspended by the impact of the blast on the desert floor"—were to some extent related to the topography of the test sites. The "uneven terrain," as Brady observed, caused radioactive dust clouds to envelop observers at Yucca Flat and radioactive particulate matter to be dispersed throughout portions of the Great Basin.[22] But if the citizens and elected officials in nearby Las Vegas worried about nuclear explosions, they left little record of their concern. Quite the opposite: The record shows that they generally supported the nearby nuclear testing and many watched the detonations with rapt fascination. An Atomic Energy Commission official helped calm any concerns about potential radiation and accidental explosions—concerns that might adversely affect tourism—by reassuring residents that the mountains "would 'shield' Las Vegas from any danger."[23]

Nuclear energy is so reminiscent of both the power of creation and the ability of God to destroy that it is cast in religious terms. The writer Walter Miller used biblical language in criticizing those who wield and support nuclear energy. In his Cold War-era novel *A Canticle for Leibowitz,* "one of the Magi was like unto Judas Iscariot, and his testimony was crafty, and having betrayed his brothers, he lied to all the people, advising them not to fear the demon Fallout."[24] So potent was nuclear energy, and so religious the apocalyptic message that it suggested, that biblical terminology was also called upon to characterize its peacetime use—as in the injunction to turn swords into plowshares. The name "Project Plowshare" was coined in the mid-1950s for a program advocating the peaceful use of nuclear energy. Appropriately enough for a program that had a subliminally biblical connection, its first proposal was named Project Chariot. The 1962 explosion at the Sedan test site in Nevada was, according to one interpreter, "probably the high point of the Plowshare excavation program," adding that the crater itself "sits as a testament to the brief glory of Plowshare."[25]

Constantly embroiled in protests, Project Plowshare's ambitious testing program never really materialized. Plans included detonations at other locations in the Great Basin, such as Pahute Mesa in the Nevada Test Site and at Nellis Air Force Base, adjacent to the test site. By 1969, the American public was becoming disenchanted with nuclear energy because of probable health risks as well as nuclear energy's association with military excess. As the historian of science David Kirsch noted, "Plowshare ended with a whimper, rather than a bang."[26]

More recently, a proposed nuclear waste site at Yucca Mountain has elicited a strong response nationally and locally. To dramatize the dilemma, Frank Bergon wrote the novel *The Temptations of St. Ed and Brother S,* which he also excerpted in a provocative essay, "Demons, Monks, and Nuke Waste." *The Temptations of St. Ed and Brother S* is a modern allegory about two contemporary monks who, "like us, grope for a vision commensurate with the gargantuan promises and fears of our nuclear age." Set in the Great Basin, Bergon's eerie tale deals with what he calls "a people caught in a conflict between spiritual energy and nuclear energy." To convey his message, Bergon uses religious symbolism and religious characters caught in a modern spiritual drama involving the landscape. Bergon characterizes Trappist monk Edward St. John Arrizabalaga as "abbot of a remote desert hermitage that is now threatened by the installation of a high-level nuclear waste dump" in a place fictionally named Shoshone Mountain. As depicted in the novel, this mountain, which "hovered in the distance, a barren, flat-topped, bluish ridge in the white desert. . . . looked almost peaceful." However, Bergon reveals that Shoshone Mountain "had been pierced, trussed, tunneled, and disemboweled." Its "belly . . . would become the repository of plutonium too dangerously explosive for nuclear weapons and too radioactive to stay in power plants." This scheme, St. Ed notes, was "an idea so wildly cancerous by now that it had consumed its human hosts, a faith in unseen priests in white lab coats behind the walls of research facilities. . . . That was the religion of the times he could not abide."[27]

I note with considerable interest three elements that are embedded in Bergon's novel, for they pertain directly to the spiritual geography of the Great Basin. First, the landscape itself is *alive.* Shoshone Mountain is described as a "beast" which is "not dead" at all but has "shifted in surprising ways" as "water bled through [its] fissures." One scientist skeptical of the planned disposal of nuclear waste in this mountain describes it using metaphors: "My opinion about Shoshone Mountain," he testifies, "is that it's in the nature of the beast to go whacko."[28] This living quality of the mountain is animism, in which things normally considered inanimate by science are living and may even have spirits or souls. Shoshone Mountain is an appropriate name for this geographic feature: historically, these indigenous Great Basin people believe mountains to be alive.

The second issue in Bergon's novel involves that perennial component of religion, chronology. At the Shoshone Mountain repository, not "just ten thousand years, but millions of years would pass while radioactive waste remained hazardous." St. Ed notes that a "thousand years in the desert affected the land no more than a minute." As he ponders the antiquity of the mountain, he increasingly feels "the past surrounding him," and he comprehends: "Ten thousand years. A million years. A billion years. In the dark rocks around him, atoms were still popping from the time of the earth's creation."[29] Here Bergon conflates scientific and religious concepts of time.

The third major issue in Bergon's novel is *faith.* Those who believed nuclear energy was safe felt that they would "in the future . . . have all the energy we need without any of the waste." Although they did not yet have evidence to support this claim, they believed it anyway. As St. Ed notes, "I'd call it faith." Bergon put it this way in describing his novel: "*We live by faith.* We all believe in something." People on both sides of the nuclear is-sue had faith in something. With the first law of thermodynamics in mind, Bergon speculated about what he called "the Great Religion Principle." In Bergon's words, "While forms of religion constantly change in society, the amount of religion remains relatively constant."[30] This revelation helps Bergon reconcile the clash in values between the two opposing forces—pronuclear and prospiritual—in his novel.

Building on several great traditions of faith in this region, namely, Na-tive American, Christian, and scientific, Bergon's novel concludes with an apocalyptic—or rather atomic—revelation. Brother S realizes that "[a]ll the bodily atoms of the first desert monk, St. Anthony, still existed. . . . so that some of those atoms certainly existed within each living human being" and within everyone. That also "meant that the atoms of Lao-tzo were also within him, the atoms of Buddha, . . . and the atoms of Jesus." Bergon con-nects spirituality to the atom, which was the true miracle despite—perhaps because of—its consisting mostly of empty space. Bergon's revelation is that both the universe and the divine heart pulse simultaneously, and he leaves us with the book's concluding lines, "O Radiant Energy! O Radiant Love!"[31]

Like Bergon's, my beliefs about the Great Basin revolve around the po-tency of physics, which is to say science, and the ethereal, or rather spiri-tual. The landscape's very form is constantly changing under the cataclys-mic forces of tectonics and subaerial erosion; but human kind also plays a major role in shaping it, even to the point of making it uninhabitable. About twenty-five years ago, I flew over the Great Basin on a United Air-lines night flight from Chicago to San Francisco. The lights of communi-ties densely filling the Midwest gave way to the scattered lights of the min-ing camps and tourist towns of the Rockies. But over the Great Basin, bathed in eerie pale moonlight, huge stretches of open space stood blank. With a drink in my hand as Wagner's Götterdämmerung played over the headset, I pondered the immensity that seemed absolutely oceanic. My God, I thought, whether mankind is really alone in the universe or not, places like the Great Basin give us a glimpse of both infinity and eternity here on earth.

Into Sacred Spaces

We have forgotten who we are....
We have alienated ourselves from the
unfolding of the cosmos.
—UN Environmental Sabbath Program

These words are fresh on my mind as I pull into Battle Mountain, Nevada, in late May of 2000. For the last two hundred miles, I've rolled along the enigmatic Humboldt River, which twists and turns like a green satin ribbon that someone casually dropped across the sagebrush-covered landscape of central Nevada. This time of year the desert is beginning to heat up, but there is still a hint of winter in the air as a stiff northwest wind blows, keeping the temperature in the sixties. Although the sun climbs high in the sky, the mountains are still covered with snow above about 7,500 feet. I'm thinking about a sentence in a book entitled *Earth Prayers from Around the World*: "In every religion we find the need to consecrate our participation in the natural world."[1]

It's just before noon and I've got a 1:30 meeting with Bernice Lalo of the Battle Mountain Shoshone; that gives me a couple of hours to grab lunch and explore the town and its surroundings. I'm especially interested in the name Battle Mountain, which resonates with conflict. At the local museum, I learn that it derives from a skirmish between Shoshone Indians and whites—either migrating settlers or a road-building party—traveling through the area in 1857.[2] Symbolically, perhaps, the name "Battle" is plastered all over the map hereabouts, as in the town of Battle Mountain itself. Huddled along the railroad and interstate, lying in the shadow of the Battle Mountain Range, which looks like piles of sagebrush-covered coffee grounds, this town once served as a connection to the outside world for the nearby Battle Mountain Mining District, which boomed about a century ago.

Mining is still an important activity hereabouts, and that suggests an enduring conflict that I am here to discuss with Ms. Lalo. I will ask her how the Shoshone peoples are faring in their ongoing battle to preserve their land—all of which is deemed sacred—in the face of mining and other interests. For their part, the mining companies claim a right to mineralized lands under the Mining Act of 1872. On the phone, Ms. Lalo told me her office is in the Shoshone band's small enclave at the edge of Battle Mountain. Following her directions I spot a local landmark, the Smoke Shop, where tobacco is sold and considerable revenue generated for the Shoshone. Turning left near the shop, I drive into a cluster of neat homes sheltered under shade trees. The sequestered setting reminds me that this Shoshone band village is a refuge from the rapid economic development that is transforming the landscapes here. Just north of Battle Mountain, mining is turning the hills inside out, and Bernice Lalo is in charge of ensuring that it does not permanently destroy her peoples' ancestral lands. After Ms. Lalo welcomes me, I provide her a copy of my book *Hard Places* as a gift to the band's library. I do so in hopes that, as the tribal coordinator of environmental affairs, she may find its references to mining landscapes of interest. I confess and apologize that it neglected Native American views toward mining. That's why I'm here, I admit, to learn, remembering Claus Biegert's proposal that a "board of listeners" be established to listen, rather than lecture, to Native peoples. As Biegert puts it, "Tribal peoples possess the knowledge of the past that could help heal and restore the earth. . . . By resisting the repeated incursions of industrial society into their lands, their cultures and their religions, they have heroically preserved a worldview, which carries the concept of sacred earth. . . . It's time we listened."[3]

Bernice Lalo's eyes are illuminated and her manner serene but determined. Interviewing her, I quickly realize that the standard question-and-answer format will not work here. Instead I simply listen as she reveals her place in a drama that has been unfolding for about 150 years. The drama has several themes and subthemes. It is between Indian and non-Indian, between private property and public space, between technology and spiritualism. As environmental coordinator, Ms. Lalo must balance the Battle Mountain band's need for economic livelihood, including job creation, with the need for preservation of the environment. There is an irony here, for like those who have earned their living as environmental planners, her work is assisted by federal funds yet her strongest concern is the well-being of her people and the long-term health of the region in which they live.

With the scene set, Ms. Lalo tells me a story that begins at the time of initial contact. It is a story forged in conflict, for she describes the inherent difference in the way non-Indians and Shoshone view the land. To those who arrived as settlers or miners in the 1800s, the land was considered impoverished. But that depended on one's beliefs. The Shoshone knew the land intimately and harvested its bounty carefully; every plant and animal had a place in their livelihood. By contrast, the early miners and ranchers believed in short-term gain based on aggressive exploitation. The economic interests of the newcomers, rather than Indian interests, were supported by the federal government—which, Lalo claims, reneged on the 1863 Treaty of Ruby Valley. This issue—whether the Shoshone own some 24 million acres of land or it was illegally taken in 1872 by the federal government—remains a battleground into the twenty-first century.[4]

I find the date 1872 ironic and crucial. In that year, the federal laws that favored private mining interests on public lands were cast in stone. With virtually no significant changes, these permissive laws remain in effect to this day. The Shoshone's battle has been a long one, but not without hope. Although the U.S. Indian Claims Commission announced in 1979 that it had awarded $26,145,189 to the Western Shoshone Nation as reimbursement for their land, the Shoshone have refused to accept the money. Their reasoning: you can't pay us for something we never agreed to sell you in the first place. The Shoshones' refusal to accept the payment gives some credence to characterizations of the situation as "The Theft of Nevada" from the Indians. Looking around Lalo's neat office, I see files that go back half a century, to the Cold War: The Shoshone's legal action had begun in 1951, when the numerous Shoshone bands contended that they "had lost not only their treaty lands, but also their aboriginal land extending into Death Valley, California."[5]

The moral of Bernice Lalo's story is fraught with irony. Upon arriving here, the whites not only found the land "impoverished"—they rapidly degraded the land so that Indian subsistence became impossible. Lalo's claim is substantiated by the historic record, which documents aggressive cutting down of pine trees for mining interests (charcoal for smelting and wood for mine props), as well as ranching that overgrazed much of the region. She is quick to point out, however, that the actions of the mining industry resulted in degradation on the one hand and economic opportunity on the other. A number of the Battle Mountain band's members in fact work in the mines. Like those miners, I know the importance of keeping a family fed and clothed, and the fraternity that having a trade nurtures. I know, too, that not all Native American people agree with the strong antimining and antiprogress philosophy that one encounters in parts of this region. But, like Lalo, I am ambivalent about the power of mining to both create and destroy.

Mention "power" in relation to "place" in the Great Basin and someone is likely to bring up the name Corbin Harney. We've encountered him before, but let's look a bit more closely at this man who, Lalo says, helps the Shoshone people comprehend more than the present. A Western Shoshone Indian in his sixties, Harney has attained the revered status of an elder. His close association with efforts to protect his people's ancestral lands from desecration makes him an elder statesman of sorts, even though his arguments are not embraced by all. He is, however, one of a growing number of Indians who now openly talk about the close spiritual connection between place and Indian culture. Harney reckons that he has "been a spiritual person since the day I was born, I guess." He adds, "I got my power from my people. I get it off the canyon wall, or wherever I'm at. Things sing to me, and that's how I pick it up."[6]

All of the lands formerly and presently occupied by Shoshone are sacred to Harney, but one place—Rock Creek Canyon in north-central Nevada (fig. 11.1)—generates very strong feelings. As Harney puts it, "Sometimes we have feelings about what's out there. Some of us have a good, strong feeling from this canyon; you can pick up songs, visions, and medicine from here." Called *Bah-tza-gohn-bah* ("otter water"), Rock Creek Canyon has been used by the Shoshone for thousands of years as a sacred burial ground. In this regard, it joins many other places in Nevada—Ione, Midas, Kern Creek, and another near Austin—that have the power to heal. Rock Creek Canyon is located in the Sheep Creek Mountain Range; as Harney describes it, Rock Creek flows "through a small, ancient canyon and is fed by natural springs oozing out of the earth in the middle of the desert."[7]

Standing at the canyon's entrance is a topographic feature called Eagle Rock. It is appropriately named, for it not only looks like the profile of an eagle's head (fig. 11.2), it is associated with the spiritual power of that impressive bird: according to Harney, "This eagle head rock here works with a spirit, the spirit of an eagle works in this place"—which is to say, gifted medicine people possessing good visions "would pray for somebody" who is ill, and "put them up on that rock in order for them to gain strength." Here, then, "the spirit takes over with its healing power to heal you from your sickness, from all kinds of sickness."[8]

The entire Rock Creek Canyon became the focus of a controversy pitting the Shoshone against Lander County officials. According to Harney, these officials "have proposed building a multi-use recreational reservoir/dam that would bulldoze Eagle Rock, flood the canyon, and violate ancestral

Fig. 11.1. Sacred Places: Responding to a request by a representative of the Battle Mountain Shoshone band, the author opted to sketch, rather than photograph, Rock Creek Canyon in north-central Nevada. This site contains many elements—a freely flowing watercourse, heart-shaped pond, and evocatively shaped rock formations—that are considered sacred by the Shoshone Indians.

burial grounds." Harney has some very pointed words for those who would desecrate this site—words that summarize several centuries of conflict between Indian and non-Indians: "All they actually wanted to do was to take the whole place away from the Indian people. That's the only logic I can see. So like I always say, they're taking a little bite at a time, and now it seems like they're going after the sacred spots, as a way to weaken our people. They know we become weakened without our spirituality."[9]

The proposal to build this dam appears to be the catalyst that galvanized resistance locally just as resistance to dams is growing throughout the West. More and more non-Indians are rethinking the validity of damming the region's watercourses, and this opposition represents a sea change in attitude. After all, dams permitted the development of much of the area, enabling the desert to blossom like the rose. Yet these same dams disrupted the region's ecology. Some Indians put it this way: All water may seem to be life giving, but the method by which it has been obtained, and is used, results in its deterioration and the deterioration of the region. Harney says that the water itself is "not clean" because it is being desecrated by chemicals and siltation. His "Prayer to Water" urges "Be pure and clean, so that when we use you, you keep us healthy, and so you can continue to be clean for us and all living things." Almost incomprehensible to whites is the idea that "this water has a spirit. It's got a life like we do, the same thing."[10] At this point, it is wise to recall that there is no separation between animate and inanimate in Native religions. Everything has a soul.

Concern about mining and opposition to dams are only two of the issues affecting the Native's spiritual geography. One other land use—nuclear testing and nuclear waste dumping—is polarizing the Great Basin's residents. According to Corbin Harney, nuclear energy is "Our One Big Enemy." As Western Shoshone Bill Rosse Sr. puts it, "We've created a monster, with no means of destroying it or neutralizing its effects, and we have no place to plant it."[11] I see the nuclear landscape as central to the region's spiritual geography. Its roots are deep-seated in our belief in aggressive applied

Fig. 11.2. Spirit and Site: Rather than reproduce a photograph which might reveal its location, the author sketched this view of Eagle Rock in north-central Nevada. Named for its similarity in appearance to an eagle's head, this site is sacred because, according to Shoshone spiritual leader Corbin Harney, "the spirit of an eagle works in this place."

science and religion. I think it ironic that our newest "star wars" defense system (2001) is an attempt to protect us from the nuclear missiles that two types of powers—evil rogue governments and evil religious fanatics (including the very people we originally helped arm against the Soviet Union during the Cold War)—might now fling at us.[12]

But the word evil here comes back to haunt proponents of nuclear test sites and waste dumps in the Great Basin. Like many Shoshone, Bill Rosse believes that the United States has never honored the Ruby Mountain Treaty of 1863 and is "doing all this damage" without "a permit from the Shoshone Nation. . . . They never had permission, and we feel it's the wrong thing what they're doing out there." "It doesn't," Rosse concludes, "go according to our beliefs and our religion."[13] In a sense, this dilemma is spiritual indeed. Although some may question the Native Americans' rights here, those Native claims are strong enough to engage serious legal discussion and action.

Upon leaving Bernice Lalo's office, I suspect that the issue of claims by both the Indians and the United States to the landscape of the Great Basin is misunderstood as simply Native versus white, mythical versus logical, oral versus legal. Back on the interstate headed east, I see that this issue has both *spiritual* and cultural roots: I reflect on the Native claim that we cannot own the land but are simply users of it—users with a responsibility to ensure that it remains for future generations. This area is called *Newe Sogobia*—a sacred portion of Mother Earth—by the Native Americans. A Western Shoshone educator put it this way: "The redmen are the last people on earth who speak on behalf of all living things. The bear, the deer, the sagebrush have no one else to speak for them. The animals and plants were put here by the Great Spirit before he put the humans here."[14] Bill Rosse further observes that "in my understanding from working with Corbin [Harney], our Native peoples' religion is like the Old Testament. The Natives don't understand Jesus Christ's coming, but they do know there was a Creator who created all of this, and they give thanks for that."[15] I like Rosse's attempt to conflate Native and Old Testament ideology, but need to remind readers that there are some structural differences between these two traditions' spiritualities. Although the Judeo-Christian tradition is also based on the belief that a supreme being created everything before man, it has another component, the belief that mankind had dominion over those creatures.

Rolling along the Humboldt Valley's sweeping landscapes after leaving Battle Mountain, I stop to hike into some intriguing, basalt-covered hills. Here, in the heart of the Great Basin, I am reminded of an epiphany experienced by Jerry Mander. As the "Ralph Nader of advertising" and Senior Fellow at the Public Media Center in San Francisco (the country's only non-profit advertising agency), Mander confesses that he, like most people, once thought of the desert along I-80 in Nevada as only "hour after hour of dull, brown wasteland from Reno to Elko." But Mander's perception changed: "Then once in 1978 I hiked off the highway into that desert world of juniper and sagebrush flats and strange, bare, folded mountains." Mander was surprised to find that "the light is alive there" and "the moods and colors change dramatically from hour to hour. Soon . . . the power of the land begins to dominate urbanite preconceptions." After this experience, Mander was able to agree with a Shoshone woman who told him, "All of this land, everything in it, is medicine."[16]

This conversion, based in part on topophilia—sudden encounter with the landscape—can happen to unsuspecting travelers in the Great Basin. The region has attracted converts who seek in its openness a kind of spiritual communion with nature. That conversion, not coincidentally, is based in part on an appreciation of Native American sentiments and beliefs. As Mander puts it, the "roots of the current New Age Indian revival lie in the hippie period of the 1960s, and in early drug explorations." Its practitioners are generally "non-acquisitive, spiritually oriented, non-hierarchical, tribal, [and] communal." Yet this fascination is often predicated on a lop-sided interpretation of Native American culture. As Mander further notes, "We have managed to isolate one or two aspects of Indian life—the spiritual aspect and sometimes the art—and to separate these from the rest of the Indian experience"—a classically exploitative, appropriative "lifting" of others' cultures to suit our needs.[17]

According to the recent literature on the subject, "Native people understood that they had to live within the balance" of the cosmos. More to the point, "When you are no longer part of it, the world goes out of balance." I think of Shoshone prophecy that the earth will tip, and that only those who have such grounded beliefs will survive—by holding onto the sagebrush. Here I sense that indigenous thinking, like any philosophy that integrates spiritual and ideological values, is right on target in warning about ecological imbalances. Who can dispute the truism that "[w]hen the life of the intellect and the life of the spirit grow apart, terrible things become possible."[18] Yet it is too easy to think that Native peoples are "centered" and the rest of humanity hopelessly lost.

In fact, Native American culture is not monolithic; different Indian peoples held, and still hold, widely differing beliefs. And even *within* any one tribe, wide differences of opinion exist. That is true even among the

Battle Mountain band of Shoshone, for example, where some members strongly oppose mining while others implicitly support it by working for mining companies. Then, too, the volatile issues of nuclear waste disposal reminds me of how divided Native peoples in this region can be. Some, like Corbin Harney, are vocal in their opposition, but not all Shoshone side with him. A recent decision by the Skull Valley Goshute Indians just across the state line in Utah's West Desert underscores the diversity of Native Americans' attitudes on this issue. The Skull Valley Goshutes recently startled their fellow Utahans, and Utah governor Mike Leavitt, by supporting a plan to store nuclear waste on their 8,000-acre reservation for forty years. The Goshutes' stand may seem incomprehensible to outsiders, and the governor himself vowed to fight their decision. However, a majority of the tribe's members contend that they have a sovereignty over such issues and can negotiate the contract directly with the federal government. The stakes are not only political: The contract would mean substantial financial benefit for the 124-member Goshute tribe.[19]

Native American culture is rife with strong tensions, not the least of which involve assimilation (i.e., emergence and acceptance into white mainstream society) versus traditionalism (the maintaining of prewhite traditions, beliefs, lifestyles). The dilemma resonates on many levels. However, the need to provide for one's family, which may mean taking a job with a mining company, working on a ranch, or even being on the payroll of a nuclear waste disposal company, is very powerful. Like those miners mentioned in the Book of Job, Native American miners bring to light things hidden in darkness. But the wise among them know that this light should not be confused with the real light—the truth, and that truth leads back to faith and spirituality—a spirituality that, for an Indian, may stress the sacredness of all things, even rocks, just as truth for a Christian means the truth of Jesus' words and the enduring quality of God as the "rock of ages."

There is a fascinating connection—perhaps conflation—between Native Americans' beliefs and the pre-Christian beliefs of the British Isles: "The core beliefs of Celtic tradition are based upon animistic understanding. The other-worlds interpenetrate mortal realms in all departments of life: spirits, creatures, faeries, ancestors and deities associate regularly with human; omens of the elements of plants, animals and people predetermine outcomes."[20] If this seems familiar, it should, for portions of it could fit seamlessly into descriptions of both Native spirituality and New Age spirituality. New Agers owe a lot not only to Native American, Celtic, and other spiritualities, however, but also to the Judeo-Christian tradition. That even old-style, hard-line Christians could be awed by nature is evident in the words of a Great Basin explorer in the mid-nineteenth century: "From this peak [I] had a most magnificent view of the mountains in every quarter of the horizon—the Humboldt range, to the east of north, showing its white snowy summits far above the intervening ones. These distant views have, at least in my mind, a decidedly moral and religious effect, and I cannot but believe that they are not less productive of emotions of value than they are of use in accustoming the mind to large conceptions, and thus giving it power and capacity."[21]

When J. H. Simpson wrote these words in 1859, he was in charge of an official expedition across the Great Basin. That expedition's report—all 518 pages of it—is totally scientific, except for one provocative page of philosophical speculation. On this lone page, Simpson indulged himself on thoughts about religion and nature. Clearly moved by the vast vistas that he experienced in the Great Basin, Simpson wrote: "The mysterious property of nature to develop the whole man, including the mind, soul, and body, is a subject which I think has not received the attention from philosophers which its importance demands." Surrounded by the vast landscape of mountains and desert basins, Simpson further pondered, "Do we rise from the contemplation of nature to nature's God, and therefore to a realization of the amplitude and reach to which our minds are capable, by our own unaided spirit; or is it by the superinduced Spirit of the Almighty Himself, which we have received, it may be on account of His only Son?" Aware that he was venturing far from the realm of science, Simpson quickly added: "But these speculations may be considered as foreign to the necessary rigor of an official report; and I, therefore, will indulge in them no further than to say that, according to my notions, the latter I believe to be the true theory."[22]

As both a scientist and a religious man, Simpson was aware of the feelings of awe generated by magnificent works of creation; yet, as a Christian, he by necessity found these works to be subservient to God—and more particularly, God's son, Jesus. Although Christianity has deep roots in pagan traditions, it continually distanced itself from nature (and nature worship) by stressing one's responsibility to behave (and believe) properly—that is, in relation to commandments and admonitions that elevate the pure over impure, spiritual over corporeal. And yet, even during Simpson's time as later, many began to view nature as a direct window into creation. In this view, nature is itself godlike in that it reveals the workings of creation and has its own laws (rather than humankind's).

Simpson built on an expanding Western tradition that increasingly embraced nature as ennobling the human spirit. Consider the words of Alexander von Humboldt, who stated in characteristic nineteenth-century prose: "Nature is a free domain; and the profound conceptions and enjoyments she awakens within us can only be vividly delineated by thought clothed in exalted forms of speech, worthy of bearing witness to the majesty and greatness of the creation."[23] We should not expect less from a man who was one of the true geniuses of his generation, a scientist, philosopher, and multilingual scholar.

Von Humboldt was on my mind in the late 1980s as I paralleled the river that bears his name. It was an unseasonably cold late September, and I was Greyhound-bound from Salt Lake City to Reno. As the bus rolled off the miles near Winnemucca, the sky was in command, unsettled and fitful as lenticular clouds sheared the tops of the Humboldt Range. Snow dusted the tops of the hills and a frosty night loomed. But first we were treated to one of those magnificent, turbulent, flaming sunsets that can make even the dead take notice.[24]

Here's what I remember of this encounter with things spiritual on that Greyhound bus, headed into the setting sun. The bus driver clicked on his mike to announce, "We're nearing Winnemucca, Nevada," then added, "Look toward the front of the bus at that sunset." At this point I expected a brief lecture on how wonderful it is to travel by bus. However, the driver took me—and all of us—completely by surprise. "When I see a sunset like this," he stated, "I am sure that Jesus Christ is my personal Lord and Savior." Whoa! I thought as I realized the man had crossed the line separating the secular from the religious; yet it was his heartfelt testimony to the power of this scene, and it brought out my admiration. A sunset like this must trigger some spiritual effect in even the most jaded traveler. This bus driver's declaration of faith was startling; first, because the last thing you'd expect from an operator of a public conveyance is a religious sermon; second, because we were within sight of the river, mountains—even within the very Nevada county!—named after Alexander von Humboldt, a man who helped shape nonreligious (although deeply spiritual) attitudes toward nature in the first half of the nineteenth century.

For several minutes, as the sunset hung like an open doorway into creation, I was drawn more deeply into words; not words from the Bible, but a passage from von Humboldt's landmark 1849 book *Cosmos*: "The earnest and solemn thoughts awakened by a communion with nature intuitively arise from presentiment of the order and harmony pervading the whole universe, and from the contrast we draw between the narrow limits of our own existence and the image of infinity revealed on every side."[25]

Within a few miles, the glow faded from the western sky, and we continued rolling westward into twilight. With evening yielding to night, I was reminded that von Humboldt wrote *Cosmos* in what he himself called "the late evening of an active life." In it, he described subjects like botany, geognosy,[26] and astronomical determinations. Although these subjects had engaged him for most of his life, now he also engaged in "the earnest endeavor to comprehend the phenomena of physical objects in their general connection, and to represent nature as one great whole, moved and animated by internal forces." He now sought to prove "that a certain degree of scientific completeness in the treatment of individual facts, is not wholly incompatible with a picturesque animation of style." Von Humboldt was passionate about what he called the "enjoyment to be derived from nature, and the knowledge of the laws by which the universe is governed."[27]

For von Humboldt, the rational study of nature revealed a "unity in diversity of phenomena; a harmony, blending together all created things, however, dissimilar in form and attributes; one great whole." He believed that "mere communion with nature, mere contact with the free air, exercise a soothing yet strengthening influence on the wearied spirit" can work wonders. It will, Humboldt claimed, "calm the storm of passion, and soften the heart when shaken by sorrow to its inmost depths."[28] Those words make me see that the bus driver's impromptu testimonial was really far more understandable as *agape*—the emotion that accompanies a sense of wonder. That emotion is as catalytic to spiritualism based on nature as it is to spiritualism based on revealed testimony.

At just about the time von Humboldt's *Cosmos* became popular, Walt Whitman wrote a series of poems that became the famed *Leaves of Grass*. In "Proto-Leaf," Whitman offers a prophecy: "O I see the following poems are indeed to drop in the earth the germs of a greater Religion." Also in *Leaves of Grass*, "Salut au Monde!" reveals Whitman awed by the powerful forces of nature: "I see mountain peaks. . . . I see the vast deserts of Western America, I see the Libyan, Arabian and Asiatic deserts. . . . I see the temples of the deaths of the bodies of Gods—I see the old signifiers." Sophisticated, imaginative, and bisexually charged, Whitman was writing no less than what he called, in a notebook entry, "The Great Construction of the New Bible." It was to become a "third religion," much like Emerson what called the "doings of the miraculous spirit of life that everywhere throbs and works."[29]

The "old signifiers" would indeed take form in diverse, almost unimaginable new attitudes that we take for granted today as we seek inspiration in nature. This "wilderness effect" is potent, and it has a long and vibrant tradition as an alternative to traditional religion. Those searching for spirituality in nature are often eloquent in their recollection of what happened when, as one put it, "we had found 'the place.'" Encountering nature in this ethereal mood, "[w]e fell silent at the sight, knowing somehow that this would be the turning point, 'the most sacred,' the place of deepest wilderness."[30] These words reveal how seamlessly worship of the sacred in nature conflates with the protection of wilderness.

Seeking to protect such sacred places, the conservation movement flowered under the "inspired" premise of protecting jewels of creation. In the Great Basin, these included stunning areas like Death Valley National Monument (1933) and Joshua Tree National Monument (1936). Both of these national monuments were redesignated as national parks in 1994 in a further recognition of both their uniqueness and sacredness. Other places set aside from development include the Malheur National Wildlife Refuge in eastern Oregon, the Desert National Wildlife Range in southwestern Nevada, and the bird refuges in the marshy lands near the Great Salt Lake. In what may have been the last of the large landscape-protection programs for some time to come, Congress passed and President Clinton signed into law the California Desert Protection Act of 1994, which created the 1.4-million-acre Mojave National Preserve.

Although these gems featured spectacular scenery, ardent conservationists had long envisioned permanently protecting a large section of typical Great Basin landscape from mining and other developments. That dream finally materialized when Great Basin National Park was created in 1986. Located in eastern Nevada, the Great Basin National Park includes not only typical basin and range country, but also the magnificent Lehman Caves, which had become a national monument in 1922. This area encompasses some of the very topography traversed by the Mormons on their search for sanctuary in the late 1850s, so it also has considerable historical significance as a site associated with more mainstream spiritual geography. Before the Mormons' arrival, the Indians also looked with awe on the artifacts of the Great Creator here. As a legacy of these thoughts and actions, the new worship of nature joins age-old forms of belief. Although he chose to express religion in a more prescribed manner, this is the spirit that energized a bus driver to proclaim a belief in a greater being and purpose. In my bewilderment at the driver's testimony, I lost an opportunity to ask him a question that goes to the heart of spirituality and geography: Why did you make that statement in that particular place at that particular time? His answer would have shed light on the bigger question: How do place and belief cooperate to so inspire thoughts of the divine here on earth?

I now see that the only line the bus driver crossed was imposed by our strict separation of religion and secular in public life. For his part, he simply responded to the subliminal religious message that, as psychotherapist James Hillman puts it, *"There's another here."* In his book *The Soul's Code,* Hillman calls these messages "'the invisibles' . . . that ordinary people in most cultures pay attention to." He elaborates, "It's why they light a candle, or why they cross themselves, why they pick up little pebbles on the beach and take them home and put them somewhere special." Hillman concludes, in words the bus driver and most of the passengers (a couple of whom responded "Amen" to his words) would implicitly understand: *"There's this sense that there's something else involved in life all the time."*[31]

This "something else" is indefinable, but I sense that it is what many people who venture into the Great Basin are looking for. It accounts for a number of manmade features out there that attempt to express something transcendental about place. Consider one of the more traditional icons— Desert Christ Park—located at the southern fringe of the region in Yucca Valley, California. I first stumbled upon this site while conducting research for my master's degree in 1968. Here, on a desert hillside overlooking the community of Yucca Valley, is a remarkable group of white concrete structures that were reportedly designed "not as a religious display, but as the sculptor's pleas for peace." One might be easily convinced that this is simply a "World Peace Shrine," as a website claims.[32] It certainly could be, for when it was created in the 1950s during the height of the Cold War, many people were profoundly concerned about nuclear proliferation and possible annihilation. But a closer look at the site (fig. 11.3) reveals thirty life-sized statues depicting the life of Jesus Christ, the "Prince of Peace." There is something incredibly potent about the snow-white statues, which dazzle in the desert sun. As I gazed upon them, I realized that they have both a classical quality and a sepulchral aura. Frozen in stone, Christ blesses the children or prays on Mount Gethsemane while the apostles sleep. These alabaster-white statues are somehow at home here, reminding me of Julene Bair's observation that "[t]he desert parches dead things until the bones shine like statuary."[33] Designed and sculpted by Antone Martin, Desert Christ Park's figures confirm that Christianity is both a living religion and a repository of icons.

That those religious icons can inspire as well as infuriate becomes apparent to me when I read the startling headline "VANDALS ATTACK RE-LIGIOUS STATUES AT DESERT CHRIST PARK." On March 16, 2000, van-dals "knocked over the Christ figurine in a scene depicting him talking to

Fig. 11.3. The Prince of Peace: Reportedly originally designed as a shrine to world peace, Desert Christ Park in Yucca Valley, California, has become a sacred place for some people due to its iconography's close association with Christian/biblical stories. (Photograph by Honor Fowler)

a woman at a well." To leave little doubt that this was not a random prank, they left a calling card: "The numbers '666' were written on the statue's forehead." For those versed in the Book of Revelation, 666 is considered the mark of the Antichrist. So potent has this numerical symbol become that conservative legislators in Arizona recently changed the number of State Highway 666 to something less disturbing; legislators in New Mexico, evidently less concerned with such matters, have let the "triple six" designation stand. Written long after Christ's death, Revelation still stirs passions with its predictions of woe.

Even though I think I'm immune from such superstitious numerology, I note with some fascination my behavior at a café after reading the vandalism story. The tab comes to $5.66, and I absentmindedly add a dollar tip as I fill out my Visa card bill; but as I start to total the numbers, I quickly—and inexplicably—raise the tip to two dollars, feeling a sense of relief at tipping the waitress better—and at seeing that the total is $7.66 instead of $6.66. Tucking my receipt into my wallet, I speculate that both the cashier and the waitress will have a better day.

Denied both inspiration and imagination, the Desert Christ Park site's vandals likely anticipated the outraged reaction that their hammer blows and triple sixes prompted. They certainly got the attention of Yucca Valley residents, who now patrol the site night and day. The newspaper report notes something important about the site, which has become a sacred place to many: "The place feels serene even with high winds blowing sand around the parking lot." For some residents, the park's value transcends the Christianity it evokes and is more broadly socio-spiritual. As outraged Yucca Valley resident Larry Willingham put it, Desert Christ Park is "a symbol of the appreciation of what this brother [Martin] had for what the Lord had done for him and the human race." Willingham added that "for us to forget this man's contribution is to woefully shortchange the next generation."[34] Thus it is that sacred places are linked to past, present, and future much like those other locales honoring individuals' memories—monuments and cemeteries.

The idea of monuments in the desert brings to mind the "Burning Man" ritual enacted in northwestern Nevada (fig. 11.4). Originating as a quirky prank on the beach in San Francisco when a rejected lover burned of life-sized replica of the victorious suitor, Burning Man soon became a cult ritual. Although the first event, in 1986, drew only a few curious onlookers, talk of it drew several hundred when it was repeated a year later. Like other sacrificial burnings, this one had spiritual overtones and was irresistible to those who found art in such "happenings." Within a short time, the event drew so much attention that San Francisco authorities outlawed it—a surprising move for a city that cultivates its reputation as tolerant, arty, and innovative. Undeterred, Burning Man's following soon surfaced in a locale guaranteed not to disturb any local residents—the middle of a dry lakebed in Nevada's Black Rock Desert. In the last decade, the event has drawn up to 25,000 people. In fact, so many pilgrims flock to it that authorities voice concern about adverse environmental impact on the site. Over the years, the Burning Man effigy increased not only in popularity, but also in physical stature, now towering about fifty feet tall (fig. 11-4).

Burning Man's founders and supporters stress the event's ethereal, ceremonial quality. An enthusiastic contributor to the Burning Man website confirms both the tribal and spiritual nature of the event: "You're here to celebrate. On Saturday night, we'll burn the Man. As the procession starts, the circle forms, and the man ignites, you experience something personal, something new to yourself, something you've never felt before. It's an epiphany, it's primal, it's newborn. And it's completely individual."[35] Note here the religious word epiphany seamlessly integrated with the more pa-

Fig. 11.4. Sacrifice and Renewal: The "Burning Man" event in northwestern Nevada is closely associated with its stark desert site and annually draws up to 25,000 people wishing to experience and participate in this "sacrificial" rite. (Photograph entitled "Burning Men" by Sean Christopher)

gan primal. Note also the emphasis on individual experience in what is also a subcultural or tribal celebration. Perhaps in keeping with its concept of total conflagration, as well as Bureau of Land Management requirements that sites not be permanently disturbed, Burning Man's practitioners insist that nothing remain after the ceremony. For many who venture to the event, Burning Man provides a first encounter with the landscape of the Great Basin. Others return year after year, much like those who travel to sunrise Easter services.

Burning Man is now intimately associated with the desert experience. The website proclaims that "you've touched the terrain of what feels like another planet." Descriptions of encounters with nature here, from searing heat to dust storms to mirages, only add to the mysticism. This is the Black Rock Desert, where "the colors paint themselves like a spice cabinet—sage, dust, slate gray."[36] Then, too, the emotion-charged event of the huge Burning Man effigy borders on orgiastic. To New Agers searching for unstructured ritual, Burning Man's locale serves as a combination of temporary Stonehenge and Mecca. The lakebed site itself only adds to the mystery; many comment on its almost unnatural flatness and stark whiteness.

With virtually every sign of the gathering gone by the time I reach the Black Rock playa on a hot summer day a few weeks after the Burning Man spectacle, I ponder the forces that bring people here for an event as frenetic as the spawning of ephemeral brine shrimp after a desert downpour and as enduring as any sacred ceremony that transforms place into story.

These pilgrimages to the Black Rock Desert reinforce its status as a place of communion with nature and a locale in which to ponder spirituality. It is the site of a fascinating artwork that appears both archaeological and ceremonial (fig. 11.5). As might be suggested by its name—Ground Zero—this wheel-like ring of stones by DeWayne Williams is meant to be seen from the air. Williams enhanced the religious quality of this sculpture by adding words from the Bible and the Koran, as well as stories and poetry. All of the selected passages suggest the futility of confrontation and non-negotiation. Williams's use of religious quotes suggests the Judeo-Christian roots of nuclear proliferation. But the form Williams uses also fascinates me, for I've seen it before. Ground Zero is actually a medicine wheel, a sacred feature associated with Native American prehistory (fig. 11.6). As a design that suggest both centripetal and centrifugal forces, the medicine wheel apparently represents the design of the universe. Its circularity suggests a type of mandala, though instead of indicating four cardinal directions, the wheel further subdivides the circle. Williams's use of the medicine wheel suggests Native American thinking as an alternative to Western thinking—and ultimately, Native American spirituality as an alternative to Judeo-Christian/Western spirituality.

These sculptures and thoughts are on my mind a few days later on a night drive through the heart of the Great Basin from Caliente to Tonopah, Nevada. I turn off the dashboard lights. Except for the intense blue bead of light on the dashboard confirming that my high beams are on, the car's interior is pitch black. Outside, my headlights are now the only thing illuminating the star-filled, moonless night. I like this feeling of being discon-

Fig. 11.5. Circle as Symbol: Ground Zero was created by DeWayne Williams in Nevada's Black Rock Desert and epitomizes humankind's search for meaning in environmental design. (Photograph by Peter Goin)

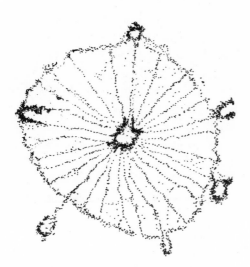

Fig. 11.6. Circle as Mandala: About seventy feet in diameter, the Medicine Wheel in Wyoming is a Native American archaeological feature suggesting the design of the cosmos. (Sketch by author, based on drawing in John A. Eddy, "Astronomical Alignment of Big Horn Medicine Wheel," *Science* 184, no. 4141 [June 1974])

nected from the interior lights, with no speedometer to tell me how fast I'm
going, no tachometer, no temperature gauge: just me and the movement of
the vehicle. At one place, I pull off the "Extraterrestrial Highway," as it has
been dubbed by the Nevada Highway Department. The name seems appropriate, given some of the goings-on hereabouts. These include the UFO
sightings by scores of otherwise rational people (and scores of irrational
people too) and the federal government's widely scattered secret military
installations that pockmark this part of Nevada. Satisfied that I've driven
far enough down this lonely unpaved road, I stop, turn off my headlights,
and shut off the motor. Swallowed in silence and darkness, I step out of the
car feeling the Great Basin's immensity embrace me. I perform this ritual
every once in a while. I am not sure what, if anything, will happen, but as I
look up into the night sky, I'm half hoping for answers—and visitors. Although I've never had any luck with the latter, I'm primed by two generations of Cold War-era science fiction movies and paperback novels to experience *something* out there.

I'm not alone. In my travels across the Great Basin, I've encountered
other people who periodically search the night sky. According to William
Fox, UFO watchers have something in common with environmental artists
like Mike Heizer. A visionary of sorts drawn to the region's open spaces,
Heizer has created several stunning large-scale earthworks in the Great
Basin. To me, they not only are art, but also resonate as spiritual places.
They both help define the "negative space" of the Great Basin and evoke its
mysterious past. Fox notes that "the UFO watchers also draw lines in time
and space, insisting, 'This is when the Other came from up There to visit
down Here.'" Many of the UFO faithful are apparently convinced that Heizer
is "a tool of the aliens, building landing strips for the invasion and refus-
ing to let them in on the secret." Interestingly, Heizer's father, archaeolo-
gist Robert Heizer, encountered similar attitudes about the deeper meanings of the Native American petroglyphs that he studied hereabouts. As
Fox puts it, "This conflation between the ancient and the alien is one that
the artist's father coped with in his professional life as well, noting in one
of his reports on the petroglyphs of Nevada that the prehistoric rock art of
the West would always attract practitioners of pseudoscience." The elder
Heizer acknowledged something intriguing about the Great Basin, "that
there always seemed to be 'two worlds—the real and the imaginary, and this
duality is for some reason necessary.'"[37] In one sense, Native traditions are
indeed easily conflated with alien because we've quite deliberately distanced Natives from our modern, technologically oriented society, assuming that there is a primitive, which is to say natural, communion between

Native peoples and the Cosmos. Like ancient earthworks consisting of straight lines and recognizable forms, Mike Heizer's giant environmental works assume a celestial view of earth and a communication of privileged information.

That idea of a privileged view reminds me of this region's association with government secrecy, and hence grand theories of conspiracy. In this regard, the region shines as a beacon to those who believe in UFOs and mistrust anything that the government says about them. Although the frenzy about UFOs was first kindled elsewhere in 1947 (note that Cold War start-up date very carefully) with "sightings" at Roswell (New Mexico) and in Washington State, no area galvanized the UFO advocates more than the Great Basin with its wide-open spaces and transparent atmosphere. And no area continues to engage persistent UFO theorists more than the Great Basin's own mysterious "Area 51" in southwestern Nevada.

Since I began traveling through the Great Basin in the 1960s, I've noted (1) the area's magnetic attraction for UFO searchers and (2) the fact that many of these searchers share a deep suspicion of governmental authority—that is, they are either farther right or left politically than most folk. I've noticed something else, too: These people, on both political fringes, seem to have a propensity to believe in spiritual phenomena. In interviewing people at the Giant Rock UFO headquarters in the Mojave Desert in 1968, I noted that most were outspoken in their belief that "something out there" was "connecting with us." This contact was occurring in order to confirm both "what we should believe, and how we should live our lives." Many cited the passage from Ezekiel about "flaming wheels in the sky"; that is, they connected these modern phenomena with ancient sightings and the human race's enduring need for spiritual guidance. Others less prone to believe the Bible per se nevertheless attributed the presence of UFOs to extraterrestrials who could "teach us about what *really* matters." Note that both groups posit a search for truth and a need for answers, and both tend to believe that those in authority stifle this flow of information because it will undermine their power.

Back on the highway and driving toward Tonopah after midnight, I realize that I haven't seen another car for an hour. I recall why the Great Basin is so closely tied to "far out" thoughts and beliefs—why, as William Fox observes, "legions worshiping the otherworldly gather therein." Fox says that emptiness itself is the attraction: "Only in the void, a disorienting space we conceive of as being vacant and thus a landscape of open possibilities, can we imagine ourselves to step outside the boundaries of what we know and receive intelligence from some other place, somewhere alien to the egocentric pivot of our bodies."[38] So it is that the void of the desert, with its bowl-shaped sky ever ready for observation, excites thoughts of the other-worldly.

It also helps us connect with our innermost thoughts and beliefs. In an essay that begins with an ode to the "extraterrestrial" saline flats on the floor of Death Valley, Yi-Fu Tuan puts it this way: "Of all the places I have lived in, without doubt the one for which I have the greatest affinity is the desert." Tuan observes that "I know this to be true at the conscious level," but he quickly adds that "the affinity goes deeper than that, for it is true even in dreams." For Tuan, who was not born or raised in the desert, it was "love at first sight." He links the desert to transcendent thoughts of life, death, and individuality: its appeal for him lies in "barrenness itself—in the presentation of absence that enables me to wipe out in one clean sweep sex, biological life and death." The desert's "mineral purity free of death's reminders" will permit Tuan a death that is "merely a process of wizening—of drying up" without "the pungent odor of decay" that would be expected in more humid areas. Then, too, the desert frees Tuan from "the pungent odor of sex" and other reminders of procreation—he is by choice celibate and childless, and thus will be "good for just one season."[39]

Yi-Fu Tuan's frank admission earns my admiration but not my emulation. The desert may be sinewy and tough, and some might see its topography as skeletal, but the same desert landscapes that "dramatize the ephemerality of life" for Tuan remind me of life's ability to endure, even thrive, under harsh circumstances. The deserts of the Great Basin are never lifeless; scratch the surface of even a dry lake and you will find tiny brine shrimp waiting for that glorious moment when nature will set them free to reproduce. Their chance may be a dozen or more years coming, but it does come. This, however, is beside the point, and I return to Tuan's profound central insight: "Strange to think that the question 'Who am I?' can be answered by a landscape."[40] That confirms how deeply place is linked to both identity and spirituality, for the question Who am I? ultimately incorporates both body and soul—which is to say that it also asks Where am I? and, ultimately, Why am I?

Believing in Place

As science breaks out of its narrow mechanistic view and approaches a more holistic view of nature, fruitful interaction between science and the spiritual will become more possible.

—RUPERT SHELDRAKE, biologist, 2001

The convergence of science and spirituality is on my mind as I head out into one of the most forbidding locales in North America. Craving silence, I've driven my white rental car out onto the porcelain-like surface of a dry lakebed in northwestern Nevada. There is no shade here, and the brightness of the light is both ethereal and overpowering. I rarely venture out onto these isotropic surfaces that remind me of thin ice and starched bed sheets, but when I do I am always aware that I can never get farther from civilization. Bone dry now, this playa could be covered by a lake of turbid, muddy water if the weather changed. There is something delightfully eerie about a place that seems so eternally dry yet can become aquatic in no time. I ponder the irony of having technology whisk me out to a spot where I can so readily commune with nature, and in turn think about humanity's place in the cosmos.

Standing next to the rental car in blue jeans and a white t-shirt, I feel the sun pound down on my face and bare arms. The breeze has shifted slightly; it's now coming out of the southeast, and I sense that the weather may be changing. It's hot and dry now, but at this time of year—the nether zone between late summer and early fall—thunderstorms can move in or build up quickly. Brushing my face on the sleeve of my t-shirt, I accidentally touch my tongue to the hot skin on my upper arm. Although I'm not aware that I'm perspiring, I taste salt. My tongue instinctively reacts with ambivalence, repelled by the salinity yet drawn to the sodium, magnesium, and calcium salts that I need to replenish my metabolism. It occurs to me that these salts on my skin are similar in composition to the salts on this dry

228

lakebed. I take comfort in this reaffirmation of the similarity between the inorganic world of geology and the organic world of physiology. Our ambivalence toward salt is revealed by the fact that wages were once paid in it (as in "worth his salt" or even the word salary) and that Lot's wife was turned into a pillar of it—the ultimate tribute to desiccation—for defying God's command and witnessing the destruction of Sodom and Gomorrah. Salt figures in storytelling here, too, as these dry lakebeds are legendary in their desolation: picture someone dying of thirst and a place like this pancake-flat playa will come to mind.

Out here on the Black Rock playa, I can never forget another image that keeps returning like the replay of a favorite film that I can't resist watching on video from time to time. The image is of the crystalline sterility of a salt lakebed, and the film is *Vanishing Point* (1971). At one level a tribute to the self-absorbed, drug-centered (or is it self-centered and drug-absorbed?) late 1960s, this film resonates as a serious spiritual drama. Like a number of quirky, even risky American productions, this film is pretty much forgotten in the United States but has a passionate following in Europe. It even has a dedicated worldwide website[1] that keeps it from complete obscurity and total oblivion in the land of its making.

The premise of *Vanishing Point* is simple enough: a driver named Kowalski ("no Christian name") accepts a challenge to drive a souped-up (but street legal) 1970 white Dodge Challenger from Denver to San Francisco at breakneck speed—about 1,300 miles in less than sixteen hours, which translates into an average speed of over 80 miles per hour. As he breaks the speed limits in the process, Kowalski is chased by highway patrol officers of four states (Colorado, Utah, Nevada, and California). During this chase, he attracts nationwide attention as "the last American hero to whom speed means freedom of the soul." In a not-so-subtle play on words, the speed here refers to both Kowalski's rapid pace and the methamphetamines that he consumes like candy along the way. As Kowalski enters the Great Basin in the speeding Challenger, he tunes into a radio station broadcast featuring Super Soul, a black disc jockey in Goldfield, Nevada. Through a type of supplemental telepathy, Kowalski and Super Soul begin to communicate; Super Soul, in fact, takes on no less a mission than guiding the speeding American hero to freedom.

Vanishing Point set a new standard for high-speed-chase driving films, and its use of the Great Basin's wide-open roads and dry lakebeds for race scenes is exhilarating; however, the film is equally noteworthy for its spiritual messages. As *Vanishing Point* evolves, we learn that Kowalski has had several careers (soldier, policeman, race car driver, and motorcycle racer) and that one pivotal event—the drowning of his wife in a surfing accident—has left him suspended in nothingness. In one sense, Kowalski's nihilism symbolizes the isolation of modernity; yet that very nihilism also makes him a modern American hero. *Vanishing Point* uses Nevada's stunning scenery of mountain passes, sweeping vistas, and sun-baked playas as a stage upon which Kowalski risks all for the freedom of unfettered mobility.

As the state highway patrol and county sheriffs close in on Kowalski, he simply leaves the road and roars off into the desert, leaving the bewildered police behind. Out in the desert, he meets an assortment of characters, including a prospector who leads him to a Christian revivalist commune. The prospector gives Kowalski some lessons in desert survival and helps him find his way west. Though they have never seen each other, Kowalski and Super Soul continue to communicate telepathically. It is in the desert that Kowalski's spiritual connection with Super Soul intensifies. However, Kowalski remains resistant to Super Soul's well-intentioned messages. When the disc jockey warns him that "You can beat the road, you can beat the clock, but you can't beat the desert," the jaded Kowalski's response is simple and to the point: "Go to hell." Yet, as Kowalski's plight worsens, Super Soul continues to inform him of the highway patrol's whereabouts and the roadblocks they are setting up. Although Super Soul is beaten by rednecks and hounded by the authorities, his message remains clear. He broadcasts to Kowalski as a minister might, and his tone is both pragmatic and metaphysical. To help Kowalski, who he tells listeners is "the last beautiful free soul on this planet," Super Soul declares: "But it is written: If the evil spirit arms the tiger with claws, Brahman provided wings for the dove. Thus spake the Super Guru."

Vanishing Point is clearly countercultural and highly spiritual. Its Christian spirituality is conflated with Buddhist messages, its soundtrack rich in Christian gospel songs such as "You Got to Believe," "I Believe," and "Sing Out for Jesus." Fans of this cult classic film will tell you, as actor Barry Newman did, that about seven minutes were cut from the supposedly final version. In the scene that wound up on the cutting-room floor, Kowalski picks up a mysterious young woman hitchhiker, with whom he makes love in the desert. The young woman then disappears before his eyes— a foreboding of death. Fans lament the loss of this scene, for it was stylishly symbolic. They also point out that it was so peremptorily cut that the young woman's name still appears in the film's credits! Like all films, *Vanishing Point* is a testimony both to the compromises that film companies make and to the values of the period in which it was made. Yet it joins a long tradition of using the desert as a spiritual testing ground.

My favorite scene in *Vanishing Point* comes to mind as I stand next to my rental car out on the playa. In it, Kowalski brings the muscle car to a stop after racing along the lakebed, only to realize that he has crossed his own tracks (fig. 12.1). The camera pans to reveal these crisscrossed tracks, and we realize that both Kowalski and the automobile are inconsequential compared to the vastness of the desert. He is lost. It is here, in the middle of nowhere, that Kowalski meets the prospector, who in turn brings him into contact with a host of characters who are also searching for freedom or redemption.

As the film unwinds, Kowalski is running from himself and the confines of his shrinking world. He manages to cross the Great Basin, only to be confronted by a roadblock in California. Not to be outdone by Kowalski, the California Highway Patrol has erected the ultimate roadblock—two ponderous bulldozers pulled up with their blades touching, completely blocking the highway. As police cars close in on Kowalski from behind, he makes the ultimate choice—and ultimate sacrifice for freedom. After a smile briefly crosses Kowalski's weary face, he accelerates at a ferocious rate, slamming into the bulldozers in a crash that sends a fireball skyward. Kowalski's suicide is the reaffirmation that *Vanishing Point* is about oblivion, but like most westerns (which I define as morality plays acted out on the fringes of civilization) it is also about escape and redemption. Characters like Kowalski never die, they become myths, as the film's (and the website's) enduring cult popularity attest.

Fig. 12.1. Crisis: In a crucial scene from the film *Vanishing Point* (1971): Kowalski realizes that he has crossed his own tracks on the barren playa. (Sketch by author)

Never leaving well enough alone, or a film without a sequel, about twenty-five years after *Vanishing Point* was released in 1971, Hollywood remade it into a TV movie, updating it with a new premise. In the 1997 version, Kowalski is also delivering a white 1970 Dodge Challenger, but now it is a vintage collector's item. And Kowalski himself is reinvented as a husband dutifully racing to his ailing wife's side in the hospital. Along the way, he is deterred by authorities who are cast in the conservative late 1990s as *federal* agents, complete with black helicopters that would warm the soul of any right-winger who sees government conspiracies everywhere. The authorities' pursuit prevents Kowalski from reaching his wife before she dies. Devastated, the updated Kowalski chooses the same spectacular alternative (Hollywood can never resist vehicular mayhem), but in the remake he is then reunited with his wife, who stands angelically dressed in white on the highway beyond the bulldozers. The remake proved two things about American pop culture vis-à-vis spirituality in the 1990s: That the original's gritty nihilism was deemed too hard to take, and that the film's conclusion had to be uplifting in its suggestion of heaven rather than oblivion as Kowalski's ultimate fate.

Both versions of Kowalski are on my mind as I crank up the rental car and roar off the lakebed like a rocket. It occurs to me that I, too, have changed since my first encounter with this playa in 1964. Like the Kowalski in all of us, I've lived sequential lives that converge as a series of film clips running through my mind. That is the miracle of life in the early twenty-first century; we've had several generations of film to prepare for a sort of personal cinematic stardom that no one else ever sees on screen. I look in the rearview mirror at the clouds of dust swirling behind, at the white lakebed ahead, and I'm entranced by the fact that I, like the three cameras filming Kowalski's escape, can simultaneously see the car from several vantage points—looking down on it as if it's one of those cars roaring across dry lakes in a TV commercial; from the side, as the car rockets along the level playa; and from the back seat like an angel looking over Kowalski's shoulder through the windshield to the snow-white desert beyond.

I've always felt exhilarated and guilty about my love of driving, but out here there's no one to judge. Leaving the lakebed, I drive along a winding road that weaves its way across a saltbush flat. Feeling the rental car surge ahead as I step on the gas coming out of one of the curves, I think about power in relationship to spirituality. I recall that spirituality connects us to a force inherent in things, and that gets me to thinking about the *bbooha* or *pooha* of the Paiute and Shoshone. That force is inherent in things; people are said to experience, perhaps even possess, it only when they have been empowered, which is to say entitled, to do so by developing a mystical connection with the universe.

It is here that I sense a major difference between the Native American and Judeo-Christian heritage. Rolling toward Pyramid Lake on an arrow-straight section of highway at 75 mph, I realize that Judeo-Christian thinking diverged from earlier roots sometime about 5,000 years ago when Egyptian priests translated power from something that came to us miraculously into something we could possess. This step translated knowledge (for example, knowledge about the seasonal flow of the Nile) into knowledge of shaping the environment (for example, controlling the labor of humankind to erect huge stone obelisks and pyramids). The Greeks and Romans erected stone buildings to gods (albeit for different reasons), and the Jewish, Christian, and Islamic faiths erected edifices of worship—temples, churches, and mosques—to their God. These religions create tangible works to reflect God's power, and in so doing empower their builders.

The Protestant ethic took that power another step, from centralized ecclesiastical power to the empowerment of the individual. Thus pursuits like reading, writing, and recordation—formerly the domain of priests and shamans—now spread to individuals who first used it to create a work ethic bound to the soul, then secularized it through public and private education systems. So it is that anyone—even a normally mild-mannered college professor pretending to be an outlaw like Kowalski—can wield such power with near impunity today. The Judeo-Christian tradition is at the root of this individualism (individual salvation being the ultimate goal of Christianity), and so I'm riding the technological wave of a universalizing religious system that has diffused into daily life; all the time knowing, somehow, that I would never have been able to do this earlier; that throughout world history, only priests or gods could be empowered to command the equivalent of 200 horsepower over a road that, until 500 years ago, would have been constructed only for the movement of armies or for the pilgrimages of thousands. I'm humbled by this power, feeling it course through my entire being as I lead the car through curves at high speed, feeling my hands guide my fate and my right foot summon power that both humbles and thrills me; yet I'm also chagrined to know that it means nothing to those who seek its distant ancestor—the spirit within, the spirit that we've now thoughtlessly, even joyously, liberated at great exhilaration and great peril.

As I swing onto Highway 97 in a cloud of dust, I see the road, straight as a landing strip for miles ahead, stretching away toward a mountain on the distant horizon. Inexplicably, I feel motivated to move into the scene at higher and higher speed, my foot pressing the accelerator down toward the floorboard. Like Kowalski, I've got an unexplainable self-imposed urgency to fly low as I accelerate to 80, 90, 100, 110. At this speed, the roadside vegetation blurs and my attention focuses only on the road ahead. At 120, the parallax effect transforms this experience from driving to tunneling. With my foot almost to the floorboard, the car seems to be rocketing toward that one point on the horizon. At 125, the car responds differently; it's trickier to control because it's lighter. I could probably take it up to 130, maybe even a little faster, but I've exceeded the aerodynamic design of the car and it's trying to take off. Then, too, that light wind is magnified at this speed, and it puts a limit on how fast I can drive this vehicle in a straight line. At this speed, another factor enters into the equation: My tires are heating up way beyond their design specifications. And besides, one screw-up at this speed and they'd have to sweep the wreckage off a thousand linear feet of highway, which I'm traversing in less than five seconds. Exhilarated but at the edge of catastrophe, I gently let off the gas and coast down through the speedometer dial: 120, 110, 100, 90, 80. When I reach 65, down 60 miles per hour from my breakneck pace a minute before, it seems that I'm driving so slow I could get out and run next to the car. Though quantifiable, even speed is relative here in the Great Basin, where land speed records are routinely set, then broken. I've slowed down here because, unlike Kowalski, I've got something to live for, a wonderful wife back home in Texas who's been waiting for my phone call.

Even slowed to a sane pace, I keep replaying my adventure with speed on my private viewing screen. The thrill of driving that fast is not only kinetic, but visually entrancing. At that speed, something fascinating happens. As the landscape in my peripheral vision blurs, the pavement becomes a triangle. Although I am on pretty much level land, as I rush toward the vanishing point up ahead, I feel that I am moving *upward* toward the apex of a pyramid. The highway is in reality a straight band of uniform width, but it becomes a pyramid because the lines converge at the vanishing point. With this in mind, I begin to understand why straight lines are associated with death, or as Paul Devereux puts it, "the association among spirits, death and straightness was fundamental, spanning cultures and times and the route to eternity—as are triangles."[2] The straight line signifies a linear connection to "the end." The triangle points the way to that end, which is infinity, and eternity.

Up ahead, the road curves a bit and I slow to 55, driving like a law-abiding citizen. I decide to take a graded road marked on the map as it looks like a cutoff that will save time. On this road I maintain about 55, bouncing over the corrugations in the road surface, hanging onto the car at the outside edge of control, looking out for coyotes and jackrabbits. Then, just as quickly as it happened in the original *Vanishing Point* movie, my reverie is broken as I hear a loud "bang" and feel the steering turn to jelly in my hands. My right front tire has blown out, and the car, rattling and shuddering violently, wants to lurch off into the desert like a crazed stallion. But I keep it reined in, going pretty much straight ahead. As coolly as Kowalski, I settle to a stop while the cloud of dust following me now catches up and envelops the car. Like Kowalski, I get out to survey what's left of the tire—very little—and get ready to change the flat. Then I notice that whatever I hit, which must have lurked just below the surface of the dusty road, has actually bent the rim of the wheel, almost cut the steel-belted radial tire in two, and sent the hubcap flying off into the sagebrush. Apparently the hubcap also sheared off the chrome strip along the side of the car, tearing into the fender's sheet metal as it skyrocketed into the air. This vehicle, I realize, is beginning to look like what was left of Kowalski's Challenger after a very rough drive across Nevada.

Replacing the flat with one of those small spare tires that looks like a Radio Flyer wagon wheel, I limp back to Reno at about 50 miles per hour to a rental car agent who insists, "You've sideswiped something," but nevertheless gives me a new car because the one I've brought back "looks like it has been in a demolition derby." Swapping cars, I prepare to head east on another day's drive before I return the rental car in Salt Lake.

About halfway to Zion, I realize I'm traveling a road I've been on (in a car and bus), next to (on a train), and over (on numerous flights) so many times that I'm finally beginning to fathom its serpentine geography. It's Highway 80, and it parallels the Humboldt River for much of its route in Nevada. From Elko, I call my wife back in Texas. Her voice, like the desert wind, is music to my ears. It calms me, yet always secretly thrills me. But after we talk for a couple of minutes, I sense that something isn't right. Her voice somehow sounds different, vulnerable. I know her well enough to ask if something is wrong. "No," she says, but after a pause, she tells me that her most recent mammogram revealed a "suspicious mass," one she couldn't even feel. That mass, she tells me, is enough of a concern to her doctor to warrant a biopsy. I tell her I'll be on the next flight out of Salt Lake City, and jump back into the rental car a different man than the one who had dialed that phone just ten minutes before. Driving with one eye on the mirror and one on the road ahead, I make record time across the eastern Great Basin on the interstate, where the highway patrol is ever on the lookout for speeders. I fantasize that if I get pulled over, I'll tell the cop about the phone call to my wife—then I remember the 1997 version of *Vanishing Point* and realize that this tactic might be to no avail.

Rolling through the desert of eastern Nevada, I think a lot about this woman whose soul is as deep as Lake Tahoe, whose breasts are part of the familiar topography of home. This is the woman to whom I once dedicated a book with the words "To Ellen, who is always There"—and I deliberately capitalized the *T* in There because she is both a person and a place to me. As I enter Utah, I'm swept by guilt as I come to the realization that the Great Basin has been my mistress for the same length of time—four decades—that I've known this woman, whose name means light and who constantly finds the bright side of things while her husband explores everything, even darkness; a woman whose husband has heard the siren's call out in the vast open spaces, where he's gone to worship like a pilgrim while life goes on in his absence.

Returning the rental car at the Salt Lake City Airport, I quickly jot down the "mileage out" and the "mileage in." When added to the mileage in the earlier ill-fated rental car, the car's digital odometer in this one reveals I've driven 2,147 miles—all of it in the Great Basin—in less than a week. That translates to a far slower pace than Kowalski's, but then again I've lived to tell about it. As I hand the keys to the attendant, I quickly calculate that I've traveled well over 135,000 miles in the Great Basin over the last forty years in search of information, stories, and inspiration. That does not count the fifty times I've flown across it, round trip.

But these thoughts recede as I strap myself into the plane headed for Dallas-Fort Worth International Airport and what promises to be one of the biggest challenges of my—our—life. As we roar down the runway and take flight, we swing off to the northwest over the brooding waters of Great Salt Lake. Continuing our climb in a sweeping arc for a few minutes, now heading east by southeast, we soar over the Wasatch Mountains and this trip to the Great Basin becomes both another memory and another chapter waiting to be written.

Back home, my wife and I look at the mammogram with the doctor. As we hold it up to the light, we strain to see a few minute specs that look like distant stars in a nebula. The doctor draws our attention here because the technician has circled several dusty spots with a blue marker. Looking at the x-ray, the doctor is more silent than I like, and my suspicions are confirmed when he recommends a biopsy. Something makes me suspect that his intuition is better than his attempt to downplay what we may find during the surgery, and I'm right. With my wife still unconscious after the biopsy surgery less than a week later, Dr. Kennard Clark walks into the hospital room where I've waited: "She's doing fine," he tells me, "but the initial biopsy was positive." The word positive has a strange effect on me, delivering a one-two punch that numbs me yet strikes me as ironic because I know he means something negative. "Cancer," he adds after a pause that somehow stresses his humanity and our mortality. "Tell me," I ask this man who is victorious in extracting tissue that yields such a defeating outcome, "you knew beforehand just by looking at the x-ray, didn't you?" "Yes," he says, but he can't really explain why, for he's not Mr. Analytical like the husband standing nonplused before him. When my wife awakens from the biopsy, I'm the one she asks about the verdict. When I tell her, she lets out a long moan, not for her own suffering but because, as her next words remind me, "Now we'll have to tell [our daughter] Heather *this* is in her family history." That's motherhood, and its roots are instinctive.

Within two weeks, my wife is back in the hospital for surgery to remove the mass of malignant tissue; she's in the hands of the same doctor, with whom I've become partners in a effort to reverse the chain reaction that will very likely kill her in a few years if we don't prevent it. Looking at us both, the doctor informs us that the chances of recovery are about 95 percent, but then, after a pause, adds, "if followed by radiation and chemotherapy." After another pause so that this can sink in, he says something that reminds me how specialized the medical profession has become: "But the oncologist will be the one who makes that determination." Radiation! Chemotherapy! My God, I think, those are the biggest guns in the arsenal. Before they wheel my wife into surgery, I look into her sapphire-blue eyes, hold her hand, and tell her I'll always be with her. It's true. She's ready for anything, even waking up to find herself missing a breast if the doctor determines we need to go that far. That's trust, and its roots are spiritual.

Two hours later, the relieved doctor tells me he's got "good news—we got a clear margin around the malignant tissue, and so we didn't have to remove your wife's breast." Upon waking up after surgery, she's even more relieved than I, for make no mistake about it, breasts are as much a part of woman's reality as they are a man's fantasy. She was willing to sacrifice one, but only to save her life. We've stared a dragon down and come out pretty much in one piece; but the long process of medical treatment will now begin, throwing my wife and me into the hands of professionals who prescribe radiation one step away from lethal and administer chemotherapy that brings her to death's doorstep, but always just this side of the threshold. It's a razor-thin margin that makes me realize how fine a line we walk between life and death.

I can't help thinking there's a reason for everything, and this proves it—or makes me want to believe it proves it. Our community just happens to have one of the best cancer treatment centers in the country, but there's something else, too. Ellen's radiation is scheduled to begin on the same day I receive several books about Nevada's bombardment by nuclear radiation; her chemotherapy begins just when I read Corbin Harney's words about the poisoning of our environment by chemicals and I receive information about the tainted water that may be causing misery in Fallon, Nevada. Like the landscape of the Great Basin, my wife will feel the diffuse rays of atoms spin out of control, feel the tinge of chemicals running rampant—working both their blessed and demonic magic in hopes of a cure. I remember the adage "What doesn't kill you makes you stronger," but don't smile at its ironic truth.

So now this woman who finds sagebrush so regenerative that she collects clusters of it on our occasional trips through the Great Basin together, later steams it to savor its magical fragrance, and feels its healing powers; now this woman who friends and associates tell me is so serene and so "centered"; now this woman, who has always felt that she is in the hands of God, is also in the hands of medical technology—for that sage and that serenity hasn't prevented the cellular stampede that can silently spread to other organs and trample the life out of her. She's done everything, or just about everything, right, yet it still did not help. In what I understand is a natural reaction, I'm shaken, for I instinctively question my own ability to protect my wife from harm. Summoning all my powers, I gently lay hands upon her in a loving caress that should—but somehow can't—protect her from harm. I touch her body, trying to reach her soul, hoping that somehow, some way, my shamanic powers will work magic to stop the disease in its tracks. But we've already come face to face with the realization that we are virtually powerless to stop this silent killer ourselves.

At this point, I'm left with two alternatives. I begin with the first, questioning—make that accusing—modern society, which reaps almost constant blame in the media and the literature for polluting water, air, and food. Like Terry Tempest Williams, who links nuclear testing in the Great Basin with her mother's cancer, I search for blame in the environment—anything including Ellen's taking birth control pills in the mid-1960s (pills that were then deemed safe, but are now linked with breast cancer). But I don't stop there, even blaming myself for traveling the radioactive Great Basin with her in the mid-to-late 1960s. But then I realize: Why stop there? I can blame anything from Burger King Whoppers to McDonald's milkshakes, but the truth is there may be no blame at all other than the luck of the draw. To many people, I'd imagine, this is incomprehensible. Someone or something *must* be to blame for our misfortunes. But blame is the easy way out in something this complex. Then, too, I could simplify things and blame God for this affliction, but that would also be an easy out. Truth is, the very science that enables us to escape death's grip from childhood diseases, beat the grim reaper during adolescence, and survive into maturity now keeps us living long enough to bring us face to face with growing odds the older we get.

As I try to learn more about the causes of breast cancer, I discover something fascinating: There are as many ways of interpreting its cause(s) as there are beliefs about why and how places are created. These beliefs run the gamut from purely mechanistic (carcinogens added to the environment) to spiritual (such diseases strike when one is "out of touch" with cosmic forces). But although everyone has a theory that *something* causes this disease, I take some solace in the fact that this simply means a trickster like Coyote has thrown a monkey wrench in our lives—lives that we thought we had some control over but now realize are beyond, or certainly almost out of, our control. We pray, we meditate, we do everything nonphysical we can; but we ultimately realize that both the doctor's statistics ("There is a strong likelihood this will be fatal without treatment") and the powers he can summon (the oncologist, Alfred DiStefano, confirms that "there's a 95 percent likelihood of beating this with surgery followed by aggressive treatment") reaffirm that we've made a wise choice to also pursue a medical solution. As the oncologist draws sketches of breasts in various stages of healing for us, I realize that these images are his petroglyphs that reveal what happens when great powers are summoned.

I suspect that all but the most antiscientific, pro-natural-cure people realize this inevitable reliance on medicine has validity. That may account for Native peoples' demands for improvements in Indian health care in both the Great Basin and elsewhere—because better doctors, better technology, better treatment facilities equal a longer life. Here I intuitively, if reluctantly, recognize the power of doctors as shamans who can affect outcomes, add years to our lives, and otherwise alter the inevitable. They do not guarantee your life will have any greater value; only you and your spirituality can guarantee that. They do, however, give you some extra time to contemplate what it all means and what you are going to do about it.

But I'm still apprehensive about this medical treatment, for at this point I recall the words of Native American scholar Vine Deloria Jr., who claims that "[l]ike any other group of priests and politicians, . . . scientists lie and fudge their conclusions as much as the most distrusted professions in our society—lawyers and car dealers." To support this assertion, Deloria cites "several instances of false or doctored [note that use of the word here!] research reports, one a very serious manipulation of cancer research on women's breasts."[3] Yet here I wonder: does a fraudulent researcher or two really invalidate science? If so, does a fraudulent minister or two invalidate religion? Does a fraudulent Native American leader invalidate his (or her) people's beliefs?

I suspect not, and take solace in something that Deloria barely hints at— that there can be a convergence of ideologies based on the best—that is, truest—of what *all* belief systems offer. These include a wide range of belief systems, among them spiritual and religious beliefs. I sense this as my wife agrees to undergo the procedure that will lead us from purely structural (surgery) to physical (radiation), chemical (chemotherapy), nutritional (diet), and spiritual (prayer, meditation). But the words of a friend who also happens to be an oncologist—and can give me a second opinion— remind me of his role as both doctor and shaman. When I tell him about my wife's apprehension about chemotherapy, he moves closer to me and looks me straight in the eye. In words that reveal the suffering he has seen in the past and the suffering he can predict in the future based on his beliefs, he begins, "Richard," his words chosen carefully, "encourage her to get chemotherapy." I later learn that Britain's high rate of breast cancer fatality is directly linked to their system's not encouraging women to follow up breast surgery, and radiation, with chemotherapy. Vastly improved, Ellen is to receive chemotherapy in six separate doses three weeks apart—each dose administered by a battery operated microcomputerized pump that is a miracle of silicon chip technology. And so we embark on an adventure that fuses all the world's great traditions of faith—including science and spirituality. Some time later, a woman undergoing "chemo" tells us that the beautiful pomegranate-juice-colored fluid Adriamycin is called, for good reason, the "red devil." It's so caustic that it is administered through a tube directly into a vein; so powerful that it casts a pall over everything, dimming the light in Ellen's eyes during each three-day period it's administered.

This bout with cancer and the grueling follow-up with radiation and chemotherapy bring me face to face with science and technology vis-à-vis spirituality. In the popular press, science and spirituality are portrayed as polar opposites, especially when technology is blamed for everything from diseases to the despiritualization of our lives, but it is too easy to blame scientists for our woes. I realize this as I watch the radiation therapists embrace my wife after mysterious treatments that yield side effects like sunburned skin and phantom nerve twitches. I watch the chemotherapy staff monitor my wife's blood with a battery of scientific tests that assure she'll stay this side of that line between life and death; console her, like I do, as her gorgeous honey-colored hair falls out in clumps and her appetite flags. She's being poisoned by chemicals that compromise her immune system but act with deadly accuracy on those rampant cells that might have—we have no evidence of this—set out on a journey through her bloodstream. We have, in other words, *faith* in the technology's ability to heal despite its grave risks.

About the time that Ellen is three-quarters of the way through chemo, she experiences some throbbing pain through her chest and arms. Concerned that this might indicate a blood clot, the doctor authorizes a special Doppler sonogram. I'm allowed to witness this procedure, and am not prepared for the wonders it reveals. As the technician runs a scanning device across Ellen's chest and arms, I watch the monitor screen reveal images in black and white. Intrigued by the circular patterns that show up on the sonogram, I realize that I am observing cross-sections of Ellen's veins and arteries, which are now showing in vivid color, the former are neon turquoise blue, the latter flaming sunset orange. Then, with the technician's flip of a switch, I'm now looking longitudinally along Ellen's veins and catheter, which are also pulsing rhythmically in the same psychedelic color. Occasionally, the technician switches to close-up views and gets incandescent red images and pulsing noises that sound like they are coming from the bottom of the sea. We've been talking all the time, he sharing arcane secrets that reveal the wonders of Ellen's most intimate anatomy. I am awed by the revelations I see on the screen, somehow realizing that few people have ever seen their lover's bodies in such exquisite detail.

Privy to these mysteries, I'm pondering the wonders of the human circulatory system and the magnificence of the electronic cartography underway before me. This technician is mapping my wife's circulatory system in the twenty-first century, but something about the images seems strangely familiar to me. To compare the images, the medical technician constructs a three-dimensional model of my wife's subcutaneous topography, and what I see reminds me of Mrs. Hugh Brown's classic description of a three-dimensional map of a mine at Tonopah, Nevada:

On thin glass slides, some of which hung vertically in slender grooves while others lay horizontally on tiny cleats, all the workings of the mine were traced to scale in colored inks. When you stood in front of the model and looked into its serried sections, you seemed to be looking into the earth with a magic eye. Here the shaft dropped down from level to level through ore and country rock; here were 'drifts' and 'stopes' and 'crosscuts' with every foot of ore blocked out; and here you traced the meandering vein, noted where it petered out or widened into richness unimagined as it continued into regions still unexplored.[4]

With Mrs. Brown's vivid subterranean cartographic description in mind, I keep one eye on Ellen and the other on the computer screen, entranced and yet apprehensive. This mapping exercise once again suggests both a visceral and a spiritual connection between body and place; between human curiosity and the workings of creation; between the wisdom of humankind and the wisdom of the Great Creator. Followed up by an elaborate infusion of radioactive iodine, it reveals the source of Ellen's pain: A lozenge-shaped blood clot has formed in the vein near the catheter. Undaunted, Ellen seconds the surgeon's recommendation that this catheter be removed and a new one inserted in another location so that she can stay on schedule with the chemotherapy.

In the midst of it all, even as the chemotherapy makes her weak and listless, Ellen looks at me and says: "Compared to the suffering that many people face, I still feel blessed and protected." Her faith is unshakable as she cherishes the lyrics of the song "Wash Your Spirit Clean" by the Native American (Cherokee) group Walela: "Be grateful for the struggle. Be thankful for the lessons." Most of the way through the journey to cancer recovery, I awaken at all hours, mostly sure we've chosen the right course, but sometimes doubting. This journey, however, is now underway and there's no turning back. In addition to seeing the connections between our bodies and place, this journey also enables me to see the deep connections, rather than differences, between Native and Western thought. After a trip to the aptly named chemotherapy "infusion center," where three patients talk openly about faith and a poster on the wall with the title "The Courage to Be Myself" encourages women to "Favor the Mystery of Spirit" as they reorder their lives, I realize that medicine and faith, which is to say science and spirituality, are moving closer together. Medical schools are integrating courses on spirituality into their curricula, and many patients now openly invite their doctors to pray with them. Looking around me at this center, I see that scientific and spiritual philosophies are converging, but realize that this can only happen if we let them—let them converge without fear of assimilation, fear of melting into a pot in which we'll lose our identity. I want to be part of that remarkable amalgam that, like a miner's crucible, re-enacts procreation. Let this fusion occur; open the dialogue; revel in the alchemy that fuses the best of cultural contact with divine inspiration.

Deep in the night, I recollect how important this fusion is, and how many of its messages I've ignored. I find recent discoveries by scientists fascinating and somehow reassuring—for example, that microbes may have survived 250 million years in a crystal of salt much like that which underlies some playas in the Great Basin.[5] Then, too the idea that microorganisms also inhabit rocks at unheard of depths—say ten thousand feet underground—helps substantiate Corbin Harney's claim that the rocks are living. This revelation, based on a microscopic analysis, reveals a previously unknown form of life, similar to bacteria, that feeds on constituents in otherwise solid rock. It may explain something that has always fascinated me: the strangely organic smell that emanates from otherwise lifeless igneous rocks as they are hammered or breathed on. Some scientists claim that these microbes thrive in temperatures as high as 200 degrees and may "have been here for 2 billion years."[6] Consider, too, this surprising revelation: the estimated biomass of these life-forms locked underground in rocks may very well *exceed* the biomass of all plants and animals living on the earth's surface. That gets me to thinking that life may abound deep under the Great Basin in contrast to the scant vegetation that clothes its surface—that the very rocks are, in a sense, alive.

I'm also thinking about the arbitrary separation between living and nonliving (that is, animate versus inanimate). According to Vine Deloria Jr., "The major difference between American Indian views of the physical world and Western science lies in the premise accepted by Indians and rejected by scientists: the world in which we live is alive." Deloria elaborates: "Many scientists believe this idea to be primitive superstition and consequently the scientific explanation rejects any nuance of interpretation which could credit the existence of activities as having partial intelligence or sentience." This thought fascinates me, for it suggests different layers of belief about the same phenomena. According to Deloria, "Indians thus obtain information from birds, animals, rivers, and mountains which is inaccessible to modern science." I like Deloria's concept that there are "certain kinds of correspondences between the Indian way and modern scientific techniques," such as the desire to create rain. The difference, as Deloria puts it, is that scientists mechanistically "force nature" while Indians perform ceremonies "asking the spirits for rain."[7] I suspect that much healing needs to occur before the Native and the scientific traditions fuse into a rich amalgam, but this can't happen soon enough for my wife and me. We are at the juncture of embracing both science and spirituality—of recognizing the convergence between animate and inanimate—as she nears the end of her chemotherapy, both of us thankful for the treatment that—we hope—will give us another forty years of love and friendship together.

By spring, Ellen is better enough for me to feel comfortable making a trip to Reno to present a paper on spirituality and landscape in the Great Basin. I had submitted the paper's abstract before learning about Ellen's condition, but over the last seven months, I've prepared the paper thinking about the changing relationship between Native spirituality, Judeo-Christian religion, and scientific technology. These potent beliefs are in conflict in the Great Basin today, but may someday come closer together. Driving to Dallas-Forth Worth International, I realize that I've engineered another trip to the Great Basin. Although I will cut it a bit shorter to get home where I'm needed, I'll still be able to drive out into the region to take a few photos for this book. Walking through the airport concourse toward the departure gate, I see a large, illuminated advertisement that stops me in my tracks. It's in the form of a newspaper headline that reads "Bacteria Tested as Digital Circuit." Its subheading, "Use in Chips May Dwarf Silicon,"[8] again makes me question the classification of things into binary categories like organic and inorganic. I sense the inherent truth in Corbin Harney's belief, though neither of us can prove it—yet.

Upon entering the plane, I glance to the left to see a myriad of illuminated dials and switches in the cockpit. Each of these is in some way connected to, or controlled by, circuits pulsing through silicon chips. These instruments not only provide information; many of them are interactive systems of artificial intelligence that communicate with the pilots, and the pilots with those systems. If and when these miraculous silicon chips are ever replaced by bacteria, I wonder if we'll then call such systems "real," rather than "artificial," intelligence. But even now, as we roar down the runway and lift off at 165 miles per hour, I sense that the separation between inorganic and organic—and even between artificial and real—no longer holds. That message—that inorganic and organic are one—is embedded in Native American history, ethics, and spirituality. I now see these elemental substances as so many forms of expression, so many representations of creation.

As always, I'm in a window seat where I can watch the panorama unfold below. Remarkably, the plane is only about three-fourths full, and there's even a row of unoccupied seats across from me so that I can hop over and gaze out the window on that side from time to time. After a couple of hours, the plane reaches that magic point not far from where Brigham Young probably said, "This is the place," where the landscape opens up into the magnificent Great Basin. Leaving the Wasatch Mountains behind, we fly

over the "West Desert," as photojournalist Craig Denton joined generations of latter-day pioneers in calling the vast area straddling the Utah-
Nevada border. Here the Great Basin confirms its reputation as a land of
religious and spiritual experimentation. Within the space of just a few
minutes, my American Airlines jet flies over several religious settlements
where people search for alternatives to mainstream spirituality. There,
just off the wing, I recognize Eskdale of the United Aaronic order, an ex-
perimental, patriarchal, music-loving community where the houses are set
in two semicircles around a common ground. Land is held in common, and
the settlement recently began "opening itself to anyone from any faith who
seeks peace and meditation in a family environment." A glance northward
reveals another settlement, the apostolic community of the Fraternity
Preparation at Vance Spring. This group "had looked for a place where they
could be as far as possible from the seductive lures of government, and
they found it at a wellspring inside a dense piñon-juniper forest about 16
miles from the Utah-Nevada border." Most had been Mormons but either
left the church or were excommunicated. Believing their land to be held in
trust with God, their leader, Talmadge Weis, sees parallels between "this
notion of land ownership and the Native American claim that humans
can't really own the land," or as he puts it: "All the land belongs to the Great
Spirit."[9]

With this fusion of beliefs on my mind, I realize we're also almost flying
over the School of the Natural Order at Home Farm, near Baker, Nevada, a
"'center of light,' a beacon or resting place for people stopping by on their
individual paths of personal discovery." Looking down from this altitude, I
recall Craig Denton's statement that "the teaching of the School of Natural
Order . . . is like water on a West Desert playa." It is both "fluid and capable
of wandering on its own," and "elusive, too, until its earthly momentum
stops and it quietly slips into the cracks of a thirsty soul." I am here once
again reminded of how human belief expresses itself in the landscape: "Because of the fluidity," Denton observed, "the Home Farm compound sometimes looks like an aluminum-sided caravan as it grows outward from the
original small cluster of buildings circling the orchard" at its center.[10]

Flying over eastern Nevada at 450 miles per hour, I realize that I've got
the manuscript for this book nearly completed but am still pondering a
conclusion that brings 165,000 square miles of geography and 10,000
years of history together. I'm jotting down sentences but also almost constantly looking out the plane's small plastic windows for fear I'll miss
something of interest. Below, the Great Basin continues to heave and
stretch under a partly cloudy sky that causes large patches of light and

shadow to migrate across the corrugated landscape below (fig. 12.2). I've come to know the region well enough to recognize physical features like the Toiyabe Mountains. Far off to the northeast I can barely make out the Ruby Mountains and recall cowboy poet Jack Walter's poem about them. The opening lines reveal a deep spiritual connection that make this rancher sound more like Walt Whitman than the Marlboro Man:

> I am part of this range of waving grass
> Part of the evening breeze, the gentle rains that pass,
> I am the horse or range cow that moves out there so free,
> Deep down within, they seem a part of me.[11]

These words remind me that even those who use the region's resources may deeply—and spiritually—love the place.

Still looking northward, I can discern the Humboldt River Valley, where the main routes of travel, rail and highway, girdle the region. Along the Southern Pacific line here, the Danish-born wife of a track work-crew manager raised a family in the 1920s, pausing to write a poem about how this region had become connected to her very being:

> A desert moon—a starlit sky,
> A merciless blazing sun.
> The Heart of the desert has claimed my love.
> With it I may now be one.[12]

These words confirm how strongly the spirit of place grips our souls. As we continue our westward flight, I recognize the once-booming mining town of Austin, which is now almost directly under the plane. Squinting to sharpen the focus of my view, I look down and see the pockmarked hill behind Austin where miners brought underground secrets into the light for an instant, the intersection where the town's Catholic church still stands after more than a century, just a barely visible speck among the cluster of specks that is Austin, the same memorable intersection where Kowalski hung a wild turn with the Nevada Highway Patrol in hot pursuit.

As the whine of the jet engines changes pitch about twenty-five minutes out of Reno, we begin a slow descent, continuing over range after serrated range of mountains that help define the region's personality and soul. Just off the right, Fallon appears as a series of emerald-green rectangular patches embroidered into the beige desert landscape. Here, amidst the desert that settlers found chaotic, I recognize Fallon as a quilt whose makers believed, and believe, in an ordered cosmos. Here, too, a community asking the perennial question of why cancer has stricken so many of its children looks

Fig. 12.2. Unfolding Panorama: Viewed from a commercial airliner nearing the Utah-Nevada border, the distinctive Great Basin landscape unfolds as a series of snow-clad mountain ranges alternating with desert valleys. (May 2000 photograph by author)

both inward and skyward for answers. Those questions involve both fate and faith, and I am reminded how much like our own bodies these places are, subject to both analyses and incantations.

In a few minutes, we begin a gentle turn to the left and I get another full view to the north. Spread out before me is one of the West's most magnificent sights—Pyramid Lake. From here, the lake looks like an oblong cerulean-blue jewel studded with a triangular fleck of white—the namesake pyramid-shaped island that enchanted mid-nineteenth-century explorers bent on translating the Great Basin into the "American Sahara." The transformation didn't end there. In the mid-1960s, the producers of the biblical epic film *The Greatest Story Ever Told* transformed Pyramid Lake into the Sea of Galilee in a tribute to the Holy Land. But try though we may to appropriate Pyramid Lake into our ever-questing Judeo-Christian philosophy—and to immortalize the Holy Land in landscapes we encounter here—this place still resonates deeply with Native American mythology, history, and spirituality. I now see the lake in a new light—not only as a body of water marooned after the desiccation since the Pleistocene, but also as a result of human (and animal) actions that left water in the wake of tragedy. I take comfort in the thought that out of our failings and tragedies we construct places that endure. They do so through our beliefs in their creation and our beliefs about their creator(s). Three Nevada authors recently noted that Pyramid Lake's "spiritual qualities are well known to Paiutes," and that they themselves find solace here. Despite the lake's "mysterious and fearful quality," it "heals both psychically and physically."[13]

With the Sierra Nevada Range now edging into view as the plane begins another long, gentle turn toward the left, I comprehend the deeper meaning of places like Pyramid Lake and environs. Believing in place means believing in the stories we tell about it, but it means far more than that. It also means integrating places into our deepest beliefs. I now see places as reflections of the human bodies we love and lose, the human souls we cherish in memory, the plants and animals with whom we inhabit the earth, and the god(s) we worship. Through place we are woven into the tapestry of creation. A beautiful desert lake that is filled by a woman's tears seems a fitting tribute to the joys we experience and the losses we suffer. As the Sierra Nevada range now swings into full view, I feel uplifted knowing that places connect us with our spiritual history and help point us toward spiritual fulfillment. The Truckee River appears below us as we glide toward Reno, the city huddling around it for sustenance, and I think again how this river flowing into the desert has nurtured both body and soul.

I'm still writing as the plane touches down with a familiar "thump . . . thump" of tires hitting, then gripping, the runway. That ritual always brings me back to Earth, but I am somehow energized by a revelation that the Great Basin has taught me as much about belief as it has geography. As the pilot pulls up to the gate, shuts down the engines, and turns off the Fasten Seat Belt sign, passengers bolt out of their seats as I finish my last thought. With this manuscript in my briefcase, I leave the plane, pick up a rental car, and drive into Reno, wondering if I could ever find another place as inspirational to write about, or another woman as inspired to love.

Notes

Introduction

1. When seen from a distance, these beams appear to be blue, and this further conveys the sense that they connect the site to the heavens. About 300 miles west of Ground Zero, the Pennsylvania site where a United Airlines jet crashed when passengers attempted to thwart its hijacking was also designated as a sacred place.

2. James Redfield, "Our Rediscovery of the World's Mysteries" *Utne Reader* no. 102 (November-December 2000): 78-79.

3. As might be expected, this search for spirituality is accompanied by a spate of books. Among them is the poignant *Soul Mountain* by Gao Xingjian, which was described as part of the current "ascent into the spiritual."

4. Mary Clearman Blew, *Bone Deep in Landscape: Writing, Reading, and Place* (Norman: University of Oklahoma Press, 1999), joins a growing list of books that examine place from the inside out, as it were: place as it affects, and is affected by, history and fate.

5. In introducing a new book series called "The Spiritual Traveler," editor Jan-Erik Guerth notes that "[s]acred journeys and sacred sites have been at the center of humankind's spiritual life from the very beginning." Other publishers' new offerings pretty much summarize the gamut of books that focus on the spiritual aspects of place. *Divine Landscapes: A Pilgrimage through Britain's Sacred Places,* by Ronald Blythe (Norwich, U.K.: Canterbury Press, 2000), offers a revealing look at the British landscape through the eyes of those who search for spiritually in place. *Pilgrimage: Adventures of the Spirit,* by James O'Reilly (Travelers' Tales Guides, 2000), and *A Woman's Path: Women's Best Spiritual Travel Writing,* by Lucy McCauley et al. (Travelers' Tales Guides, 2000), confirm that spiritual places are often associated with quests—and that a person's age, gender, and other factors are important elements in how he or she pursues spirituality. Lastly, *Holy Personal: Looking for Small Private Places of Worship,* by Laura Chester et al. (Bloomington: Indiana University Press, 2000) reveals something of the complexity of sacred places as interpreted by Americans of diverse faiths.

6. For an excellent discussion on this subject, see chapter 2, "Modern Definitions of the Great Basin," in Donald K. Grayson, *The Desert's Past: A Natural Prehistory of the Great Basin* (Washington, D.C.: Smithsonian Institution Press, 1993), 11-42.

7. William C. Sturtevant et al., *Handbook of North American Indians: Great Basin* (Washington, D.C.: Government Printing Office, 1986).

8. See John Logan Allen, *North American Exploration,* vol. 3, *A Continent Comprehended* (Lincoln: University of Nebraska Press, 1997).

9. See Page Smith, *As a City upon a Hill: The Town in American History* (New York: Knopf, 1966).

10. James Griffith, *Beliefs and Holy Places: A Spiritual Geography of the Pimería Alta* (Tucson: University of Arizona Press, 1992). In this landmark book, Griffith interprets southern Arizona and northern Sonora in light of the folklore and beliefs of both indigenous peoples and newcomers.

11. Keith Basso, Wisdom Sits in Places: Landscape and Language among the Western Apache (Albuquerque: University of New Mexico Press, 1996), reaffirms the importance of listening to Native voices and appreciating the deeper meanings of place names. Basso studied the Western Apache of Arizona, but his methodology works elsewhere.

12. See Bruce S. Feiler, *Walking the Bible: A Journey by Land through the Five Books of Moses* (New York: W. Morrow, 2001).

1. Landscape and Storytelling

1. Steve Schmollinger, *Desert Railroading* (Forest Park, Ill.: Heimburger House, 1999), 15-16.

2. For an excellent discussion of travelers'' accounts of the arid West, see Patricia Nelson Limerick, *Desert Passages: Encounters with the American Deserts* (Albuquerque: University of New Mexico Press, 1985).

3. Mark W. Hemphill, *Union Pacific Salt Lake Route* (Erin, Ontario: Boston Mills Press, 1995), 47.

4. J. H. Simpson, *Report of Explorations across the Great Basin in 1859,* 30.

5. Martha Knack and Omer C. Stewart, *As Long as the River Shall Run: An Ethnohistory of Pyramid Lake Indian Reservation* (Berkeley: University of California Press, 1984), 16-18, 19.

6. Corbin Harney, *The Way It Is: One Water . . . One Air . . . One Mother* (Nevada City, Calif.: Blue Dolphin, 1994), 41, 71.

7. Michael Hittman, *A Numu History: The Yerington Paiute Tribe* (Yerington, Nev.:Yerington Paiute Tribe, 1984), 15.

8. Ibid.

9. Ibid.

10. Phil Robinson, *Sinners and Saints: A Tour across the States, and round Them; with Three Months among the Mormons* (Boston: Roberts Brothers, 1883), 183; Georgiana M. Stisted, *The True Life of Capt. Sir Richard F. Burton* (London: H. S. Nichol, 1896), 265; John Charles Frémont, *Memoirs of My Life* (Chicago: Belford, Clarke, 1887), 438.

11. Larry Prosor et al., *Nevada: Desert Lows and Mountain Highs: A Photo Essay,* ed. Laurel Hilde (Truckee, Calif.: Fine Line Productions, 1994), 11.

12. See Yi-Fu Tuan, *Topophilia: A Study of Environmental Perception, Attitudes, and Values* (Englewood Cliffs, N.J.: Prentice-Hall, 1974).

13. See Lawrence K. Hersh, *The Central Pacific Railroad across Nevada, 1868 and 1997 Photographic Comparatives* (Los Angeles: Lawrence K. Hersh, 2000).

14. Union Pacific since 1997.

15. D. W. Meinig, *The Interpretation of Ordinary Landscapes* (New York: Oxford University Press, 1979), 33-48.

16. Michael Conzen, ed., *The Making of the American Landscape* (New York: Routledge, 1990), 3.

17. See Ferenc Morton Szasz, *Religion in the Modern American West* (Tucson: University of Arizona Press, 2000), xi-xvi.

18. See James Griffith, *Beliefs and Holy Places* (Tucson: University of Arizona Press, 1992).

19. Wallace Stegner, *The Preacher and the Slave* (Boston: Houghton Mifflin, 1950), 193.

20. See John G. Mitchell, "The Way West," *National Geographic,* September 2000, 58-59.

21. Mark Wheeler, "When Magma's on the Move," *Smithsonian,* February 2000, 48.

22. Blew, *Bone Deep in Landscape,* 7.

23. See Victoria Dickenson, *Drawn from Life: Science and Art in the Portrayal of the New World* (Toronto: University of Toronto Press, 1998), 66-67; see also 4-17.

24. See Sidney J. Jansma Sr., *Six Days* (Grand Rapids, Mich.: Sidney J. Jansma, 1985).

25. See John McPhee, *Annals of the Former World* (New York: Farrar, Straus and Giroux, 1998).

26. See Denis Wood, *The Power of Maps* (New York: Guilford Press, 1992), 145-81, for a study of how different cultures depict hills and mountains.

27. Richard Poulsen, *The Pure Experience of Order: Essays on the Symbolic in the Folk Material Culture of Western America* (Albuquerque: University of New Mexico Press, 1982), 125.

28. Anne M. Smith, comp., *Shoshone Tales* (Salt Lake City: University of Utah Press, 1993), 42.

29. From "Deep Springs College: Loyalty to a Fault?" by L. Jackson Newell, Deep Springs College president, on the college website: <http://www.deepsprings.edu/whatis/newell1.html>, as viewed October 31, 2000.

30. See Richard Moreno, *Roadside History of Nevada* (Missoula, Mont.: Mountain Press, 2000),169.

2. Darkness and Light

1. Dorcas S. Miller, *Stars of the First People: Native American Star Myths and Constellations* (Boulder: Pruett, 1997), 124-35.

2. Mary L. Pope, *Let Me Tell You a Story: Adapted Paiute Tales,* from stories told by Frank Quinn, Hazel Quinn, and Russell Dick (N.p.: Yerington Paiute Tribal Council 1981), 1-3.

3. From "Let Me Tell You a Story," adapted from the collection of Numu tales by Isabel Kelly, in *Numu Ya Dua'* 3, no. 19 (February 5, 1982): 3.

4. William L. Fox, *The Void, the Grid, and the Sign: Traversing the Great Basin* (Salt Lake City: University of Utah Press, 2000), 185.

5. See Mark Q. Sutton, "The Numic Expansion As Seen from the Mojave Desert," in

Across the West: Human Population Movement and the Expansion of the Numa, ed. David B. Madsen and David Rhode (Salt Lake City: University of Utah Press, 1994), 133-40.

6. Moreno, *Roadside History of Nevada,* 3.

7. "The Cave," in Mary L. Pope, *Let Me Tell You a Story: Adapted Paiute Tales,* from stories told by Frank Quinn, Hazel Quinn, and Russell Dick (N.p.: Yerington Paiute Tribe 1981), 45-46.

8. Frémont, *Memoirs,* 436-37.

9. Moreno, *Roadside History of Nevada,* 112-13.

10. Clifford L. Stott, *Search for Sanctuary: Brigham Young and the White Mountain Expedition* (Salt Lake City: University of Utah Press, 1984),165-66.

11. Ibid., 167.

12. Ibid., 169-70.

13. Ibid., 166.

14. Terry Tempest Williams, *Refuge: An Unnatural History of Family and Place* (New York: Vintage Books, 1992), 237.

15. Ibid., 237-38.

16. Ibid., 50.

17. Luella Adams Dalton, comp., *History of Iron County Mission and Parowan: The Mother Town* (Parowan, Utah: N.p., n.d.), 2-3.

3. Water and Memory

The UNICORN, words and music by Shel Silverstein TRO–© copyright 1962 (Renewed), 1968 (Renewed) Hollis Music, Inc., New York, NY; used by permission.

1. Richard Moreno, *Roadside History of Nevada* (Missoula, Mont.: Mountain Press, 2000), 3.

2. Stephen Trimble, *The Sagebrush Ocean: A Natural History of the Great Basin* (Reno: University of Nevada Press, 1989).

3. Samuel Clemens, *Roughing It* (Hartford, Conn.: American, 1872), 143.

4. For an excellent discussion of Lake Lahontan, see Richard L. Orndorff, Robert W. Wieder, and Harry F. Filkorn, *Geology Underfoot in Central Nevada* (Missoula, Mont.: Mountain Press, 2001), 83-96.

5. "Let Me Tell You a Story," told by Corbett Mack, *Numu Ya Dua'* 3, no. 1 (July 3, 1981): 4.

6. See Hittman, *A Numu History,,* 12.

7.Ibid., 2.

8. Julia Panguish in Anne M. Smith, comp. and ed., *Shoshone Tales* (Salt Lake City: University of Utah Press, 1993), 108.

9. Ibid., 78-79.

10. Hittman, A Numu History, 2.

11. Ibid.

12. Solomon Nunes Carvalho, *Incidents of Travel and Adventure in the Far West . . .* (1857; reprint, Philadelphia: Jewish Publication Society of America, 1954), 213.

13. Ibid.

14. Ibid., 213-14.

15. John Pulsipher's History in "Pulsipher Family History Book," unpublished family

history dated December 22, 1961, arranged and typed by Eva H. Allan, 57-58 [copy in possession of author as provided by Nancy Grace].

16. Dorothea Theodratus, "A Perspective on Traditional Sites," *Proceedings of the Society for California Archaeology* 6 (1993): 46.

17. Consider, for example, the Bavispe earthquake in Sonora, Mexico, in 1887; it resulted in new springs appearing and the disappearance of others, as well as changes to the flow of the San Pedro River in Arizona.

18. Robert Dawson, Peter Goin, and Mary Webb, *A Doubtful River* (Reno: University of Nevada Press, 2000), 133

19. Yi-Fu Tuan, *Escapism* (Baltimore: John Hopkins University Press, 1998), 66.

20. John Cowper Powys, *The Art of Happiness* (London: John Lane, Bodley Head, 1935), 46-47, 74.

21. "A Horse with No Name," song by America, 1972.

22. Mary Austin, *The American Rhythm* (New York: Harcourt, Brace, 1923). See also Leah Dilworth, *Imagining Indians in the Southwest: Persistent Visions of a Primitive Past* (Washington, D.C.: Smithsonian Institution Press, 1997), 180-81.

23. Angie Wagner, "Cluster of Child Cancer Cases Bewilders Small Nevada Town," *Dallas Morning News,* Monday, February 5, 2001, 4a.

24. Howard Stansbury, *Exploration of the Valley of the Great Salt Lake,* ed. Don D. Fowler (Washington, D.C.: Smithsonian Institution Press, 1998), 119.

4. Stories in Stone

1. See "Flashes of Light: Meteors and Railroad Valley," in Robert D. McCracken and Jeanne Sharp Howerton, *A History of Railroad Valley, Nevada* (Tonopah: Central Nevada Historical Society, 1996), 199-205.

2. Originally quoted in John McPhee, *Basin and Range* (New York: Noonday Press, 1981); also in Joseph V. Tingley and Kris Ann Pizarro, *Traveling America's Loneliest Road: A Geologic and Natural History Tour through Nevada along U.S. Highway 50* (Reno: Nevada Bureau of Mining and Geology, 2000), 6.

3. Fox, *The Void, the Grid, and the Sign,* xi , ix.

4. See Tingley and Pizarro, *Traveling American's Loneliest Road.*

5. John Stewart, *Geology of Nevada: A Discussion to Accompany the Geologic Map of Nevada* (Reno: Nevada Bureau of Mines and Geology, University of Nevada, 1980), 110.

6. Bill Fiero, *Geology of the Great Basin* (Reno: University of Nevada Press, 1986), 127.

7. Donald L. Baars, *The Colorado Plateau; A Geologic History* (Albuquerque: University of New Mexico Press, 2000), 191.

8. See Stott, *Search for Sanctuary,* 141.

9. Richard L. Orndorff, Robert W. Wieder, and Harry F. Filkorn, *Geology Underfoot in Central Nevada* (Missoula, Mont.: Mountain Press, 2001), 213.

10. Howard Stansbury, *Exploration of the Valley of the Great Salt Lake,* ed. Don D. Fowler (Washington, D.C.: Smithsonian Institution Press, 1988), 90, 100-101.

11. Yi-Fu Tuan, "The Desert and I: A Study in Affinity," *Michigan Quarterly Review* 40, no. 1 (winter 2001): 16.

12. Harney, *The Way It Is,* 26.

13. Ibid., 8-9.

14. See Thomas Clements, "Leonardo da Vinci as a Geologist," in *Language of the Earth,* ed. Frank H. T. Rhodes and Richard O. Stone (New York: Pergamon Press, 1981), 313.

15. Harney, *The Way It Is,* 11, 12.

16. Ibid, 12.

17. Szasz, *Religion in the Modern American West,* 63-64.

18. Helen Carlson, *Nevada Place Names: A Geographical Dictionary* (Reno: University of Nevada Press, 1974), 221.

19. Ibid., 177.

20. Ibid., 120.

21. Carvalho, *Incidents of Travel and Adventure in the Far West,* 268-71.

22. Ibid.

23. Carlson, *Nevada Place Names,* 97.

24. Helen Carlson, ibid., notes that this is a local name for Diana's Punchbowl.

25. "Discovering Millard County & West Central Utah, 2001-2002 Edition" (N.p.: n.p., n.d), 12.

26. See Eric Haseltine, "Apparitions: Did You Just See a Ghost?" *Discover* 23, no. 2 (February 2002): 88.

27. Prosor et al, *Nevada: Desert Lows and Mountain Highs,* ed. Hilde, 169.

28. Samuel Bowles, *Our New West: Records of Travel between the Mississippi River and the Pacific Ocean . . .* (Hartford, Conn.: Hartford Publishing, 1869), 277-78.

29. See J. Douglas Porteous, *Landscapes of the Mind: Worlds of Sense and Metaphor* (Toronto: University of Toronto Press, 1990), 69-70.

30. Williams, *Refuge,* 109.

31. Catherine Fowler, "Ethnography and Great Basin Prehistory," in *Models and Great Basin Prehistory: A Symposium,* ed. Don Fowler (Reno and Las Vegas: Desert Research Institute Publications in Social Science, #12, 1978), 11-48; also cited in Pat Barker and Cynthia Pinto, "Legal and Ethnic Implications of the Numic Expansion," in *Across the West: Human Population Movement and the Expansion of the Numa,* ed. David B. Madsen and David Rhode (Salt Lake City: University of Utah Press, 1994), 18-29.

32. Barker and Pinto, "Legal and Ethnic Implications of the Numic Expansion," 18-29.

33. See Frank Wendell Call, *Gandydancer's Children: A Railroad Memoir* (Reno: University of Nevada Press, 2000).

34. Carlson, *Nevada Place Names,* 49-50.

5. Encounters with the Wind

1. In a wetter climate, those basins would fill with water, and the overflow would run to the sea; the rivers flowing outward would erode the rims of the basin.

2. Dan De Quille [William Wright], *The Big Bonanza* (New York: Alfred A. Knopf, 1953), 86.

3. William O. Vanderburg, *Mines of Lander and Eureka Counties* (Las Vegas: Nevada Publications, 1988), 10

4. "Songs of Life Returning," originally translated by James Mooney, and referenced

in *Earth Always Endures: Native American Poems,* comp. Neil Philip (New York: Viking, 1996), 86.

5. B. M. Bower, *The Parowan Bonanza* (Boston: Little, Brown, 1923), 19-20.

6. Maureen Whipple, *The Giant Joshua* (Boston: Houghton Mifflin, 1942), 194.

7. Carlson, *Nevada Place Names,* 244.

8. *Dictionary of American Regional English,* Vol. 2, 45, 240.

9. William Least Heat Moon, *Blue Highways: A Journey into America* (Boston: Little, Brown, 1982), 156.

10. See Don D. Fowler and Catherine S. Fowler, *Anthropology of the Numa: John Wesley Powell's Manuscripts on the Numic People of Western North America, 1868-1880* (Washington, D.C.: Smithsonian Institution Press, 1981), 132.

11. Jan Deblieu, *Wind: How the Flow of Air Has Shaped Life, Myth, and the Land* (Boston: Houghton Mifflin, 1998), 26. See also James Kale McNeley, *Holy Wind in Navajo Philosophy* (Tucson: University of Arizona Press, 1981).

12. Blew, *Bone Deep in Landscape,* 170.

13. Richard Francaviglia, "Learning from 'The Spirit of Place,'" *Fronteras* 9, no. 1 (spring 2000), 3-4.

14. "Memories of T.A.A.F, Part IV," *Central Nevada's Glorious Past* 18, no. 2 (November 1995): 34-35.

15. J. Ross Browne, "Washoe Revisited," in *Adventures in Apache Country: A Tour through Arizona and Sonora, with notes on the Silver Regions of Nevada,* (New York: Harper and Brothers, 1868). This piece was originally published in *Harper's New Monthly Magazine,* 1864.

16. Deblieu, *Wind,* 13.

17. Carlson, *Nevada Place Names,* 250.

18. See Sarah Ann Davis et al., *Guide to Virginia City, Nevada, and the Comstock Lode Area* ... (Sausalito, Calif.: Pages of History, 1959), 42.

19. Deblieu, *Wind,* 25-26.

20. "Songs of Life Returning," in *Earth Always Endures,* comp. Philip, 86.

21. John Randolph Spears, *Illustrated Sketches of Death Valley and Other Borax Deserts of the Pacific Coast* (Baltimore: Johns Hopkins University Press, 2000), 128, 44.

22. Harney, *The Way It Is,* 73.

23. Carvalho, *Incidents of Travel and Adventure in the Far West,* 267.

24. Smith, comp., *Shoshone Tales,* 186-88.

6. In Search of the Great Spirit

1. Herbert E. Bolton, *Pageant in the Wilderness: The Story of the Escalante Expedition to the Interior Basin, 1776* (Salt Lake City: Utah State Historical Society, 1950), 243.

2. Ibid., 244, 188.

3. Simpson, Report of Explorations, 460-61.

4. John Wesley Powell and George W. Ingalls, *Report of Special Commissioners J. W. Powell and G. W. Ingalls on the Condition of the Ute Indians of Utah; the Paiutes of Utah, Northern Arizona, Southern Nevada, and Southeastern California; the Northwestern Shoshones of Nevada; and Report Concerning Claims of Settlers in the Mo-a-pa Valley, Southeastern Nevada* (Washington, D.C.: Government Printing Office, 1874), 114.

5. Simpson, Report of Explorations, 463.

6. Ibid., 462.

7. Ibid., 18, 461.

8. Ibid., 36.

9. Ibid., 459.

10. Ibid.

11. Julian H. Steward and Erminie Wheeler-Voegelin, *The Northern Paiute Indians* (New York: Garland, 1974), 309.

12. Ibid.

13. Gae Whitney Canfield, *Sarah Winnemucca of the Northern Paiutes* (Norman: University of Oklahoma Press, 1983), 11-13.

14. David S. Whitley, "Shamanism, Natural Modeling, and the Rock Art of Far Western North American Hunter-Gatherers," in *Shamanism and Rock Art in North America,* ed. Solveig A. Turpin, Special Publication 1 (San Antonio, Tex.: Rock Art Foundation, 1994), 4. See Carling Malouf, "The Goshiute Indians," in *The Shoshone Indians, American Indian Ethnohistory: California and Basin-Plateau Indians* (New York: Garland, 1974), 25-172.

15. See <http://www.doitnow.org/pages/525.html>.

16. Paul Devereux, *The Long Trip: A Prehistory of Psychedelia* (New York: Penguin Arkana, 1997), 3.

17. See Carobeth Laird, *The Chemehuevis* (Banning, Calif.: Malki Museum, 1976), 84, and Whitley, "Shamanism, Natural Modeling, and the Rock Art," 22.

18. Whitley, "Shamanism, Natural Modeling, and the Rock Art," 22-23.

19. Lawrence Biemiller, "Clambering Up a Cliff to Record the Handiwork of Man," *Chronicle of Higher Education,* February 23, 2001, A64.

20. See Tuan, "The Desert and I," 7-16.

21. Michael Hittman, *Wovoka and the Ghost Dance,* ed. Don Lynch (Lincoln: University of Nebraska Press, 1997), 75-85.

22. Ibid., 107, 111, 108, 124-25.

23. Paul Dayton Bailey, *Ghost Dance Messiah* (1970; reprint, Tucson: Westernlore Press, 1986), 66-71.

24. Robbie Robertson and the Red Road Ensemble, *Music for the Native Americans* (Capitol Records, Inc., 1994), jacket notes.

25. Hittman, *Wovoka,* 91.

26. Ibid., 95-96, 98.

27. Ibid., 7-8.

28. Ibid., 143, 173.

29. Ibid., 182-83.

30. Interview of Marlin Thompson with author, Yerington, Nev., May 30, 2000.

31. Hittman, *Wovoka,* 186 .

32. Ibid., 185.

33. Ibid., 194.

34. Jan Deblieu, *Wind,* 14-15.

35. See Frantz Klaus, *Indian Reservations in the United States: Territory, Sovereignty, and Socioeconomic Change* (Chicago: The University of Chicago Press, 1999).

36. Szasz, *Religion in the Modern American West,* 11.

37. Don Hardesty, "Ethnographic Landscapes: Transforming Nature into Culture," in Arnold R. Alanen and Robert Z. Melnick, *Preserving Cultural Landscapes in America* (Baltimore: Johns Hopkins University Press, 2000), 177.

38. Quoted in Hardesty, "Ethnographic Landscapes," as originally in Catherine S. Fowler, "Subsistence," in William C. Sturtevant et al. *Handbook of North American Indians: Great Basin* (Washington, D.C.: Government Printing Office, 1986).

39. Ronald J. Taylor, *Sagebrush Country: A Wildflower Sanctuary* (Missoula, Mont.: Mountain Press, 1992), 18-21.

40. Carvalho, *Incidents of Travel and Adventure in the Far West,* 305.

41. Whipple, *Giant Joshua,* 50-51.

42. Ibid., 322.

43. Ibid., 555.

44. Ibid., 22.

45. See Tim Folger, "From Here to Eternity," *Discover* (December 2000): 54-61.

46. Ibid.

7. Chosen People, Chosen Land

1. The commercial was broadcast on national television December 2000-January 2001.

2. Robert D. McCracken and Jeanne Sharp Howerton, *A History of Railroad Valley Nevada* (Tonopah: Central Nevada Historical Society, 1996), 130-31.

3. See Wayne Muller, *Sabbath: Finding Rest, Renewal, and Delight in Our Busy Lives* (New York: Bantam Books, 2001).

4. Michael Hittman, *Corbett Mack: The Life of a Northern Paiute as Told by Michael Hittman* (Lincoln: University of Nebraska Press, 1996), 95.

5. Ibid., 76-77.

6. Ibid., 128.

7. For a good summary of the Pyramid Lake Wars, see Ronald James, *The Roar and the Silence: A History of Virginia City and the Comstock Lode* (Reno: University of Nevada Press, 1997), 38-42.

8. Myron Angel, ed., *History of Nevada* (Oakland, Calif.: Thompson and West, 1881), 151.

9. See Hayden White, "Forms of Wildness: Archaeological of an Idea," in Edward Dudley and Maximillian E. Novak, *The Wild Man Within: An Image in Western Thought from the Renaissance to Romanticism* (Pittsburgh: University of Pittsburgh Press, 1972), 3-38.

10. See Hittman, *A Numu History,* 17.

11. Robinson, *Sinners and Saints,* 278, 280-81.

12. "History of Charles Pulsipher" ["Written mostly by himself"], in "Pulsipher Family History Book," 73-74.

13. Newell G. Bringhurst, "The 'Descendants of Ham' in Zion: Discrimination against Blacks along the Shifting Mormon Frontier, 1830-1920," *Nevada Historical Society Quarterly* 24, no. 4 (winter 1981): 305, 308.

14. Ibid., 309.

15. See Michael Adas, *Machines as the Measure of Man: Science, Technology, and Ideologies of Western Dominance* (Ithaca, N.Y.: Cornell University Press, 1990).

16. Hugh N. Mozingo, *Shrubs of the Great Basin: A Natural History* (Reno: University of Nevada Press, 1987), 19.

17. Heidi J. Nast "Mapping the 'Unconscious': Racism and the Oedipal Family," *Annals, Association of American Geographers* 90, no. 2 (June 2000): 215-55.

18. Denis Cosgrove, *Apollo's Eye: A Cartographic Genealogy of the Earth in the Western Imagination,* (Baltimore: Johns Hopkins University Press, 2001), 80.

19. Samuel Bowles, *Across the Continent: A Summer's Journey to the Rocky Mountains, the Mormons, and the Pacific States* (Springfield, Mass.: Samuel Bowles; New York: Hurd and Houghton, 1865), 69.

20. Ibid., 79-80.

21. Ibid., 82.

22. Juanita Brooks, *John Doyle Lee: Zealot, Pioneer Builder, Scapegoat* (Logan: Utah State University Press, 1992), 11.

23. Simpson *Report of Explorations,* 35.

24. Stott, *Search for Sanctuary,* 49, 80.

25. Ibid., 89, 90, 100-101.

26. Ibid., 119, 141, 143.

27. Ibid., 142.

28. Ibid.

29. Ibid., 143.

30. Michael Cohen, *A Garden of Bristlecones: Tales of Change in the Great Basin* (Reno: University of Nevada Press, 1998), 10.

31. Ibid., 15.

32. Stott, Search for Sanctuary, 58.

33. Stanley W. Paher, *Nevada Ghost Towns and Mining Camps: Illustrated Atlas* (Las Vegas: Nevada Publications, 1999), 45.

34. Robinson, *Sinners and Saints,* 68-71.

35. L. P. Brockett, *Our Western Empire; or, The New West beyond the Mississippi: The latest and most comprehensive work on the states and territories west of the Mississippi* (Philadelphia: Bradley, Garretson, 1882), 33.

36. Ibid., 1183.

8. Vanishing Cities of Zion

1. Henry Howe, *The Great West: Containing Narratives. . . .* (New York: Geo. F. Tuttle, 1858), 48.

2. Robinson, *Sinners and Saints,* 67.

3. J. H. Beadle, *Western Wilds and the Men Who Redeem Them* (Cincinnati: Jones Brothers, 1878), 371.

4. Richard Poulsen, *The Landscape of the Mind: Cultural Transformations of the American West* (New York: Peter Lang, 1992), 104-105.

5. Hosea Stout, *On the Mormon Frontier: The Diary of Hosea Stout, 1844-1861,* ed. Juanita Brooks (Salt Lake City: University of Utah Press, 1964), vol. 1, 326-27.

6. Richard F. Burton, *The City of the Saints and across the Rocky Mountains to California*, ed. Fawn Brodie (New York: Alfred A. Knopf, 1963), 210-15.

7. Stout, *On the Mormon Frontier*, vol. 2, 456.

8. G. D. Watt and J. W. Long, "Prosperity of Zion &c, Discourses Delivered by Elder George A. Smith, in the Tabernacle, Great Salt Lake City, March 10, 1861," *Journal of Discourses Delivered by President Brigham Young, His Two Counselors, the Twelve Apostles, and Others* 9 (1862): 71.

9. Leonard Arrington, *Great Basin Kingdom: An Economic History of the Latter-day Saints, 1830-1900* (Lincoln: University of Nebraska Press, 1958), 64-66.

10. See William Mulder and Arlington Russell Mortensen, eds., *Among the Mormons: Historic Accounts by Contemporary Observers* (New York: Alfred A. Knopf, 1958), 345.

11. See Charles Sharon Peterson, "The Americanization of Utah's Agriculture," *Utah Historical Quarterly* 42, no. 2 (summer 1974): 108-25.

12. See Doug Stewart, "Imagining the Orient," *Smithsonian,* September 2000, 60-70.

13. Ibid., 68.

14. Gustav Niebuhr, "Latter-day Saints to Play Down the Term 'Mormon,'" *Dallas Morning News,* March 3, 2001, 4-G.

15. Scott Anderson, *The 4 O'clock Murders*: The True Story of a Mormon Family's Vengeance (New York: Doubleday, 1993), 5.

16. F. A. Bailey, *My Summer in a Mormon Village* (Boston: Houghton Mifflin, 1894), 3-4.

17. Lowry Nelson, *The Mormon Village: A Pattern and Technique of Land Settlement* (Salt Lake City: University of Utah Press, 1952).

18. D. W. Meinig, "The Mormon Culture Region: Strategies and Patterns in the Geography of the American West, 1847-1964," *Annals, Association of American Geographers* 55 (June 1965): 191-220.

19. "A Leap toward a Living Faith," *Oregon Quarterly* 80, no. 2 (winter 2000): 5-6.

20. Robert Raleigh, *In Our Lovely Deseret: Mormon Fictions* (Salt Lake City: Signature Books, 1998).

21. "Discovering Millard County & West Central Utah, 2001-2002 Edition" (N.p.: n.p., n.d), 14-15.

22. Ibid., 22.

23. John Codman, *The Mormon Country: A Summer with the Latter-day Saints* (New York: United States Publishing, 1874).

24. Richard Francaviglia *The Mormon Landscape: Existence, Creation, and Perception of a Unique Image in the American West* (New York: AMS Press, 1978).

25. John Reps, *Town Planning in Frontier America* (Princeton, N.J.: Princeton University Press, 1969), 413.

26. *Images of Parowan's Past* (Parowan, Utah: Parowan Main Street, 1998), 22.

27. William Clayton, *The Latter-day Saints' Emigrants' Guide ... From Council Bluffs to the Valley of the Great Salt Lake* (St. Louis: Mo. Republican Steam Power Press—Chambers & Knapp, 1848), 80.

28. Maureen Whipple, *This Is the Place: Utah* (New York: Alfred A. Knopf, 1945), 84.

29. G. W. James, *Utah, the Land of Blossoming Valleys* (Boston: Page, 1922), 25-26.

30. J. B. Jackson, *Discovering the Vernacular Landscape* (New Haven: Yale University Press, 1984), 12.

31. Preston Nibley, *Brigham Young: The Man and His Work* (Salt Lake City: Deseret News Press, 1937), 181.

32. Historical Records of Nephi, Utah, 1851-1862, Church Historian's Office, Salt Lake City.

33. Codman, *Mormon Country*, 144.

34. See Reps, *Town Planning in Frontier America*, 413.

35. See Lowell "Ben" Bennion, "A Geographer's Discovery of the *Great Basin Kingdom*," in *Great Basin Kingdom Revisited: Contemporary Perspectives*, ed. Thomas G. Alexander (Logan: Utah State University Press, 1991), 109-32.

36. Richard Francaviglia, "The City of Zion in the Mountain West," *Improvement Era* 72, no. 12 (December 1969): 10-17.

37. Historical Records of Parowan, Utah, 1856-59, 3, Church Historian's Office, Salt Lake City.

38. Ibid., 19. The underscorings are the original recorder's.

39. S. L. Richards, "Chapels and Temples Held Monuments to Progress of Man," *Deseret News*, October 25, 1953, 1-2.

40. E. Hopper, "The Church Spire," *Improvement Era* 63 (1959): 271.

41. Thomas Wolfe, *A Western Journal: A Daily Log of the Great Parks Trip, June 20-July 2, 1938* (Pittsburgh: University of Pittsburgh Press, 1951), 32-34.

42. Wallace Stegner, *Mormon Country* (New York: Duell, Sloan and Pearce, 1942), 21.

43. Whipple, *This Is the Place*, 31-32.

44. Thomas F. O'Dea, *The Mormons* (Chicago: University of Chicago Press, 1957), 1.

45. Richard Francaviglia, "The Passing Mormon Village," *Landscape* 22, no. 2 (spring 1978): 40-47.

46. I am indebted to University of Texas at Arlington student Nancy Grace, who visited Parowan in 2000 with my book *The Mormon Landscape* in hand. Ms. Grace wrote a fine paper updating Parowan. I later visited Parowan (June 2002) to confirm these findings.

9. Pilgrimages to Babylon

1. "Lost in Las Vegas," a&e Special, April 29, 2001.

2. "Las Vegas Uncovered," television special on Travel Channel, March 26, 2001.

3. Ralph J. Roske, "Gambling in Nevada: The Early Years, 1861-1931" *Nevada Historical Society Quarterly* 33, no. 1 (spring 1990): 28.

4. . Simpson, *Report of Explorations*, 461.

5. "Las Vegas Uncovered."

6. Jerome E. Edwards, "Nevada Gambling: Just Another Business Enterprise," *Nevada Historical Society Quarterly* 37, no. 2 (summer 1994): 110.

7. See Eugene Moehring, *Resort City in the Sunbelt: Las Vegas, 1930-2000* (Reno: University of Nevada Press, 2000).

8. See Page Smith, *As a City upon a Hill: The Town in American History* (New York: Knopf, 1966).

9. Richard Francaviglia, *Hard Places: Reading the Landscape of America's Historic Mining Districts* (Iowa City: University of Iowa Press, 1991).

10. Robinson, Sinners and Saints, 68-69.

11. See James, *The Roar and the Silence,* 95-96.

12. Job 28:3.

13. From the *White Pine (Nev.) News,* April 10, 1869, as cited in W. Turrentine Jackson, *Treasure Hill: Portrait of a Silver Mining Camp* (1963; reprint, Reno: University of Nevada Press, 2000), 53.

14. Job 28:3-4.

15. Robinson, Sinners and Saints, 260-61.

16. Wilbur S. Shepperson, ed., *East of Eden, West of Zion: Essays on Nevada* (Reno: University of Nevada Press, 1989).

17. See William D. Rowley, "People of Good Hope in the Land of Nod," *Nevada Historical Society Quarterly* 42, no. 1 (spring 1999): 3-20.

18. See Carlson, *Nevada Place Names,* 181-82, and Paher, *Nevada Ghost Towns,* 16, 17, 35, 42.

19. See M. Guy Bishop, *Henry William Bigler: Soldier, Gold Miner, Missionary, Chronicler, 1815-1900* (Logan: Utah State University Press, 1998).

20. Ferenc Morton Szasz, *Scots in the North American West, 1790-1917* (Norman: University of Oklahoma Press, 2000), 85.

21. "Lost Tribes of Israel to Get Bullfrog Mines," *Bullfrog Miner,* August 8, 1907.

22. See Richard Francaviglia, "In Her Image: Some Comments on Power and Gender in Mining History," *Annual Journal, Mining History Association* (1998).

23. "Telegraph Saloon!" Dun Glen, Nev., Advertisement dated May 10, 1867 as reproduced in Paher, *Nevada Ghost Towns,* 139.

24. George Gordon, Lord Byron, *Don Juan,* clxxix; this passage concludes, "without their sap, how branchless were the trunk of life's strange tree, so fruitful on occasion."

25. Carlson, *Nevada Place Names,* 98, 43, 133.

26. Paher, *Nevada Ghost Towns,* 126.

27. Carlson, *Nevada Place Names,* 234.

28. Paher, *Nevada Ghost Towns,* 115.

10. Landscapes of Armageddon

1. Lewis Mumford, *Faith for Living* (London: Secker and Warburg, 1941).

2. Ibid., 16-17.

3. Catherine Fowler, *In the Shadow of Fox Peak: An Ethnography of the Cattail-eater Northern Paiute People of Stillwater Marsh,* U.S. Fish & Wildlife Service, Cultural Resource Series #5 (Washington, D.C.: U.S. Dept. of the Interior, 1992).

4. Hardesty, "Ethnographic Landscapes," 177.

5. Vivian Gornick, *The Romance of American Communism* (New York: Basic Books, 1977), 3, 8, 13.

6. J. Edgar Hoover, *Masters of Deceit: The Story of Communism in America and How to Fight It* (New York: Henry Holt, 1958), v.

7. Ibid., 14-15.

8. Ibid., 125.

9. Ibid., 319-20.

10. Ibid., 320.

11. Ibid.

12. Ibid., 322.

13. Ibid., 321, 323-24.

14. Ibid., 328.

15. John A. Stormer, *None Dare Call It Treason . . . 25 Years Later* (Florissant, Mo.: Liberty Bell Press, 1990), vii, 1.

16. See S. Gladstone and P. Dolan, eds., *The Effects of Nuclear Weapons* (Washington, D.C.: Government Printing Office, 1977).

17. See B. L. Cohen, *Nuclear Science and Society* (New York: Doubleday, 1974).

18. Written by P. F. Sloan, sung by Barry McGuire, Dunhill Records, 1965.

19. Harney, *The Way It Is*, 24-25.

20. Matthew Coolidge, *The Nevada Test Site: A Guide to America's Nuclear Proving Ground* (Los Angeles: Center for Land Use Interpretation, 1996), 9, 7.

21. Sue Rabbitt Roff, "Mock Turtle Arithmetic, Public Trust, and the Nevada Test Site," in *Science, Values, and the American West,* ed. Stephen Tchudi (Reno: Nevada Humanities Committee, 1997), 180-82.

22. See Carole Gallagher, *American Ground Zero: The Secret Nuclear War* (New York: Doubleday, 1993), and Roff, "Mock Turtle Arithmetic," 182-83.

23. Eugene P. Moehring, *Resort City in the Sunbelt: Las Vegas, 1930-2000* (Reno: University of Nevada Press, 2000), 98.

24. Walter Miller, *A Canticle for Leibowitz* (New York: Bantam Books, 1959).

25. David A. Kirsch, "Project Plowshare: The Cold War Search for a Peaceful Nuclear Explosive," in *Science, Values and the American West,* ed. Tchudi, 200.

26. Ibid., 219.

27. Frank Bergon, "Demons, Monks, and Nuke Waste" in *Science, Values, and the American West,* ed Tchudi, 245-47.

28. Ibid., 250.

29. Ibid., 247, 254.

30. Ibid., 249, 251, 253.

31. Ibid., 255-56.

11. Into Sacred Spaces

1. Elizabeth Roberts and Elias Amidon, *Earth Prayers from Around the World: 365 Prayers, Poems, and Invocations for Honoring the Earth,* (San Francisco: Harper, 1991), xxi.

2. See also Carlson, *Nevada Place Names,* 47.

3. Claus Biegert, quoted in Jerry Mander, *In the Absence of the Sacred: The Failure of Technology and the Survival of the Indian Nations* (San Francisco: Sierra Club Books, 1991), 386.

4. For the Shoshone interpretation of this issue, see Western Shoshone National Council, "Outline of Western Shoshone National Government's Finding of Facts against the United States," (Indian Springs, Nev.: January 1998), n.p.

5. See Mander, *In the Absence of the Sacred,* 303–18.

6. Harney, *The Way It Is,* 92, 108.

7. Ibid., 84, 80, 79.

8. Ibid., 86.

9. Ibid., 79, 117.

10. Ibid., 37, 31.

11. Ibid., 131.

12. In March of 2001, the Taliban destroyed centuries-old Buddhist sculptures because, in their view, those icons were sullying a pure fundamentalist Islamic locale in violation of Islam's belief against idolatry.

13. Harney, *The Way It Is,* 141.

14. Mander, *In the Absence of the Sacred,* 318.

15. Harney, *The Way It Is,* xvii.

16. Mander, *In the Absence of the Sacred,* 305.

17. Ibid., 207, 208.

18. Joseph Bruchac, "Introduction," in *I Become Part of It: Sacred Dimension in Native American Life,* ed. D. M. Dooling and Paul Jordan-Smith (San Francisco: Harper San Francisco, 1989), 6.

19. Rich Vosepka, "Indian Tribe Banking on Nuclear Waste Storage Proposal," *Fort Worth Star-Telegram,* May 5, 2002, 29A.

20. Caitlain Matthews and John Matthews, *The Encyclopedia of Celtic Wisdom* (Shaftsbury, Dorset; Rockport, Mass.: Element, 1994), 2.

21. Simpson, Report of Explorations, 69.

22. Ibid.

23. Alexander von Humboldt, *Cosmos* (London: Henry G. Bohn, 1849), vol. 1, p. B[1].

24. Carlson, *Nevada Place Names,* 138.

25. Von Humboldt, *Cosmos,* vol. 1, p. 3.

26. Now archaic, the term *geognosy* is defined as the study of rocks and minerals and the orderly succession of geological formations.

27. Von Humboldt, *Cosmos,* vol. 1, ix–xii.

28. Ibid., 3–4.

29. Walt Whitman, *Leaves of Grass,* with an Introduction by Roy Harvey Pearce (1860; reprint, Ithaca, N.Y.: Great Seal Books, 1961), 13, 246–47, xix.

30. Robert Greenway, "The Wilderness Effect and Ecopsychology," in *Ecopsychology: Restoring the Earth, Healing the Mind,* ed. Theodore Roszak, Mary E. Gomes, and Allen D. Kanner (San Francisco: Sierra Club Books, 1995), 126.

31. Steve Perry, "Waking Up with the House on Fire: An Interview with James Hillman," *Utne Reader,* January–February, 1997, 55.

32. As seen on the Yucca Valley Chamber of Commerce "Quality of Life" website, <http://www.yuccavalley.org/Quality_of_Life.htm> (January 17, 2001).

33. Julene Bair, "Night in the Mojave," *Michigan Quarterly Review* 40, no. 1 (winter 2001): 165.

34. As seen on website for thedesertsun.com, a product of the Desert Sun Publishing Company, <www.thedesertsun.com/news/stories/local/954559647.shtml> (January 17, 2001).

35. <http://www.burningman.com/whatisburningman/> (September 12, 2000).

36. Ibid.

37. Fox, *The Void, the Grid, and the Sign,* 5

38. Ibid., 4.

39. Tuan, "The Desert and I," 7, 12-13, 15.

40. Ibid., 8-9.

12. Believing in Place

1. <http://www.mnsinc.com/kowalski/vpoint.html> (June 26, 2000).

2. See Devereux, *The Long Trip,* 232, regarding spirits universally traveling in straight lines.

3. Vine Deloria Jr., *Red Earth, White Lies: Native Americans and the Myth of Scientific Fact* (New York: Scribner's, 1995), 41.

4. Mrs. Hugh Brown, *Lady in Boomtown: Miners and Manners on the Nevada Frontier* (Palo Alto: American West, 1968), 126.

5. Sue Goetnick Ambrose, "Microbes May Have Survived 250 Million Years in Crystal," *Dallas Morning News,* October 19, 2000, 1A.

6. Kevin Krajick, "To Hell and Back," *Discover,* July 1999, 78.

7. Vine Deloria Jr., *Red Earth, White Lies,* 55-56.

8. Advertisement by Accenture-Consulting Technologies.

9. Craig Denton, *People of the West Desert: Finding Common Ground,* (Logan: Utah State University Press, 1999), 63-65, 71-77.

10. Ibid., 81-85.

11. Jack Walter, "Ruby Mountains" in *Buckaroo: Visions and Voices of the American Cowboy,* ed. Hal Cannon and Thomas West (New York: Simon & Schuster, 1993), 27.

12. From a poem by Johanne Call in Frank Wendell Call, *Gandydancer's Children,* 133.

13. Robert Dawson, Peter Goin, and Mary Webb, *A Doubtful River* (Reno: University of Nevada Press, 2000), 127.

Bibliography

Adams, Melvin R. *Netting the Sun: A Personal Geography of the Oregon Desert.* Pullman: Washington State University Press, 2001.

Adas, Michael. *Machines as the Measure of Man: Science, Technology, and Ideologies of Western Dominance.* Ithaca, N.Y.: Cornell University Press, 1990.

Adkinson, Stephen. "Coffee, Doughnuts, and Atomic Bombs." In *Science, Values, and the American West.* Ed. Stephen Tchudi, 151–55. Reno: Nevada Humanities Committee, 1997.

Alanen, Arnold R., and Robert Z. Melnick, eds. *Preserving Cultural Landscapes in America.* Baltimore: Johns Hopkins University Press, 2000.

Alexander, Thomas G. *Great Basin Kingdom Revisited: Contemporary Perspectives.* Logan: Utah State University Press, 1991.

———. *Mormonism in Transition: A History of the Latter-day Saints, 1890–1930.* Urbana: University of Illinois Press, 1996.

Alexander, Thomas G., and James B. Allen. *Mormons and Gentiles: A History of Salt Lake City.* Boulder: Pruett, 1984.

Allen, James B., and Glen M. Leonard. *The Story of the Latter-day Saints.* Salt Lake City: Deseret Books, 1976.

Allen, John Logan. *A Continent Comprehended.* Vol. 3 of *North American Exploration.* Lincoln: University of Nebraska Press, 1997.

Angel, Myron, ed. *History of Nevada.* Oakland, Calif.: Thompson and West, 1881.

Arrington, Leonard. *Brigham Young: American Moses.* New York: Alfred A. Knopf, 1985.

———. *Great Basin Kingdom: An Economic History of the Latter-day Saints, 1830–1900.* Lincoln: University of Nebraska Press, 1987.

Austin, Mary. *The American Rhythm.* New York: Harcourt, Brace, 1923.

Bailey, F. A. *My Summer in a Mormon Village.* Boston: Houghton Mifflin, 1894.

Bailey, Paul Dayton. *Ghost Dance Messiah.* 1970. Reprinted, Tucson: Westernlore Press, 1986.

Bair, Julene. "Night in the Mojave." *Michigan Quarterly Review* 40, no. 1 (winter 2001): 153–65.

Beadle, J. H. *Western Wilds and the Men Who Redeem Them.* Cincinnati: Jones Brothers, 1878.

Bennion, Lowell C. "Ben.""Mormondom's Deseret Homeland." In *Homelands: A Geography of Culture and Place across America.* Ed. Richard L. Nostrand and Lawrence Estaville, 184-209. Baltimore: Johns Hopkins University Press, 2001.

————. "A Geographer's Discovery of the *Great Basin Kingdom.*" In *Great Basin Kingdom Revisited: Contemporary Perspectives.* Ed. Thomas G. Alexander, 109-32. Logan: Utah State University Press, 1991.

Bergon, Frank. "Demons, Monks, and Nuke Waste." In *Science, Values, and the American West.* Ed. Stephen Tchudi, 245-56. Reno: Nevada Committee for the Humanities, 1997.

Bigler, David L. *Forgotten Kingdom: The Mormon Theocracy in the American West, 1847-1896.* Logan: Utah State University Press, 1998.

Bishop, M. Guy. *Henry William Bigler: Soldier, Gold Miner, Missionary, Chronicler, 1815-1900.* Logan: Utah State University Press, 1998.

Blew, Mary Clearman. *Bone Deep in Landscape: Writing, Reading, and Place.* Norman: University of Oklahoma Press, 1999.

Bolton, Herbert E. *Pageant in the Wilderness: The Story of the Escalante Expedition to the Interior Basin, 1776.* Salt Lake City: Utah State Historical Society, 1950.

Bowen, Marshall E. *Utah People in the Nevada Desert: Homestead and Community on a Twentieth-Century Farmers' Frontier.* Logan: Utah State University Press, 1994.

Bower, B. M. *The Parowan Bonanza.* Boston: Little, Brown, 1923.

Bowles, Samuel. *Across the Continent: A Summer's Journey to the Rocky Mountains, the Mormons, and the Pacific States.* Springfield, Mass.: Samuel Bowles and Co.; New York: Hurd and Houghton, 1865.

————. *Our New West: Records of Travel between the Mississippi River and the Pacific Ocean. Over the Plains—Over the Mountains—Through the Great Interior Basin—Over the Sierra Nevadas—To and Up and Down the Pacific Coast.* Hartford, Conn.: Hartford Publishing, 1869.

Bradley, Richard. *An Archaeology of Natural Places.* London: Routledge, 2000.

Bringhurst, Newell G. "The 'Descendants of Ham' in Zion: Discrimination against Blacks along the Shifting Mormon Frontier, 1830-1920," *Nevada Historical Society Quarterly* 24, no. 4 (winter, 1981): 298-318.

Brady, Margaret K. *Mormon Healer and Folk Poet.* Logan: Utah State University Press, 2000.

Brockett, L. P. *Our Western Empire; or, The New West beyond the Mississippi: The latest and most comprehensive work on the states and territories west of the Mississippi.* Philadelphia: Bradley, 1881.

Brooks, Juanita. *John Doyle Lee: Zealot, Pioneer Builder, Scapegoat.* Logan: Utah State University Press, 1992.

————, ed. *On the Mormon Frontier: The Diary of Hosea Stout, 1844-1861.* Vol. 1. Salt Lake City: University of Utah Press, 1964.

Browne, J. Ross. "Washoe Revisited." In *Adventures in Apache Country: A Tour through Arizona and Sonora, with Notes on the Silver Regions of Nevada.* New York: Harper and Brothers, 1868. Originally published in *Harper's New Monthly Magazine,* 1864.

Burton, Richard F. *The City of the Saints, and Across the Rocky Mountains to California.* Ed. Fawn Brodie. New York: Alfred A. Knopf, 1963.

Call, Frank Wendell. *Gandydancer's Children: A Railroad Memoir.* Reno: University of Nevada Press, 2000.

Canfield, Gae Whitney. *Sarah Winnemucca of the Northern Paiutes.* Norman: University of Oklahoma Press, 1983.

Carlson, Helen. *Nevada Place Names: A Geographical Dictionary.* Reno: University of Nevada Press, 1974.

Carvalho, Solomon Nunes. *Incidents of Travel and Adventure in the Far West: With Col. Fremont's last expedition across the Rocky Mountains; including three months' residence in Utah, and a perilous trip across the Great American desert to the Pacific.* New York: Derby and Jackson, 1857. Reprinted, Philadelphia: Jewish Publication Society of America, 1954.

Cervantes, Fernando. *The Devil in the New World: The Impact of Diabolism in New Spain.* New Haven: Yale University Press, 1994.

Christensen, Scott R. *Sagwitch: Shoshone Chieftain, Mormon Elder, 1822–1887.* Logan: Utah State University Press, 1999.

Clayton, William. *The Latter-day Saints' Emigrants' Guide . . . From Council Bluffs to the Valley of the Great Salt Lake.* St. Louis: Mo. Republican Steam Power Press—Chambers & Knapp, 1848.

Clemens, Samuel. *Roughing It.* Hartford, Conn.: American, 1872.

Codman, John. *The Mormon Country: A Summer with the Latter-day Saints.* New York: United States Publishing, 1874.

Cohen, B. L. *Nuclear Science and Society.* New York: Doubleday, 1974.

Cohen, Michael. *A Garden of Bristlecones: Tales of Change in the Great Basin.* Reno: University of Nevada Press, 1998.

Conzen, Michael, ed. *The Making of the American Landscape.* New York: Routledge, 1990.

Coolidge, Matthew. *The Nevada Test Site: A Guide to America's Nuclear Proving Ground.* Los Angeles: Center for Land Use Interpretation, 1996.

Cosgrove, Denis. *Apollo's Eye: A Cartographic Genealogy of the Earth in the Western Imagination.* Baltimore: Johns Hopkins University Press, 2001.

Culin, Stewart. *Games of the North American Indians.* Lincoln: University of Nebraska Press, 1992.

Dalton, Luella Adams, comp. *History of Iron County Mission and Parowan: The Mother Town.* Parowan, Utah: N.p., 1962.

Davis, Sarah Ann, Mary Hill, Elisabeth Egenhoff, and Elinor Rhodes. *Guide to Virginia City, Nevada, and the Comstock Lode Area. . . .* Sausalito, Calif.: Pages of History, 1959.

Dawson, Robert, Peter Goin, and Mary Webb. *A Doubtful River.* Reno: University of Nevada Press, 2000.

Deblieu, Jan. *Wind: How the Flow of Air Has Shaped Life, Myth, and the Land.* Boston: Houghton Mifflin, 1998.

Deloria, Vine, Jr. *Red Earth, White Lies: Native Americans and the Myth of Scientific Fact.* New York, Scribner, 1995.

———. "Out of Chaos." In *I Become Part of It: Sacred Dimensions in Native American Life.* Ed. D. M. Dooling and Paul Jordan-Smith, 259–68. San Francisco: Harper San Francisco, 1989.

————. *God Is Red.* New York: Dell, 1974.

Denton, Craig. *People of the West Desert: Finding Common Ground.* Logan: Utah State University Press, 1999.

De Quille, Dan [William Wright]. *The Big Bonanza.* New York: Alfred A. Knopf, 1953.

Devereux, Paul. *The Long Trip: A Prehistory of Psychedelia.* New York: Penguin Arkana, 1997.

Dickenson, Victoria. *Drawn from Life: Science and Art in the Portrayal of the New World.* Toronto: University of Toronto Press, 1998.

Dilworth, Leah. *Imagining Indians in the Southwest: Persistent Visions of a Primitive Past.* Washington, D.C.: Smithsonian Institution Press, 1997.

Dooling, D. M., and Paul Jordan-Smith, eds. *I Become Part of It: Sacred Dimensions in Native American Life.* San Francisco: Harper San Francisco, 1989.

Dudley, Edward, and Maximillian E. Novak. *The Wild Man Within: An Image in Western Thought from the Renaissance to Romanticism.* Pittsburgh: University of Pittsburgh Press, 1972.

Durham, Michael S. *Desert between the Mountains: Mormons, Miners, Padres, Mountain Men, and the Opening of the Great Basin, 1772–1869.* New York: Henry Holt, 1997.

Edwards, Greg, and Mary Jane Edwards. *Bet on It! The Ultimate Guide to Nevada.* Memphis: Mustang, 1992.

Edwards, Jerome E. "From Back Alley to Main Street: Nevada's Acceptance of Gambling." *Nevada Historical Society Quarterly* 33, no. 1 (spring 1990): 16–27.

————. "Nevada Gambling: Just Another Business Enterprise." *Nevada Historical Society Quarterly* 37, no. 2 (summer 1994): 101–13.

Fiero, Bill. *Geology of the Great Basin.* Reno: University of Nevada Press, 1986.

Findlay, John. *People of Chance: Gambling in American Society from Jamestown to Las Vegas.* New York: Oxford University Press, 1986.

————. "Suckers and Escapists: Interpreting Las Vegas and Post-war America." *Nevada Historical Society Quarterly* 33, no. 1 (spring 1990): 1–15.

Fowler, Catherine, *In the Shadow of Fox Peak: An Ethnography of the Cattail-eater Northern Paiute People of Stillwater Marsh.* U.S. Fish and Wildlife Service, Cultural Resource Series #5. Washington, D.C.: Dept. of the Interior, 1993.

————. "Ethnography and Great Basin Prehistory." In *Models and Great Basin Prehistory: A Symposium.* Ed. Don Fowler. Reno and Las Vegas: Desert Research Institute Publications in Social Science, no. 12, 1978.

Fowler, Don. *Great Basin Cultural Ecology: A Symposium.* Reno and Las Vegas: Desert Research Institute Publications in the Social Sciences, no. 8, 1972.

Fowler, Don D., and Catherine S. Fowler, eds. *Anthropology of the Numa: John Wesley Powell's Manuscripts on the Numic People of Western North America, 1868–1880.* Washington, D.C.: Smithsonian Institution Press, 1981.

Fox, William L. *The Void, the Grid, and the Sign: Traversing the Great Basin.* Salt Lake City: University of Utah Press, 2000.

Francaviglia, Richard. "The City of Zion in the Mountain West." *Improvement Era* 72, no. 12 (December 1969): 10–17.

————. *Hard Places: Reading the Landscape of America's Historic Mining Districts.* Iowa City: University of Iowa Press, 1991.

————. "In Her Image: Some Comments on Power and Gender in Mining History." *Annual Journal, Mining History Association* 5 (1998): 118-26.

————. "Learning from 'The Spirit of Place.'" *Fronteras* 9, no. 1 (spring 2000): 3-4.

————. "Mormon Central-Hall Houses in the American West." In *Baseball, Barns, and Bluegrass: A Geography of American Folklife.* Ed. George O. Carney, 56-64. Lanham, Md.: Rowman & Littlefield, 1998.

————. *The Mormon Landscape: Existence, Creation, and Perception of a Unique Image in the American West.* New York: AMS Press, 1978.

————. "The Passing Mormon Village," *Landscape* 22, no. 2 (spring 1978): 40-47.

Frantz, Klaus. *Indian Reservations in the United States: Territory, Sovereignty, and Socioeconomic Change.* Chicago: University of Chicago Press, 1999.

Frémont, John Charles. *Memoirs of My Life.* Chicago: Belford, Clarke, 1887.

————. *Report of the Exploring Expedition to the Rocky Mountains in the Year 1842, and to Oregon and North California in the Years 1843-44.* Washington, D.C.: Blair and Rives, 1845.

Gallagher, Carole. *American Ground Zero: The Secret Nuclear War.* New York: Doubleday, 1993.

Gladstone, S., and P. Dolan, eds. *The Effects of Nuclear Weapons.* Washington, D.C.: Government Printing Office, 1977.

Goin, Peter. *Nuclear Landscapes.* Baltimore: Johns Hopkins University Press, 1991.

Goodwin, S. H. *Mormonism and Masonry.* Salt Lake City: Grand Lodge, F.&A.M. of Utah, 1938.

Gornick, Virginia. *The Romance of American Communism.* New York: Basic Books, 1977.

Griffith, James. *Beliefs and Holy Places.* Tucson: University of Arizona Press, 1992.

Grayson, Donald K. *The Desert's Past: A Natural Prehistory of the Great Basin.* Washington, D.C.: Smithsonian Institution Press, 1993.

Gulliford, Andrew. *Sacred Objects and Sacred Places: Preserving Tribal Traditions.* Boulder: University Press of Colorado, 2000.

Hardesty, Don. "Ethnographic Landscapes: Transforming Nature into Culture." In Arnold R. Alanen and Robert Z. Melnick, *Preserving Cultural Landscapes in America.* Baltimore: Johns Hopkins University Press, 2000.

Hardesty, Donald L. *The Archaeology of Mining and Miners: A View from the Silver State.* Ed. William Turnbaugh. Special Publication Series, no. 6. (Ann Arbor: Society for Historical Archaeology, 1988).

Harney, Corbin. *The Way It Is: One Water … One Air … One Mother.* Nevada City, Calif.: Blue Dolphin, 1994.

Harris, Beth Kay. *The Towns of Tintic.* Denver: Sage Books, 1961.

Heat Moon, William Least. *Blue Highways: A Journey into America.* Boston: Little, Brown, 1982.

Hemphill, Mark W. *Union Pacific Salt Lake Route.* Erin, Ontario: Boston Mills Press, 1995.

Hersh, Lawrence. *The Central Pacific Railroad across Nevada, 1868 and 1997 Photographic Comparatives.* Los Angeles: Lawrence K. Hersh, 2000.

Historical Records of Nephi, Utah, 1851-1862. Church Historian's Office, Salt Lake City.

Historical Records of Parowan, Utah, 1856-59. Church Historian's Office, Salt Lake City.

Hittman, Michael. *Corbett Mack: The Life of a Northern Paiute.* Lincoln: University of Nebraska Press, 1996.

————. *A Numu History: The Yerington Paiute Tribe.* Yerington, Nev.: Yerington Paiute Tribe, 1984.

————. *Wovoka and the Ghost Dance.* Edited by Don Lynch. Lincoln: University of Nebraska Press, 1997.

Holt, Ronald L. *Beneath These Red Cliffs: An Ethnohistory of the Utah Paiutes.* Albuquerque: University of New Mexico Press, 1992.

Hopkins, Sarah Winnemucca. *Life among the Piutes: Their Wrongs and Claims.* 1883. Reprint, Reno: University of Nevada Press, 1994.

Hoover, J. Edgar. *Masters of Deceit: The Story of Communism in America and How to Fight It.* New York: Henry Holt, 1958.

Howe, Henry. *The Great West: Containing Narratives. . . .* New York: Geo. F. Tuttle, 1858.

Humboldt, Alexander von. *Cosmos.* London: Henry G. Bohn, 1849.

Iber, Jorge. *Hispanics in the Mormon Zion, 1912-1999.* College Station: Texas A&M University Press, 2000.

Jackson, J. B. *Discovering the Vernacular Landscape.* New Haven: Yale University Press 1984.

Jackson, Richard H. "The Mormon Experience: The Plains as Sinai, the Great Salt Lake as the Dead Sea, and the Great Basin as Desert-cum-Promised Land." *Journal of Historical Geography* 18, no. 1 (1992): 41-58.

————. "Mormon Perception and Settlement," *Annals, Association of American Geographers* 68 (1978): 317-34.

————, ed. *The Mormon Role in the Settlement of the West.* Charles Redd Monograph in Western History no. 9. Provo: Brigham Young University Press, 1978.

James, G. W. *Utah, the Land of Blossoming Valleys.* Boston: Page, 1922.

James, Ronald. *The Roar and the Silence: A History of Virginia City and the Comstock Lode.* Reno: University of Nevada Press, 1997.

Jansma, Sidney J., Sr. *Six Days.* Grand Rapids, Mich.: Sidney J. Jansma, 1985.

Jennings, Jesse D. *Prehistory of Utah and the Eastern Great Basin.* Salt Lake City: University of Utah Press, 1978.

Kay, Jeanne. "Mormons and Mountains." In *The Mountainous West: Explorations in Historical Geography.* Ed. William Wyckoff and Lary M. Dilsaver, 368-95. Lincoln: University of Nebraska Press, 1995.

Kelly, Isabel. "Let Me Tell You a Story." Adapted from the collection of Numu tales by Isabel Kelly. In *Numu Ya Dua'* 3, no. 19 (February 5, 1982).

————. *Paiute Indians II—Southern Paiute Ethnography.* New York: Garland, 1976.

Kersten, Earl W. "Landscapes and Landscape Change in Nevada," *Nevada Public Affairs Review* no. 1 (1988): 54-63.

Kirsch, David A. "Project Plowshare: The Cold War Search for a Peaceful Nuclear Explosive." In *Science, Values, and the American West.* Ed. Stephen Tchudi, 191–222. Reno: Nevada Humanities Committee, 1997.

Kirsch, Scott. "Peaceful Nuclear Explosions and the Geography of Scientific Authority." *Professional Geographer* 52, no. 2 (May 2000): 179–92.

Kliner, James. "The Trinity of Physics in Nevada." In *Science, Values, and the American West.* Ed. Stephen Tchudi, 153–74. Reno: Nevada Humanities Committee, 1997.

Knack, Martha, and Omer C. Stewart. *As Long as the River Shall Run: An Ethnohistory of Pyramid Lake Indian Reservation.* Berkeley: University of California Press, 1984.

Laird, Carobeth. *The Chemehuevis.* Banning, Calif: Malki Museum, 1976.

Lane, Belden C. *Landscapes of the Sacred: Geography and Narrative in American Spirituality.* Mahwah, N.J.: Paulist Press, 1998.

Lanner, Richard M. *The Piñon Pine: A Natural and Cultural History.* Reno: University of Nevada Press, 1981.

Lautensach, Hermann. *Das Mormonenland als Beispiel eines sozialgeographischen Raumes.* Bonn: Im Selbstverlag des Geographischen Instituts der Universität Bonn, 1953.

Limerick, Patricia Nelson. *Desert Passages: Encounters with the American Deserts.* Albuquerque: University of New Mexico Press, 1985.

Littlejohn, David, ed. *The Real Las Vegas: Life beyond the Strip* New York: Oxford University Press, 1999.

Madsen, David B., and David Rhode. *Across the West: Human Population Movement and the Expansion of the Numa.* Salt Lake City: University of Utah Press, 1994.

Madsen, David B., and J. F. O'Connell. *Man and Environment in the Great Basin.* Washington, D.C.: Society for American Archaeology, 1982.

Mander, Jerry. *In the Absence of the Sacred: The Failure of Technology and the Survival of the Indian Nations.* San Francisco: Sierra Club Books, 1991.

McCracken, Robert D., and Jeanne Sharp Howerton. *A History of Railroad Valley Nevada.* Tonopah: Central Nevada Historical Society, 1996.

McNeley, James Kale. *Holy Wind in Navajo Philosophy.* Tucson: University of Arizona Press, 1981.

McPhee, John. *Basin and Range.* New York: Noonday Press, 1981.

Meinig, D. W. *The Interpretation of Ordinary Landscapes.* New York: Oxford University Press, 1979.

———. "The Mormon Culture Region: Strategies and Patterns in the Geography of the American West, 1847-1964," *Annals, Association of American Geographers* 55 (June 1965): 191–220.

Miller, Dorcas S. *Stars of the First People: Native American Star Myths and Constellations.* Boulder: Pruett, 1997.

Miller, Walter. *A Canticle for Leibowitz.* New York: Bantam Books, 1959.

Misrach, Richard. *Bravo 20: The Bombing of the American West.* Baltimore: Johns Hopkins University Press, 1990.

Moehring, Eugene P. *Resort City in the Sunbelt: Las Vegas, 1930-2000.* Reno: University of Nevada Press, 2000.

Moreno, Richard. *Roadside History of Nevada.* Missoula, Mont.: Mountain Press, 2000.

Mozingo, Hugh N. *Shrubs of the Great Basin: A Natural History.* Reno: University of Nevada Press, 1987.

Mulder, William. *Homeward to Zion: The Mormon Migration from Scandinavia.* Minneapolis: University of Minnesota Press, 1957.

Mulder, William, and Russell A. Mortensen. *Among the Mormons: Historic Accounts of Contemporary Observers.* New York: Alfred A. Knopf, 1958.

Muller, Wayne. *Sabbath: Finding Rest, Renewal, and Delight in Our Busy Lives.* New York: Bantam Books, 2001.

Mumford, Lewis. *Faith for Living.* London: Secker and Warburg, 1941.

Nast, Heidi J. "Mapping the 'Unconscious': Racism and the Oedipal Family." *Annals, Association of American Geographers* 90, no. 2 (June 2000): 215-55.

Nelson, Lowry. *The Mormon Village: A Pattern and Technique of Land Settlement.* Salt Lake City: University of Utah Press, 1952.

Newman, William M., and Peter L. Halvorson. *Atlas of American Religion: The Denominational Era, 1776-1990.* Walnut Creek, Calif.: AltaMira Press, 2000.

Nibley, Preston. *Brigham Young: The Man and His Work.* Salt Lake City: Deseret News Press, 1937.

Notarianni, Philip F. *Faith, Hope, and Prosperity: The Tintic Mining District.* Eureka, Utah: Tintic Historical Society, 1981.

O'Dea, Thomas F. *The Mormons.* Chicago: University of Chicago Press, 1957.

Orndorff, Richard, Robert W. Wieder, and Harry Filkorn. *Geology Underfoot in Central Nevada.* Missoula, Mont.: Mountain Press, 2001.

Paher, Stanley W. *Nevada Ghost Towns and Mining Camps: Illustrated Atlas.* Las Vegas: Nevada Publications, 1999.

————. *Nevada Ghost Towns and Mining Camps.* Berkeley: Howell-North Books, 1970.

Peterson, Charles Sharon. "The Americanization of Utah's Agriculture." *Utah Historical Quarterly* 42, no. 2 (spring 1974): 108-25 .

Peterson, John Alton. *Utah's Black Hawk War.* Salt Lake City: University of Utah Press, 1998.

Philip, Neil, comp. *Earth Always Endures: Native American Poems.* New York: Viking, 1996.

Poll, Richard D., Thomas G. Alexander, Eugene E. Campbell, and David E. Miller, eds. *Utah's History.* Provo: Brigham Young University Press, 1978.

Pool, Peter E., ed. *The Altered Landscape.* Published by the Nevada Museum of Art in association with University of Nevada Press, Reno, Las Vegas, 1999.

Pope, Mary L. *Let Me Tell You a Story: Adapted Paiute Tales.* From stories told by Frank Quinn, Hazel Quinn, and Russell Dick. N.p.: Yerington Paiute Tribal Council, 1981.

Porteous, J. Douglas. *Landscapes of the Mind: Worlds of Sense and Metaphor.* Toronto: University of Toronto Press, 1990.

Poulsen, Richard. *The Landscape of the Mind: Cultural Transformations of the American West.* New York: Peter Lang, 1992.

————. *The Pure Experience of Order: Essays on the Symbolic in the Folk Material Culture of Western America.* Albuquerque: University of New Mexico Press, 1982.

Powell, John Wesley, and G. W. Ingalls. *Report of Special Commissioners J. W. Powell and G. W. Ingalls on the Condition of the Ute Indians of Utah; the Paiutes of Utah,*

Northern Arizona, Southern Nevada, and Southeastern California; the Northwestern Shoshones of Nevada; and Report Concerning Claims of Settlers in the Mo-a-pa Valley, Southeastern Nevada. Washington, D.C.: Government Printing Office, 1874.

Prosor, Larry, et al. *Nevada: Desert Lows and Mountain Highs.* Ed. Laurel Hilde. Truckee, Calif.: Fine Line Productions, 1994.

"Pulsipher Family History Book." Arranged and typed by Eva H. Allan. Unpublished family history dated December 22, 1961. Copy in possession of author as provided by Nancy Grace

Raleigh, Robert. *In Our Lovely Deseret: Mormon Fictions.* Salt Lake City: Signature Books, 1998.

Raymond, Elizabeth. "Sense of Place in the Great Basin." In *East of Eden, West of Zion.* Ed. Wilbur S. Shepperson, 17-29. Reno: University of Nevada Press, 1989.

———. "Desert/Paradise: Images of Nevada Landscape." *Nevada Public Affairs Review* no. 1 (1988): 12-18.

Redfield, James. "Our Rediscovery of the World's Mysteries." *Utne Reader* no. 102 (November-December 2000): 78-79.

Reeve, W. Paul. "Cattle, Cotton, and Conflict: The Possession and Dispossession of Hebron, Utah." *Utah Historical Quarterly* 67, no. 2 (spring 1999): 148-75.

Reps, John. *Town Planning in Frontier America.* Princeton, N.J.: Princeton University Press, 1969.

Rhodes, Frank, Harold Trevor, and Richard O. Stone, eds. *Language of the Earth.* New York: Pergamon Press, 1981.

Richards, S. L. "Chapels and Temples Held Monuments to Progress of Man." *Deseret News,* October 25, 1953.

Riebsame, William E., ed. *Atlas of the New West: Portrait of a Changing Region.* New York: W. W. Norton, 1997.

Roberts, Elizabeth, and Elias Amidon. *Earth Prayers from Around the World: 365 Prayers, Poems, and Invocations for Honoring the Earth.* San Francisco: Harper, 1991.

Robinson, Phil. *Sinners and Saints: A Tour across the States, and round Them; with Three Months among the Mormons.* Boston: Roberts Brothers, 1883.

Roff, Sue Rabbitt. "Mock Turtle Arithmetic, Public Trust, and the Nevada Test Site." In *Science, Values, and the American West.* Ed. Stephen Tchudi, 175-90. Reno: Nevada Humanities Committee, 1997.

Roske, Ralph J. "Gambling in Nevada: The Early Years, 1861-1931." *Nevada Historical Society Quarterly* 33, no. 1 (spring 1990): 28-40.

Roszak, Theodore, Mary E. Gomes, and Allan D. Kanner, eds. *Ecopsychology, Restoring the Earth, Healing the Mind.* San Francisco: Sierra Club Book, 1995.

Rowley, William D. "People of Good Hope in the Land of Nod." *Nevada Historical Society Quarterly* 42, no. 1 (spring 1999): 3-20.

Schenker, Heath. "Desert Sculpture: Nevada Earthworks Update." *Nevada Public Affairs Review* no. 1 (1988): 19-24.

Schmollinger, Steve. *Desert Railroading.* Forest Park, Ill.: Heimburger House, 1999.

Shepperson, Wilbur S., ed. *East of Eden, West of Zion: Essays on Nevada.* Reno: University of Nevada Press, 1989.

Simons, Sarah. *Around Wendover: An Examination of the Anthropic Landscape of the*

Great Salt Lake Desert Region. Los Angeles: Center for Land Use Interpretation, 1998.

Simpson, J. H. *Report of Explorations across the Great Basin of the Territory of Utah ... in 1859.* Vintage Nevada Series. Reno: University of Nevada Press, 1983.

Smith, Anne M. *Shoshone Tales.* Salt Lake City: University of Utah Press, 1993.

Smith, Page. *As a City upon a Hill: The Town in American History.* New York: Knopf, 1966.

Sopher, David. *Geography of Religions.* Foundations of Cultural Geography Series. Englewood Cliffs, N.J.: Prentice-Hall, 1967.

Stansbury, Howard. *Exploration of the Valley of the Great Salt Lake.* Ed. Don D. Fowler. Washington, D.C.: Smithsonian Institution Press, 1988.

Stegner, Wallace. *Mormon Country.* New York: Duell, Sloan and Pearce, 1942.

———. *The Preacher and the Slave.* Boston: Houghton Mifflin, 1950.

Steward, Julian H., and Erminie Wheeler-Voegelin. *The Northern Paiute Indians.* New York: Garland, 1974.

Stewart, John. *Geology of Nevada: A Discussion to Accompany the Geologic Map of Nevada.* Reno: Nevada Bureau of Mines and Geology, University of Nevada, 1980.

Stisted, Georgiana M. *The True Life of Capt. Sir Richard F. Burton.* London: H. S. Nichol, 1896.

Stott, Clifford L. *Search for Sanctuary: Brigham Young and the White Mountain Expedition.* Salt Lake City: University of Utah Press, 1984.

Stout, Hosea. *On the Mormon Frontier: The Diary of Hosea Stout, 1844-1861.* Ed. Juanita Brooks. Salt Lake City: University of Utah Press, 1964.

Sturtevant, William C., et al. *Handbook of North American Indians: Great Basin.* Washington, D.C.: Government Printing Office, 1986.

Sutton, Mark Q. "The Numic Expansion as Seen from the Mojave Desert." In *Across the West: Human Population Movement and the Expansion of the Numa.* Ed. David B. Madsen and David Rhode. Salt Lake City: University of Utah Press, 1994.

Szasz, Ferenc Morton. *Religion in the Modern American West.* Tucson: University of Arizona Press, 2000.

Taylor, Ronald J. *Sagebrush Country: A Wildflower Sanctuary.* Missoula, Mont.: Mountain Press, 1992.

Theodratus, Dorothea. "A Perspective on Traditional Sites." *Proceedings of the Society for California Archaeology* 6 (1993).

Thursby, Jacqueline S. "Mormon Temple Reproductions on Cemetery Markers." *Markers: Annual Journal of the Association for Gravestone Studies* 20 (2003): 312-32.

Thybony, Scott. *Dry Rivers and Standing Rocks: A Word Finder for the American West.* Albuquerque: University of New Mexico Press, 2000.

Tingley, Joseph V., and Kris Ann Pizarro. *Traveling America's Loneliest Road: A Geologic and Natural History Tour through Nevada along U.S. Highway 50.* Reno: Nevada Bureau of Mining and Geology, 2000.

Titus, A. Costandina. "A-Bombs in the Backyard: Southern Nevada Adapts to the Nuclear Age, 1951-1963." *Nevada Historical Quarterly* 26, no. 4 (winter 1983): 235-54.

———. *Bombs in the Backyard: Atomic Testing and American Politics.* Reno: University of Nevada Press, 1986.

Trimble, Stephen. *The Sagebrush Ocean: A Natural History of the Great Basin.* Reno: University of Nevada Press, 1989.

Tuan, Yi-Fu. "The Desert and I: A Study in Affinity," *Michigan Quarterly* 40, no. 1 (winter 2001): 7-16.

———. *Escapism.* Baltimore: John Hopkins University Press, 1998.

———. *Topophilia: A Study of Environmental Perception, Attitudes, and Values.* Englewood Cliffs, N.J.: Prentice-Hall, 1974.

Vanderburg, William O. *Mines of Lander and Eureka Counties.* Las Vegas: Nevada Publications, 1988.

Vosepka, Rich. "Indian Tribe Banking on Nuclear Waste Storage Proposal." *Fort Worth Star-Telegram,* May 5, 2002, 29A.

Walter, Jack. "Ruby Mountains." In *Buckaroo: Visions and Voices of the American Cowboy.* Ed. Hal Cannon and Thomas West. New York: Simon & Schuster, 1993.

West, Ray B. *Kingdom of the Saints: The Story of Brigham Young and the Mormons.* New York: Viking Press, 1957.

Whipple, Maureen. *The Giant Joshua.* Boston: Houghton Mifflin, 1942.

———. *This Is the Place: Utah.* New York: Alfred A. Knopf, 1945.

Whitley, David S. "Finding Rain in the Desert: Landscape, Gender, and Far Western North American Rock-Art." In *The Archeology of Rock-Art.* Ed. Christopher Chippindale and Paul S. C. Taçon, 11-29. New York: Cambridge University Press, 1998.

———. "Shamanism, Natural Modeling, and the Rock Art of Far Western North American Hunter-Gatherers." In Solveig A. Turpin, *Shamanism and Rock Art in North America.* Special Publication 1, Rock Art Foundation, San Antonio, Tex., 1994.

———, ed. *Handbook of Rock Art Research.* Walnut Creek, Calif.: AltaMira Press, 2001.

Whitman, Walt. *Leaves of Grass.* With an Introduction by Roy Harvey Pearce. 1860. Reprint, Ithaca, N.Y.: Great Seal Books, 1961.

Wieners, Brad, ed. *Burning Man.* San Francisco: HardWired, 1997.

Williams, Terry Tempest. *Refuge: An Unnatural History of Family and Place.* New York: Vintage, 1991.

Wolfe, Thomas. *A Western Journal: A Daily Log of the Great Parks Trip, June 20-July 2, 1938.* Pittsburgh: University of Pittsburgh Press, 1951.

Wood, Denis. *The Power of Maps.* New York: Guilford Press, 1992.

Wyckoff, William, and Lary M. Dilsaver. *The Mountainous West: Explorations in Historical Geography.* Lincoln: University of Nebraska Press, 1995.

Index

Note: Italic page numbers refer to illustrations.